Taking the Fifth

Taking the Fifth

**The Supreme Court and the Privilege
Against Self-Incrimination**

Mark Berger
University of
Missouri—Kansas City
School of Law

LexingtonBooks
D.C. Heath and Company
Lexington, Massachusetts
Toronto

Library of Congress Cataloging in Publication Data

Berger, Mark, 1946-
 Taking the Fifth.

 Bibliography: p.
 Includes index.
  1. Self-Incrimination—United States. 2. United States. Supreme
Court. 3. Self-Incrimination—United States—Cases. I. Title.
KF9668.B47   345'.73'056   78-55953
ISBN 0-669-02339-6

Published simultaneously in Canada.

Printed in the United States of America.

International Standard Book Number: 0-669-02339-6

Library of Congress Catalog Card Number: 78-55953

To Kathy, Kerren, and Claire

Contents

Preface and Acknowledgments

No person . . . shall be compelled in any criminal case to be a witness against himself.

—United States Constitution, Amendment V

The Fifth Amendment occupies a very special place in the American public consciousness. It was at the center of attention during the McCarthy era when witness after witness invoked the privilege against self-incrimination before congressional committees investigating communist influence in areas as diverse as the State Department, the army, and the Hollywood movie industry. During the 1960s it was again a source of controversy, this time reflected in the bitterly received *Miranda* rules requiring that suspects in a custodial police interrogation be warned of their constitutional rights. Indeed, a unique language has developed around this provision of the Bill of Rights so that simply "taking the Fifth" has come to mean assertion of the self-incrimination clause of the Fifth Amendment of the U.S. Constitution. No other provision of the Constitution is referred to in quite that way.

Considering its illustrious past and controversial present, it is rather strange that the privilege against self-incrimination has not been given book-length treatment for approximately twenty years. Ewrin Griswold's *The Fifth Amendment Today* and Lewis Mayers' *Shall We Amend the Fifth Amendment?*, both written during the 1950s, have not been followed since then with anything of comparable quality or depth. There are of course evidence treatises that consider the privilege against self-incrimination— those by Dean John Wigmore and Dean Charles McCormick being the most helpful—as well as innumerable articles on the subject in legal and nonlegal journals alike. Yet the more generalized emphasis of a treatise on the entire corpus of evidence law and the narrow focus reflected in an article on a particular facet of the Fifth Amendment do not cover every need. Surely there is room for a book on the Fifth Amendment that seeks both an overview of its history, policy, and contemporary application as well as a more detailed treatment of its evolutionary development in the courts. That is the task I set for myself, and it is my hope that the result is valuable to the practitioner, teacher, student, and general reader.

Although this book reflects a broad cross-section of Fifth Amendment issues, it is not and was not meant to be treatise-like in its coverage. Notes have been kept to a minimum, consistent with sound scholarship, in order to avoid diverting the reader's attention. Both the table of cases and the bibliography, however, were intended to assist the researcher in locating the important primary and secondary Fifth Amendment sources. And, although the subject matter of this book is the self-incrimination clause of the Fifth Amendment, it is variously referred to throughout as "the privilege against self-incrimination," "the Fifth Amendment," and "the right to remain silent." Hopefully, these labels will not prove confusing, particularly with reference to the other protections encompassed by the Fifth Amendment. Additionally, the term *defendant* here denotes parties originally charged with a criminal offense even though the correct label at the appellate level might be "petitioner," "respondent," "appellant," or "appellee." It is hoped that this usage will improve clarity for the general reader. Finally, some of the theories expressed in this book have been the subject of articles previously published by the author in legal periodicals. The articles are cited in the bibliography, but I wish to acknowledge the permission granted by the *Journal of Criminal Law and Criminology* to revise and reprint the article "Burdening the Fifth Amendment," which appears herein as chapter 8.

It is with deep appreciation that I express my thanks for the assistance I received from many sources. Deborah Lane, Peggy O'Hare Scott, and Kerry Myers, students at the University of Missouri-Kansas City School of Law, contributed valuable help as research assistants. Linda Stephenson managed to secure every resource I needed through the magic of interlibrary loans. Jackie Capranica was more patient than I had a right to expect in handling the typing of far too many drafts. And finally, my wife, Kathy, gave me her fullest support and encouragement in this project, assisting in everything from substantive editing of the text to proofreading the manuscript. I hope this book is worthy of so many efforts.

1 The Historical Framework

The Fifth Amendment of the U.S. Constitution provides, in part, that "[n]o person . . . shall be compelled in any criminal case to be a witness against himself." The First Congress proposed the addition of this language to the Constitution as part of the Bill of Rights in order to ensure the existence of a privilege against self-incrimination that would be protected against interference by the newly created federal government. Behind the effort to establish an American self-incrimination privilege, however, lay an Anglo-American legal tradition dating back to at least the thirteenth century. In fact, there exist biblical references to a duty to refrain from subscribing to oaths, suggesting even earlier origins of the concepts underlying the modern privilege against self-incrimination. Clearly the principle derives from an established historical background of substantial duration.[1]

The history of the privilege against self-incrimination is so rich and dramatic and so frequently referred to in court opinions that it simply cannot be overlooked in any treatment of the right to remain silent. There is a danger, however, that the particular abuses that prompted the development of the privilege and dominate its history will be used to define the limits of the privilege today. Indeed, the very repetition of the important historical events behind the development of the privilege in case after case may well serve to reinforce the notion that the self-incrimination clause of the Fifth Amendment is circumscribed by its sources and traditions. In light of the absence of formal standards governing the role of history in the interpretation of the privilege against self-incrimination, the risk of overvaluing the available historical evidence is significant.[2]

There is, however, no inflexible tradition limiting the interpretation of the scope of the privilege against self-incrimination to its historical sources, nor would such an approach be advisable. The obvious consequence of a historical barrier would be to halt further development of the privilege and encourage the government to devise techniques to circumvent existing Fifth Amendment limitations. The ultimate outcome of such a process would be the severe dilution of self-incrimination protection. Elsewhere, the U.S. Supreme Court has recognized the need to retain the ability to adapt constitutional doctrine to contemporary needs in order to both prevent the dilution of constitutional protections and regulate unanticipated government conduct. The Eighth Amendment ban against cruel and unusual punishments, for example, is said to "draw its meaning from the evolving

1

standards of decency that mark the progress of a maturing society."[3] Similarly, the Supreme Court has demonstrated its willingness to apply the Fourth Amendment's protection against unreasonable searches and seizures to problems not faced by the American colonists, as in the case of wiretapping, and has observed that the "[f]ramers were men who focused on the wrongs of that day but who intended the Fourth Amendment to safeguard fundamental values which would far outlast the specific abuses which gave it birth."[4] The same logic is equally persuasive when applied to the Fifth Amendment and strongly supports the view that the privilege against self-incrimination need not be limited to curing the abuses from which it grew. Rather, as Judge Jerome Frank observed, we should view the right to remain silent as a "noble privilege [that] often transcends its origins, . . . account[ing] for some of our most cherished values and institutions."[5]

At the other extreme, it could be argued that the history of the privilege is largely irrelevant to determining its proper scope in contemporary American criminal procedure. Presumably, after eliminating the historical sources of the self-incrimination clause, its interpretation would then rest upon the particular language used by the framers of the Fifth Amendment, a sense of the policy objectives that the right to remain silent seeks to further, and legal precedent. Interpreting the self-incrimination clause without reference to its history, however, would produce results as sterile as those obtained from a decision-making perspective in which history was the sole criterion. The language of and policies behind the privilege against self-incrimination, as well as prior Fifth Amendment decisions, derive much of their content from history and tradition. Eliminating the sources of the privilege from the process of interpreting its scope would leave the doctrine without a firm foundation and more easily subject to manipulation.

In light of the ease with which the historical background of the privilege can be misused, it is important to stress that the privilege's history must be understood as neither a determinant of the contemporary meaning of the Fifth Amendment nor as an academic exercise having no bearing upon the process of interpreting its scope. Rather, the sources of the privilege constitute an important body of evidence upon which the courts must rely in determining the proper role of the right to remain silent. The historical evidence should thus be considered as highly relevant but not controlling. It may well be true, as Justice Frankfurter observed, that "[t]he privilege against self-incrimination is a specific provision of which it is peculiarly true that 'a page of history is worth a volume of logic.' "[6] While it is not true that history provides all the answers, it is also not true that the privilege can be understood without a thorough appreciation of the context in which the right to silence arose. Its appropriate role was perhaps best stated by Dean Wigmore, whose views on the privilege have been extremely influential in shaping its development:

If we can throw the light of history upon this rule from its first appearance down to the time when it received its final shape, we shall be better able to judge how firm is its basis in our system of law, and how strong a claim, merely by virtue of its history and its lineage, it ought to have upon our respect. We may then weigh intelligently the various contesting considerations and be prepared to make a final adjustment of the claims of this principle to the important place which it now occupies. . . . If our verdict is favorable, let us carry the principle to its logical extent and enforce it thoroughly; if unfavorable, let its influence be discouraged and let its operation be modified to the extent which our conclusion may require.[7]

Early English Sources

The signing of the Magna Carta by King John in 1215 has been regarded as a momentous event in the development of English law. Yet while King John was forced by the barons at Runnymede to assent to a variety of legal principles, on the whole the document he executed broke little new ground. Rather, the Great Charter was a reaction to the king's legal excesses, and its real importance lay in its reaffirmation of traditional limitations on the authority of the sovereign. Among the issues it addressed were criminal procedure matters such as the requirement in chapter 28 of formal accusation by presentment. No specific mention, however, was made of anything remotely resembling the privilege against self-incrimination. The best argument that can be made for the position that the Magna Carta encompassed a restriction on the power of the government to compel self-incriminatory evidence stems from chapter 29, which ensures freedom from punishment "unless by the lawful judgment of his peers, or by the law of the land." And, while proponents of the principle that an individual should not be forced to accuse himself would later claim the "law-of-the-land" provision of the Magna Carta as the legal authority for their position, history does not support their argument. The evidence suggests to the contrary that the barons who confronted King John were not particularly concerned with the problem of compelled self-incrimination nor was the compelling of self-incrimination an especially widespread practice. Instead, the historical sources of the privilege against self-incrimination reflect a process of development partly predating the Magna Carta but largely independent of it.[8]

At the outset some understanding of the basic features of Anglo-Saxon criminal procedure is necessary to appreciate the evolution of the right to remain silent. The Norman Conquest found a largely informal system of criminal justice prevalent in England, but it was nevertheless a system characterized by accusatorial procedures. The process involved an accusation or charge being made against the alleged offender, followed by a decision as to the form of trial to be employed. During this era such trials assumed three essential modes. "Trial by compurgation" encompassed a sworn oath by the accused attesting to his innocence, supported by the oaths of some number of other persons, the so-called compurgators. However, the latter oaths became merely assertions of the credibility of the accused and did not have to come from people who knew the facts underlying the charge. "Trial by ordeal" required the accused to undergo a physical test to establish his innocence. Carrying a hot iron, inserting one's hand or arm into boiling water, or being bound and then cast into a pool of cold water were the most frequently used techniques. Finally, the Normans added to this array the concept of "trial by battle." Much like trial by ordeal, the system of trial by battle depended upon divine intervention to protect the innocent and was ultimately used in only the more serious criminal cases.[9]

The modes of proof utilized in early Anglo-Saxon criminal procedure were concededly primitive in character. Nevertheless, they were an accurate reflection of the profound religious faith placed in divine intervention and in the sanctity of oaths. They satisfied the need to resolve disputed issues of fact in a manner very much in keeping with the character of the times. Their critical weakness, of course, and the reason for the growth of disenchantment toward their continued use, was the nearly total unreliability of the results produced.

For purposes of the development of the privilege against self-incrimination, however, early Anglo-Saxon criminal procedure is relevant for its overwhelmingly accusatorial characteristics. More particularly, before being put to trial in whatever form, the defendant was the recipient of a public accusation by an identified accuser. The court's role was to determine the mode of trial—it was not to decide guilt or innocence. Finally, the three forms of trial did not exclusively depend upon the presentation of evidence to resolve factual disputes between the parties. Instead, the verdict was based upon the results of the compurgation oath, ordeal, or battle procedures. In the context of such a system, self-incrimination problems were largely irrelevant. Since the procedures of that period did not rely upon factual evidence as such, there was no special need to obtain self-incriminatory admissions from the accused and no effort was made to secure them. The system's indifference to acquiring self-incriminatory evidence was simply part of its general lack of reliance upon evidentiary support for criminal verdicts other than that supplied by the compurgation oath, ordeal, or battle procedures.

The post-Norman Conquest period, extending past the signing of the Magna Carta in 1215, witnessed little change in the accusatorial character of the criminal procedure system. However, the beginnings of an inquest system were developing in the legal structure governing civil matters. But the civil inquest was far different from the full-scale inquisitional proceeding later introduced by ecclesiastical law. Its major characteristic was the fact that decision-making authority was placed in the hands of a jury and the outcome did not depend upon the result of compurgation oaths, ordeals, or battles. Consequently, there was greater dependence upon the presentation of evidence to support the verdict, but still no effort was made to compel the production of evidence that might be criminally damaging. Nevertheless, the movement toward a procedure of trial by jury, a trend that ultimately reached criminal matters, increased the need for the collection of evidence to be used at trial, and fostered a system in which self-incriminatory evidence obtained from the accused might be especially critical.[10]

While Anglo-Saxon law was developing a system that would accommodate self-incriminatory evidence, canon law had already made the change from an accusatorial format to an essentially inquisitorial mode of procedure. Church law had suffered from the same reliability problems that plagued the early English criminal law system, but the shift to an inquisitorial style does not appear to have been undertaken for the purpose of improving verdict reliability. Rather, the development of the inquisitorial process represented a procedural accommodation to permit the church to more effectively and efficiently pursue its sacred mission of identifying and prosecuting religious heretics.

Although the church had generally been lax in its efforts to root out heresy, its perspective dramatically changed in the thirteenth century primarily as a result of both the zealousness of Pope Innocent III and what was felt at the time to be a growing danger of mass heresy. However, the traditional accusatorial procedures were inadequate to aggressively root out heretics. The *accusatio* form of prosecution depended upon an individual making the accusation and becoming a party to the prosecution, as well as bearing the risk of being punished if the prosecution failed. The *denunciatio* procedure permitted the judge to exclusively undertake the prosecution after receiving an accusation, which he then kept secret. The fact that the accuser in a *denunciatio* proceeding was not revealed and did not bear the risk of failure nor the burden of prosecution served to encourage the filing of an accusation. Nevertheless, the system was still tied to the willingness of some private person to assume at least the moral responsibility of becoming an accuser.[11]

The church had at its disposal one additional mode of prosecution with a far greater potential for successfully guarding the true Christian faith, the so-called *inquisitio* proceeding. Here the court functioned as accuser, prosecutor, judge, and jury; one individual had the authority to make the charge, determine whether to prosecute it, and assess whether there was sufficient proof of guilt. The absence of a dependence upon any other official or private party meant that there was no barrier to church defense of established doctrine other than providing for the selection of diligent and loyal judges. In formal terms it was true that the judge was obligated to satisfy himself that grounds for an *inquisitio* proceeding existed in the form of the canon law requirement of *infamia*. However, suspicion or rumor would suffice, and the judge had unreviewable discretion in determining whether the standard was met.[12] Support for the increased utilization of the *inquisitio* procedure, moreover, was given by the Fourth Lateran Council in 1215, ironically the same year the Magna Carta was signed. The council established the oath *de veritate dicenda* to which a suspect was required to swear.[13] The form of the oath was a model of compulsory self-incrimination in that it required truthful answers to all questions directed to the suspect. With the establishment of the oath and given the freedom to conduct a prosecution without waiting for a private complaint, the basic structure of the modern inquisitorial system was complete.

In one sense, the power to investigate possible offenses and the imposition of a requirement that anyone questioned give only truthful answers might not seem out of line with legitimate needs. The reality, however, was that the inquisitorial proceeding coupled with the administration of the oath created an insidious trap for all those unfortunate enough to be ensnared in it. First, the *infamia* requirement presented no real obstacle to subjecting anyone to the *inquisitio* proceeding. Beyond that, once an individual had been chosen as an inquisition victim and presented with the oath, his chances of escaping were slight. The accused was not informed of the charges, his accusers, nor the evidence against him. He was condemned if he refused to take the oath, condemned if he supplied the sought-after admissions, and risked perjury if he failed to tell the truth. In the hands of a skillful interrogator, the inquisitional proceeding and oath were extremely powerful tools and nearly foolproof in securing the conviction of those against whom they were directed.

It was not long before the inquisitorial reforms of the church were introduced into the ecclesiastical law of England. In 1236 upon the marriage of Henry III to his French wife, a number of Catholic clergy migrated to England. Among them was Cardinal Otho, the legate of Pope Gregory IX. Otho convened a meeting of the English bishops and issued a series of constitutions on ecclesiastical matters, including questions of proper procedure to be followed in ecclesiastical courts. Included in the directives was the introduction of the oath *de veritate dicenda*, ultimately better known in England as the "oath *ex officio*" because the judge compelled its execution by virtue of his official office.[14] But, although initially introduced into ecclesiastical procedure, the oath *ex officio* was not limited to use against the clergy. In 1246 Bishop Robert Grosseteste undertook an inquisitorial investigation into immorality in Lincoln and made wide use of the oath. Subjects were intensively questioned about themselves and others, and ultimately protests were lodged against the entire procedure. Henry III responded by limiting use of the oath against civil subjects to matrimonial and testamentary matters, but the evidence suggests that far wider use continued, even by Bishop Grosseteste.[15]

Protests against the use of the oath were a part of a larger controversy over the jurisdictional division between ecclesiastical and civil courts. Common law judges resisted the encroachment of ecclesiastical courts by issuing writs of prohibition against proceedings conducted by church officials. Meanwhile the church sought to conduct its affairs pursuant to constitutions such as those issued by Archbishop Boniface in 1272, which threatened excommunication for anyone who refused to swear to the oath or hindered its administration. By the early 1300s this practice led to the statute "De Articulis Cleri," which sought to clarify the jurisdictional reach of the ecclesiastical courts, prohibit their activities beyond the established jurisdictional limits, and bar administration of the oath *ex officio* to laymen other than in matrimonial or testamentary cases. It appears, however, that even parliamentary controls on the oath were not fully respected.[16]

While the ecclesiastical uses of the inquisitional oath generated some opposition, it must still have been readily apparent how powerful and effective the oath procedure was. It provided a means for compelling even the most powerful people to submit to official questioning. There was no implicit obligation to inform the suspect of the charges against him, nor did his accusers have to be named. He could be interrogated about his own activities or be forced to implicate others, or both. And he faced possible penalties for refusing the oath, committing perjury, or supplying incriminating information. Given the advantages of the procedure, perhaps the only flaw from the crown's perspective was that it had been used by ecclesiastical courts in matters over which the crown wished to retain authority.

In fact, in matters over which the king did have jurisdiction, the civil law system began to copy aspects of ecclesiastical procedure, including utilitzation of the inquisitorial oath. This is best illustrated by the activities of the King's Council. The council was an immensely powerful institution that exercised its authority in the name of the king. Its membership comprised the foremost officers of the time, many of whom were church officials who naturally relied upon ecclesiastical procedure. The council exercised executive, legislative, and judicial authority and ultimately evolved into many important British political institutions, including the Court of Star Chamber, a body whose name derived from the fact that the facilities it used were ornamented with stars. During the fourteenth century the council developed procedures for handling its judicial role, which included anonymous accusation, secret proceedings, and examination by oath *ex officio*. Even opposition by Parliament, including charges that the oath violated the law-of-the-land provision of the Magna Carta, was to no avail. Inquisitorial procedures clearly worked too efficiently to be willingly given up.[17]

Resistance to the early ecclesiastical and civil law uses of the oath procedure constitutes a significant starting point in the evolution of the privilege against self-incrimination. Yet the extent of that early resistance was limited. Nothing like the church inquisitions on the continent appeared in England during this early period, and it would have taken more substantial use of the procedure to stiffen opposition. Instead, resistance to the oath at this time was more a means than an end, its role during this era being primarily that of a focal point in the struggles between ecclesiastical and civil courts. Yet all that could readily have changed if a zealous campaign to root out heresy had been undertaken, but that appeared unnecessary in England, at least until the appearance of John Wycliffe and the Lollards in the late fourteenth century.

The spread of Lollardry in England was aggressively fought by the Catholic clergy. They viewed the Lollards as a heretical sect and even petitioned Parliament for its assistance. Parliament responded in 1401 with the statute "De Haeretico Comburendo," providing for the burning of heretics. Opposition was limited, but there were instances in which suspected Lollards challenged their subjection to the inquisitorial features of the oath. In particular, in 1407 Willard Thorpe was ordered to swear to the oath prior to his interrogation, but he refused. Thorpe was therefore questioned without the oath, and in 1408 Archibishop Arundel issued a decree providing that there should be no future challenging of the oath procedure in such cases.[18]

The statutory enactment of 1401 effectively introduced the Inquisition to England. It entailed the utilization of the state's power to support ecclesiastical efforts to control heresy, and it meant the emergence of the oath interrogation as an important, if not dominant, procedural technique. Moreover, much like its counterpart on the continent, the English Inquisition produced its share of martyrs. Professor Leonard Levy has estimated that during the period from 1401 to 1534, when the statute on heretics was repealed, approximately fifty people were burned at the stake while many thousands were subjected to lesser persecutions, including substantial terms of imprisonment. Victims were selected on the basis of suspicion and subjected to a wide-ranging interrogation in which they were forced not only to admit their own guilt but also to provide names for future proceedings. But despite the significance of the oath in the inquisitorial process, it does not appear to have led to widespread resistance. Objection to taking the oath such as that of Willard Thorpe was apparently rare or at least not widely reported. Similarly, only a few writers protested against the oath, and they faced the opposition of the influential Sir Thomas More.[19]

One can only speculate as to what might have happened with respect to resistance to the inquisitorial oath had not Henry VIII broken with the Church of Rome. The king had received a petition from Parliament in 1532 that objected to the broad ecclesiastical inquisitions and the procedures they employed, but Henry passed it on to the clergy officials for reply. Moreover, he himself appeared to be orthodox in his religious beliefs and committed to the suppression of opposing views. But in seeking to establish himself as head of the Church of England, it became useful to Henry to accept the parliamentary petition, which led him to approve the repeal of the statute on the burning of heretics in 1534. But, lest there be any doubt that Henry had not changed character, it should be noted that he then mercilessly pursued those who sided with the Church of Rome and refused to swear to the Act of Supremacy recognizing him as "Supreme Head of the Church of England." Failure to execute the oath recognizing Henry VIII as the leader of the church in place of the pope brought with it risk of the death penalty. Such was the case even for Sir Thomas More who had, ironically, supported the oath procedure so vigorously in his pursuit of opponents of official Catholic dogma.[20]

The history of the evolution of the privilege against self-incrimination is, up to this point, very much the story of the struggles between ecclesiastical and civil courts. Opposition to inquisitorial procedures was clearly tied to efforts to restrict the infringements of the ecclesiastical judges who were using them. When, however, the crown placed itself behind the movement to crush heresy, opposition appeared to dwindle. Subsequently the papal-crown controversies during the reign of Henry VIII changed the character of the dispute. The crown took control over church as well as civil law, and the rift between the two dimmed in importance. Replacing it, however, was a new struggle between the Church of Rome and the Church of England, with Anglicans now using inquisitorial techniques against their Catholic originators.

The use of the oath *ex officio* during the reign of Edward VI, Henry's son, does not appear to have been extensive. But, upon his death, the crown passed to Queen Mary who instituted a Catholic restoration and a reign of terror to ensure its success. Widespread use was made of inquisitional proceedings, and the statute "De Haeretico Comburendo" was reenacted for additional support. To further aid her cause, Mary also created a new institution, which ultimately became the Court of High Commission. Its purpose was to ensure vigorous action against heresy, and Mary commanded that it use the oath *ex officio* in the performance of its duties. Many more "heretics" went to the stake and suffered persecution for their beliefs during Queen Mary's reign than in comparable periods under her predecessors, and perhaps for this reason challenges to the authority to extract the oath were more frequently made.[21]

Elizabeth I's ascendancy to the English throne meant a return to efforts to establish an independent Anglican church. Queen Mary's legislation against heresy as such was repealed, and the capital punishment of heretics virtually ended. Officially disapproved beliefs were still banned, but under the label of "treason" rather than "heresy," and the enforcement of this state policy was generally far more lenient than had previously been the case. But, although efforts to root out opposing views were less intense during the Elizabethan era, they did exist and, in fact, encompassed a broader array of victims. The previous pattern had been one in which a Catholic sovereign had sought to root out anti-Catholic heresy. Now, in the person of Elizabeth, the anti-Catholics had wrested control of the monarchy. Not unexpectedly they commenced to use the tools their predecessors had created against them. In addition, however, the Anglican hierarchy directed some of its energies to the suppression of emerging Puritan heresies. The result was a seemingly evenhanded policy of persecution. But the Catholics, having previously used the self-incriminatory oath procedure, less frequently objected to its legality while the Puritans, always its victims, were more likely to complain.[22]

Queen Elizabeth's policy of relative toleration came under great pressure as a result of Catholic threats to the security of her throne. These included a papal-supported rebellion and the excommunication of Elizabeth by Pope Pius V in 1570. It became necessary to use the secular treason laws to protect Protestant England in much the same way that Catholic orthodoxy had used heresy as a means of preserving the purity of the Catholic faith. Especially after Elizabeth's excommunication, which absolved subjects from allegiance to her and commanded that her laws not be obeyed, every Catholic became a potential traitor, unlike Puritan nonconformists who at least presented no similar external threat. Activist English Catholics were vigorously pursued and placed in the traditional dilemma of an inquisition victim. Refusal to take the oath meant punishment just as surely as an admission of Catholicism. A few did resort to the traditional maxim *nemo tenetur seipsum prodere*, that no man is bound to accuse himself, but they were a very small minority of the Catholics investigated. And for those who did resist the oath, there remained the fact that Catholicism had been responsible for the development of the *ex officio* procedure and that it was an established part of canon law. The objections that were made tended to reflect refusals to answer based upon conscience or the more limited principle that compelled self-incrimination was proper only after formal accusation and could not serve as an open-ended opportunity to question uncharged suspects. Most Catholics, however, did not challenge the procedure, thereby either passively accepting their fate or glorying in their imminent martyrdom.[23]

During a period of very deep concern as to the loyalty of English Catholics, it was understandable that the crown did not undertake aggressive pursuit of the Puritans despite their severe criticisms of the Anglican faith. The Puritans approached their religion with the utmost sincerity and intensity and were willing to challenge issues as diverse as proper priestly attire and the choice of a prayer book. Nevertheless, they were allies of the throne in opposition to the Catholic threat and, indeed, would have been far more merciless in their treatment of the Romanists had the charge been theirs. It is doubtful, moreover, that they would have been any more indulgent to the Anglicans had they been given the opportunity to pursue them. The character of the early Puritan opposition to Anglican practice, however, was largely limited to minor procedural matters. Moreover, the Puritans maintained their allegiance to Elizabeth even in the midst of their criticism. But, in the final analysis, the queen saw the Puritan movement as a fundamental challenge to her sovereignty since Puritan faith simply did not accept civilian supremacy in ecclesiastical matters. In 1583 Elizabeth took the first major step toward bringing the Puritan challenge under control with the selection of John Whitgift as archbishop of Canterbury.

Archbishop Whitgift zealously undertook his responsibility to ferret out dangerous Puritan nonconformists. Of particular importance to the development of the privilege against self-incrimination was the fact that he used the device of the special commission created by Queen Mary in his enforcement efforts. This mechanism, constituted on authority of the crown, had been used sporadically in ecclesiastical matters. The increasing judicial character of commission proceedings and its more regularized use turned it into a more formal institution, which came to be known as the "Court of High Commission" or, more simply, the "High Commission." It was reconstituted by Elizabeth with Whitgift as its president and given vast authority over religious matters, including the power to interrogate upon oath. Only the discretion of the commissioners restricted the High Commission in its activities.[24]

The High Commission proceedings covered both private and public religious matters. In private matters such as a complaint of adultery lodged by a spouse, the defendant would be brought in for interrogation and tendered the oath. His responses were secured without the benefit of counsel and without being presented with formal charges. The High Commission, however, could also proceed *ex officio mero*, that is to say, on its own authority. Here the court was itself the accuser, but it could not proceed without some suspicion, albeit slight, directed against the accused. The procedure was particularly appropriate against the religious dissent of Catholics and Puritans. And it too relied heavily on the administration of the oath *ex officio* for the acquisition of evidence. Despite opposition to High Commission tactics and petitions for relief, no change in its procedure was made.

Puritans were far more vocal in their resistance to High Commission inquisitional proceedings than their Catholic victims. If nothing else, they, unlike the Catholics, had no tradition of ecclesiastical use of the oath *ex of-*

ficio behind them. Perhaps the most notable case during this period involved Robert Beale, clerk of the privy council, and a bitter opponent of interrogation by oath. Beale was one of the early advocates of the view that the Magna Carta itself barred the oath. He argued that the common law prohibitions of the thirteenth century against ecclesiastical court encroachments upon the jurisdiction of the civil courts demonstrated the illegality of the oath procedure. Others similarly took the position that the law did not permit them to be forced to take the oath. They argued that under the common law, no one was bound to accuse himself, nor was he obligated to subscribe to an oath requiring that he answer all the questions put to him without first being informed of the charges. But the Puritan position failed to undercut Elizabeth's support of Archbishop Whitgift. And with the defeat of the Spanish Armada in 1588, as a result of which the Catholic threat was drastically reduced, the Puritans' hope for gentle treatment at the hands of the High Commission diminished.[25]

The practical consequences of being selected for High Commission interrogation and facing the oath *ex officio* during this period are aptly illustrated by the proceedings against John Udall in 1590. As described by Professor Leonard Levy, Udall was arrested as part of a crackdown stemming from the publication of a number of seditious works. Udall refused to answer questions relating to the authorship of two tracts and refused to take the oath. In response to repeated urgings from his interrogators that he swear to answer all questions truthfully, Udall remained adamant. Moreover, he offered a perceptive insight into the consequences of taking the oath, noting that he had done so two years previously and thereby provided self-incriminatory evidence with respect to a charge that could not otherwise have been proven. Udall's refusal to take the oath, however, resulted in his imprisonment. He was examined again six months later but persisted in his refusal to swear to the oath. He was then brought to trial for the publication of seditious matter where he was again challenged to take the oath and establish his innocence; indeed, his failure to do so was urged as proof of his guilt. Nevertheless, Udall clung to the view that he could not be compelled to accuse himself. The result was a verdict of guilty and, after a refusal to admit guilt in writing, the imposition of the death sentence. The execution, however, was never carried out. A series of delays occurred during which time Udall's submission was sought in return for a pardon. Udall maintained his stance, however, and wound up dying in prison during the negotiation process.[26]

Certain critical aspects of High Commission procedure and the resistance to it during this era are especially important in tracing the history of the privilege against self-incrimination. The Commission, pursuant to the crown's directive, functioned only in the realm of ecclesiastical matters. It seemed to view itself, therefore, as immune from common law restrictions. This meant not only the power to utilize *ex officio* inquisitorial procedures but also freedom from the common law prerequisite of a formal presentment or charge. Opposition to the High Commission, and particularly to its use of the oath *ex officio*, stressed several distinct positions. The legalistic objections were based upon the absence of a common law history of compelled interrogation by oath as well as the tradition of common law court resistance to ecclesiastical encroachment. The absence of formal accusation or presentment prior to the interrogation was also singled out. The law-of-the-land clause of chapter 29 of the Magna Carta provided additional authority. Finally, opponents raised fundamental moral objections to forcing self-incrimination and the incrimination of others as part of the inquisitorial process.[27]

The vast authority of the High Commission, despite its pervasiveness, was not without limits. In particular, it could seek to coerce its victims into executing the oath, but if that failed, its proceedings were thwarted. The Commission did have the power to imprison for failure to swear to the oath, but it had no power to render a conviction. That step required referral of the matter to the Court of Star Chamber where the oath could be administered in all except capital cases, but only after formal presentment. Other common law protections such as the right to call witnesses were also available in the Star Chamber. The remainder of Queen Elizabeth's reign, during which Whitgift continued in his role as archbishop of Canterbury, saw both institutions work hand in hand to serve the crown's interests. Inquisition procedures and interrogation by oath remained important in both the High Commission and Star Chamber; opposition was largely futile.[28]

The ascension of James I to the English throne had little impact on the by now extensive use of inquisitorial procedures. Indeed, the new sovereign left little doubt that he fully supported the oath *ex officio*. Puritan opposition to the administration of the oath meanwhile remained strong and found an ally in the common law courts. The latter joined the struggle against the oath *ex officio* as part of a larger effort to control the scope of ecclesiastical court jurisdiction, an objective dating back to the thirteenth century. The tactic employed, again reaching back into history, was the writ of prohibition barring administration of the oath by the ecclesiastical courts. By the early seventeenth century common law prohibitions were increasingly used against the oath to the consternation of church officials. But even their formal complaints failed to stem the use of the writ.[29]

The appointment of Sir Edward Coke as chief justice of the Court of Common Pleas in 1606 led to even more resistance to the compulsory self-incrimination procedures of the ecclesiastical courts. In 1607 he took the position that the High Commission lacked the authority to imprison without action of Parliament and ruled:

[n]o man ecclesiastical or temporal shall be examined upon secret thoughts
of his heart or of his secret opinion. . . . No layman may be examined *ex
officio* except in two causes . . . for laymen for the most part are not let-
tered, wherefore they may easily be inveigled and entrapped, and principally in heresy and errors of faith.[30]

Yet behind his opposition to the oath *ex officio* was a more significant
challenge to the prerogative of the crown, which lay behind the High Commission and its procedures. Coke went so far as to suggest to James that he lacked
the authority to personally decide cases and therefore could not take prohibition matters away from the common law courts. James was enraged, and accounts have Coke begging his pardon for the affront. Whether or not this incident occurred, Coke continued to support the use of the writ of prohibition
against the ecclesiastical oath *ex officio* procedure. Even James' action in issuing new letters patent for the High Commission and naming Coke as a commissioner failed to alter his stance; Coke simply refused to serve. Coke's elevation
to the position of chief justice of the King's Bench was similarly ineffective, and
he was ultimately dismissed from office by King James in 1616. With his
removal the common law courts virtually abandoned their use of prohibitions
against High Commission oaths. Yet Coke, along with common law judges and
members of Parliament, as well as the Puritan victims of the High Commission, had contributed to the greater general acceptance of the Latin maxim
nemo tenetur seipsum prodere, that no one was bound to accuse himself.[31]

The Proceedings against John Lilburne

By the early part of the seventeenth century, a substantial history of opposition to the oath *ex officio* in High Commission proceedings had already
developed. Concededly, the resistance to the oath was part of a larger pattern of struggles between the crown, Parliament, common law and ecclesiastical courts, and religious dissidents. One might speculate whether,
absent these tensions, any significant opposition to the inquisitorial process
would have emerged. However, history demonstrates that the oath was
often a focal point of controversy, undoubtedly at least partly because of its
effectiveness as a prosecution tool. Nevertheless, history has not accorded
to any one opponent or incident up until this period any unique credit in the
development of the privilege against self-incrimination. That judgment is,
instead, reserved for a remarkable young Puritan named John Lilburne,
known in his own day as "Freeborn John."

Lilburne was, himself, a clothier's apprentice with relatively little formal education. Yet he possessed a tenacity of spirit and single-mindedness
of conviction rare for individuals of any age or level of sophistication.
Simply reading the reports of the proceedings against him amply
demonstrates how unrelenting he was in the pursuit of his objectives, important among which was the elimination of the oath *ex officio* procedure.

A variety of factors related to the historical period in which Lilburne undertook his crusade against the oath were of assistance, but history quite appropriately recognizes Lilburne's service as a special catalyst in the movement to abolish the oath.

Lilburne's difficulties arose during the ill-fated reign of Charles I, particularly after 1633 when William Laud was appointed archbishop of Canterbury. The era was characterized by a renewed zeal in efforts to preserve the Anglican faith from all potential threats, a task well suited to Laud's aggressive inclinations. To accomplish this sacred mission, new letters patent for the High Commission were obtained from the king, and the Commission itself was increased in size and thereby enabled to function within a larger geographical jurisdiction. In a sense, Laud was no different than many of his predecessors in utilizing the High Commission and its oath *ex officio* procedure to attack dissident beliefs. However, he was particularly aggressive in his methods and scope and did not have to face significant opposition from the common law judges who, since Coke's removal, remained under control, nor from Parliament, which was kept in recess for eleven years. In fact, the commission was now a more powerful institution as a result of a change in procedure permitting it to view a refusal to take the oath as an admission of the charges *pro confesso*. What Archbishop Laud did not realize, however, was that his unrelenting persecution of dissidents was creating a body of sympathizers for the victims of the repression. And, while the sympathizers were probably most disturbed by both the punishments the High Commission imposed and the overall scope of its activities, they were also available to lend support to attacks on Commission procedure. It was to this body of public opinion that John Lilburne made his most effective appeal.[32]

The year 1637 marked the opening round in Lilburne's crusade against the oath *ex officio*. In December of that year he was arrested along with John Wharton, a book dealer, for having sent seditious books from Holland to England. After three days of imprisonment, he was taken before a Mr. Cockney, chief clerk to the attorney-general, John Banks. Cockney proceeded to question Lilburne about his general background, presence in Holland, and awareness of the seditious tracts he allegedly helped smuggle into England. After a short period of such questioning, and as the interrogation began to stray, Lilburne ceased to cooperate. When asked about conversations he might have had with another suspect, he launched into a reply setting the framework for his later objection to the administration of the oath *ex officio*. He inquired,

> [W]hy do you ask me all these questions? these are nothing pertinent to my imprisonment, for I am not imprisoned for knowing and talking with such and such men, but for sending over Books; and therefore I am not willing to answer you to any more of these questions, because I see you go about by this Examination to ensnare me: for seeing the things for which I am im-

prisoned cannot be proved against me, you will get other matter out of my examination . . . and of any other matter that you have to accuse me of, I know it is warrantable by the law of God, and I think by the law of the land, that I may stand upon my just defense, and not answer to your interrogatories; and that my accusers ought to be brought face to face to justify what they accuse me of.[33]

Cockney persisted in his efforts to secure responses from Lilburne, but he continued "unwilling to answer any impertinent questions, for fear that with my answer I may do myself hurt."[34] Lilburne was then taken before Banks, but there was no change of heart, and he was recommitted.

One can only be impressed by the courage Lilburne displayed in challenging the authority of his interrogators despite his youth and inexperience. He resolutely maintained that the questions propounded were impertinent and contrary to the laws of God and England. Yet, beyond that, an analysis of the character of Lilburne's position reveals a far more astute and particularized objection to the proceedings. Lilburne was being subjected to preliminary interrogation prior to a formal Star Chamber trial. The tradition of resistance to compulsory interrogation was, however, associated with High Commission proceedings. It was in the realm of the ecclesiastical courts that appeals to the maxim *nemo tenetur seipsum prodere* were made. By invoking a right against self-accusation, dissidents sought to confine ecclesiastical jurisdiction within appropriate limits. Even Coke, who opposed the High Commission oath except in matrimonial or testamentary matters, or in proceedings involving priests, accepted the legality of the procedure in the Court of Star Chamber. His only qualifications were that witnesses were to be protected from the oath and that it could not be employed in serious trials for life or limb. Lilburne could not draw on legal tradition, therefore, to support total opposition to interrogations that might be self-incriminatory. Instead, his objections to Cockney and Banks were more precise than a general resistance to being questioned. Since the interrogation was preliminary to a Star Chamber trial, common law procedures were presumably necessary. In particular, this would mean a requirement of formal presentment or accusation prior to the administration of the oath. Since formal accusation had been made that Lilburne had sent seditious matter into England, he expressed his willingness to answer questions related to that charge. He objected specifically to responding to interrogatories he felt were not germane to that accusation, and he recognized that answering the questions might serve to ensnare him by providing the state with its only usable source of evidence. Simply stated, therefore, Lilburne sought merely to limit the interrogation, not to end it. And, while common law tradition supported his position, his reliance on the law of God and the Magna Carta's law-of-the-land language was a dubious foundation.

Two weeks after Lilburne's confrontation with Banks and his clerk, he was brought to the Star Chamber office and told that he would be examined *before* the drawing of a bill of complaint setting forth the charges. To Lilburne, this meant that "they had no grounded matter against me for to write a bill, and therefore they went about to make me betray my own innocence, that so they might ground the bill upon my own words."[35] Pressed to take the oath, he responded that "before I swear, I will know to what I must swear";[36] Lilburne would have no part of an oath demanding truthful answers to all questions without first knowing the subject matter of the questions. It is not clear whether or not Lilburne perceived that High Commission tactics were being used in a Star Chamber proceeding, but it is certain that Lilburne would not cooperate.

Some time thereafter Lilburne and Wharton were brought to trial before the Star Chamber Court for sending seditious books into England and refusing to take the oath. Not surprisingly, Lilburne persisted in his refusal to be sworn. He was recommmitted to prison, but later returned to court. This time the affidavit of his accuser was read to him and the oath again tendered. Lilburne's refusal to take the oath on this occasion set forth his reasons: "I understand, that this Oath is one and the same with the High Commission Oath, which Oath I know to be both against the law of God, and the law of the land; and therefore in brief I dare not take the oath, though I suffer death for the refusal of it."[37] Although he rejected administration of the oath, Lilburne nevertheless defended himself against the specific claims in the affidavit read to him, categorically denying the charges and questioning the veracity of his accuser who "is known to be a notorious lying fellow, and hath accused me for the purchasing of his own liberty, which he hath got."[38]

Lilburne's obstinacy was rewarded by the court with a contempt conviction. Interestingly, the court chose not to take the sedition charge as proven *pro confesso*. The punishment, however, was severe, including a £500 fine and an apparently savage whipping as he was wheeled in a cart to the pillory. Yet Lilburne would still not hold his tongue and used the occasion of his punishment to launch into a speech against his mistreatment at the hands of the bishops. That action caused his reimprisonment under conditions that he "should be laid alone, with irons on his hands and legs, in the Wards of the Fleet, where the basest and meanest sort of prisoners are used to be put; and that the Warden of the Fleet take special care to hinder the resort of any persons whatsoever unto him."[39]

Lilburne remained imprisoned for over two years but saw his opportunity for release arrive when King Charles called Parliament into session after a break of eleven years. The king's objectives may well have focused upon the raising of revenue, but Parliament was after concessions. Immediately upon the convening of Parliament in 1640, Lilburne presented it with a petition for his release, in response to which the Commons resolved "that the Sentence of the Star Chamber given against John Lilburne is illegal" and that "reparation ought to be given to Mr. Lilburne for his imprisonment, sufferings, and losses sustained by that illegal sentence."[40] Beyond remedying the specific injustices done to Lilburne and others like him, Parliament also addressed complaints against the crown's methods. It being too late for compromise, Parliament in 1641 enacted legislation abolishing both the Star Chamber and High Commission and specifically barred the administration of oaths by ecclesiastical courts.[41] Lilburne himself enlisted in the parliamentary forces when civil war broke out and was committed to their cause. Through it all he gained great popularity among the citizenry.

Lilburne's character was such that he could not abandon principle even though he had become part of the triumphant resistance. For him, the right against self-accusation was more than an issue to be used in challenging the crown; it was an end in itself rather than the means to an end. Soon enough this brought Lilburne into conflict with the parliamentary forces, and he ultimately was arrested in 1649, this time charged with high treason. He was brought to trial before an Extraordinary Commission of Oyer and Terminer whose members included the lord mayor of London, a number of aldermen, and seventeen special appointees. But despite the number and stature of the officials arrayed against him, Lilburne was in command. He objected, obstructed, and interfered with the proceedings at every opportunity. Asked at the very commencement of the trial to simply hold up his hand, Lilburne launched into an extended speech criticizing the proceedings and demanding "the liberty of every free-born Englishman."[42] Resistance to the court's proceedings included, of course, objection to compelled interrogation. Lilburne commented that he had been brought in for examination despite the fact that he saw "no accuser, no prosecutor, no accusation, no charge nor indictment,"[43] and could not avoid noting the irony of the fact that his interrogator, John Bradshaw, had represented him in his efforts to secure reparations for his Star Chamber treatment. His continual interruptions brought frustration to the court. At one point when Lilburne asked to be heard, Lord Keble responded, "I pray you hear me a word."[44] Shortly thereafter when Lilburne asked for one word more, Judge Jermin answered: "Mr. Lilburne, pray spare a word, and hear the court."[45] It must have taken hours before Lilburne raised his hand as initially requested and stated, "I am John Lilburne, son of Mr. Richard Lilburne."[46]

It had been twelve years since Lilburne had resisted the oath *ex officio* in the Star Chamber and suffered a harsh contempt sentence for his actions. In the intervening years, Parliament had abolished the Courts of Star Chamber and High Commission as well as ecclesiastical use of the oath *ex officio*. Moreover, it had voted his Star Chamber sentence illegal. The impact of these developments on Lilburne's 1649 trial were evident. When called upon to plead to the charge, for example, the following exchange is reported.

> Mr. Broughton: What say'st thou, John Lilburne, art thou guilty of this treason whereof thou standest indicted, or not guilty?
>
> ***
>
> Lilburne: . . . Then, Sir, thus by the Laws of England, I am not to answer to questions against or concerning myself.
> Lord Keble: You shall not be compelled.
> Another Judge: Mr. Lilburne, is this to answer against yourself, to say, you are not guilty? By the Laws of the Land you are to plead to your Charge, and it is no accusing of yourself to say Guilty, or Not Guilty.
>
> ***
>
> Lilburne: Sir, by the Petition of Right, I am not bound to answer to any questions concerning myself. . . . I find there is a great deal of nicety and danger in locking a man up to single formalities, in answering Guilty or Not Guilty.[47]

Apparently, the court was willing to accept the proposition that it could not compel answers to incriminatory questions. Lilburne, however, was extending this to the notion that there was a sufficient risk of danger to justify a refusal to even plead to the charge. He prodded the court to grant him counsel and other rights so that the proceedings would not "ensnare me, and take away my life for punctilios."[48] Later when the statement was made that Lilburne had "pleaded Not Guilty and confessed something," he responded: "I have never confessed any thing, neither did I plead Not Guilty; for my plea was conditional, grounded upon your promises, not to take any advantage of my ignorance in your formalities."[49] His concern as to the consequences of pleading was, therefore, not totally ill-founded, but, nevertheless, the view that he was not bound to enter a plea was without legal support.

Self-incrimination problems also arose during the course of the trial. Lilburne was confronted with a witness who asserted that Lilburne was the author of a treasonous tract. The report of the trial describes the exchange:

> Lord Keble: Mr. Lilburne, do you acknowledge it to be your own handwriting? Shew it him.
> Lilburne: I am too old with such simple ginns to be catched; I will cast mine eyes upon none of your papers, neither shall I answer to any questions that concern myself: I have learned more law out of the Petition of Right, and Christ pleading before Pilate, than so.
> Mr. Attorney: Would you had learnt more gospel!
> Judge Jermin: You may answer a question, whether it be true or false; and confess and glorify God.
> Lilburne: I have said, Sir; prove it: I am not to be catched with such fooleries.

Lord Keble: You see the man, and the quality of the man; this is the paper that he delivered into his own hand, and that is sufficient, as well as if it was of his own hand-writing.

***

Mr. Attorney: My lord, you may see the valiantness of this champion of the people's liberties, that will not own his own hand; although I must desire you, gentlemen of the jury, to observe that Mr. Lilburne implicitly confesseth it.

Lilburne: Sir, I deny nothing: and what now can be proved mine, I have a life to lay down for the justification of it, but prove it first.[50]

The court did not, as had the Star Chamber in 1639, imprison Lilburne for his refusal to answer. Rather, they sought to pressure and mock him into a response and suggested the applicability of the *pro confesso* rule deeming the lack of a response to be an implicit admission. Lilburne, however, stood firm.

Much of Lilburne's trial consisted of the reading of his allegedly seditious tracts. Lilburne, however, interrupted the proceedings frequently to question the legality of the court and its tactics, claiming that he was "denied, and that upon my life, all the privileges of an Englishman, and with your insinuations and great words drawn on by my ignorance to ensnare myself."[51] He gave an impassioned speech in his defense, rambling far afield and causing Lord Keble to comment that the court was not there "to hear you tell the story of all your life."[52] The conclusion of Lilburne's monologue, however, was greeted with audible approval from the gallery, enough so that more troops had to be summoned.[53] But the tumult apparently did not approach the intensity of the reaction when the jury returned its verdict of not guilty.[54] Two weeks later Lilburne was released from the tower a hero.

Even Lilburne's successful treason defense did not end his troubles. In 1651 he was brought before the House of Commons, charged with attacking the reputation of a member of Parliament. There he was summarily convicted and fined as well as banished. He fled to Holland but subsequently returned whereupon he was arrested. Violating his banishment merely required that he be proven to be John Lilburne. He was nevertheless acquitted but kept under confinement where he died in 1657. Two years later Parliament revoked his illegal sentence.[55] However, Lilburne's life had given meaning to a principle in a way few others could claim. Thereafter, although judges might seek to pressure a suspect into self-incriminatory revelations, the principle that answers could not be compelled seems to have become an accepted fact.

The Constitutional and Colonial Background

Given that the American colonies were principally settled by British subjects, it should not be suprising to find that English legal traditions appeared very quickly in the colonial experience. The transition, however, particularly as it affected the development of the privilege against self-incrimination, was not an entirely smooth one. After all, some of the colonies were established prior to Parliament's abolition of the Star Chamber and High Commission in 1641 while others were settled after; legal principles in the separate settlements might well differ because of that fact. In addition, the colonists were largely political and religious dissidents seeking escape from the persecution they suffered in England. To the extent that the oath *ex officio* and the inquisitorial process contributed to their oppression, they might be expected to have supported the right to remain silent. On the other hand, the single-mindedness of many of the religious groups of that era could have lead them to employ any means at their disposal to suppress differing views.

The colonial response to the concept of a right against self-incrimination reflected both legal developments up until the Lilburne trials as well as those that followed. In particular, the post-Lilburne era in England had seen widespread recognition of the right against self-accusation, eventually leading to the enactment of a statute in 1662 barring administration of the oath *ex officio* in any proceeding.[56] During the same period the civil rules disqualifying a party in interest from testifying were being extended to English criminal procedure.[57] This served to make compulsory interrogation fruitless since an accused could not testify either for or against himself. The witness disqualification theory was based upon the untrustworthiness of an interested party's testimony while the opposition to the oath was premised upon the unfairness of compelled self-accusation. The result of both, however, was an end to forceable questioning of an accused upon threat of imprisonment for failure to respond. The colonial legal systems were influenced by these trends.

The American colonies, however, respected the tradition against compulsory self-incrimination with considerable inconsistency. This was true both before and after 1641, the point at which the Star Chamber and the High Commission courts were abolished. Indeed, the very fact that both institutions were never brought over to the colonies deprived the American legal system of the kind of symbol it would have taken to prompt a concerted movement against self-incriminatory questioning. The passage of time, however, along with periodic efforts by colonial officials to suppress opposition brought more support to the principle of a suspect's right to silence. Professor Levy's exhaustive analysis of pre-revolutionary trial transcripts and statutes reflects frequent mention of and deference to the *nemo tenetur* principle.[58]

In the context of the steady progression toward a right of silence in the colonial legal systems, instances where the right was denied stand out dramatically. The Salem witch trials of 1692 deserve particular mention. The Salem judges not only felt that no freedom from self-incrimination existed but to the contrary believed that torture and death for the recalcitrant were appropriate. Similarly, in New York a statute was enacted in 1722 requiring suspects in certain cases to take an oath that they had not traded in violation of the existing commerce laws. Refusal to take the oath meant conviction *pro confesso*. The resulting objection to the procedure, however, led to the abolition of the oath requirement. Even the future president of the Continental Congress, John Hancock, may have been the victim of inquisitorial proceedings in his trial on smuggling charges.[59]

The end of the Revolutionary War failed to bring with it the formation of a strong national government. Instead, the newly freed colonies were loosely united under the Articles of Confederation with each colony retaining authority over its own affairs. Since they had experienced what was perceived to be widespread British violations of the common law, colonial leaders largely avoided relying upon legislative and judicial officials to protect fundamental rights; rather, written constitutions appeared to be necessary. The widespread resistance to the oath *ex officio* in England and the overutilization of inquisitorial procedures in the colonies made the right to remain silent one such issue to be addressed in these new constitutions.

George Mason drafted the language of the self-incrimination privilege in the Virginia Declaration of Rights, providing in the context of enumerating the rights of an accused that no man could be "compelled to give evidence against himself."[60] His wording was closely followed in the constitutions of Pennsylvania, Delaware, Maryland, North Carolina, Vermont, Massachusetts, and New Hampshire, all of which enacted a separate bill of rights.[61] Of these, Maryland and Delaware incorporated language to the effect that the right was not to be exclusively restricted to criminal matters, something Mason might have intended but did not state. The New York, New Jersey, Georgia, and South Carolina constitutions did not have separate bills of rights, but this does not mean that freedom from self-incrimination did not exist, particularly since the English common law was kept in force.[62] Finally, Rhode Island and Connecticut did not at this time replace their colonial charters with a written constitution, but again not necessarily intending by their inaction to imply that they subscribed to compulsory self-incrimination.

In 1787 representatives met in Philadelphia as a constitutional convention to form a national government and replace the unsatisfactory Articles of Confederation. Their attentions, however, did not turn to the establishment of a bill of rights, and the convention adjourned without providing for any written protection of fundamental liberties. George Mason's suggestion that the delegates adopt a bill of rights was defeated by the negative votes of all the state delegations voting as states. Nevertheless, it became apparent during the ratification process that a bill of rights was needed to allay popular suspicions about the new federal government. When the First Congress convened in 1789 Congressman James Madison undertook to see that such a document was framed. His initial proposal with respect to the right to silence provided that no person "shall be compelled to be a witness against himself." Although similar in language to Mason's Virginia Declaration of Rights formulation, Madison's version clearly had no limitation to criminal matters. That, however, was changed as a result of an amendment in the House and no further alterations were made in the Senate. Thus with relatively little discussion or debate, the self-incrimination clause was incorporated into the Bill of Rights. In its final form, it provided that "[n]o person . . . shall be compelled in any Criminal Case to be a witness against himself." The transformation of the Latin maxim *nemo tenetur seipsum prodere* into a protected right was now complete.[63]

2 The Policy Perspective

Although the Fifth Amendment privilege against self-incrimination can trace its roots back several centuries and point to sources in many dramatic confrontations between men of conscience and their persecutors, its history does not totally define the contemporary scope of the right to remain silent. The proceedings against Lilburne, Udall, and others were for the most part official investigations in which the suspect was required to answer all inquiries upon threat of either contempt for failure to respond, conviction of the charge being investigated, or torture to overcome his resistance. The methodology was direct, and subtlety was unnecessary. Efforts to duplicate these features of seventeenth-century British procedure are rarely encountered today, however, partly as a result of the success of the movement to achieve freedom from compelled self-accusation. Instead, indirect techniques to acquire self-incriminatory information are used in attempting to circumvent Fifth Amendment restrictions. History fails to reveal that the *nemo tenetur seipsum prodere* principle barred the use of such tactics because the state did not have to rely upon them. Twentieth-century American society must decide for itself whether the application of the Fifth Amendment privilege is to be limited to the specific abuses from which it grew or be expanded beyond its narrow historical focus. The answer to this question lies not in history but rather in the Fifth Amendment's policy objectives.

The identification of the policy interests served by the privilege against self-incrimination is not a new undertaking.[1] Jeremy Bentham's *Rationale of Judicial Evidence* analyzed the supporting justifications for the right to remain silent well over a century ago as did Wigmore's classic *Treatise on the Anglo-American System of Evidence in Trials at Common Law* more recently. Other authors have contributed additional valuable insights, addressing questions presented by the application of the Fifth Amendment to situations not previously confronted. It would seem that since the Fifth Amendment has moved beyond its initial focus of barring contempt penalties for an accused who refused to answer self-incriminatory questions at trial, one might anticipate extensive judicial analysis of the policies behind the privilege. The absence of clear historical support for other than a narrow right to remain silent at trial seemingly dictates a substantial judicial effort to develop other supporting rationales for a wider privilege. Surprisingly, such has not been the case. This is not meant to imply that the courts have failed to identify the objectives the privilege might serve to further, for they have not. Rather, court opinions to date are deficient in failing to undertake a meaningful Fifth Amendment policy analysis, the result of which is a shopping list of rationales without any hint as to the relative importance of the identified policy objectives and without any indication of how the principles are to be applied.

The Supreme Court bears the greatest responsibility for the general judicial inattentiveness to Fifth Amendment policy analysis. Supreme Court decisions have been woefully deficient in piercing the language of the Amendment to develop principles for its application, despite the fact that it is the tribunal to which all others look for guidance. The Court has, for example, given inconsistent signals in formulating a basic strategy in Fifth Amendment decisions. On the one hand, it has urged that the privilege "is not to be interpreted literally,"[2] nor in "a hostile [n]or niggardly spirit"[3] and is "as broad as the mischief against which it seeks to guard."[4] Elsewhere, the Court has stated that in interpreting the privilege, it "cannot cut the Amendment completely loose from the moorings of its language."[5] Such inconsistency only deprives lower courts of a starting point from which to approach Fifth Amendment problems.

Even more serious, however, has been the Supreme Court's superficial treatment of the supporting rationales behind the privilege in its one major effort at analyzing Fifth Amendment policy. Justice Goldberg, writing for the Court in *Murphy v. Waterfront Commission*, labeled a portion of his opinion "The Policies of the Privilege" and stated that the privilege

> reflects many of our fundamental values and most noble aspirations: our unwillingness to subject those suspected of crime to the cruel trilemma of self-accusation, perjury or contempt; our preference for an accusatorial rather than an inquisitorial system of criminal justice; our fear that self-incriminating statements will be elicited by inhumane treatment and abuses; our sense of fair play which dictates "a fair state-individual balance by requiring the government to leave the individual alone until good cause is shown for disturbing him and by requiring the government in its contest with the individual to shoulder the entire load," 8 Wigmore, Evidence (McNaughton rev., 1961) 317; our respect for the inviolability of the human personality and of the right of each individual "to a private enclave where he may lead a private life," *United States v. Grunewald*, 233 F.2d 556, 581-582 (Frank, J., dissenting), rev'd 353 U.S. 391; our distrust of self-deprecatory statements; and our realization that the privilege, while sometimes "a shelter to the guilty," is often "a protection to the innocent." *Quinn v. United States*, 349 U.S. 155, 162.[6]

The language has been quoted and applied by other courts but never critically evaluated. This is the task to which we must turn.

The Innocent and the Guilty

One of the most intense debates in the analysis of the privilege against self-incrimination has centered upon its role as either a protector of the innocent or the guilty.[7] The Supreme Court at one time took the position that the privilege partly serves the goal of protecting innocent individuals from unjust convictions. Quoting from *Quinn v. United States*, Justice Goldberg included this rationale in his opinion in *Murphy*,[8] but failed to explain how the privilege might achieve this goal, at what cost, and why the issue was even relevant to Fifth Amendment analysis. Former Harvard Dean and Solicitor-General Erwin Griswold provided support for the same objective,[9] but the background of the McCarthy investigations during which he wrote no longer prevails, and the position has been criticized by commentators as well as qualified by Dean Griswold himself.[10]

At first glance, it is difficult to comprehend how anyone who is innocent could fear being exposed to a risk of criminal prosecution as a result of complying with the state's demand to provide information. The suspect's answers in such circumstances should be entirely consistent with his innocence because there is nothing of a self-incriminatory character to be obtained. To the contrary, assertion of the privilege is more suggestive of the suspect's guilt since only the guilty are likely to have self-incriminatory information to reveal. Bentham reflected this view in his observation that "between delinquency on the one hand, and silence under inquiry on the other, there is a manifest connection; a connection too natural not to be constant and inseparable."[11] Concisely stated, his position was that innocence and silence do not mix.

Conceding that self-incriminatory responses will not usually come from suspects who are in fact innocent,[12] it is nevertheless true that an individual might well criminally damage himself if forced to respond to any question asked of him even though he may not have committed a specific criminal offense. Dean Griswold's argument to this effect was directly tied to the dragnet anticommunist investigations of the post-World War II and Korean War period. The techniques employed by the House Un-American Activities Committee and similar legislative investigating committees of that time were those of an inquisition seeking, in particular, to identify the communist affiliations of the witnesses called to testify. In many instances the questioning was intense and heavy-handed, reminiscent of High Commission interrogations during the Elizabethan era. Although the proper purpose of such proceedings lies in the need to acquire information in order to enact legislation, the investigations of that period were arguably directed instead toward the humiliation of those who had had communist ties, as well as their social isolation. The question as to whether the hearings were pursuing a legitimate purpose and thus directed toward their legislative function, though present, was, however, only a minor concern in the public mind. Of far greater significance was the fact that so many witnesses chose to invoke the Fifth Amendment rather than respond. What had they to fear if they were innocent of any wrongdoing?[13]

Dean Griswold responded to this concern by positing the case of a college instructor in the 1950s who had been a member of the Communist party during the 1930s. Joining the party at that time was perfectly legal, and the disclosure of that fact would seemingly represent no danger of self-incrimination. Moreover, the hypothetical assumed that no espionage nor treasonous activities were undertaken by the individual in question, nor did he by specific deed aid in any way in the overthrow of the government by force or violence. Nevertheless, Dean Griswold maintained that the privilege could be properly invoked to questions directed at discovering the instructor's past Communist party membership. His view that innocence and invocation of the privilege against self-incrimination were not inconsistent in such a case relied heavily upon the consequences of an accumulation of suspicious circumstantial evidence. Under the Smith Act barring advocacy of the violent overthrow of the United States, Communist party membership *per se* could not be used to support a conviction, but membership along with proof of other activities would suffice. Although the hypothetical posited no such other activities, one might well fear that sufficient circumstantial evidence would serve to overcome the absence of direct evidence. As a result, revelation of prior Communist party membership would contribute incriminatory force to the circumstantial evidence of other illegal activities, which would constitute enough of a link in the chain of proof to warrant a refusal to provide the information. Innocence, in short, was no guarantee that information furnished by the accused would not help to convict him.[14]

There is merit to Dean Griswold's argument that one who is innocent may, in appropriate circumstances, validly invoke the privilege. Yet, conceding the possibility of such a case does not necessarily lead to the conclusion that the central purpose of the privilege is to protect the innocent from unjust convictions. It may well be that the special context of government intrusion into matters of belief and conscience reflected in Griswold's hypothetical creates only the illusion that the Fifth Amendment is protecting innocence. In fact, it may be duplicating a role more appropriate to the First Amendment in safeguarding freedom of belief. If so, the provisions of the First Amendment should perhaps be applied so that Fifth Amendment doctrine is not distorted by being tied to an objective it cannot fulfill. Nevertheless, there remains one aspect of the privilege that does appear to be clearly linked to the goal of shielding innocence. By virtue of the Fifth Amendment, the defendant at his own trial need not take the witness stand,[15] but his refusal to testify may not be taken as a sign of guilt. As recognized by the Supreme Court,

> [i]t is not every one who can safely venture on the witness stand though entirely innocent of the charge against him. Excessive timidity, nervousness when facing others and attempting to explain transactions of a suspicious character, and offenses charged against him, will often confuse and embarrass him to such a degree as to increase rather than remove prejudice against him. It is not every one, however honest, who would, therefore, willingly be placed on the witness stand.[16]

However, the fact that this argument cannot be applied to witnesses who must testify but can assert the privilege in response to specific incriminatory questions[17] suggests its limited utility.

The view that the privilege serves to protect the innocent from unjust convictions has been subjected to criticism on a number of fronts. Opponents of the privilege have questioned whether any protection of the innocent is achieved as a result of the Fifth Amendment.[18] Others recognizing the possible application of the privilege to this problem nevertheless see the "protection of the innocent" rationale as a diversion from the assessment of the Fifth Amendment's primary objectives.[19] Even Dean Griswold later concluded that defending the privilege on the grounds that it is a protector of the innocent was a "mistake."[20] At the very least, such situations are in a distinct numerical minority, and it is difficult to effectively justify so broad a rule in light of so narrow an impact. But the most important retreat from the view that the Fifth Amendment's function is to shield the innocent has come from the Supreme Court. In *Tehan v. United States ex rel. Shott*, the Court refused to retroactively apply the rule barring comment on the defendant's failure to take the stand, in contrast to what one might expect if the privilege truly guarded the innocent. Instead, Justice Stewart succinctly stated that "the basic purposes that lie behind the privilege against self-incrimination do not relate to protecting the innocent from conviction."[21] It may have such an effect in selected circumstances, but attempting to explain the privilege and define its scope on the basis of this rationale simply will not work.

The Promotion of Truth

Arguing that the privilege against self-incrimination serves the goal of promoting the truth-seeking function of the criminal process suffers from many of the same weaknesses as the protection of the innocent rationale. More particularly, although there may well be situations in which a refusal to answer relevant questions will promote the search for truth, often exactly the reverse will be true. This in turn presents us with the difficulty of justifying the privilege in light of a rationale that may well be inapplicable more often than it is relevant. Here too criticism has been substantial, and the Court has itself retreated from a reliance on this justification.[22]

How then can the privilege against self-incrimination promote truth? Arguably, if the state compels answers to incriminatory questions, the answers may be given undue weight by the trier of fact. Contrary evidence, even if logically more probative, will thus tend to be ignored in the face of a defendant's damaging admission. To prevent this, one might wish to deprive the state of the power to compel a response in much the same way that evidence is excluded from the jury when its prejudicial impact outweighs its probative force.

Independent of the undue weight issue is a more practical concern as to the likelihood of receiving truthful responses to self-incriminatory questions when the subject has no option to remain silent. The absence of a privilege against self-incrimination creates an obligation to respond to all inquiries. Some individuals may still remain silent, but they face being adjudicated in contempt of court.[23] Those who provide incriminatory information may well ensure the certainty of their conviction. But if the suspect chooses instead to provide perjurous answers, he faces only a *risk* of detection and punishment for perjury; indeed, perjury may well be the least risky alternative. That some will choose it is illustrated by the facts of *United States v. Wong*,[24] a 1977 Supreme Court decision. The suspect, Rose Wong, was indicted for giving false testimony to a grand jury. She had been born in China and her primary language was Chinese. Although given a Fifth Amendment warning, her language difficulty caused the lower court to accept her testimony that "she had thought she was required to answer all questions."[25] The Supreme Court, however, was not willing to excuse her perjury even under these circumstances, but it is significant to note that feeling compelled to provide an answer to the grand jury, Wong chose a perjurous response she thought would not incriminate her.

Analyzing the pursuit-of-truth rationale is a difficult proposition. First of all, we have no empirical data suggesting whether we are more likely to receive truthful or false responses to incriminatory questions. Nor do we have any idea how heavily self-incriminatory responses are weighted in a jury's deliberations. Bentham vehemently argued that what he called "self-disserving testimony" produced "evidence of the best, most trustworthy, most satisfactory kind."[26] Indeed, exclusion of such evidence in his judgment resulted in reliance upon other evidence of a far inferior character. Yet he wrote during an age in which oaths may well have been taken more seriously than today. Recent commentators and the Supreme Court have largely disclaimed reliance upon the promotion of truth as a rationale behind the self-incrimination privilege. Dean McKay called it "scarcely realistic"[27] while McNaughton labeled it a "makeweight" argument.[28] Justice Stewart's opinion in *Tehan* maintained that "the Fifth Amendment privilege against self-incrimination is not an adjunct to the ascertainment of truth."[29] Ultimately the modern view of the privilege appears prepared to accept the right to silence even if in its absence truthful testimony would be promoted. While this might appear to be a sign of firm support for the Fifth Amendment, it is in reality a danger signal. If the privilege interferes with the truth-seeking function, one can expect the right to be narrowly confined.

Inhumanity and Cruelty

The privilege against self-incrimination serves a variety of interests seemingly directed at the prevention of cruel and inhuman treatment.[30] The logic underlying this argument reflects several distinct points. Initially, it may be asserted that without the privilege the state would be encouraged to attempt truly offensive tactics to secure information. Absent a right to remain silent and assuming, nevertheless, a subject's refusal to respond, the state is entitled to the information it seeks and will be tempted to secure it by fair means or foul. In contrast, the presence of a right to remain silent establishes the principle that a certain category of information, more particularly that which might prove self-incriminatory, is not owed the state. Granting that the state may seek to obtain it anyway, perhaps as a result of a voluntary waiver of the privilege, it nevertheless must recognize that it has no absolute right to what it seeks and will, as a result, be restrained in its choice of methods.

The prevention-of-cruelty rationale also applies even where the state does not resort to torture or bullying interrogation techniques to extract a confession. Both methods entail overt state efforts to overcome the suspect's will to remain silent. The state might instead accept the refusal to answer but choose to impose a sanction rather than attempt to extract a response. The result is a far more dignified process, but one that is no less cruel. The imposition of harsh penalties in a gentlemanly manner can reflect as much inhumanity as the utilization of overt force. In fact, analytically both represent the same fundamental tactic of subjecting the suspect to the choice of responding or else. Separate mention of the less overt sanctions is necessary, however, because there is no consensus as to their acceptability.

As we have already seen, the major English inquisitorial institutions, the Star Chamber and High Commission courts, were invested with authority to compel the production of even self-incriminatory information. This occurred upon administration of the oath *ex officio*, which required truthful responses to all questions asked, regardless of their character or subject matter. The most obvious technique to ensure that answers were provided in accordance with the subject's legal obligation was, of course, to torture him. But, while torture was by no means unknown during this era, it seems, particularly after the abolition of the Star Chamber and the High Commission, to have become a disfavored and less frequently used technique. That, along with an unmistakable modern rejection of physical abuse, prevents its classification as an acceptable sanction.[31]

But the common law and ecclesiastical courts had other tools at their disposal to deal with recalcitrant witnesses besides the application of physical force. The proceedings against John Lilburne provide ample illustration of the nonphysical sanctions available at that time. After Lilburne's very first confrontation with the crown, he was convicted of contempt for his rejection of the oath and punished by a £500 fine and imprisonment.[32] Subsequent proceedings saw Lilburne again resist compulsory self-incrimination. In these later confrontations the prosecutor sought to take advantage of his recalcitrance by suggesting to the jury that his refusal to respond might either justify an inference as to the subsidiary issues the state was seeking to establish or a complete finding of guilt.[33] In modern-day terminology these techniques would be labeled the "civil" or "criminal contempt sanction," the "adverse inference," and a "full confession of guilt." Although not entirely the same as the remedies available during the Elizabethan era, there can be little dispute that such sanctions have a substantial history behind them and simply cannot be included in the same category as torture. Whether they are truly cruel and inhuman tactics that the right to remain silent seeks to thwart is thus a debatable question. Indeed, with the exception of physical abuse, there is little agreement as to the specific tactics the state should be barred from employing as a consequence of their cruelty.

But there is also the moral aspect of the cruelty rationale. Its essence is that it is simply wrong to depend upon self-incriminatory testimony in a civilized criminal justice system. But why, in Dean Wigmore's words, does a procedure that relies heavily upon self-accusation "suffer morally?"[34] The answer lies in the position that forcing an individual to be the instrument of his own undoing degrades the dignity of man. Justice Douglas reflected this view of the Fifth Amendment in observing that the "evil to be guarded against was partly self-accusation under legal compulsion. But that was only part of the evil. The conscience and dignity of man were also involved."[35] Similarly, Justice Fortas observed that the privilege "historically goes to the roots of democratic and religious principle. It prevents the debasement of the citizen which would result from compelling him to 'accuse' himself before the power of the state."[36] Pushed to its extreme, the position might justify barring *all* self-incriminatory testimony, even if completely voluntary. Justice Douglas' footnote reference to the

Halakhah, which "discards confessions in toto, and this because of its psychological insight and concern for saving man from his own destructive inclination,"[37] expresses this view.

The supporting arguments behind the prevention of cruelty and inhumanity rationale have not enabled it to escape criticism. Bentham gave it the label of the "old woman's" or "lawyer's reason" and went on to maintain:

> The essence of this reason is contained in the word *hard*: 'tis hard upon a man to be obliged to criminate himself. Hard it is upon man, it must be confessed, to be obliged to do anything he does not like. That he should not much like to do what is meant by criminating himself, is natural enough; for what it leads to, is, his being punished. What is no less hard upon him, is, that he should be punished: but did it ever yet occur to a man to propose a general abolition of all punishment with this hardship for a reason for it?[38]

The core of his argument, that the obligation to answer is not too harsh a duty in light of the fact that even more demanding obligations are imposed by society, has been taken up by others. Judge Henry Friendly, for example, citing Lewis Mayers' *Shall We Amend the Fifth Amendment?*, suggested the weakness of justifying the privilege by the harshness it avoids in light of the even more difficult choices we force people to make.[39] A mother revealing incriminatory information about her child is deprived of a shield to resist disclosure although the pain may be more severe than that which the child would experience if forced to reveal the information himself. The general point is of course well taken, but it may mean that we need a parent-child privilege rather than the abolition of the self-incrimination privilege.

Aside from the comparative illogic of existing evidentiary privileges, the proposition that compelled self-incrimination is unduly harsh is obviously subject to dispute. Professor McNaughton observed both religious and moral issues in the breaking of an individual's will to remain silent, potentially pushing him into perjury and subjecting him to what might prove to be substantial anguish. He maintained, however, that the argument was "not too important" and was unconvinced that the "increment of cruelty, by itself, comes to much."[40] Concededly, the issue calls for highly subjective judgments as to the kind and intensity of pressure a state should be allowed to bring to bear upon a suspect, and it may well not be an entirely convincing rationale in and of itself, but totally dismissing the argument is an overreaction.

We have all been confronted by interrogators who seek admissions, beginning with parents wanting to know, "Did you do that?" Many such situations, however, reflect no legal obligation to respond and no state-imposed sanction for a refusal. Nevertheless, they can be wrenching experiences whose intensity increases with the seriousness of the information sought. Where, however, the inquiring party is the state, and it seeks to use the force of law to compel a response, some limits are appropriate. The state's legitimate need for information justifies allowing it to compel answers, but it is not irrational to conclude that the line separating self-incriminatory information represents a logical point at which state authority must be limited. It might be theoretically preferable to impose such restrictions on an individualized, case-by-case basis, analyzing the character of each disclosure sought by the state, but that would represent an impossible system to administer. Thus the fact that some required nonincriminatory disclosures may in particular cases entail a greater degree of hardship should not undercut the propriety of a general restriction limited only to state power to compel self-incriminatory testimony.[41]

But what is it that makes the state demand for this information unreasonable and the resulting choice given to the subject a "cruel trilemma of self-accusation, perjury or contempt?"[42] One must recognize that the issue arises in the context of state efforts to acquire information from an individual to be used to secure a criminal conviction against him. This is possibly the most serious and grave action the state can take with respect to its citizens and, therefore, the most appropriate place to impose limits on state power. In a similar sense, the seriousness and gravity of the criminal process supports the position that citizens should have the widest protection when they are its potential objects. Forcing such hard choices in light of the environment in which they must be made is a very special problem requiring a special solution. But even if this is not the situation in every case, it occurs often enough to warrant a general privilege against compelled self-incrimination.

It is more difficult, however, to justify the notion that the privilege against self-incrimination protects against the inhumanity reflected in the tactics the state might employ to acquire information, as opposed to the inhumanity intrinsic in the obligation to provide it. If the state is willing to stoop to the level of barbarity to obtain self-incriminatory information, it is doubtful that the privilege will have much of an effect. Officials willing to coerce admissions in the absence of the privilege will do so in its presence. Beyond that, the privilege against self-incrimination is not the only source of constitutional authority to control such cruelty. The same Fifth Amendment that encompasses the privilege also provides that the federal government must act in accordance with "due process of law," a requirement imposed upon the states by virtue of the Fourteenth Amendment. It can be argued that due process provides a superior mechanism to keep inhumane government pressure tactics in check because of its wider perspective. In contrast, the privilege narrowly focuses on pressure directed toward self-incrimination. Thus if the cruelty rationale has any validity, it lies in the immorality that is inherent in compelled self-incrimination, not what it may lead to.

Tradition and Abuse

The evolution of the privilege against self-incrimination represents a process that can be traced back several centuries. History, in its wisdom, has led us to the right to remain silent as a solution to a variety of problems. Historical development, therefore, supports the Fifth Amendment. However, as straightforward as that logic is, it would take very frequent and rapid repetition in order to accept it uncritically. Rather, as suggested by Professor McNaughton, the relevance of history is to put the burden of proof on those who would abolish the privilege and to provide illustrative analogies for the contemporary interpretation of its scope.[43] Yet the historical background of the privilege provides another rationale supporting its continuation. The privilege evolved not out of thin air but rather as a response to particular abuses. Thus, so the argument runs, the right to remain silent provides us with protection against a revival of those abuses. Its abolition would lead government to utilize techniques of criminal procedure that have, over time, fallen into disfavor.[44] Concededly, history does support the view that the right to silence was an important tool in controlling government repression, but that is no guarantee that it is as critical today in performing the same task.

Much of the weight of the argument relating to the privilege's role in preventing abuse revolves around the use of governmental power in relation to First Amendment protected activities. When those who express unpopular political or religious ideas are swept into the criminal justice process because of conduct related to their views, even if the substantive charge against them is a traditional offense rather than a Smith Act type crime directed at their dissent, the specter of repression arises. The special weight our democratic society attaches to freedom of speech, however, mandates extra protection when its values are threatened. Compelled self-incrimination, if tolerated, might well prove to be too tempting a tool for use against minority views. Its value in other spheres is thus outweighed by the risks posed to the right of dissent.

Even if one concedes the special flavor of the right to remain silent when considered in relation to activities protected by the First Amendment, as critics of the privilege like Judge Friendly have done,[45] that still does not determine the form the protection should take. To provide a shield by way of the Fifth Amendment may well be an inferior solution. Indeed, as Professor McNaughton has observed, the entire rationale may serve only to saddle the privilege with a "First Amendment albatross."[46] The consequences of tying freedom of speech, religion, press, and assembly issues to the privilege against self-incrimination may well be to create a remedy that doesn't fit the need. Bentham's observations on this point are still relevant:

[B]y the effect of this impunity-giving rule, undue suffering has probably in some instances been prevented. Prevented? but to what extent? To the extent of that part of the field of penal law which is occupied by bad laws. . . . Applying with equal force and efficiency to all penal laws without distinction—to the worst as well as to the best, it at the same time diminishes the efficiency of such as are good.[47]

Thus if one accepts the view that the right to silence is only appropriate in a narrow sphere, its general application may do more harm than good.

Judge Friendly's solution, and one that Professor McNaughton also looked to, was the development of something akin to a First Amendment right to silence. Support for this proposition is found in a 1963 Supreme Court decision demanding that "the State convincingly show a substantial relation between the information sought and a subject of overriding and compelling state interest"[48] when seeking constitutionally protected evidence in the context of a legislative investigation. Judge Friendly's hope, however, that the principle would develop into a fully effective shield, can no longer be sustained. Recent decisions of the Supreme Court amply demonstrate that First Amendment protections are easily overriden by state claims. Newsmen, in particular, have repeatedly failed in their efforts to resist the disclosure of information on First Amendment grounds.[49] Seemingly, only application of the privilege against self-incrimination can serve to provide a measure of relief, despite the fact that the relief is not total and appears to suffer from overbreadth.

Beyond abuses incident to the application of criminal sanctions to constitutionally protected activities, there are possibly additional institutional abuses a right to silence may thwart. Bentham called this rationale "the reference to unpopular institutions" and appropriately criticized it for its lack of analysis.[50] The argument does no more than link compelled self-incrimination with such discredited institutions as the Star Chamber, High Commission, and Inquisition and then proceed to reject the technique because we reject the institutions. It fails to isolate the abuses of these institutions, which arguably were not related to the legal obligation to provide self-incriminatory information but rather to the bullying tactics they frequently employed. Critical analysis will not support a blind adherence to the right to remain silent based on guilt by association.

The Inquisitorial-Accusatorial Dichotomy

It has been frequently asserted that the privilege against self-incrimination plays a major role in the Anglo-American accusatorial system of justice. The right to remain silent is seen as a cornerstone, firmly anchoring our system of criminal procedure to principles that have evolved over centuries and dramatically contrast with the inquisitorial features of continental criminal procedure. From this perspective, the Fifth Amendment privilege and its interpretation should reflect the need to maintain the accusatorial character of our criminal process. The abolition of the privilege, or its narrow construction by the courts, might thus permit too much of a flavor of the inquisitional tradition to engraft itself upon the accusatorial framework history has given us.[51]

Why, however, are we so firmly set against an inquisitorial system of justice? If continental jurisdictions employ it, and granting that they are civilized members of the Western community of nations, it would seem that it must at least be an acceptable form of criminal procedure. Perhaps, given the widespread use and respectability of inquisitorial techniques, it is a superior process, and thus our attempted justifications of the privilege in order to preserve an accusatorial system of justice are misguided. And, if quality judgments are removed, the privilege appears left to the role of protecting the accusatorial system of justice simply because that is what we have, not because there is something about the inquisitorial system to be avoided. If so, the accusatorial-inquisitorial rationale of the privilege winds up more of an inertia justification than a soundly reasoned argument.

Any consideration of the inquisitorial system of justice in its modern form cannot avoid recognition of the roots such procedures have in the Roman Inquisition.[52] And if the privilege against self-incrimination represents the most effective way of preventing accusatorial procedures from tolerating anything like the Inquisition, it would be an important protection indeed. But, it may be argued, the abuses of the Inquisition are largely irrelevant to the question of whether or not an indiviudal should have a privilege of refusing to answer incriminating questions. The Inquisition was directed at the identification and punishment of religious dissent. If we feel such objectives are impermissible, there are far better ways than a right to remain silent to ensure against prosecutions of that kind. Similarly, the Inquisition made use of torture as a matter of policy to extract admissions. Yet as long as we permit suspects to waive the privilege and provide such admissions voluntarily, there is no guarantee in the Fifth Amendment against instances of torture today. To the extent accusatorial procedures accept into evidence incriminating statements from the accused, there will remain some incentive for employing tactics of physical abuse; only a total bar to such evidence would eliminate the utility of torture. And finally, the Inquisition was characterized by the imposition of grotesque penalties, including death at the stake, with even ignorance of little use as a defense. Once again, it must be conceded that the privilege against self-incrimination has little to offer in controlling such punishments.

Inquisitional procedures, however, encompassed a variety of other characteristics having a more direct bearing on the privilege against self-incrimination. Unlike the common law system in which an accusation was a precondition to trial, the inquisition process permitted the *inquisitio* procedure to go forward on the court's own initiative. All that was required was suspicion, the so-called *publica fama*, which was not a demanding criterion. Beyond justifying the commencement of proceedings, the *publica fama* served further to effectively shift the burden of proof to the defendant, branding him guilty until he established his innocence. Additionally, the procedure was entirely secret, and the suspect did not learn the names of his accusers, nor was he assisted by an advocate. The system, in operation, produced few acquittals.[53] Moreover, it relied heavily, though not exclusively, on interrogations to produce evidence of heresy. The suspect sealing his own doom helped to make the system an efficient self-contained unit. And the other characteristics of the Inquisition virtually ensured that the interrogation would be successful. Barring compulsory self-incrimination might well have made it difficult to retain the other heavy-handed techniques used by the church since it would have meant the need for substantially more effort to acquire the evidence needed to prove heresy.

Modern supporters of the privilege against self-incrimination have recognized that its role in preserving an accusatorial system of justice is not that of a last barrier against a return to the use of inquisitions. Forces that might seek such an objective would undoubtedly find the privilege a minor obstacle, easily circumvented. The more serious concerns, in contrast, focus upon features of the inquisitorial process that vary from common law tradition. The seeming absence of restraint on the initiation of an inquisitorial proceeding and the shifting of the burden of proof to the defendant are, in particular, aspects of the pure inquisitorial form that are out of line with current conceptions of the proper limits of state authority. These characteristics would simply make it too easy to bring the power of the state to bear upon those suspected of deviant behavior. No controls are present other than the exercise of informal restraint by criminal justice officials, and that is too unreliable a mechanism for society to depend upon. Yet it must be conceded here too that the privilege against self-incrimination does not necessarily prevent the criminal justice system from adopting such disfavored modes of procedure, nor would its abolition necessarily mean that other limits on state power to enforce the criminal sanction would disappear. Fundamentally, while recognizing that the right to remain silent is a mainstay of the accusatorial system of justice, it must find its justification in the inherent superiority of a system that does not depend upon the accused involuntarily contributing to his own conviction.

But is it true that a system of justice that does not depend upon the compelled testimony of the accused to secure his conviction is a superior mode of criminal procedure? The Supreme Court apparently ascribes to such a view, having stated its preference for an accusatorial system in its 1964 *Murphy v. Waterfront Commission* opinion as well as its rejection of the most immediate consequence of compulsory self-incrimination, the so-called "cruel trilemma of self-accusation, perjury or contempt."[54] Moreover, this principle was reaffirmed in 1966, with Justice Stewart writing that the privilege ensures "preserving the integrity of a judicial system in which even the guilty are not to be convicted unless the prosecution 'shoulder the entire load.' "[55] The logic behind such an approach demands analysis.

Part of the reason for requiring that the entire burden of establishing guilt be made the responsibility of the state ties in with many other rationales behind the privilege. If self-incriminatory admissions can be compelled from the accused, prosecutors will naturally resort to securing them. Other forms of investigation are often more cumbersome and expensive, and it is unreasonable to expect that they would be used if so easily avoided. But why should the state be forced to use the more cumbersome and expensive techniques of investigation when others are available? Surely there is nothing intrinsically valuable in promoting state inefficiency. The answer is, perhaps, that there is something to be gained by avoiding what might otherwise become a bitter confrontation over efforts to extract incriminatory evidence from the accused. Cruel trilemmas, browbeating interrogations, and the like do not present a favorable image of our criminal justice system.[56] They would, however, be inevitable in a system of compulsory self-incrimination.

There is a value far more basic to our social fabric that may provide a better explanation of both the privilege and our emphasis on accusatorial procedures. Our system of government represents an attempt at accommodating the often opposing interests of the citizen and the state. In a very general sense, it accords high regard to the individual and seeks to protect him against unwarranted state interference. Beyond that, it protects the individual against methods of intrusion that may violate his individuality and integrity, even though the intrusion itself may be warranted. The Fifth Amendment very clearly promotes these goals and is justified by them. It is essential to maintaining what Professor McNaughton called the "fair state-individual balance."[57] Without it, as recognized by Dean Wigmore, our system of justice would be weakened since the power to compel answers can lead only to a "forgetfulness of the just limitations of that power."[58]

The argument in favor of the privilege against self-incrimination does not end with the simple assertion that it is necessary to a fair balance of power and that its absence would lead to abuses of state authority. Rather, the point demands analysis in light of the realities of criminal law enforcement. And those realities clearly demonstrate how awesome a machine the criminal justice system can be. The power of the state includes a virtual army of law-enforcement officers at every level of government, often specialized by the nature of the crime under investigation. Their authority to investigate is not without limits, but those limits can sometimes be evaded and often are not very demanding. State authority encompasses the power to compel the attendance and testimony of witnesses and the production of physical evidence. The only practical restraints on the entire system seem to be restricted to two basic characteristics. First, the system is innundated by the sheer weight of the caseload it must process. Second, the suspect need not cooperate; literally, he can sit back and say, "prove it." Removing the ability of the accused to refuse to cooperate and thereby shifting away from an accusatorial format undercuts the fairness of the battle between the state and the defendant. But this is not merely undesirable because it removes the sporting quality of the conflict, what Bentham critically labeled the "fox-hunter's rationale."[59] Concededly, there is a substantial state interest in the control of crime, and the procedures used to achieve that goal are not a game. Rather, the fairness issue is intimately tied to our conception of how much power the state should have in its relationship to the individual. When it can compel the individual to incriminate himself and proceed to apply criminal sanctions based upon the information it obtains, its control is virtually complete. As Justice Fortas observed:

> A sovereign state has the right to defend itself, and within the limits of accepted procedure, to punish infractions of the rules that govern its relationships with its sovereign individuals. But it has no right to compel the sovereign individual to surrender or impair his right of self-defense.[60]

In that sense the privilege against self-incrimination is essential to the maintenance of a fair balance of power between the individual and the state. And the law's preference for an accusatorial system of justice simply reflects a commitment to retain that balance.

In the final analysis, the argument boils down to the question of where the line limiting state power should be drawn. One can easily accept the principle that government power demands control but that a right to remain silent is an irrational way to achieve that end. Judge Friendly, indeed, framed his criticism of the privilege along just such lines, conceding only that the contempt sanction should not be applied to the recalcitrant defendant.[61] But why even make that concession? Presumably the reason is that there is something wrong in forcing an individual to secure his own conviction; if not, the sanction of contempt would be appropriate. The problem is that taking away the right to stand mute leaves the defendant helpless before the power of the state. That other controls on state power might be warranted or that the fair state-individual balance principle does not tell us with mathematical precision how the privilege should be interpreted in various contexts does not undercut the fact that it is a basic control mechanism that must be applied to the administration of criminal justice. Without it, and in light of the state's extensive investigatory power and vast array of criminal prohibitions, the result would be a grant of too much authority to control the individual and too little power to prevent excesses. Requiring the state to "prove it" limits opportunities for abuse and provides the defendant with some protection against the state.

The price of self-incrimination limits on state power to compel the production of evidence is, of course, inefficiency in crime control. No doubt that factor looms large in efforts to restrict the scope of the Fifth Amendment. Whether the price is worth it is a judgmental question, involving a balance between state and individual interests. The weighing, moreover, becomes increasingly difficult as more novel applications of the Fifth Amendment are urged. But the process of balancing must not ignore what it means to the individual to be a criminal defendant with an obligation to aid the state. The cost is one that society, if it is to retain a minimum of control on state authority, must bear.

A Private Enclave

One of the rationales cited by Justice Goldberg in *Murphy v. Waterfront Commission* in support of the privilege against self-incrimination, quoting from Judge Jerome Frank's dissenting opinion in *United States v. Grunewald*, is the notion that the Fifth Amendment provides us with "a private enclave where [we] may lead a private life."[62] The same position was urged by Justice Stewart who observed that the privilege against self-incrimination "like the guarantees of the Fourth Amendment, stands as a protection of quite different values—values reflecting the concern of our society for the right of each individual to be let alone. To recognize this is no more than to accord those values undiluted respect."[63] The Fifth Amendment is thus part of what Dean Robert McKay has labeled the "new privacy."[64] As such, it is a principle very closely related to the fair state-individual balance theory. But, whereas the fair-balance approach argues against compulsory self-incrimination because it represents too great an allocation of power to the state, the privacy rationale focuses on the obstacles compelled self-incrimination would create to the ability of individuals to shut out certain forms of government intrusion.

If the evaluation of the private enclave rationale for the privilege against self-incrimination is related to the Supreme Court's general support for a constitutionally founded right to privacy, the justification is today on shaky ground indeed. During the early 1960s, the Court was able to hint at privacy interests in the Fifth Amendment because it was a period during which the privacy concept was developing. Arguably, the Court used privacy language to test the water and establish a proper scope for the privacy doctrine despite the fact that the Constitution contains no specific words creating it. The Supreme Court's decision in *Griswold v. Connecti-*

cut[65] was the high point of this technique. There, in invalidating a Connecticut statute prohibiting licensed physicians from providing information about contraception to married persons and barring their use of contraceptives, Justice Douglas wrote that "specific guarantees in the Bill of Rights have penumbras" and create "zones of privacy."[66] More specifically, the "Fifth Amendment in its Self-Incrimination Clause enables the citizen to create a zone of privacy which the government may not force him to surrender to his detriment."[67] *Griswold* thus provided a general framework for a privacy rationale to support the privilege the Court later built upon in its *Murphy* and *Tehan* opinions.

Privacy, however, has not fared nearly as well before the Supreme Court recently. That is not meant to imply that the Court has retreated from the *Griswold* decision itself, which struck down state interference with married persons' access to contraceptives. To the contrary, there has been further development of this principle to the point where the state is now barred from interfering with a woman's decision to undergo an abortion during the first trimester of pregnancy.[68] Intrusion upon privacy in the home has also received special consideration from the Supreme Court, as evidenced by its ruling prohibiting the punishment of the private possession of obscene material in one's own home.[69] Home, marital privacy, and the decision to have a child, however, seem to reflect the limits of constitutional privacy that the Court is currently willing to accept. Elsewhere, constitutional provisions are being read narrowly to provide only so much privacy protection as the specific language demands, an approach that helps to explain Supreme Court decisions allowing the state to regulate private consensual sexual conduct[70] and barring a federal cause of action for the publication of criminal records.[71]

The Supreme Court's curtailment of the privacy doctrine in other spheres has understandably led it to restrict the privacy implications of the Fifth Amendment. Without rejecting the decisions in *Murphy* or *Tehan*, the Supreme Court has nevertheless ruled that the privilege offers no general privacy protection even if the privacy sought represented a reasonable expectation on the part of the subject. Rather, such privacy as the privilege affords is tied to the "limits imposed by the language of the Fifth Amendment."[72] The result is that the privilege does not protect private information obtained from an individual, but rather only a strictly construed version of the concept of compulsory self-incrimination. The Court's current view is that informational privacy is addressed in the Fourth Amendment's ban against unreasonable searches and seizures. The framers "did not seek in still another Amendment—the Fifth—to achieve a general protection of privacy but to deal with the more specific issue of compelled self-incrimination."[73]

That the Court now views privacy as a disfavored, or at least incidental, justification for the privilege may only be a temporary phenomenon. Indeed, the Supreme Court's current approach is in fact a reversal of long-standing precedent. In its 1886 *Boyd v. United States* decision, the Court held there to be an "intimate relation"[74] between the Fourth and Fifth Amendments and that they apply to "all invasions on the part of the government and its employee's of the sanctity of a man's home and the privacies of life."[75] A change of philosophy might well cause the Court to revive the Fifth Amendment privacy rationale as a major foundation principle for the privilege against self-incrimination. That possibility, however, does not necessarily mean that a change is warranted.

Is it important that the Fifth Amendment accept as a supporting rationale the principle that the privilege against self-incrimination serves to provide privacy protection in the realm of criminal procedure? The case in favor is a strong one emanating from two sources. First, the intrusive character of contemporary society is such that privacy is a difficult objective to achieve. There is thus a pragmatic need to provide what little privacy protection we can whenever possible. Second, the intrinsic value of privacy is such as to demand support from those sources of authority that are relevant.

The position that privacy is inherently important to American society is concededly a value judgment. However, it is one with significant support behind it, particularly Justice Brandeis' classic dissent in *Olmstead v. United States*:

> The makers of our Constitution undertook to secure conditions favorable to the pursuit of happiness. They recognized the significance of man's spiritual nature, of his feeling and of his intellect. . . . They sought to protect Americans in their beliefs, their thoughts, their emotions and their sensations. They conferred as against the government, the right to be let alone—the most comprehensive of rights and the right most valued by civilized men.[76]

The importance of privacy relates to its core element, the control over our own personal integrity. That in turn encompasses the ability to withhold information about ourselves, or reveal it, as we choose.[77] Permitting the state to compel the production of self-incriminatory information entails a vast inroad upon individual integrity in the sensitive arena of "the mea culpa, the public admission of private judgment of self-condemnation."[78] Moreover, that compulsion can be applied even if the state lacks a firm basis for suspicion that criminal activity has been engaged in. As a result, privacy values can be interfered with even though the state is engaged in a fishing expedition for whatever may turn up.

There is a certain inconsistency in the privacy rationale reflected in the fact that the privilege only protects privacy when there is an issue of self-incrimination. On occasion this may result in the forced revelation of information more private in character than an admission of minor criminal misdeeds. There is also concern that the protection is most often given to the guilty. Both points are true, but not necessarily conclusive. Can we truly be sure that granting the state the power to compel self-incrimination will cause it to confine the exercise of that power to the guilty? How are the guilty to be identified until the effort to extract such admissions has been made? With all due respect to Judge Friendly's forceful critique,[79] the privilege must either apply fully in all relevant situations or not at all, and the consequences of the latter approach are too risky to warrant taking the chance. This is true despite the fact that the privilege gives criminals the chance to hide information and, at other points, is inapplicable despite the need for privacy protection.

Finally, it is hard to question the increasing intrusiveness of contemporary society. We are an urban, crowded, and technologically complex system in which there is much information available for those who desire it. This is an environmental consideration the framers could not be expected to have anticipated. Affirmative steps are required to protect privacy today although they were not needed previously. The alternative is to allow the dossiers and public information gathered by the state to be used beyond justification. A privacy rationale behind the privilege against self-incrimination simply prevents the state from employing a far too simple technique to add to its stock of information. It may not constitute a complete shield, but its contribution in a world so beset by intrusions is a significant one. It establishes at a minimum the right to be let alone when the state seeks self-incriminatory information from an individual facing the possibility of a criminal conviction. Privacy is thus one of the central concerns reflected in the right to remain silent. Along with the other major Fifth Amendment policy objectives of limiting the enforcement powers of the state and eliminating the cruelty of self-accusation, the privacy rationale helps to focus attention on the values reflected in the privilege and ensure its continued viability.

3 The Contours of the Privilege

The privilege against self-incrimination as reflected in the language of the Fifth Amendment is a deceptively simple concept. The words provide that "[n]o person . . . shall be compelled in any criminal case to be a witness against himself." Yet they in no way define what constitutes unlawful compulsion, nor do they delineate what is meant by a criminal case. Indeed, a large number of issues cannot be resolved solely by reference to the language of the amendment. Since clues as to the framers' intent are noticeably lacking, courts have had to give content to the privilege with only fifteen words and scant legislative history to guide them. The result has been an evolutionary process in which the basic contours of the right to remain silent have been defined. Most are now firmly entrenched in the case law, but their settled character tends to obscure the controversy that attended their establishment.

Incorporation

One of the "great debates" in American constitutional law has centered on the application of the Bill of Rights as a restraint upon the power of state governments. Initially, the matter was not in dispute since the first eight amendments to the Constitution were clearly and concededly aimed at the powers of the federal government. Protection of individual liberties against state infringement was left to state constitutions.[1]

The end of the Civil War and the passage of the Reconstruction amendments, particularly the Fourteenth Amendment, raised the issue anew. Section 1 of the Fourteenth Amendment contained two provisions that suggested a relationship between the Bill of Rights and the control of state power. First, the amendment barred any state from abridging the "privileges or immunities of citizens of the United States." If the privilege against self-incrimination, as well as other Bill of Rights guarantees, was within the scope of that provision, it could not be subjected to state interference. Second, the Fourteenth Amendment precluded any state from depriving any person of "life, liberty or property without due process of law." Arguably, the concept of due process of law encompassed through incorporation the specific guarantees of the Bill of Rights or at least those provisions of the first eight amendments which, like the privilege against self-incrimination, were deemed fundamental to our liberty.

Whether or not the Fifth Amendment controls the exercise of state as well as federal power is a matter of great concern. The absence of such control would leave self-incrimination protection to a wide variety of differing state constitutional language.[2] Concededly, most parallel the provisions of the Fifth Amendment, but there is enough variation in wording to support a number of alternative interpretations of essentially the same core concept. In fact, even identical language would very likely be subject to different interpretations by at least some of the fifty state supreme courts. True, inconsistency is not an inherent evil, particularly in a system of government committed to federalism. Nor can we ensure complete uniformity in self-incrimination rights given the Supreme Court's willingness to permit the states to extend greater coverage under the aegis of their own constitutional requirements. Nevertheless, the incorporation of the Fifth Amendment by the Fourteenth Amendment's provisions, and its resulting application to the states, would at least ensure a uniform minimum of constitutional protection for the right to silence beyond which federalism would be free to operate.[3]

The Supreme Court first confronted the applicability of the privilege against self-incrimination to the states in its 1908 *Twining v. New Jersey*[4] decision. Twining and a codefendant had been convicted of deceiving state banking examiners as to the financial condition of a bank they ran. They did not take the stand at their own trial, thus exercising the right to remain silent granted by New Jersey law, but their failure to deny certain critical features of the state's case was commented on by the judge who instructed the jury that it could draw an adverse inference based upon the defendants' silence. They conceded before the Supreme Court that the specific Fifth Amendment guarantee against self-incrimination was not applicable but instead urged that drawing an adverse inference from a defendant's exercise of his state-granted right to remain silent both abridged a privilege or immunity of U.S. citizenship and offended the principles of due process of law. Neither position was successful.

Twining's argument was that the privileges and immunities clause of the Fourteenth Amendment barred state interference with the same liberties protected against federal encroachment by the Bill of Rights. Such was said to be the intent of the framers and the only interpretation that would not render the phrase meaningless. The same argument, however, had been unsuccessfully made to the Court in the *Slaughter-House Cases*.[5] The *Twining* majority simply reiterated the view expressed there that "privileges and immunities of citizens of the United States . . . are only such as arise out of the nature and essential character of the National Government, or are specifically granted or secured to all citizens or persons by the Constitution of the United States."[6] The Court concluded that freedom from compulsory self-incrimination was plainly not encompassed within that definition and thus was left to state protection. The decision was a reflection of the Court's consistent position that "the Fourteenth Amendment did not forbid the States to abridge the personal rights enumerated in the first eight Amendments, because those rights were not within the meaning of the clause 'privileges and immunities of citizens of the United States.' "[7]

The Supreme Court similarly rejected Twining's incorporation theory, which argued that the due process clause of the Fourteenth Amendment had the effect of making specific guarantees of the Bill of Rights applicable against the states. Virtually no discussion was deemed necessary to support this point. However, more extended analysis was required to determine whether the concept of due process inherently encompassed individual freedom from compulsory self-incrimination. This was a reflection of the Court's view that the due process clause was a source of independent authority to evaluate the fundamental fairness of state procedures, not a shorthand formula to justify applying the specifics of the Fifth Amendment to the states. As a result, the Fifth Amendment privilege against self-incrimination was largely irrelevant to the decison, except for illustrative purposes. Instead, the Court deemed it necessary to look to "settled usages and modes of proceedings"[8] to define the scope of due process protection for individuals against arbitrary action by the state. Pursuant to this standard, the Court concluded that the privilege was not sufficiently supported by historical precedent to be deemed an element of due process of law. Of particular significance to the Court was the absence of reference to the privilege in the great landmark documents of English history: the Magna Carta (1215), the Petition of Right (1629), and the Bill of Rights (1689). And beyond what the Court deemed to be an inadequate supporting history, it felt the concept was simply not an "immutable principle of justice which is the inalienable possession of every citizen of a free government."[9]

Although the doctrine surrounding the privileges and immunities clause has continued to bar its use as a vehicle to apply the Fifth Amendment to the states, the same has not been true of the due process requirement. In the years following the *Twining* decision, renewed efforts were made to have the Court accept incorporation of the Bill of Rights as the guiding principle behind the Fourteenth Amendment's due process clause. In the view of Justice Black, the language of and proceedings surrounding the adoption of the Fourteenth Amendment "conclusively demonstrate[d]"[10] that such was the intent of the framers. The alternative was to utilize the Fourteenth Amendment as a reservoir of "boundless power under 'natural law' periodically to expand and contract constitutional standards to conform to the Court's conception of what at a particular time constitutes 'civilized decency' and 'fundamental liberty and justice.' "[11] Yet despite Justice Black's forceful views, the Court at first continued to reject the doctrine of incorporation. Justice Frankfurter's position that the due process clause "neither comprehends the specific provisions by which the founders deemed it appropriate to restrict the federal government nor is it confined to them"[12] continued as the dominant philosophy, and the privilege against self-incrimination remained without federal protection against state infringement. This was illustrated in 1947 as a result of *Adamson v. California*[13] in which the Court reaffirmed its 1908 decision in *Twining*.

The Supreme Court's rejection of the incorporation doctrine in *Adamson*, however, was an extremely narrow victory. Four dissenters would have reversed *Twining* and applied the Fifth Amendment as a controlling principle over state criminal procedure rules. But the decision did not lay the issue to rest. The concept of applying the specific guarantees of the Bill of Rights to regulate state activities remained in the background, ultimately to resurface during the 1960s. And, as described by Justice White, the reemergence was coupled with the development of a more contemporary standard for the interpretation of the due process clause, which served to explain the Court's adoption of the essence of the incorporation theory at that time:

> Earlier the Court can be seen as having asked, when inquiring into whether some particular procedural safeguard was required of a State, if a civilized system of justice could be imagined that would not accord the particular protection. . . . The recent cases, on the other hand, have proceeded upon the valid assumption that state criminal processes are not imaginary and theoretical schemes but actual systems bearing virtually every characteristic of the common-law system that has been developing contemporaneously in England and in this Country. The question thus is whether given this kind of system a particular procedure is fundamental. . . .[14]

The new approach did not mean limiting due process to the specifics of the Bill of Rights, but rather their incorporation as part of the due process clause's larger scope.[15]

Finally, in 1964 the Supreme Court fully incorporated the Fifth Amendment privilege and held it binding on the states. Writing for the Court in *Malloy v. Hogan*,[16] Justice Brennan noted that the principles underlying *Twining* and *Adamson* had been substantially undermined by Court decisions incorporating other provisions of the Bill of Rights via the due process clause. He observed that incorporation was necessary because "the American system of criminal prosecution is accusatorial, not inquisitorial, and . . . the Fifth Amendment privilege is its essential mainstay."[17] The same result was compelled by the due process rules prohibiting coerced confessions; without a privilege against self-incrimination, the state might seek coerced testimony of the type that due process forbids. Finally, the Court's prior incorporation of the Fourth Amendment, arguably based in part upon

Fifth Amendment principles, demanded the unequivocal incorporation of the Fifth Amendment as well. And to remove any question about uniformity of standards, the Court observed that the incorporation of the privilege meant that "the same standards must determine whether an accused's silence in either a federal or state proceeding is justified."[18] As a result, the shape of the right to remain silent became almost entirely a federal question with Supreme Court decisions controlling state as well as federal court practice.

Witnesses, Defendants, and the Criminal Case

The specific wording of the Fifth Amendment purports to limit its applicability to compelled self-incrimination arising in "any criminal case." It is odd, however, that the Fifth Amendment, which establishes important substantive rights in all of its provisions, restricts the self-incrimination clause to a particular procedural context. It is as though the framers viewed the protections against double jeopardy and due process as too important to confine to selected proceedings while the problem of compelled self-incrimination was an evil only when it occurred in the realm of a criminal case. Viewed in this light, there is nothing inherently wrong with the process of compulsory incriminatory interrogation; instead, there is merely a need to confine it so that such questioning would not emerge in the subject's own criminal trial.

The seemingly second-class status of the privilege within the overall structure of the Fifth Amendment receives some support from the history surrounding the adoption of the self-incrimination clause. The Virginia Declaration of Rights, for example, in which the immediate roots of the self-incrimination clause lie, spoke in terms of "capital or criminal prosecutions." A vast array of proceedings were excluded by this language. Perhaps recognizing the restrictiveness of such an approach, James Madison offered a version of the self-incrimination clause to the First Congress that did not specify the nature of the proceedings in which the right would exist. His proposal remained intact through committee consideration but was amended in the full House. Objection was made to the absence of limitations on the privilege, and it was altered to encompass the "criminal case" restriction. No records exist to indicate exactly what considerations prompted the change, although it has been suggested that there may have been some concern that Madison's language would have extended the privilege beyond its common law heritage by barring parties in civil proceedings from being compelled to produce evidence that would adversely affect their civil claims.[19]

If the criminal case restriction is applied to the self-incrimination clause and taken at face value, the result is a confusing and illogical dimension for the right to silence. The limitation would bar only compelling self-incriminatory testimony from the defendant at his own trial. He could, however, be compelled to provide such information in another proceeding under this interpretation, and presumably the prosecutor would not run afoul of the privilege if he then introduced the adverse evidence at a later criminal trial against the party from whom it had been compelled. Indeed, nothing would apparently prevent the prosecutor from staging such proceedings in order to acquire evidence not otherwise obtainable from the defendant at the criminal trial stage. The right to remain silent would as a result become an easily circumventable obstacle. However, it is questionable why anyone would have bothered with the privilege if its scope were truly limited to compelled testimony from the accused at his criminal trial. By the time the First Congress was considering the adoption of the Bill of Rights, the defendant was barred by law from testifying at his own trial on the theory that his interest in the outcome of the proceedings made his testimony too unreliable to consider. Thus a narrow construction of the privilege leaves it in control of testimony that could not be given anyway.

It is possible that the framers were concerned that Congress might alter the rules disqualifying the defendant as a witness. If so, the privilege would have prevented a legislative reversal aimed at reintroducing compulsory trial interrogation. This would explain why constitutional protection was needed to cover an area already limited by common law tradition but does not clarify the reason the framers would have been satisfied by a provision so easily avoided. Those who support a narrow construction of the privilege have arugued that the widespread practice of preliminary examination by magistrates at that time, and the fact that court decisions subsequent to the adoption of the Bill of Rights looked to the common law rather than the Fifth Amendment as the source of the broadest protection of the right to remain silent, suggest that the framers intended only the most limited constitutional privilege of silence. But as long as defendants as a class remained disqualified to be witnesses in their own behalf, the issue did not have to be resolved. The demise of witness disqualification rules in the late nineteenth century, however, forced the courts to confront the problem of defining the scope of the Fifth Amendment's self-incrimination protection.[20]

The issue was first addressed in an 1892 Supreme Court decision, *Counselman v. Hitchcock*,[21] involving a grand jury probe of railroad rate manipulation. Charles Counselman had been summoned to testify about shipping rates paid by him in connection with his Chicago grain business. He refused to respond to specific questions directed to whether he had shipped his goods at less than the approved tariffs or had received rebates on transporation charges for shipping grain with particular railroads. Such actions would have constituted criminal violations under federal law, and

Counselman declined to answer because of the potential incrimination, even after being ordered to do so by the lower court. The result was a finding of contempt, imprisonment, and a fine of $500 plus court costs.

In reviewing Counselman's contempt sentence, the Supreme Court confronted the argument that the grand jury proceeding before which Counselman appeared did not constitute a criminal case for purposes of the Fifth Amendment, and therefore he had no privilege of refusing to respond. Reliance was placed on the fact that no indictments had as yet been issued nor charges filed against him. The proceeding was, instead, one to determine whether a crime had been committed and, if so, who should be charged. Moreover, the New York Court of Appeals had interpreted the privilege against self-incrimination of the New York State Constitution involving language identical to the Fifth Amendment as limited to the prosecution of an offense,[22] thereby excluding grand jury investigations. In the Supreme Court's view, however, the Fifth Amendment could not be so narrowly construed. When the framers wanted to convey the idea of a criminal prosecution, they used appropriate language. Indeed, the Sixth Amendment rights to speedy trial, impartial jury, compulsory process, and assistance of counsel were qualified by language specifically limiting their applicability to criminal prosecutions. The Court saw significance in the choice of different language for the Fifth Amendment and felt that the words "criminal case" encompassed a broader scope. The fact that the matter under inquiry was criminal and that Counselman was himself liable to prosecution for the activities the grand jury was investigating was sufficient to place the entire proceeding within the criminal case boundaries of the Fifth Amendment.

Much of the language of the Court in its *Counselman* opinion reflects only a limited effort to give content to the privilege against self-incrimination despite the criminal case restriction of the Fifth Amendment. This is seen in the Court's analysis of the grand jury proceeding as in reality the first step in what could well have led to a criminal charge. Given the fact that the grand jury before which Counselman testified might have indicted him for activities that were the subject of its investigation, the extension of the criminal case requirement to cover Counselman's grand jury appearance was hardly an open-ended decision. On the other hand, however, there is a reading of *Counselman* that suggests far broader applicability of the Fifth Amendment stemming from the Court's statement:

> It is impossible that the meaning of the constitutional provision can only be, that a person shall not be compelled to be a witness against himself in a criminal prosecution against himself. It would doubtless cover such cases; but it is not limited to them. The object was to insure that a person should not be compelled when acting as a witness *in any investigation*, to give testimony which might tend to show that *he himself had committed a crime*.[23] (Emphasis added)

This portion of the Court's opinion focused on the incriminatory character of the statements called for, not the context in which they were sought. State-directed civil as well as criminal investigations would clearly fit such a view of the privilege, as long as incrimination with respect to a criminal offense might result. And there is room to include entirely civil matters between private parties, such being investigations in a broad sense. Followed to its logical conclusion, the Court was setting out the framework of a structure for the privilege that would ensure its role as the guarantor of a substantive right to remain silent rather than a limited obstacle to compulsory interrogation applicable solely to the criminal trial itself.

Although the Court's 1892 *Counselman v. Hitchcock* decision would permit either a broad or narrow reading of the scope of the Fifth Amendment, by 1924 it was clear that the privilege was to be expansively construed. In that year the Court held that the Fifth Amendment privilege against self-incrimination could be asserted by an involuntary bankrupt under examination by a special commissioner civilly investigating the bankrupt's assets pursuant to federal law.[24] The risk of self-incrimination was clearly present in the proceeding, but the context was hardly that of a criminal case as seemingly called for in the Fifth Amendment. Nevertheless, in response to the government's claim that the privilege against self-incrimination was inapplicable to civil proceedings, the Supreme Court responded:

> [T]he contrary must be accepted as settled. The privilege is not ordinarily dependent upon the nature of the proceeding in which the testimony is sought or to be used. It applies alike to civil and criminal proceedings, wherever the answer might tend to subject to criminal responsibility him who gives it.[25]

The same kind of approach characterized the application of the Fifth Amendment to legislative investigations, the Court simply asserting that "[w]itnesses cannot be compelled to give evidence against themselves."[26] And most recently, in holding that the privilege applies to juvenile court proceedings, the Court thought it "clear that the availability of the privilege does not turn upon the type of proceeding in which the protection is invoked."[27]

The Supreme Court can be criticized for resolving so critical a feature of the Fifth Amendment without undertaking a substantive analysis of the issue. Nevertheless, its final interpretation is readily supportable since absent a broad scope for the Fifth Amendment, its protections would be far too easily circumvented. The fruits of compelled self-incrimination obtained in civil proceedings would be available to the state for use in criminal trials, thus converting the privilege into a mere conditional right to silence.

Restricting the settings in which the privilege could be asserted, even though potential incrimination was present, would only make the right to remain silent an illusory guarantee. Although it might be argued that such a limited right was intended by the framers, the position is debatable as a matter of history and unwise as a matter of policy. In the context of our modern criminal procedure systems, the vices of compulsory interrogation at trial are equally present when the questioning occurs in another arena. If so, the privilege must be available in such other proceedings.

The criminal case restriction, however, has not been entirely read out of the Fifth Amendment. But rather than limiting the context in which the privilege may be raised, it serves instead to define the risk against which the right to silence may be asserted. The effect is to retain the principle that the privilege is not unlimited in scope but at the same time avoid tying it to formalistic procedural distinctions. As a result, whatever the character of the proceeding in which the questioning takes place, the privilege prevents a compelled response if the answer would be incriminating to the subject. The controlling principle then becomes "the nature of the statement or admission and the exposure which it invites"[28] rather than the procedural setting of the questioning. Isolating when the exposure risk is sufficient to call for Fifth Amendment protection, however, is not always an easy task. The simplest of the situations with which the Fifth Amendment must deal involves statements relating to activities barred by criminal statutes. Here the exposure risk is concededly criminal, and the privilege clearly applies. Many other proceedings, however, may entail aspects of criminality without possessing the label. How are they to be treated in terms of the Fifth Amendment?

As early as 1886 the Supreme Court confronted the issue of the applicability of the privilege to such "quasi-criminal" matters. In the setting of a forfeiture proceeding to seize property allegedly brought into the country in violation of the customs laws, the Court held the Fifth Amendment protection available.[29] Important to the decision were the facts that the actions leading to forfeiture were in themselves criminal and that the forfeiture could have been imposed as part of the criminal penalty had criminal proceedings been instituted. It struck the Court that the forfeiture proceeding was "in substance and effect a criminal one" and that the prosecutor's decision to waive criminal charges could not "deprive the claimants of their immunities as citizens, and extort from them a production of their private papers, or, as an alternative, a confession of guilt."[30] The Court had little difficulty concluding that labels were not controlling for purposes of the Fifth Amendment and that the substance of the impact of the proceedings would govern.

The Supreme Court's 1967 decision in *In re Gault*,[31] applying the Fifth Amendment to a juvenile court hearing to determine a delinquency commitment, raised the same issue in a different context. On the one hand, juvenile court commitments result in incarceration that is just as confining as a prison sentence imposed upon an adult. Although efforts are theoretically made to provide more constructive rehabilitation opportunities for juvenile offenders, the result is often no real difference in programming for adult and juvenile prisoners. Nor would an actual program difference necessarily be controlling since there remains the inescapable fact that both forms of confinement entail the loss of the individual's freedom of movement. On the other hand, the proceedings are not formally criminal in character, nor do they necessarily entail the risk of criminal prosecution. The only qualification is that the juvenile court may waive jurisdiction and permit the case to be handled by an adult criminal court. However, the Supreme Court did not rely on this potential criminal risk in its decision. It accepted the noncriminal and nonpunitive model of the juvenile court system, yet still held the privilege applicable. Simply being threatened with the loss of liberty in the context of a delinquency commitment was deemed sufficient to call into play the protective shield of the privilege against self-incrimination.

While the Supreme Court has resolved the role of the Fifth Amendment in the context of two specific quasi-criminal proceedings, there are a wide variety of others where the applicability of the privilege cannot readily be determined on the authority of existing Court decisions. Are Fifth Amendment protections available in commitment hearings for addicts and alcoholics, in treble-damage actions under the Sherman Act, in a license-revocation proceeding, or in a prison disciplinary hearing because of the exposure entailed in such proceedings? If labels are not controlling in assessing the risk, as they should not be, what then is determinative? The problem is not a new one. The structure of both the Fifth and Sixth Amendments creates an amalgam of procedural and substantive rights governing criminal procedure. They serve to make conviction more difficult, and there is an obvious temptation to avoid them. If minor tinkering were sufficient to avoid the classification of "criminal," more than just the privilege against self-incrimination would be undercut. Most desirable, of course, would be a clear line of demarcation between sanctions or proceedings sufficiently criminal to warrant a Fifth Amendment shield and those outside the scope of its coverage. Such unambiguous rules are rare, however, and we must content ourselves instead with the delineation of factors relevant to the unavoidable classification decision. These in turn should reflect the special concerns that lie behind the right to silence including ensuring a proper balance between the power of the state and the rights of the individual, and permitting the individual to refuse to assist the state to his own detriment when the negative consequences are sufficiently serious to warrant the protections normally associated with the imposition of the criminal sanction.

One effort of this kind was undertaken in the Supreme Court's 1963

Kennedy v. Mendoza-Martinez[32] decision. There, two native-born Americans were stripped of their citizenship for remaining outside the jurisdiction of the United States in time of war to avoid military service. The loss of citizenship was, moreover, automatic and without any prior judicial or administrative review. Recognizing that no criminal label was attached to the provision, the Court nevertheless held the sanction to be essentially penal in character and as such required due process procedures prior to its imposition. Of controlling significance was the penal intent behind the legislation, but the Court suggested other criteria:

> Whether the sanction involves an affirmative disability or restraint, whether it has historically been regarded as a punishment, whether it comes into play only on a finding of *scienter*, whether its operation will promote the traditional aims of punishment—retribution and deterrence, whether the behavior to which it applies is already a crime, whether an alternative purpose to which it may rationally be connected is assignable for it, and whether it appears excessive in relation to the alternative purpose assigned.[33]

Obviously, such criteria are expansive and offer substantial room for assertion of the privilege. Yet they suggest a valuable direction to take in determining the scope limits of the Fifth Amendment by ensuring the dominance of substance over form without precluding the existence of a truly civil context in which the privilege need not be held to apply. Moreover, they are consistent with the Supreme Court's exhortation that "[t]his constitutional protection must not be interpreted in a hostile or niggardly spirit."[34]

There has been forceful opinion voiced that the Fifth Amendment ought not to encompass a criminal or penal risk theory. Justice Field commented that "[i]t is contended, indeed, that it was not the object of the constitutional safeguard to protect the witness against infamy and disgrace. It is urged that its sole purpose was to protect him against incriminating testimony with reference to the offense under prosecution. But I do not agree that such limited protection was all that was secured."[35] Sixty years later, during the McCarthy era, Justice Douglas echoed these thoughts with respect to the infamy to which exposed ex-communists were subjected.[36] Such a view of the privilege would make it unnecessary to separate civil threats from those more properly classified as penal and thus subject to Fifth Amendment control. But with relatively little dissent, infamy and disgrace have been excluded from coverage by the privilege. This has been done to avoid creating too expansive an opportunity to decline to testify, depriving the state of needed evidence even where the state could not criminally sanction the behavior revealed. Absent the possibility of criminal punishment and assuming that criminal-type sanctions constitute the most serious consequence that can follow coerced revelations, the balance was felt to weigh in favor of compelled disclosure. Moreover, since there has been no effort to weigh the consequences of disclosure on a case-by-case basis, no different result has been held to follow even though a particular civil consequence might be more severe in an individual case than the imposition of criminal punishment. Since this would not be true in general, despite selected exceptions, all truly civil risks have been held outside the scope of the self-incrimination clause.

Given the by now settled proposition that the exposure risk, not the form of the proceeding, determines the applicability of the Fifth Amendment, it then becomes clear that the status of the subject being questioned is similarly irrelevant. No distinction should be drawn between a witness or a defendant since both face the risk of self-incrimination if compelled to respond in an official inquiry, and the Court has clearly stated that penal risk is the determinative factor. Historically, one might argue that the Fifth Amendment was only intended to shield criminal defendants. Indeed, the early federal cases extending the privilege to witnesses relied on common law doctrine, not on the Constitution.[37] Yet it is also true that there was recognition of a self-incrimination privilege for witnesses as far back as the trial of King Charles in 1649.[38] Moreover, the logic behind the privilege would not appear to vary with the status of the individual under interrogation. Whatever merit there is in the notion of a right to remain silent in the face of self-incriminatory questioning would be undercut if arbitrarily denied to witnesses. Furthermore, the creation of such a classification might well encourage the use of collateral proceedings to obtain information that a criminal defendant could not be forced to reveal. The privilege against self-incrimination must either be a complete right to silence or it might well become a valueless guarantee. If the state's interest in the acquisition of evidence, a concededly important objective, is outweighed when balanced against the criminal defendant's interest in freedom from compulsory self-incrimination, there does not appear to be enough variation in the characteristics of a witness to warrant a different result.

There is, however, an aspect of the privilege against self-incrimination whose application does vary between witnesses and defendants. Uniformly, both are permitted to decline to answer self-incriminatory inquiries. If the prerequisites are met, the subject of the question may simply assert his Fifth Amendment rights in lieu of providing the information sought. The criminal defendant has, however, the additional right to be free of any questions whatsoever. He may not be called to testify and be forced to assert the privilege as is the case for a witness. Instead, he has the additional option of not even taking the witness stand. The logic behind the criminal defendant's total freedom from any compelled interrogation was explained by Dean Wigmore as related to the privilege's role in guarding against self-incriminatory inquiries. On the assumption that the prosecution would only seek incriminatory facts from the defendant that were relevant to the charges against him, the defendant was privileged from providing any answers. Additionally, the privilege developed during the period in which the rules disqualifying a defendant from testifying in his own behalf were evolving. This also barred the prosecution from calling the defendant to the stand, and the prohibition survived the end of the disqualification principle.[39]

A Personal Right

The historical sources of the privilege against self-incrimination go back over many centuries of British common law development, and during most of that period, the focus of concern was the right of political and religious minorities to reject state inquiries into matters of conscience. In line with this, the establishment of a right to remain silent was at least partly directed toward making the suppression of dissent more difficult. The same objective is still furthered by the privilege, but to it have been added a number of contemporary goals including the preservation of human dignity through the restriction of the state's power to compel self-incrimination, and the protection of the individual's private enclave. Overall, however, the object of the privilege has very clearly been people and the protection of their liberties. Nevertheless, it is also true that unlike England in 1641, modern society depends heavily upon institutions, both formal and informal. Contemporary America has grown too large for individuals, acting alone, to successfully influence it, and thus they must associate in groups. In a sense such groupings are no more than collections of individuals who are acting for their common good. But as such groupings grow, they require a structure that will permit them to function with an acceptable level of efficiency. The response to this need has been to accord formal status to a wide variety of organizational entities and to set ground rules to govern the way in which they operate. As legal entities they exist apart from the individuals who form them, but, of course, they can function only through some human agency. No doubt, the framers did not anticipate that such a dramatic alteration of American society would occur and bring with it unique Fifth Amendment problems, but such has been the case.

The language of the Fifth Amendment itself provides that "[n]o person" may be subjected to compulsory self-incrimination. That individuals are included is clear, but it is not readily apparent how organizations, corporations, partnerships, associations, and the like are to be treated. It is on the one hand established that corporate and other legal entities may be deemed persons for some constitutional purposes. Thus, for example, the Supreme Court had no difficulty concluding that the Fourteenth Amendment language barring the deprivation of life, liberty, or property of any "person" without due process of law included corporations within its protective shield.[40] On the other hand, there is no unbending rule that requires that language be given the same reading when used in different contexts and when there are sufficiently strong policy reasons for another interpretation.

The Supreme Court's first effort to directly address the applicability of the Fifth Amendment privilege to corporations arose in its 1906 *Hale v. Henkel*[41] decision. The context was a grand jury inquiry into antitrust violations by a corporation and a subpoena to an officer of the corporation to produce some of its books and records. The officer was protected by the federal immunity statute from any self-incrimination that could arise as a result of compliance, but he argued that the immunity was inadequate to protect the corporation even though it too was exposed to criminal liability and he was its authorized representative. The Supreme Court, however, ruled that no Fifth Amendment coverage was available, offering three separate rationales for its conclusion. The first reflected an assessment of the intent behind the Fifth Amendment. Despite the fact that the corporation would be exposed to criminal liability by the records and that compliance with the subpoena would require some human assistance, the Court stated:

> The right of a person under the Fifth Amendment to refuse to incriminate himself is purely a personal privilege of the witness. It was never intended to permit him to plead the fact that some third person might be incriminated by his testimony, even though he were the agent of such person.[42]

Since corporations must act through agents, the Court was effectively withdrawing their Fifth Amendment protection as a result of its theory. Yet no historical analysis was offered to support the Court's conclusion, and its suggestion that a corporation is not entitled to Fifth Amendment coverage stood as an unproven assertion. It is true that the long struggle to establish the right to remain silent did not concern itself with corporate entities, and the framers may thus not have had corporations in mind in adopting the Fifth Amendment. But even accepting the possible historical accuracy of the Court's conclusion, it is nevertheless true that corporate structures had come to play a far more significant role in American society than they did in 1789. History is no substitute for reasoned analysis in answering a question as to the scope of the Fifth Amendment largely unanticipated when the amendment was adopted.

The Court's second rationale constituted a more substantive justification for excluding corporations from coverage by the privilege against self-incrimination. This aspect of the opinion focused on the practical obstacle to law enforcement a corporate self-incrimination privilege would entail. Corporations act only through their agents and by written documents. Permitting the corporation to assert the privilege against self-incrimination would in many circumstances deny to the courts the only available evidence of corporate crime. Unlike individual crime where a wide variety of techniques may be employed to acquire evidence of guilt, corporate investigations present more limited opportunities. The privilege therefore might be a far more formidable investigative barrier in the corporate crime arena. Of particular concern to the Court was the antitrust context in which *Hale* itself arose. The Court stated:

> As the combination or conspiracies provided against by the Sherman Anti-Trust Act can ordinarily be proved only by the testimony of parties thereto, in the person of their agents or employes, the privilege claimed could practically nullify the whole act of Congress. Of what use would it be for the Legislature to declare these combinations unlawful if the judicial power may close the door of access to every available source of information upon the subject?[43]

At its core, the argument was one of pure expediency. If the privilege was too significant an impediment to law enforcement, at least with respect to corporations, it had to be dispensed with.

Finally, the Court found special significance in the status of corporations in their relationship to the state. Corporations are state-chartered entities whose powers are limited by law. The state permits individuals to organize them because it is in the larger social interest to do so. But after chartering a corporation, the state still retains an interest in ensuring that state-imposed obligations are followed. This is reflected in the so-called visitorial power that authorizes the state to examine corporate books and papers. The Supreme Court thought it would be a "strange anomaly"[44] if the Fifth Amendment were to become a barrier to the effective use of the state's historical authority over organizations it has itself created. Thus in subsequent decisions it found there to be no Fifth Amendment obstacle to the compulsory production of records of a dissolved or defunct corporation,[45] even though the records had been transferred to individuals. The power of the state to obtain such documents from corporate entities survives even the demise of the corporation, and constitutes a condition on the right to function in a corporate structure. The personal character of the Fifth Amendment assures that there is no interference with this power.

The impetus to organize in contemporary America, of course, has many facets beyond the option to incorporate. State law may permit alternative structures to be established, which have a recognized and formal status. In addition, individuals may organize without any intent to attain formality. The Court's approach to the applicability of the Fifth Amendment in a corporate context is not particularly helpful in determining whether other organizational entities are entitled to assert the privilege. Rather, by relying in part on the state's visitorial power over corporations, the Court suggested a theory by which other groupings might be permitted a measure of Fifth Amendment protection. In *United States v. White*,[46] however, decided by the Supreme Court in 1944, such a distinction was rejected.

A federal grand jury had been investigating payoffs and kickbacks in the construction of a naval facility in Pennsylvania. During the course of its probe, a subpoena was issued for the records of Local No. 542 of the International Union of Operating Engineers. White appeared with the douments but refused to turn them over, asserting the privilege against self-incrimination as the basis for his refusal. He offered to turn over the records in order to permit verification of his self-incrimination claim but not for grand jury use. The district court found him in contempt but was reversed by the court of appeals. The appellate court's judgment was that the books of an unincorporated labor union were the property of all its members, and that the privilege could be asserted by any union member who would be incriminated by being compelled to produce them. The U.S. Supreme Court rejected the court of appeals' theory and denied that the Fifth Amendment could be validly asserted in response to the grand jury's subpoena in such a situation.

Unincorporated labor unions are, of course, quite different from corporations, the latter being chartered by the state for special purposes. The fact that corporations were denied Fifth Amendment protection in *Hale* should not, therefore, have been deemed controlling with respect to a labor organization. The Court could have limited its withdrawal of the privilege to corporate structures because of their special features and accorded protection to the labor union in *White*. It chose instead to identify what it felt to be important similarities among organizations, regardless of their form, and to extend its rule limiting Fifth Amendment coverage to all entities sharing the relevant attributes. Most important among these was the fact that organizations of all sorts are to some extent separate from the individuals who comprise them. This was relevant because the *White* Court took as the funciton of the privilege the need "to prevent the use of legal process to force from the lips of the accused individual the evidence necessary to convict him or to force him to produce and authenticate any personal documents or effects that might incriminate him."[47] This was an objective designed to avoid physical abuse and other "equally reprehensible"[48] techniques. Since organizations could not be dealt with in that way, they did not have to fear being subjected to such force and did not warrant Fifth Amendment protection.

The Court repeated the arguments that the privilege was not intended to protect organizations and that the state had a legitimate interest in inquiring into their activities, an interest that extended beyond its visitorial power over corporations. However, it appeared to place more reliance on the degree of the organization's independence from its members. To the Court, the separate identity obviated the need to apply the privilege since the organization did not have to fear the evils the privilege was designed to control. Moreover, the Court appeared to accept the converse of its position for organizations that did not possess the requisite degree of independence from its members. This was reflected in the standard the Court established to resolve associational Fifth Amendment rights:

> The test . . . is whether one can fairly say under all the circumstances that a particular type of organization has a character so impersonal in the scope of its membership and activities that it cannot be said to embody or represent the purely private or personal interests of its constituents, but rather to embody their common or group interests only.[49]

Presumably, truly private or personal associations would be entitled to assert the privilege because they are really not separate from the interests of the individuals who comprise them. As a result, extracting information from such an entity through its agent is to effectively force him to provide his own rather than the entity's records, thereby compelling self-incrimination in violation of the Fifth Amendment.

Two factors emerge from the *White* opinion that make it an exceedingly persuasive doctrine. First, it reflects the logical principle of balancing state authority and individual rights in the application of the privilege against self-incrimination. Given the fact that individual rights are implicated to a lesser extent when the association of individuals has a truly separate identity, the state interest in the acquisition of evidence outweighs the organization's desire to withhold it. In contrast, if the organization is not in actuality independent of its members, the compulsory production of evidence interferes more with the members' interest than that of the organization, a result that would help tip the balance in favor of applying the privilege. Second, the *White* opinion can be interpreted as an acceptance of the Fifth Amendment's role in the protection of personal privacy. The *White* test to measure the application of the privilege provides coverage for organizations that most reflect the privacy interests of their members, and withholds it where the members can be legitimately held to have given up their privacy interests in joining the organization.

Despite its appeal, determining the applicability of the privilege to organizations based upon an assessment of the separability of the organization from the individuals who comprise it is risky since the standard lacks firm criteria for making the necessary judgments. The Court did not provide a clear indication as to what groups would receive Fifth Amendment protection under *White*, and consequently the test could be converted into a virtual bar to any associational privilege. The Court's actual decisions precluding typical business corporations and a fair-sized labor union from asserting the right to remain silent may reflect a reasonable accommodation of Fifth Amendment interests with the state's law enforcement responsibility. But the *White* test contained no guarantee that a different result would follow for other organizational structures. Interests reflected in the privilege against self-incrimination can of course be implicated when information is sought from an association, especially when the organization is directed toward political purposes.[50] The development of case law implementing the *White* standard, however, seemed to suggest that although the theoretical basis for an associational right to silence remained, its reality was doubtful.[51]

By 1974, in its decision in *Bellis v. United States*,[52] the Supreme Court clearly demonstrated that it intended only the most limited role for the Fifth Amendment in protecting organizations. Bellis had been a partner in a small three-attorney law firm. The firm additionally employed three secretaries and three other attorneys. Although Bellis left the firm in 1969, he did not take any of the partnership records with him, and the remaining two partners formed a new association after his departure. Bellis recovered the records in 1973 and was then served with a grand jury subpoena ordering him to appear and produce any partnership documents in his possession. His assertion of the Fifth Amendment as the basis for refusing to produce the records was rejected, and he was held in contempt. The Supreme Court affirmed in an opinion that reiterated the argument in *White* that the privilege against self-incrimination should be "limited to its historic function of protecting only the natural individual from compulsory incrimination through his own testimony or personal records."[53] Similarly, the Court pointed to the unwarranted obstacles an associational privilege would erect to legitimate state regulatory efforts, a view reminiscent of its 1906 decision in *Hale*. Finally, the Court explicitly reaffirmed the *White* view that the purposes behind the privilege do not justify its application to organizations. The opinion particularly identified individual privacy as the relevant consideration and observed that it was not implicated in the compulsory production of organizational records. The fact that such records were often strictly regulated by the state and that access to them was generally shared among members of the organization meant that the custodian of the records lacked the kind of control "which would be characteristic of a claim of privacy and confidentiality"[54] and that the records themselves did not possess "the requisite element of privacy or confidentiality essential for the privilege to attach."[55] The general theory of *Bellis* closely tracked *White* in justifying the denial of Fifth Amendment coverage to organizations on historic, practical, and functional grounds.

Like the Court in *White*, the *Bellis* majority left room for the possibility of a Fifth Amendment privilege for associations. This was most clearly indicated in its observation that the facts of *Bellis* "might be a different case if it involved a small family partnership, . . . or, if there were some other pre-existing relationship of confidentiality among the partners."[56] But the tenor of the opinion was even less hospitable to such a possibility than the *White* Court had been. It labeled the *White* test for separating organizations that represent the purely private interests of its members from those embodying their common interests as "not particularly helpful."[57] And rather than pursuing the *White* analysis in *Bellis*, the Court simply identified the criteria that satisfied it as to the separate identity of the law firm. It noted that the firm was a formal institution, state law governed its internal workings absent a partnership agreement, it maintained a separate bank account, filed separate tax returns, and it could be sued and hold property. Satisfying itself as to the firm's separate identity, the Court found it unnecessary to inquire into its personal or impersonal character.

The significance of the *Bellis* departure from the standard set out in *White* is that it substantially restricts the scope of Fifth Amendment protection for associations.[58] This stems from the fact that indicia of a separate association identity will be easy to find if reference can be made to such factors as continuity, separate bank accounts, and the like. Unlike *White*, which called for a further inquiry into the characteristics of the organization, *Bellis* ends with the determination that the group exists apart from its members, even, apparently, if it is no more than their alter ego. This was quite clearly the case for a partnership such as that reflected in the three-man *Bellis* law firm, but was also hinted at for other groupings as well. It is not true, however, that the privilege has no value when individuals join together to further their interests, and there should be a way for people to associate for common purposes without having to lose Fifth Amendment protection in the process. Whether such a possibility exists is uncertain. The best available advice is that if the privilege is to be retained, the association should be as informal and unstructured as possible or, if possible, not be formed at all.

Establishing the virtual absence of Fifth Amendment protection for organizations leads to the conclusion that the organization's agent cannot assert a privilege on its behalf in response to a state demand for incriminatory evidence. It remains possible, however, that compliance with the demand will incriminate the agent as well, and thus he may wish to assert his own rather than the organization's privilege. Under such circumstances, the *White* and *Bellis* reasoning are not conclusive.

In *Wilson v. United States*,[59] the Supreme Court was faced with an agent's claim of personal self-incrimination in response to a subpoena for corporate records. Although the Court recognized the validity of a claim of privilege for personal documents, it denied that an officer of a corporation could assert the Fifth Amendment with respect to the latter's records, which he controlled. The Court's conclusion was that "physical custody of incriminating documents does not of itself protect the custodian against their compulsory production."[60] The controlling issue was deemed to be the "nature of the documents and the capacity in which they are held."[61] If the documents are subject to scrutiny, custody alone will not permit the officer to claim the privilege. The Court characterized the situation as one in which the corporate officer has "voluntarily assumed a duty which overrides his claim of privilege."[62]

In so ruling, the Supreme Court again relied upon the practical effect of allowing the agent to claim the Fifth Amendment to support its conclusion that no privilege protection was warranted. In its view, the "reserved power of visitation would seriously be embarrassed, if not wholly defeated in its effective exercise, if guilty officers could refuse inspection of the records and papers of the corporation."[63] This detriment to state regulation was not outweighed by the value of applying the privilege in such situations. To the Court the contrary view would have been an "unjustifiable extenstion"[64] of the Fifth Amendment. The records were not those of the agent, nor were they personal papers, and thus the privilege was deemed inapplicable.

One of the consequences of *Wilson* was to require an inquiry into the ownership of the records being sought. This was not difficult in the context of the *Wilson* fact situation since the subpoena was clearly for corporate documents and the lower court offered to remove personal papers from those to be turned over. In *White* also the subpoena directed production of only official union records so that no personal claim of privilege could validly be made. In *Bellis*, however, the Court dealt with partnership records and the claim by Bellis that he had an ownership interest in the law firm's subpoenaed documents. The point, however, was brushed aside in a footnote.[65] Seemingly, the indicia of separate identity, which supports denial of Fifth Amendment coverage to the association, also supports the conclusion that the individual does not have a sufficient ownership interest in the documents to warrant a personal claim of privilege. The more identifiable the organization is as an entity apart from its members, the more likely it is that organization documents will not be deemed the property of the members. Although the Court was not explicit on this point, its overall approach does not seem to suggest a willingness to label organizational documents as personal for Fifth Amendment purposes. If, as a result, the agent is deemed to have custody in a representative capacity, his claim of privilege will fail.

The Supreme Court in *Wilson* took pains to point out the limited character of the compelled production it demanded. The opinion noted that the agent could "decline to utter upon the witness stand a single self-incriminating word,"[66] but this was true only because the subpoena sought documents alone. The decision did not necessarily mean that no oral testimony could be obtained despite the fact that compelling such testimony on top of the production of documents would have constituted a far more expansive grant of authority to the state. The issue, however, came to a head in the Court's 1957 *Curcio v. United States*[67] ruling. A grand jury investigating racketeering in the New York City garment and trucking industries had subpoenaed Curcio, a union official, to produce certain union records. Curcio appeared in response to the subpoena but did not have the records and invoked the privilege against self-incrimination when asked questions pertaining to their whereabouts.

In its decision the Court recognized that there are alternative forms of questioning that might pertain to the organization records sought from the agent. The limited form focuses on oral testimony to authenticate and identify the documents produced in response to the subpoena. Consistently, rulings from the lower courts have upheld the propriety of such questioning over Fifth Amendment objection, reliance frequently being placed on Judge Learned Hand's view that the act of producing the documents constitutes a form of implicit authentication, and making it explicit constitutes little, if any, further danger of incrimination.[68] The Court accurately observed, however, that it did not have to pass on the validity of such decisions since the government sought to compel a broader form of disclosure in seeking testimony as to the whereabouts of documents that had not been produced.

The government's argument relied heavily upon the practical consequences that had proven so persuasive in *White* and *Wilson*. Its position was that organizational records would be more readily obtained if the custodian faced contempt for refusing to testify about their location. That, however, pushed practicalities too far, and the Court responded by noting that it "need not concern [itself] with the relative efficacy"[69] of techniques for obtaining such documents. Fifth Amendment interests of the subject in the "contents of his own mind"[70] were deemed to be directly infringed by the testimony sought, there being no question that the information about the location of the records was not held in a representative capacity. In contrast, as to the corporate records themselves, the custodian "does not own the records and has no legally cognizable interest in them."[71]

In personalizing the Fifth Amendment by restricting its availability to organizations and their agents, the Court has embarked on a course that may not be fully in accord with current needs. Formal group activity is a far more significant feature of modern American life than it was in the days of the framers. Denial of virtually any Fifth Amendment protection in such circumstances may restrict the ability of individuals to freely pursue their interests in the most expedient manner. However, it is also true that the decision to extend Fifth Amendment coverage must take into account countervailing state regulatory interests. In this regard there is a basis for legitimate concern that an extensive organizational shield pursuant to the privilege against self-incrimination might unduly hamper the state's valid objectives without a significant incremental benefit to the goals served by the privilege. The Court's resolution of these countervailing considerations indicates its skepticism that much of value would be achieved by broadening the Fifth Amendment's coverage of organizations. The scales tip the other way only when agents are extensively questioned beyond the point of authenticating documents they produce. But although the balance point chosen by the Court is overly restrictive, its demand that opposing interests be weighed is surely the proper mode of analysis.

The Scope of Immunity

In providing for the privilege against self-incrimination, the First Congress very clearly sought to bar state compulsion to force an individual to assist in securing his own criminal conviction. The centuries of evolution of the right to remain silent is ample proof of that intent. More debatable, and agreed to by only a five-four vote of the Supreme Court, is the question of whether self-accusation alone is sufficient to implicate Fifth Amendment values. Although the two alternatives may initially appear indistinguishable, the differences between them are substantial. Most critical is the fact that the state might attempt to compel the production of self-incriminatory evidence but not seek to use it to the individual's *criminal* detriment. The result could then be the elimination of the risk of a criminal conviction but not necessarily the possibility of other adverse consequences. These consequences could be substantial, and could include the risk of prosecution independent of the risk of criminal conviction; the affront to human dignity and conscience; and the exposure to infamy and disgrace that self-accusation entails. Yet, although four justices of the Supreme Court in an 1896 decision would not have limited the privilege to instances of penal risk,[72] a position echoed by Justice Douglas in 1956,[73] the contrary must be taken as settled. However, accepting this principle does not resolve all related questions. In particular, if the state may compel the production of evidence from a suspect, how much protection need it provide before the Fifth Amendment is satisfied? The issue has been appropriately labeled as the problem of defining the scope of immunity sufficient to satisfy the privilege against self-incrimination.[74]

There is a significant history behind immunity and immunity-related legislation that helps to define the character of the problem.[75] As far back as 1710 an English statute was enacted to provide immunity in civil gambling cases. Its effect was to permit the loser to sue for recovery of his losses without having to face an assertion of privilege by the winner that would have obstructed the suit. An immunity statute was also enacted by Parliament to permit it to secure evidence in the impeachment trial of Lord Chancellor Macclesfield for bribery.[76] Similarly, political corruption lay behind the first federal immunity statute in the United States that provided immunity for witnesses before congressional investigating committees.[77] Immunity could also be provided by executive pardon where legislative immunity was unavailable.[78] All such efforts, however, shared the characteristic of seeking to remove the risk of criminal conviction in order to permit the compulsory production of evidence. But also shared were the difficult policy judgments the immunity issue forced since each such grant traded the opportunity of conviction for the acquisition of evidence.

Unquestionably, the reason for the importance of the scope problem lies in the dramatic consequences of an immunity grant. If the state is precluded by immunity legislation from prosecuting the recipient of an immunity grant and if that result is required by the Fifth Amendment, the decision to offer the grant must be very carefully weighed. Giving up the possibility of prosecution in return for testimony involves a difficult tradeoff of factors not clearly resolvable one way or the other. It would appear, moreover, that much of the decision must also be made in the dark since the state cannot always know the value of what it will receive until the immunity is conferred and the testimony obtained. If, on the other hand, a less extensive form of immunity would satisfy the Constitution, the state might be able to secure testimony without having to totally foreclose the option of criminally prosecuting an individual who provides incriminating evidence under compulsion. Depending upon how limited an immunity satisfies the Fifth Amendment, the result would still be a difficult balancing decision for the state but without the finality necessarily reflected in a total immunity grant.

The Supreme Court's first venture into the realm of immunity under the Fifth Amendment occurred in *Counselman v. Hitchcock*.[79] The case arose in the context of a criminal antitrust investigation. Testimony was sought under a grant of immunity, but it was contended that the immunity did not provide sufficient protection to circumvent the privilege against self-incrimination. Behind the argument and setting its contours, was the brief history of immunity law development in the federal system. Congress first enacted an immunity statute in 1857 to permit it to investigate a vote-selling scheme. The statute authorized congressional committees to grant full transactional immunity to witnesses in return for their testimony. With such an immunity grant, the witness was guaranteed that he would not "be held to answer criminally"[80] for any federal offenses about which he was compelled to testify. Indeed, the fact that transactional immunity constituted a total bar to prosecution made compulsory testimony an attractive opportunity for potential witnesses. The more crimes they disclosed, the more freedom from prosecution they obtained. Witnesses, in fact, sought the "immunity baths" Congress was authorized to give. Transactional immunity turned into a procedure far too easily abused, and Congress responded by enacting legislation to restrict the scope of its immunity grants to cover solely the use of the compelled testimony in a subsequent criminal prosecution.[81] Then in 1868 the authority to grant this form of use immunity was extended to cover judicial as well as legislative proceedings. The statutory language provided that the compelled testimony "shall not be used as evidence in any criminal prosecution against such witness,"[82] and it was this provision that was before the Supreme Court in the 1892 *Counselman* case.

Concededly, the language and history behind the privilege against self-incrimination provide no ready answer to the question of how much immunity is necessary to satisfy the Fifth Amendment. Simple use immunity would be the narrowest the privilege might allow. It removes the direct benefit the state would obtain if it could not only compel self-incriminatory testimony but also introduce it in a criminal prosecution. But use immunity provides no protection against the indirect benefits of compelled testimony, including investigatory leads, trial strategy decisions, and the like. If the privilege against self-incrimination protects against any use of compelled testimony to the witness's detriment, both direct and indirect, use immunity will not suffice to supplant the privilege.

The most relevant federal precedent available to the Court in *Counselman* was Chief Justice Marshall's views on the privilege against self-incrimination expressed in the proceedings against Aaron Burr. Burr's secretary, a man named Willie, had been called to the stand to authenticate a letter he allegedly wrote in cipher to a Dr. Bollman. He refused to provide the sought-after testimony, although recognizing that no direct and immediate incrimination would have been generated by a response. Instead, his concern was that "other elements of the crime [of treason might] be gradually unfolded"[83] as a result of his testimony. And Marshall agreed with his claim:

> Many links frequently compose that chain of testimony which is necessary to convict any individual of a crime. It appears to the court to be the true sense of the rule that no witness is compellable to furnish any one of them against himself. It is certainly not only a possible but a probable case that a witness, by disclosing a single fact, may complete the testimony against himself, and to every effectual purpose accuse himself as entirely as he would by stating every circumstance which would be required for his conviction.[84]

From this, Marshall concluded that a witness may refuse to answer and thereby "disclose a fact which forms a necessary and essential link in the chain of testimony, which would be sufficient to convict him of any crimes."[85]

Marshall's opinion did not involve a confrontation with an immunity statute, nor did it specifically hold that the privilege against self-incrimination protects against more than the direct use of compelled incriminatory testimony. However, his "link in the chain" analogy hints at such a result insofar as it suggests that the privilege may cover disclosures that are not in themselves directly incriminatory. Additionally, the *Counselman* Court was of the view that a "liberal construction . . . must be placed upon constitutional provisions for the protection of personal rights."[86] As a result, it concluded that the narrow use immunity provided by federal law was inadequate to bar a plea of self-incrimination. The federal immunity statute "could not, and would not, prevent the use of his testimony to search out other testimony," nor would it bar "the obtaining and the use of witnesses and evidence which should be attributable directly to the testimony he might give under compulsion."[87] The Court implicitly viewed the self-incrimination clause as a bar to any indirect prosecution benefit from compulsory testimony. To be a witness against oneself involves therefore both providing self-incriminatory testimony for the fact-finder's consideration and investigative leads to assist the state in acquiring incriminatory evidence from other sources. And thus the state, in an apparently broad sense, may not force an individual to testify to his possible future criminal detriment even if no direct evidentiary use will be made of his testimony.

The Court in *Counselman* did not end with a simple rejection of use immunity. Instead, it suggested that if immunity were to satisfy the demands of the Fifth Amendment, it would have to be of the transactional variety. The Court thought that a "reasonable construction" of the privilege would encompass protection against compulsory disclosure of both the "circumstances of his offense" and "the sources from which, or the means by which, evidence of its commission, or of his connection with it, may be obtained."[88] This in turn would clearly require more than use immunity since the protection offered must be coextensive with the scope of the privilege's coverage, and use immunity failed to restrict secondary employment of compulsory testimony. That the only solution would be full transactional immunity was indicated by the Court's concluding observation:

> We are clearly of the opinion that no statute which leaves the party or witness subject to prosecution after he answers the criminating question put to him, can have the effect of supplanting the privilege conferred by the Constitution of the United States.[89]

It was only sixteen days later that Congress began to consider a new immunity statute designed to satisfy the *Counselman* requirements. As finally enacted, the immunity legislation was limited to Interstate Commerce Act proceedings and offered full transactional immunity for compelled testimony. Its language provided that "[n]o person shall be prosecuted or subjected to any penalty or forfeiture for or on account of any transaction, matter or thing, concerning which he may testify, or produce evidence."[90] In 1896 the Court took up the issue of the constitutionality of the statute in *Brown v. Walker*,[91] and by a five-four vote upheld its validity. The case squarely presented the Court with the need to define the scope of the right not to be compelled to be a "witness against himself." If the phrase had been interpreted to include revelations that would expose the witness simply to unfavorable comments, then as a practical matter no testimony could be compelled. Instead, the Court read the language as providing protection only against criminal prosecution and found that transactional immunity satisfactorily removed that risk. Then, aware that it had found an immunity formula that would meet the Court's requirements, Congress proceeded to enact further compulsory-testimony legislation of the same variety as the statute upheld in *Brown v. Walker*. Three such statutes were upheld in the Court's 1906 *Hale v. Henkel*[92] decision, thus laying to rest any lingering doubts as to the constitutionality of transactional immunity. But despite the constitutional acceptabilty of transactional immunity, its practical consequences apparently caused prosecutors to use it infrequently. The "immunity bath" it provided seemed to constitute too high a price for the testimony received, but the nature of transactional immunity left no other option.

The character of the immunity problem remained static until the Supreme Court's 1964 decision in *Murphy v. Waterfront Commission*.[93] The Bistate Commission had been investigating a work stoppage at some New Jersey piers and sought to compel testimony on the matter over Fifth Amendment objection by granting transactional immunity from prosecution by New York or New Jersey. The witnesses, however, persisted in their refusal to respond on the grounds that the risk of incrimination under federal law remained. In the course of holding their refusal justified, the Court noted that the risk of federal incrimination did have to be removed. And it indicated that this could be achieved by a rule that "the compelled testimony and its fruits cannot be used in any manner by federal officials in connection with a criminal prosecution"[94] against the witnesses. Moreover, the Court added that once a witness proves he has testified under a state grant of immunity, the burden would shift to federal authorities to demonstrate that their evidence had been obtained from an independent source.

As a result of *Murphy*, the argument could now be made that something less than full transactional immunity might satisfy the demands of the Fifth Amendment. The *Counselman* decision barred use immunity and the response of Congress had been to offer grants of transactional immunity from prosecution in return for compelled self-incriminatory testimony. The compromise suggestion in *Murphy* was immunity covering both direct use of the compelled testimony and indirect use of its fruits. This would not bar future prosecution if independent evidence sufficient to convict the witness for the offense about which he was forced to testify was available from an unconnected source. The Court's opinion did not provide any elaboration of its views on the scope of immunity required by the Constitution, but Justice White, concurrring, stressed his position that the broader form of transactional immunity relied upon since *Counselman* was a "wholly unnecessary constitutional principle."[95]

In 1970 Congress responded to the opinion in *Murphy* by repealing federal transactional immunity legislation and replacing it with what has been labeled use-derivative use immunity. Pursuant to such an immunity grant, "no testimony or other information compelled under the order (or any information directly or indirectly derived from such testimony) may be used against the witness in any criminal case"[96] except, as had previously been true, for perjury, false statement, or contempt prosecutions. But it was not altogether clear that such a statute would survive constitutional attack. The reason for the doubt stemmed from the fact that *Murphy* had involved an interjurisdictional immunity problem between the states and the federal government. Where, instead, the question focused on the scope of immunity required of the jurisdiction compelling the testimony, full transactional immunity might be necessary.[97] First, the risk of future prosecution by the same jurisdiction that sought the testimony would be greater than the risk that another would seek to prosecute. This served to make the scope of immunity a more acute issue. Beyond that, no special problems of federalism would be involved, and therefore no worry that jurisdictions would be in conflict over whether the testimony was worth the immunity grant. Inherent in the conflict was pressure to provide less than full transactional immunity as a way to ensure that a jurisdiction would not be totally barred from enforcing its criminal statutes because of the immunity decisions of another jurisdiction. Finally, given the difficult problems envisioned for demonstrating the independent source of evidence after immunity had been granted, only transactional immunity would arguably suffice in a single jurisdiction context.

Ultimately, the Supreme Court resolved the dispute in the companion cases of *Kastigar v. United States*[98] and *Zicarelli v. New Jersey State Commission of Investigation.*[99] Both 1972 decisions focused on single jurisdiction grants of use-derivative use immunity and upheld their constitutionality. The Court refused to limit *Murphy* to interjurisdictional considerations and found, instead, that the privilege against self-incrimination was satisfied in all circumstances if the immunity "prohibits the prosecutorial authorities from using the compelled testimony in *any* respect."[100] This, in the Court's view, would leave the state and federal authorities "in substantially the same position as if the witness had claimed his privilege in the absence of a state grant of immunity.''[101] And the Court felt no need for a "greater margin of protection.''[102]

Recent decisions of the Supreme Court have reflected little disagreement over the principle that immunity must be coextensive with the privilege against self-incrimination in order to survive constitutional attack and that a total ban on any use of any compelled testimony would meet that requirement. Rather, the disagreement appears to focus on whether use-derivative use immunity will in practice provide the necessary protection. It appears thus far that actual prosecution of witnesses for offenses revealed in compelled testimony is rare.[103] Use-derivative use immunity may, therefore, in practice be much akin to full transactional immunity. The case law in the lower courts, however, has not yet fully developed standards for judging the independent-source requirement where prosecution has been sought, and thus it is difficult to tell whether less than full transactional immunity can in practice provide the necessary degree of protection. One decision from the Second Circuit Court of Appeals suggests a basis for legitimate concern on this point.[104] A witness compelled to testify under an immunity grant provided the sought-after evidence against the investigation's prime target as did other witnesses. Some time later the target himself pleaded guilty and testified against the witness who had been immunized. In response to a motion to exclude the testimony, the court ruled that it could be admitted if the court was satisfied that the subjective motivation behind the target's decision to implicate the witness did not result from the consequences of the witness's testimony against him. Yet a finding of an independent source based upon an assessment of the intent of a witness is a very fragile distinction upon which to authorize compulsory testimony. Any doubt in such circumstances should be resolved against an independent-source finding. Indeed, in any case where the prosecution has not identified its proof against a witness prior to immunizing his testimony, great care must be taken to ensure that its evidence is not derived from the compelled revelations. Failure to strictly enforce the independent-source rule would be inconsistent with the rationale behind the decisions upholding the validity of use-derivative use immunity statutes.

4

Official Proceedings: The Core Concept

The heart of contemporary American criminal procedure is the criminal trial. It represents the focus of the confrontation between the state and the accused as they contest the issue of criminal guilt. Each party must use its every resource at this stage to convince the trier of fact. Once the trial has resulted in a verdict, the losing party bears the burden of appeal and must overcome the traditional reluctance of appellate courts to reverse lower court judgments. The criminal trial is the point at which the stakes are highest for all participants.

The significance and consequences of the trial's outcome generate the greatest pressure on the state to seek incriminatory testimony from the accused. If the state is successful in this endeavor, it will have acquired compelling, if not conclusive, proof of guilt. But just as the state's desire for damaging evidence is greatest at this point, so too the defendant's interest in freedom from compulsory self-incrimination is most severely strained by state efforts to force him to assist in convicting himself at his own trial. Historically such efforts generated the most vehement opposition to compulsory interrogation. It is only fitting therefore that the central proceeding of the criminal process, the criminal trial itself, encompass the greatest measure of self-incrimination protection. In response, the privilege against self-incrimination has developed a core reflecting the very special considerations surrounding the criminal trial. Within the core of the Fifth Amendment's coverage, the right to remain silent receives the greatest measure of legal protection; outside, there is less consistency. But, not unexpectedly, a battleground has developed as to the reach of the privilege's core. The issue is of major significance since how its boundaries are defined along with the characteristics of the procedures surrounding its application tell us much about the Fifth Amendment's true measure of effectiveness.

The Privilege, the Accused, and the Trial

The legal development of the privilege against self-incrimination and the scholarly commentary surrounding it have reflected a fundamental distinction between the right to remain silent of an accused and that of an ordinary witness.[1] Clearly, the accused faces the more immediate threat that criminal sanctions will be applied to him. The risk of prosecution faced by a witness may be high in individual cases, but as a class, witnesses are simply not as directly and imminently confronted with the possibility of a criminal conviction. Consequently, any differentiation in self-incrimination protection should accord greater coverage to the criminally accused as compared to those who are merely witnesses. While the law has evolved in a manner consistent with these considerations, other factors may well have contributed to this result.

For the witness, the privilege against self-incrimination means that he has the right to refuse to answer self-incriminatory inquiries. When a question is propounded or a request for information made, the witness must claim the privilege as the basis of his refusal to respond. But for the criminally accused, the privilege means not merely the right to refuse to answer incriminatory questions but rather the right to refuse to answer any question whatsoever. The accused therefore need not weigh the risks of incrimination posed by each question, nor need he face the pressure of the surroundings of the interrogation in exercising his privilege against self-incrimination. A blanket refusal to respond will suffice.

One might explain the greater scope of the accused's privilege by the more immediate conviction risk he faces. However, two other factors previously noted are also relevant. First, the privilege against self-incrimination protects against the compulsory disclosure of incriminatory facts relating to a criminal proceeding. If the prosecutor makes an inquiry of an accused, it is fair to assume that the prosecutor believes that the result will be such a disclosure. All such inquiries of an accused are, therefore, appropriately barred, and there is no need to separately assess the incriminatory impact of each question.[2] The accused's privilege was also an offshoot of the now discarded rules disqualifying him from testifying in his own behalf even if he sought to. The abolition of the disqualification bar to testimony of the accused left him free to answer questions voluntarily but did not change the fact that the prosecutor could not compel him to testify.[3] The accused is thus free both to decline to respond to all questions as well as take the witness stand at his trial. Unlike the witness, he may not be forced to assert the privilege to every question, but may exercise his right to remain silent through the single act of refusing to testify at all. In so doing, the accused eliminates the risks of error entailed in individualized decisions to assert the privilege, and also avoids repeatedly calling attention to the fact that he is not testifying despite his obvious awareness of information relevant to the proceedings.

Concededly, the defendant's Fifth Amendment rights are far broader than those available to the ordinary witness. As a general principle, it has been said that "the public has a right to everyman's evidence"[4] subject only to a valid claim of privilege. Yet the defendant need not answer even nonincriminatory questions, nor is he obligated to take the witness stand and assert the privilege as is required of the witness. Neither Dean Wigmore's view that the Fifth Amendment would be a valid assertion in response to any question the prosecutor might ask nor the coincident evolution of the privilege and the defendant disqualification rules, however, provides an adequate explanation. Rather, the justification lies in policy, specifically the consequences that may follow a decision to take the stand. The witness does not necessarily have anything immediate at stake although, of course, he may fear inadvertent self-incrimination and subsequent prosecution. The defendant, however, is faced with the challenge of avoiding the thrust of the state's case against him, which is directed toward proving his guilt. He too will undoubtedly fear inadvertent self-incrimination if forced to respond to nonincriminatory questions, but beyond that the very fact of taking the witness stand will expose his character to the jury, which may be far more damaging than anything he might say. As the Supreme Court observed, "[e]xcessive timidity, nervousness when facing others and attempting to explain transactions of a suspicious character, and offenses charged against him, will often confuse and embarrass him to such a degree as to increase rather than remove prejudices against him."[5] Allowing the state to force a defendant to reveal such characteristics in front of the jury, which has the power to convict him, touches the central concerns of the Fifth Amendment and has been appropriately prohibited.

Given the greater scope of the privilege as applied to defendants, it is understandably important to accurately separate them from those in the category of witnesses. The most obvious line of demarcation would be the point of formal criminal accusation after which the subject of the criminal charge is most certainly an accused. Provision of the defendant's special privilege not to testify at this point would bar an individual from being forced to take the stand not only at his own trial but also at various pretrial proceedings such as a suppression hearing.[6] Recent cases have suggested, moreover, that the accusatorial stage may start even earlier, including the preliminary hearing and arraignment, thus prohibiting any compelled testimony at these proceedings.[7] But wherever the formal accusation line is drawn, there will undoubtedly remain a variety of procedures classified as being in the preaccusation stage. These may be investigatory in format, aimed at determining if a crime has been committed and who committed it, or they may focus on the charging decision itself and encompass an assessment of whether there is enough evidence to warrant a trial. It is not clear, however, whether any of the special Fifth Amendment protection afforded to the accused carries over to activities preceding formal accusation.

The Supreme Court's rulings on this question to date have reflected inconsistent solutions. Its decision in *Miranda v. Arizona*[8] affirmed the suspect's right to refuse to respond in a police interrogation and added the requirement that the suspect be warned of that fact and have the right to the presence of counsel during the questioning. Only if the government meets the "heavy burden" of proving a knowing and intelligent waiver will the results of such an interrogation be admissible against the accused in a later trial. Overall the result is a system more protective in Fifth Amendment terms than that normally available to witnesses. However, the Supreme Court has not placed any similar restrictions on grand jury practice. Prospective defendants have been held not to have a constitutional right to the presence of counsel when called to appear before a grand jury, nor does the status of being a prospective defendant entitle an individual to refuse to respond entirely. To the contrary, the prospective or putative defendant seems to be in a position no different from that of any witness.[9] It is not even clear whether any special warning need be given under these circumstances. As a result, it appears that the criminal suspect prior to formal accusation is not as fully protected as a postaccusation accused since some questioning may occur but may possibly stand in a somewhat better position than an ordinary witness, at least in the police interrogation room.

The utilization of a formal line of demarcation between witnesses and the accused for purposes of administering the Fifth Amendment satisfies the need for certainty in determining when an individual may refuse to answer all questions as opposed to only those that are self-incriminatory. But the price for certainty here is a degree of arbitrariness in providing Fifth Amendment protection. A prospective defendant may differ from an actual defendant only in that the state has not yet had the opportunity to indict him. Or, given the contrast in Fifth Amendment coverage applicable to each, the difference may arise from the fact that the state has delayed charging a suspect in order to take advantage of the increased opportunities for questioning present in the preaccusation stage. In both cases, however, there are more similarities than differences between the two categories thus supporting equal application of the privilege to both. Rather than sensitively weighing state interests in the acquisition of information against the policy interests the privilege is designed to further, in light of the special risks faced by individuals slated for prosecution whether or not formal charges have been filed, the law has drawn a narrow and specially protective shield around only those *formally* accused. For others, individualized assertion of the privilege on a question-by-question basis must suffice.

Acceptance of the right of a defendant to decline to testify after being formally accused has been universal in the United States. However, there has been some disagreement as to what consequences may follow the assertion of that right. The Supreme Court's 1965 decision in *Griffin v. California*[10] focused on one such consequence, a judge's adverse comment on the defendant's failure to take the witness stand. In *Griffin*, the trial judge had instructed the jury that a criminal defendant has a constitutional right not to testify, but added that appropriate adverse inferences could be drawn by the jury. The judge's language confined the permissible inferences to a suitably narrow range:

> As to any evidence of facts against him which the defendant can reasonably be expected to deny or explain because of facts within his knowledge, if he does not testify or if, though he does testify, he fails to deny or explain such evidence, the jury may take that failure into consideration as tending to indicate the truth of such evidence and as indicating that among the inferences that may reasonably be drawn therefrom those unfavorable to the defendant are the more probable.[11]

As such, the judge's comment was consistent with normally accepted evidentiary inferences, and only constitutional considerations could have altered the result.

The Supreme Court had previously considered constitutional challenges to the use of an adverse inference following a defendant's refusal to take the stand but had not found the Fourteenth Amendment due process clause to be violated by such a procedure.[12] *Griffin*, however, raised the issue under the Fifth Amendment's self-incrimination clause, which the Court had incorporated in *Malloy v. Hogan*.[13] And the Court found in the Fifth Amendment a prohibition against the trial judge's actions in *Griffin* commenting on the defendant's silence. A strict reading of the Fifth Amendment would not necessarily have led to the conclusion that a judge is barred from commenting on the accused's failure to testify. The language of the Fifth Amendment prohibits only compulsion to be a witness against oneself. While the adverse comment certainly constitutes a pressure to testify, it is hardly of the magnitude of the techniques out of which the privilege evolved. Additionally, the adverse comment does not bring to the jury's attention something of which it was not previously aware. Arguably, the instruction given in *Griffin* was more beneficial than no comment at all since it sought to confine any inference into logically relevant boundaries and directed the jury not to draw a conclusion of guilt from the defendant's silence but rather only factual inferences. Following this reasoning, the *Griffin* dissent thought that barring instructions such as that given by the trial judge "stretche[d] the concept of compulsion beyond all reasonable bounds."[14]

The majority opinion in *Griffin* did not view the trial judge's adverse comment as akin to traditional forms of interrogation compulsion. Indeed, it does not appear that an instruction such as that given to the jury would generally compel defendants to take the witness stand. And, of course, the instruction obviously didn't compel Griffin himself to testify. Rather, the Court advanced the theory that an adverse inference instruction constituted "a penalty imposed by courts for exercising a constitutional privilege. It cuts down on the privilege by making its assertion costly."[15] At least insofar as the defendant's core Fifth Amendment right not to take the stand was concerned, the Court suggested that freedom to exercise the privilege against self-incrimination could not be unduly impeded. The adverse inference instruction was too much of a burden to impose upon the defendant's decision whether to invoke or forgo his Fifth Amendment privilege. Although it did not prevent him from remaining silent, it did authorize the jury to hold his silence against him in its guilt-determination process.

Although *Griffin* barred the state from affirmatively presenting the defendant's silence to the jury as a basis for resolving factual disputes in the state's favor, it did not directly hold that the jury may not draw its own adverse inference from the defendant's silence. Similarly, the Court did not address the question of whether, as in the federal system, a jury instruction barring adverse inferences may be demanded by the defendant or refused by him. Each of these additional questions presents issues that can be analyzed in the *Griffin* framework. The defendant's decision whether or not to take the stand must take into account a variety of strategic factors, including such considerations as his credibility as a witness and the believability of his testimony. The adverse inference instruction adds an extraneous factor to the defendant's decision, an issue not intrinsic to the testimonial process itself. As such, the Court found it to be an unconstitutional penalty on the exercise of the Fifth Amendment. But the fact that the jury may draw an adverse inference without being instructed to do so is also an added factor the defendant must weigh in deciding whether to testify. The same is true with respect to the questions of whether the defendant may demand a no adverse inference instruction or whether one may be given over his objection. All these considerations are extrinsic to the likely effect the defendant's testimony might have on the jury, and therefore may be unconstitutional penalties on the exercise of the privilege against self-incrimination.

Footnote 6 of the Supreme Court's *Griffin* opinion specifically reserved decision on whether an accused had the right to demand a no adverse inference instruction, and no Supreme Court ruling has held that the jury may not generate such an inference on its own. In a 1978 decision, however, *Lakeside v. Oregon*,[16] the Supreme Court did confront a Fifth Amendment challenge to a no adverse inference instruction given over the defendant's objection, and held that the instruction given under such conditions was not unconstitutional. In so ruling, the Court rejected a literal reading of the *Griffin* requirement that there be no "comment on the refusal to testify,"[17] noting that the language referred to adverse comment. It concluded that the instruction did not amount to the same kind and degree of impermissible pressure such as had been barred in *Griffin*. More significant than the decision, however, was the fact that the Court made no reference to the *Griffin* penalty analysis. Instead, it focused on the question of whether the instruction generated impermissible compulsion pursuant to the Fifth Amendment. The manner of its application, moreover, demonstrated that the compulsion theory was likely to place fewer controls on Fifth Amendment penalties than the discarded *Griffin* penalty analysis.

The Court's decision in *Lakeside* did not suggest any departure from its 1972 ruling in *Brooks v. Tennessee*.[18] There the defendant had been faced with a Tennessee rule that required him to testify before any other defense witnesses if he chose to take the witness stand. Behind the rule lay the desire to prevent the defendant from tailoring his testimony to conform to that of his witnesses. Although the witnesses could be sequestered and thus prevented from altering their testimony, the defendant's right to be present at his own trial prevented the application of a sequestration requirement to him. But despite the state interest behind the rule, its operation served to encumber the defendant's decision whether or not to take the stand. The Court called it a "heavy burden"[19] because it forced the defendant to exercise or forgo his right to remain silent before a complete determination of the necessity of his testimony could be made. Following the *Griffin* penalty analysis, the Court held the procedure to violate the Fifth Amendment.

The invalidation of the Tennessee rule in *Brooks* on Fifth Amendment grounds stands in marked contrast to the Court's decision the previous term in *McGautha v. California*.[20] There the defendant in a capital case faced the possibility that the jury considering his guilt would also impose the death penalty as a sentence. Rather than employing a bifurcated trial procedure in which guilt and punishment are assessed in separate stages, the system under attack utilized a unitary trial for both purposes. As a result, the defendant's decision whether to take the stand was burdened by the knowledge that anything he said to mitigate possible punishment might be held against him on the issue of guilt. And as the dissent suggested in *Brooks*, the decision whether to take the stand might have been made more difficult by the unitary trial system than by the Tennessee rule requiring the defendant to testify first. Yet the *McGautha* Court upheld the unitary trial system against a Fifth Amendment challenge even in the context of a capital case.

The basis of the Supreme Court's decision in *McGautha* was a literal application of the Fifth Amendment's ban against compulsion to testify against oneself. Although the defendant had to risk self-incrimination on the issue of guilt in order to address his sentencer on the issue of punishment, the technical requirements of the privilege were not violated. One who testifies in such a system has no right to limit the impact of his testimony to the sentencing decision, while those who remain silent have obviously not incriminated themselves. What was most significant about the analysis, however, was that it did not rely on the penalty theory that had been employed in *Griffin* and would be used again in *Brooks*. And it is certainly possible that the penalty theory would have led to a different result, just as it is conceivable that the compulsion analysis would have reversed the outcome in both *Griffin* and *Brooks*. It appears that what the Court has done has been to define a narrow core of the privilege against self-incrimination within which the penalty analysis predominates and serves to protect against undue interferences with the defendant's already difficult decision whether or not to take the stand. This core has been deemed to encompass both awareness of all the testimony before a decision to testify need be made (*Brooks*) and freedom from attention being called to the fact that the defendant has chosen to remain silent (*Griffin*). As a result of *McGautha*, the core does not include the defendant's desire to limit the thrust of his testimony to the issue of punishment, and the Fifth Amendment analysis then becomes the more traditional and less protective compulsion standard. This is true despite the fact that the burden on the defendant's decision whether to testify in *McGautha* may well be greater than that created by the Tennessee rule invalidated in *Brooks* or the adverse comment rejected in *Griffin*.

It is difficult to assess why the Court chose to abandon the penalty theory in *McGautha*. Moreover, the decision offered no standard for determining the circumstances in which the theory would be held inapplicable, and the subsequent ruling in *Brooks* was silent on this question as well. In substance, however, there was more in all three cases uniting rather than distinguishing them. They shared the basic characteristic of focusing on the defendant's decision to testify at his own criminal trial, a concern that is central both to the privilege's history as well as policy, and deserved more protection than the compulsion standard allowed. It is the area in which the defendant should have the right "to remain silent unless he chooses to speak in the unfettered exercise of his own will, and to suffer no penalty . . . for such silence."[21] The core of the privilege should be sufficiently broad to encompass all such direct threats to the defendant's critical decision whether to take the stand. And the evaluation of their constitutionality should not have to rely on the weaker compulsion standard.

Incrimination

The special character of the criminal defendant's core Fifth Amendment privilege should not overshadow the vast array of other contexts in which right to silence issues arise. These other circumstances may not generate the same special protections offered to the defendant at trial, but in numerical terms they are undoubtedly a significant part of the scope of Fifth Amendment protection. Indeed, without a right to silence outside of the criminal trial, the defendant's privilege against self-incrimination at trial might be seriously undercut. Although he could not be compelled to testify at trial, nor would adverse comment on his exercise of the privilege at trial be permitted, there would still remain serious potential disadvantages stemming from the possible adverse use of pretrial silence and introduction of pretrial statements made under compulsion. Conceding the significance of the nontrial contexts in which the privilege applies does not necessarily mean, however, that the protections afforded by the Fifth Amendment must be the same as those of the criminal defendant at trial. If such were the case, the state could not obtain any information relating to criminal behavior except on a voluntary basis since suspects would refuse to respond to all questions asked of them, regardless of their content or setting. This, however, would show far too little respect for the state's legitimate need for information. An alternative approach, and the one reflected in the privilege against self-incrimination, is that outside of the postaccusation stage, the state has the authority to compel answers to nonincriminatory questions. As a result, attention must be paid to the kind of incrimination that implicates Fifth Amendment values and the manner in which the privilege must be asserted in response to such incriminatory questioning.

The language of the Fifth Amendment provides that no one may be compelled to be a witness against himself, but it is not clear what kind of barriers these words create to state efforts aimed at forcing the defendant to assist in his own conviction. Certainly included is compelled oral testimony, but perhaps also the exhibition of the defendant for identification purposes and the performance of such physical tests as fingerprinting and blood typing. Indeed, there are myriad ways in which the defendant may be used to secure his own conviction against his will. Reading the word "witness" as used in the Fifth Amendment in a literal manner, however, would effectively bar all such state tactics. It would also reflect a "broad and liberal construction"[22] of the privilege that other Fifth Amendment decisions have called for. The U.S. Supreme Court, however, has opted for an interpretation of the privilege far narrower than that permitted by the language of the Fifth Amendment. The occasion for its limiting construction was the 1966 ruling in *Schmerber v. California.*[23] There the defendant had sustained injuries in an automobile accident and was being treated at a hospital. Blood samples, obtained by a hospital physician without the defendant's consent, revealed an alcohol level indicating intoxication. Later this evidence was introduced at trial over the defendant's objection, and the Supreme Court subsequently affirmed the defendant's conviction.

The principle underlying the Court's decision was the view that the Fifth Amendment does not bar all state compulsion to obtain evidence from an accused. Rather, the Court took the position that "the privilege protects an accused only from being compelled to testify against himself, or otherwise provide the State with evidence of a testimonial or communicative nature,"[24] a standard not infringed by an involuntary blood test. Nor was this the first suggestion from the Court of such an approach to the Fifth Amendment. In a 1910 case the Court had been confronted with a challenge to a conviction obtained after the defendant had been forced to exhibit himself in a particular shirt. Justice Holmes rejected the claim that such conduct violated the privilege against self-incrimination. In his view "the prohibition of compelling a man in a criminal court to be a witness against himself is a prohibition of the use of physical or moral compulsion to extort communications from him, not an exclusion of his body as evidence when it may be material."[25]

Both a historical and a policy analysis help explain the Court's unwillingness to extend the protection of the privilege beyond testimonial communications. The historical development of the privilege clearly reflected opposition to compulsion to orally testify against oneself. The inquisitorial procedures of the Star Chamber and High Commission, particularly the utilization of the oath *ex officio*, were directed at the acquisition of testimony from the accused, and the resistance of men like John Lilburne sought to establish a right not to be questioned on matters that might be self-incriminatory. In contrast, the history of the privilege demonstrates no concern with compulsion directed at nontestimonial issues. Similarly, it can be argued, as Dean Wigmore maintained, that the policies underlying the privilege are not seriously implicated outside the sphere of testimonial communications. Compulsion as to nontestimonial matters does not intrude into an individual's privacy of thought, nor does it represent an undue allocation of power to the state according to this line of reasoning.[26]

Having established a standard of sorts, the Court in *Schmerber* proceeded to rule that compulsory blood testing did not violate the privilege against self-incrimination. And it noted with seeming approval lower federal and state court decisions holding that the privilege "offers no protection against compulsion to submit to fingerprinting, photographing, or measurements, to write or speak for identification, to appear in court, to stand, to assume a stance, to walk, or to make a particular gesture."[27] All shared the common trait that they did not purport to communicate information whose truthfulness was in question but rather constituted a physical identification of the suspect. But a majority of the Court did hold in *California v. Byers*[28] that an identifying act such as stopping and giving one's name and address after being involved in an auto accident might receive Fifth Amendment protection if that act had testimonially communicative aspects.

Nevertheless, a distinction could be drawn between the simple display of the suspect and the requirement that he perform some act for others to view. The latter obligates the suspect to affirmatively assist the state in securing his own conviction. It is what Justice Fortas characterized as "the kind of volitional act—the kind of forced cooperation by the accused—which is within the historical perimeter of the privilege against self-incrimination.''[29] In his view the privilege barred the state from such coercion since forced physical assistance differed only marginally from forced testimony. Both represented serious interferences with individual freedom to stand mute when charged with an offense and undercut the "nature of a free man and . . . his relationship to the state.''[30] Justice Fortas' view was expressed in the context of state coercion to force an accused in a lineup to utter the words spoken by the person who committed the crime, but the principle would have had wider application to other forms of forced cooperation. To the majority of the Supreme Court, however, coerced assistance for identification was no different from the mere display of the accused in assessing the applicability of the privilege. Neither were instances of testimonial communication covered by the Fifth Amendment.

That the state may compel the defendant to assist in securing his own conviction by providing nontestimonial evidence is not meant to imply the absence of controls on the coercive power of the government. Even if the privilege against self-incrimination is not violated, other constitutional provisions, particularly the due process clause of the Fourteenth Amendment, restrict the range of permissible state tactics. In *Rochin v. California*, where police used force to compel an individual to submit to a stomach pumping procedure, the Court held that the Constitution prohibits any state method which "shocks the conscience."[31] The standard is a concededly vague one, but nevertheless, it provides a clear indication that there are limits to the forms of coercion the state may employ. It is unlikely, however, to have any bearing on reasonable nonphysical forms of coercion. Thus a contempt sanction for failure to comply with a proper court-ordered identification procedure and an adverse comment on a suspect's lack of cooperation are undoubtedly constitutional forms of coercion. Some physical force, albeit a minimal amount, might also survive attack. However, it must be kept in mind that physical force has only limited utility. It may be effective in forcing a suspect to display a side view but is unlikely to be successful in coercing him to give a handwriting sample. For many of the affirmative act identification procedures, legal coercion may well be the only tool at the state's disposal.[32]

It takes more than the fact that the evidence sought is a testimonial communication to bring the Fifth Amendment into play. Additionally, that evidence must present a problem of potential self-incrimination. If not removed, such as by a grant of immunity, the risk of testimonial self-incrimination provides the individual with the right to plead the privilege against self-incrimination as a justification for his refusal to answer. But what degree and quality of incrimination is required by the Fifth Amendment before the privilege can be validly asserted? Clearly sufficient are disclosures that would in themselves reveal a completed crime. Similarly, admissions of the essential elements of an offense are within the coverage of the Fifth Amendment since they are an intimate part of the conviction process. Illustrative would be an admission of knowledge of the stolen character of goods in a prosecution for the knowing possession of stolen goods. What is less clear is the application of the privilege to facts that are only indirectly incriminatory; these may generate incriminatory inferences but are not in and of themselves the essential elements of an offense. Fifth Amendment problems are also raised by disclosures that would lead investigators to incriminatory information. There has been a long and somewhat inconsistent history in the application of self-incrimination protection to these latter two categories.

The treason proceedings against Aaron Burr, presided over by Chief Justice John Marshall, are an important chapter in the development of incrimination standards for the Fifth Amendment. There, the prosecutor sought to introduce a letter allegedly written by Burr's secretary, a Mr. Willie, in a cipher. Willie was called to the witness stand and asked if he understood the contents of the letter. In response he raised the privilege against self-incrimination, and the trial court was forced to rule on the validity of his plea. Chief Justice Marshall rejected what he considered to be the government's unduly broad claim that only admissions that would in themselves be sufficient to convict an individual of a crime were covered by the Fifth Amendment. In his view, this would make the privilege "perfectly worthless."[33] Instead, Marshall recognized the fact that "[m]any links frequently compose that chain of testimony which is necessary to convict any individual of a crime" and that if the answer sought would "disclose a fact which forms a necessary and essential link in the chain of testimony, which would be sufficient to convict him of any crime, he is not bound to answer it so as to furnish matter for that conviction."[34]

Marshall's "link-in-the-chain" theory has become an established part of Fifth Amendment doctrine. In rejecting the suggested limitation of the privilege to full-fledged criminal admissions, he recognized the obvious fact that self-incrimination can be the direct result of lesser disclosures. The potential incrimination faced by Willie was a case in point. Willie risked prosecution on a charge of misprision of treason since revelation that he understood the cipher would have demonstrated possible knowledge of treasonable matter, itself an element of the potential criminal charge. The facts of the decision, however, indicated that while protected incrimination might include the essential elements of a criminal offense, it need not necessarily extend further. Marshall referred to the special character of a "fact of this description" because "a witness, by disclosing a single fact, may complete the testimony against himself, and to every effectual purpose accuse himself as entirely as he would by stating every circumstance which would be required for his conviction."[35]

Inferential facts and investigatory leads stand on a much different footing than admissions of part or all of a criminal offense. Their incriminatory potential is a matter of risk rather than of certainty since the incriminatory inference might not be drawn and the investigatory lead could prove fruitless. To extend the coverage of the privilege against self-incrimination to such disclosures serves to protect not only that which will incriminate but also information that *may* incriminate. And as a matter of policy, it is not clear whether disclosures that have only a tendency to incriminate should be protected. The exclusion or inclusion decision must take into account not only the subject's desire to withhold information but also the state's legitimate need to obtain it. The privilege against self-incrimination is an exception to the normal obligation that "entitles the United States to the testimony of every citizen."[36] Dean Wigmore believed, as a result, that fixed boundaries for the privilege were essential and that the exception to every citizen's testimonial obligation must be narrowly circumscribed.[37] But it should also be kept in mind that exclusion of inferential facts and investigatory leads from Fifth Amendment coverage might well leave the privilege against self-incrimination devoid of any real significance. The state would have at its disposal a readily usable evasion technique; it could not obtain admissions that were in and of themselves incriminatory but would be able to question suspects for leads to enable it to acquire the same substantive proof in another manner.

Unless form is to triumph over substance, there is no choice but to apply the privilege to evidentiary as well as direct links in the chain of incrimination. And the Supreme Court indicated early on that it would take just such a broad view of the form of incrimination protected by the Fifth Amendment. In its 1892 *Counselman v. Hitchcock*[38] decision, the Court ruled that a narrow testimonial immunity statute that did not cover derivative use of the compelled testimony would not satisfy the Fifth Amendment. In discussing the flaws of the immunity statute under review, the Court noted that it "could not, and would not, prevent the use of his testimony to search out other testimony to be used in evidence against him," nor could it "prevent the obtaining and the use of witnesses and evidence which should be attributable directly to the testimony he might give under compulsion."[39] Though not part of the *Counselman* holding as such, the implication of the decision was clearly that the incriminatory potential of compelled testimony was to be liberally construed for purposes of extending Fifth Amendment coverage.

The *Counselman* approach has been followed in a number of subsequent court decisions. Judge Learned Hand observed in a 1942 case that by then it was "settled in federal courts that a witness cannot be compelled to disclose anything that will 'tend' to incriminate him, whether or not the answer would be an admission of one of the constitutive elements of the crime."[40] A 1951 Supreme Court decision stated that the "privilege afforded not only extends to answers that would in themselves support a conviction under a federal criminal statute but likewise embraces those which would furnish a link in the chain of evidence needed to prosecute the claimant for a federal crime."[41] Even English precedent as far back as 1861 accepted the privilege as broadly covering indirect incriminatory evidence.[42] Yet the principle brings with it some dangers. In particular, the administration of the link-in-the-chain theory leaves room for an imaginative mind to conjure up potential incrimination whose connection with the information being sought is tenuous and remote. While it is appropriate for the law to be concerned about a narrowly confined privilege that the state can easily evade, it must also be concerned with setting loose boundaries to the Fifth Amendment that individuals may abuse. The balance between the state's interest in the acquisition of information and the self-incrimination right to withhold it can be undone if the incrimination requirement is ignored. Without it we are left with what is essentially a right to deny information to the state upon an individual's mere desire, and that is both contrary to our tradition and a possibly serious impediment to the orderly functioning of government.

The problem was recognized in the frequently cited English case, *Regina v. Boyes*,[43] in which the Court of Queen's Bench was faced with an assertion of privilege in the context of a bribery prosecution. The defendant was alleged to have purchased votes in a parliamentary election and John Best, one of the voters allegedly bribed, was called to the witness stand and questioned as to whether he received money in return for his vote. Best declined to respond, asserting his privilege, but a crown pardon from prosecution was produced. Nevertheless, the witness continued to refuse to answer, claiming that the pardon was no protection from impeachment by the House of Commons. Eventually the witness testified to receiving the bribe and the defendant was convicted, but the Court reconsidered the propriety of compelling Best to answer the crown's inquiries. Concededly, the testimony sought was incriminatory, and the pardon provided no protection from its use for impeachment purposes. But, even assuming these facts and the applicability of the privilege to an impeachment by the House of Commons, the Court nevertheless ruled that there had been no violation of the right to remain silent. The opinion of Chief Justice Cockburn rejected the notion that a "bare possibility of legal peril"[44] was sufficient to invoke the protection of the privilege. In his view there must be "reasonable ground to apprehend danger," adding:

> [W]e are of the opinion that the danger to be apprehended must be real and appreciable, with reference to the ordinary operation of law in the ordinary course of things—not a danger of imaginary and unsubstantial character, having reference to some extraordinary and barely possible contingency, so improbable that no reasonable man would suffer it to influence his conduct. We think that a merely remote and naked possibility, out of the ordinary course of the law and such as no reasonable man would be affected by should not be suffered to obstruct the administration of justice.[45]

Lamenting the fact that the witness faced not the slightest risk of impeachment given the total inaction by the House of Commons in the numerous cases of bribery brought to its attention, the Court ruled that he was under a duty to answer and that the evidence was properly received.

The English requirement of a real and appreciable danger of incrimination was adopted by the U.S. Supreme Court in its 1896 *Brown v. Walker*[46] decision approving transactional immunity statutes. Since then it has been applied in a manner that has provoked severe criticism.[47] The reason for the standard, given the applicability of the privilege to evidence forming a link in the chain to self-incrimination, is to ensure that the right to remain silent is not abused by being claimed where there is no real danger of incrimination. Indeed, whether the information sought is directly incriminatory or may lead to incrimination, the goals of the privilege are not implicated if the criminal risk is nonexistent. The manner in which the real and appreciable danger standard is administered, therefore, does much to determine whether the privilege may be covertly extended into a right to silence outside the confines of situations posing a risk of criminal liability.

Two early twentieth-century decisions of the U.S. Supreme Court reflect a restrictive view of the incriminatory risk necessary to generate Fifth Amendment protection. The first was *Heike v. United States*[48] involving a prosecution for revenue fraud. Heike claimed that the transactional immunity he received as a result of prior testimony in an antitrust investigation of the sugar industry covered the revenue offenses he allegedly committed by fraudulently weighing sugar. Even though the same sugar was involved, the Court ruled that providing information about the sugar in the antitrust context did not sufficiently risk incrimination with respect to the fraud prosecution in order to be covered by the immunity grant. Four years later in *Mason v. United States*,[49] the Court reviewed contempt citations given to grand jury witnesses who were ordered to testify despite a claim of privilege. The grand jury had been investigating illegal gambling and inquired whether two witnesses saw card games under way at tables at which they were sitting or at nearby tables. The Court upheld the judge's ruling that there was no "reasonable cause to apprehend danger"[50] primarily because the specific revelation would not have disclosed an offense by the witness.

The contemporary law interpreting the incrimination danger requirement stands in marked contrast to the Supreme Court's earlier position. In *Blau v. United States*,[51] for example, a 1950 decision, a grand jury witness refused to answer questions concerning the Communist party of Colorado and her employment by it. Justice Black found the incrimination danger under the Smith Act was sufficiently real to allow her to refuse to disclose such information as the names of party officers, its table of organization, and the location of its records. The next year in *Hoffman v. United States*[52] the Court upheld another grand jury witness's claim of privilege in refusing to disclose the fact of recent contacts with a fugitive defendant. And more recently in *Malloy v. Hogan*,[53] a 1964 Supreme Court decision, the defendant had been called as a witness to testify about his knowledge concerning gambling activities for which he had already been tried and faced no further risk of incrimination. Yet the Court found a sufficient danger in that if forced to identify an illegal gambler he was previously connected with, "disclosure of his name might furnish a link in a chain of evidence sufficient to connect the petitioner with a more recent crime for which he might still be prosecuted."[54] The result was a virtual reversal of the position reflected in *Mason* and *Heike*.

There is no mistaking the fact that the law has become far more generous in accepting claims of incrimination danger under the Fifth Amendment. The trend is one that some commentators have decried, pointing to the consequence that the state is deprived of information it needs when the privilege is upheld. Yet the result may well be inevitable. The problems of proving incrimination or developing the indirect links to it may well be too burdensome for the courts to administer. It may also sacrifice much of the value of the privilege to require a suspect to establish the potential self-incrimination upon which his claim of privilege must rest. The simple solution, and perhaps the only feasible one, is to recognize that "obscure and unlikely lines of inquiry"[55] may prove incriminating and therefore liberality in reviewing claims of privilege is unavoidable.

These considerations may have also contributed to the Supreme Court's decision to end the separate sovereignty exception to the Fifth Amendment. This theory had permitted a state to compel testimony over a claim of privilege stemming from the fact that the testimony would be self-incriminatory in another jurisdiction. In *Murphy v. Waterfront Commission*,[56] the separate sovereignty rationale had been the basis of the lower court's rejection of a witness's claim of privilege in a state proceeding after a state grant of immunity. The Supreme Court, however, recognized the cooperative character of contemporary law enforcement and held that compelled testimony given in a state proceeding is also privileged in federal courts. So too it indicated that compelled testimony in a federal proceeding would be privileged from state use. On principle, the logic behind the separate sovereignty exception was not particularly convincing. It arbitrarily carved out an area excluded from Fifth Amendment protection despite the fact that Fifth Amendment values were implicated. With its demise, except perhaps where the incrimination risk arises under the laws of a foreign nation,[57] assertions of privilege can be analyzed in light of general requirements focusing on the sufficiency of the incriminatory danger.

The Procedural Environment

The criminal defendant's privilege against self-incrimination has evolved into a right not to take the witness stand at his own trial. For the witness, in

contrast, the privilege is a more limited right to refuse to answer incriminating questions. The constitutional violation, therefore, occurs not in
asking the question, but rather in compelling a response. This is the basis for
Dean Wigmore's observation that the privilege is an "option of refusal, not
a prohibition of inquiry."[58] And given that the questions may be asked, it
then becomes the responsibility of the witness to assert the privilege as the
basis of his refusal to respond. After all, the questioner cannot know in advance whether the answer will serve to incriminate the witness nor whether
assuming such incrimination, the witness will nevertheless choose to voluntarily respond. The fact that the assertion requirement is a well-settled
feature of Fifth Amendment doctrine, however, has not prevented other
problem areas from emerging. In particular, courts have had to confront
the issues of what constitutes a sufficient assertion of the privilege and
whether there are special circumstances where a witness must be warned of
his right to remain silent.

It appears established that if a witness specifically disclaims reliance on
the Fifth Amendment, he cannot later seek to convert a refusal to answer
into an assertion of the privilege. This problem occurred in *Hutcheson v.
United States*[59] where a witness before a congressional investigating committee relied upon a claim that the committee's questions were outside the
scope of its investigation rather than the Fifth Amendment as the basis for
refusing to answer. Although the committee indicated it would respect a
claim of privilege, the witness was concerned that such a claim could be
used to impeach him in a state trial if he chose to take the stand. The Court
held him bound by his Fifth Amendment waiver. In the Court's 1951
Rogers v. United States[60] decision, however, no such specific disclaimer of
reliance on the Fifth Amendment was made. Rogers had been summoned to
appear before a grand jury investigating the Communist party of Denver.
She admitted prior possession of the party's books and records but refused
to say to whom she gave them, stating: "I don't feel that I should subject a
person or persons to the same thing that I'm going through."[61] She refused
to answer the next day as well. The following day she appeared in court and
invoked her privilege against self-incrimination to justify her conduct but
was held in contempt of court for not answering. The Supreme Court's
position on the proceedings was that the witness had to claim the privilege in
order to secure its protection but that Rogers' assertion of the Fifth Amendment was "pure afterthought."[62] Although she did not disclaim the
privilege, she also failed to effectively assert it.

Witnesses under interrogation are in a very precarious position with
respect to the privilege against self-incrimination. They cannot exercise a
blanket assertion of the privilege but must instead claim the right not to
answer individual incriminating questions. This means that they must make
their decision under the pressures of questioning, which may lead them to
respond out of frustration. Also present is the risk that they may fail to real-

ize the incriminatory potential of the inquiry and therefore respond out of
ignorance. In light of these considerations, it is appropriate for the courts to
carefully guard the privilege and be solicitous of even halfhearted assertions. Two 1955 Supreme Court decisions are illustrative. In *Quinn v.
United States*[63] and *Emspak v. United States*,[64] witnesses in House Un-
American Activities Committee hearings on communist influence in unions
invoked their privilege by claiming "the first amendment to the Constitution, supplemented by the fifth amendment"[65] and "primarily the first
amendment, supplemented by the fifth."[66] The Supreme Court held the
language sufficient and ruled that the assertion can be made in any form
that a committee "may reasonably be expected to understand as an attempt
to invoke the privilege."[67]

The law must be generous in finding assertions of the Fifth Amendment
because of the fact that it has not required that witnesses in potentially self-
incriminatory situations be accorded the benefit of either warnings or the
advice of counsel.[68] *In re Groban*,[69] decided by the Supreme Court in 1957,
denied witnesses in a fire marshall's investigation the right to the advice of
counsel during testimony, and from this the implication was drawn that an
assertion of privilege was the sole responsibility of the witness. However,
the Court's 1966 ruling in *Miranda v. Arizona*[70] requiring warnings to
suspects in police custodial interrogations led to an erosion of the traditional doctrine, particularly in grand jury proceedings. Increasingly, appellate courts imposed warning and counsel requirements for at least prospective or putative defendants called before a grand jury.[71] At a minimum,
such a procedure ensured that neither error nor inadvertence would lead to a
waiver of the privilege. Indeed, where there was a risk of potential self-
incrimination, a warning and the right to the advice of counsel should probably have been made available regardless of the setting since the state had
no legitimate interest in securing information from individuals unaware of
or unable to assess their need to invoke the privilege against self-
incrimination. And the position was particularly persuasive before bodies
with the legal authority to compel answers.

Despite the force of the arguments calling for counsel and warnings to
witnesses faced with potential self-incrimination as a result of their
testimony, the Supreme Court has recently reaffirmed the traditional view
that both are unnecessary. In *United States v. Mandujano*,[72] a 1976 decision, the Court reviewed the perjury conviction of a defendant who had lied
under oath to a grand jury. Prior to being questioned, he was denied
counsel and received abbreviated Fifth Amendment warnings far short of
those required in police interrogations under the *Miranda* decision. The
Court held that a Fifth Amendment violation constituted no excuse for perjury but added in the course of its opinion that even a prospective defendant
had no right to counsel before a grand jury. The Court refused to rule that

any Fifth Amendment warning was required and in a subsequent case upheld the perjury conviction of a witness even on the assumption that as a result of language difficulties, she thought she was required to answer self-incriminatory questions.[73] *Miranda* warnings were confined to the realm of police custodial interrogations and approving reference was made to the absence of warnings for trial witnesses.[74] Presumably, the only inquiry left is whether the subject was compelled to incriminate himself. He need not waive his privilege as such and must be determined to have answered voluntarily; but the lack of a warning and counsel are only factors to consider in assessing the voluntariness of his response.

The Court has not yet taken the final step of holding that no Fifth Amendment warnings need be given to prospective defendants called before the grand jury, but the hints in that direction are strong. Such a step, however, would not be a wise one. Witnesses without counsel and without formal training in the law face the risk of self-incrimination through ignorance or error. A warning about the privilege might help to eliminate some of that risk. Interests of fairness in the balance of power between the state and the individual support such a procedure, as does the need to protect privacy and basic human dignity. If *Mandujano* and succeeding decisions are narrowly confined to the realm of perjury prosecutions, room is still left to otherwise require that at least some Fifth Amendment information be provided to witnesses facing potentially self-incriminatory questions.

Once the privilege against self-incrimination has been effectively asserted, and given the fact that only real and appreciable dangers of incrimination warrant a refusal to answer, it is necessary for some judgment to be made as to whether the circumstances warrant Fifth Amendment protection. The decision cannot be left entirely to the witness since this would eliminate any possibility of controlling improper assertions of the privilege. The judge is the most appropriate official to rule on the propriety of a self-incrimination claim, but he must be cautious that he does not force too much disclosure from the witness before making his ruling lest he undercut the values the privilege is designed to protect. The result is a tension between competing goals of policing the privilege and protecting it, and this tension has produced a set of principles aimed at accommodating the interests involved. The current balance is very clearly in favor of accepting claims of privilege as a result of the Supreme Court's decision in *Hoffman v. United States*.[75]

Hoffman was called before a grand jury investigating racketeering and questioned about his knowledge of another suspect. He claimed the privilege against self-incrimination in refusing to respond and was held in contempt. The court of appeals had agreed with the judge below that Hoffman had failed to support his claim of privilege. The Supreme Court, however, recognized that "if the witness, upon interposing his claim, were required to prove the hazard in the sense in which a claim is usually required to be established in court, he would be compelled to surrender the very protection which the privilege is designed to guarantee."[76] And being sensitive to the consequences of forcing the witness to prove his own self-incrimination, the Court ruled that "[t]o sustain the privilege, it need only be evident from the implications of the question, in the setting in which it is asked, that a responsive answer to the question or an explanation of why it cannot be answered might be dangerous because injurious disclosure could result."[77] Encompassed within the standard was an urging to trial judges to broadly consider the position of the witness and the character of the question in assessing the likelihood of self-incrimination. In the context of *Hoffman* itself, this meant taking into account the nature of the racketeering investigation, the implications of connecting Hoffman to a fugitive witness believed to be involved in criminal activity, Hoffman's own extensive criminal record including his public label as an underworld figure by a Senate committee, and press clippings pointing to Hoffman's imminent testimony. The Court in its analysis clearly signaled that the record in a self-incrimination ruling could be constructed from anything that would help to shed light on the issue. The result might not have been traditional, but it was necessary to ensure that the privilege was not violated in the process of determining the validity of its assertion.

In ruling on a claim of privilege, the Supreme Court further instructed that the claim must be respected unless it is " 'perfectly clear, from a careful consideration of all the circumstances in the case, that the witness is mistaken, and that the answer[s] cannot possibly have such a tendency' to incriminate."[78] The Court's language was a direct quote from an 1881 Virginia decision, Temple v. Commonwealth.[79] In that case a witness had been ordered to give self-incriminatory testimony in a lottery prosecution after the attorney for the state indicated that no prosecution against the witness was pending or intended. Recognizing the inadequacy of the protection provided by this assurance, the Court rightly ruled that the privilege was properly asserted. In effect then the result allocated the burden of proof to the state to establish the absence of an incriminatory risk where some danger of incrimination was apparent from the surrounding circumstances. Where it was not, the witness would have to establish the danger through his own efforts. Thus the standard for rejecting a claim of privilege, much like the injunction to broadly consider the factors surrounding its assertion, is highly protective of the right to remain silent. Both principles appropriately prevent a witness from being faced with an added risk of self-incrimination at the point he seeks to assert his Fifth Amendment rights.

In contrast to existing rules that accord leeway in identifying and protecting assertions of the Fifth Amendment, the Supreme Court has readily applied the doctrine of waiver and analagous principles to deal with situations in which there has not been a valid claim of privilege. The concern that the Court has sought to reflect has been the need to ensure that distorted evidence is not presented to the trier of fact as a result of allowing the witness to choose, as a matter of convenience, at what point he will assert his privilege against self-incrimination. Instead, failure to assert the Fifth Amendment promptly has been converted into a triggering mechanism that permits the court to demand further information, even over the witness's objection.

The leading constitutional decision from the Supreme Court in this area is its 1951 ruling in *Rogers v. United States.*[80] After being subpoenaed to appear before a grand jury, Rogers answered a series of questions about herself but declined to implicate others and only subsequently indicated that her refusal to respond was based upon the privilege against self-incrimination. As previously noted, the Court rejected her untimely assertion of the Fifth Amendment but went on to maintain that even a timely claim would not have sufficed. In the Court's view, having disclosed her membership, activities, and role in the Communist party of Denver, Rogers was not free to refuse to respond to more particularized inquiries on these matters. Succinctly stated, the Court ruled that "where incriminating facts have been voluntarily revealed, the privilege cannot be invoked to avoid disclosure of the details."[81] Yet strictly speaking, the result was not due to any notion that Fifth Amendment rights had been waived by Rogers' limited testimony. Rather, the Court felt that the responses sought from the witness created no real danger of further incrimination given the revelations already made and that, to the contrary, the risk was no more than a "mere imaginary possibility."[82]

The Supreme Court's approach to the Fifth Amendment implications of a decision to testify recognizes that a response to some questions does not eliminate all Fifth Amendment issues. One area where this is quite plain is the situation in which testimony is given by an accused despite the fact that in previous proceedings, he did not take the stand. At first, the Supreme Court had allowed a prosecutor in a retrial to cross-examine a defendant on his failure to take the stand at his first trial to refute an accusation that he had made incriminating out-of-court admissions to an agent. Very broad waiver language was used by the Court in reaching this result, stating that a Fifth Amendment waiver "is not partial; having once cast aside the cloak of immunity, [the defendant] may not resume it at will."[83] More recent decisions have substantially retreated from this position by holding that prior silence and current testimony are not necessarily inconsistent, thereby barring impeachment of the witness by pointing to his previous assertion of the privilege.[84] A decision by an accused to testify does not, consequently, result in a retroactive waiver with respect to a prior claim of the Fifth Amendment. Moreover, the reverse is also true in that a waiver of the Fifth Amendment by contract does not bar later retraction of the waiver.[85] The waiver problems are thus confined to the question of the permissible extent of further examination after some self-incriminatory information has been revealed.

The simplest waiver question to resolve, of course, is the issue of the defendant's Fifth Amendment right not to take the stand. Obviously, his decision to testify constitutes a waiver of that right. But it is far less clear whether the defendant's decision to testify is also a waiver of his Fifth Amendment right not to respond to specific self-incriminatory questions. Dean Wigmore's position was that the defendant's decision to take the stand amounted to a waiver of the privilege with respect to all facts relevant to the offense being tried.[86] There is even a Supreme Court decision holding that a defendant who had testified at his own trial could be questioned about offenses other than those with which he was charged if they were deemed relevant. The only self-incriminatory questioning excluded under this theory was where the answers sought were solely directed toward impeaching the defendant's credibility.[87] Apparently, where the questioning was aimed at impeachment rather than eliciting substantive evidence of guilt, the defendant's Fifth Amendment interests outweighed the state's need for the answers. Despite this concession to the defendant's privilege against self-incrimination, however, the Court's application of the waiver theory to a defendant's Fifth Amendment rights was unnecessarily harsh. There was no need to totally withdraw the protection of the privilege from a defendant who took the stand. To the contrary, all that was necessary was to prevent the jury from being left with slanted testimony as a result of the defendant's sudden invocation of the Fifth Amendment after giving his side of the story. The normal rules of evidence in cross-examination were adequate to meet this need without holding the defendant to a wholesale waiver of his Fifth Amendment rights.

Since a witness, as opposed to a defendant, has no right to refuse to take the stand, the problem of his waiver of the privilege takes on a somewhat different cast. The fact of testifying itself obviously cannot be a waiver since the witness has no right to refuse. Waiver only arises when the witness voluntarily answers an incriminatory question and only as to the incriminatory information voluntarily provided.[88] Any further questions on matters of detail stemming from a witness's voluntary disclosures must, under the *Rogers* decision, be analyzed to determine if there is a sufficient incrimination risk—a real and appreciable danger—to warrant the invocation of the privilege as to such detail. In a sense, the witness does effect a waiver of the privilege by testifying on a self-incriminatory matter, but the compelled response to further questions, the area where controversy arises, is not as much a waiver issue as it is a question of evaluating the likely answer in terms of its incriminatory potential.

Conflict at the Core: Pretrial Discovery

The fundamental requirements for the successful assertion of the privilege against self-incrimination accurately reflect the internal inconsistencies of Fifth Amendment jurisprudence. In several areas the law has evolved a rigorous standard to ensure that the privilege would be held within acceptable boundaries. The testimonial incrimination requirement and the standards for Fifth Amendment waiver are illustrative of this trend. Yet at the same time other aspects of the privilege have been liberally construed, thereby making it difficult to confine the privilege within narrow borders. This is true of the construction given to the "link-in-the-chain" and "real and appreciable danger" components of the Fifth Amendment. Each new Fifth Amendment issue relating to the core right to remain silent at an official proceeding must find its own place amid the conflicting judicial attitudes. The question of the relationship of pretrial discovery to the Fifth Amendment has had to confront this dilemma.

By way of background, pretrial discovery of the opposition's case has had a much slower development in criminal law than in civil procedure. The arguments in favor of broad pretrial discovery are the same in both spheres. In each, surprise can be minimized and the orderly conduct of trial proceedings improved if advance disclosure of at least some evidence is provided. Criminal discovery has been only reluctantly accepted, however, because many felt that the Fifth Amendment prevented it from being a two-way street. Defendants could obtain the advantages of pretrial discovery from the prosecution but were believed protected from compulsory disclosure by the privilege against self-incrimination. And since the issue of the defense's disclosure of its evidence relates closely to the core feature of the privilege, the right to remain silent at official proceedings, such a result was not an unlikely outcome.

The controversy came before the U.S. Supreme Court in a 1970 case, *Williams v. Florida*.[89] The state of Florida had enacted a notice-of-alibi rule that required the defendant, upon written demand of the prosecuting attorney, to file a notice of intent to rely on the alibi defense, furnish the names and addresses of alibi witnesses to be called by the defendant, and disclose where he allegedly was at the time of the offense. Williams voluntarily declared his intent to rely on an alibi defense but objected to any further pretrial disclosure. His objection was overruled, however, the trial court finding no interference with his Fifth Amendment privilege against self-incrimination. The Supreme Court's review of the alibi-notice rule emphasized the same Fifth Amendment issue and in the balance hung the likely direction of the movement toward nationwide reform of criminal discovery. The argument against the alibi-notice requirement was a straightforward application of the Fifth Amendment. The relevant language of the privilege bars the state from compelling an individual to be a witness against himself.

The alibi-notice rule infringed that right "because it require[d] a defendant to disclose information to the State so that the State [could] use that information to destroy him."[90] And if the notice was not provided, the defendant could conceivably have been barred from raising the defense or subjected to adverse comment and a negative inference.

In the Supreme Court's view, however, the Florida notice-of-alibi rule did not violate the Fifth Amendment. In *Williams* the rule had succeeded in forcing the defendant to reveal the name of his alibi witness whom the prosecution then interviewed. Most directly, this assisted the state in impeaching the witness's trial testimony with the results of his pretrial deposition and alerted it to the kind and amount of rebuttal evidence it would have to produce. However, the defendant was not precluded as a result of the notice from either abandoning the defense entirely or choosing not to call a particular alibi witness. The defendant merely, in the Court's words, "accelerate[d] the timing of his disclosure"[91] by complying with the notice requirement. Since the Court could grant a continuance to the prosecutor to allow him to rebut an alibi defense put on at trial, there was no difference to the Court in permitting this to be done before trial. In short, the Court saw the Fifth Amendment as a device for permitting the defendant to refuse any disclosure at all, but not as a protection against the early disclosure required by the rule.

There is an immediate attractiveness to the Court's rationale. The right to total silence does seem to be a more significant interest than the right to pick and choose when disclosures will be made, and it therefore might be appropriate to limit Fifth Amendment coverage to only the former. What is not clear, however, is whether the issue is truly only a matter of timing. If pretrial disclosure produces additional risks of self-incrimination that are real and appreciable, then there is a substantial difference between pretrial and at-trial disclosure. When the defendant presents his evidence at trial, the prosecution's only course of action is to rebut it. If this task is undertaken before trial, however, it may lead to additional evidence that the prosecution might use to prove the primary issue of guilt. Illustrative would be an alibi witness revealing a characteristic of the defendant, which when conveyed to the victim, assists him in making an identification. The case for the application of the Fifth Amendment to such a circumstance is overwhelming. The use of compelled revelations from a defendant to prove guilt as opposed to rebutting a so-called affirmative defense is the essence of compelled self-incrimination.

These considerations have prompted at least two state court cases to vary from the *Williams* decision based upon state constitutional self-incrimination clauses. The first of these was the Alaska Supreme Court's 1974 ruling in *Scott v. State*.[92] There, self-incrimination objections were raised to broad prosecution discovery orders, including an alibi notice provision similar to the one at issue in *Williams*. But the Alaska Supreme Court would permit discovery only of the alibi notice itself and barred disclosure of the alibi details and names of witnesses. It found the latter to comprise compulsion to produce testimonial communications of a potentially self-incriminatory character, and therefore in violation of the Alaska privilege. The California Supreme Court ruled to the same effect in a 1976 decision, and reaffirmed its commitment to bar compulsory production of any evidence that "conceivably might lighten the prosecution's burden of proving its case in chief."[93] Neither ruling, however, was based upon an assumption that the compelled disclosures would have been self-incriminatory in the particular cases before the courts. Rather, they suggested reliance upon the likelihood that there was a risk of self-incrimination in enough instances to prohibit such disclosure in all cases. This clearly would also prevent pretrial prosecution discovery in cases in which the witness lists and alibi details would not be self-incriminatory. However, totally barring these pretrial notices in *all* cases in an appropriate protective mechanism. It must be kept in mind that the issue is closely related to the very core feature of the Fifth Amendment, the defendant's privilege against self-incrimination at trial. As we have seen, the defendant's privilege includes the right not to take the witness stand at all at his own trial, even to answer nonincriminatory inquiries. The question of pretrial discovery requires the same extra protection because of its similar proximity to the Fifth Amendment's core. Witness lists and defense details are of a special character, encompassing sufficient risks of incrimination generally, that, as in California and Alaska, they should not be subject to compulsory discovery from any defendant.

Although the Supreme Court's decision in *Williams* upheld the principle of pretrial discovery over Fifth Amendment objection, some room may remain for at least individualized assertions of privilege. The facts of *Williams*, as the Court stressed, involved prosecution use of the notice provided by the defense only for rebuttal purposes. The state did not bolster its case in chief with the fruits of the alibi-notice rule, nor did the defendant claim a personal risk of self-incrimination. If such a claim were made, however, the *Williams* decision would not bar the denial of discovery. And maybe all *Williams* really meant was that this aspect of the defendant's right to remain silent will have to be asserted and judged by the normal Fifth Amendment standards. It is difficult to conceive of *Williams* being read to permit discovery in the face of an otherwise valid individual claim of privilege, an issue the *Williams* Court did not have to address. The role of the privilege against self-incrimination in pretrial discovery therefore has not been finally resolved but rather now must be dealt with on a case-by-case basis.

5 Confessions: The Road to *Miranda*

Some of the most intense, as well as the most bitter, debate surrounding the Fifth Amendment has focused upon the role of the self-incrimination clause in controlling nonjudicial interrogations. Of particular concern has been the process of police questioning, but the controversy extends to all forms of interrogation in which the individual from whom responses are sought is under no legal obligation to provide them. Customs inquiries and preliminary tax interviews are in this sense similar to police interrogations for Fifth Amendment purposes and have also generated special problems in the application of the right to remain silent. Judge Henry Friendly has labeled the issue the "liveliest" of the Fifth Amendment problem areas, and the characterization is an apt one.[1]

The intensity of the debate on the appropriate legal standard for out-of-court confessions is understandable. Despite the importance of courtroom proceedings in the criminal justice system, what happens before trial is undoubtedly also of critical significance. Estimates are that somewhere on the order of 90 percent of all cases slated for trial are disposed of through the plea-bargaining process. The strength of the prosecutor's case is a major factor in inducing a defendant to plead guilty, and a signed confession admissible in court is in and of itself enough to ensure that the prosecutor can bargain from a position of strength. From the law enforcement perspective, therefore, there is an interest in maintaining a standard that will not unduly burden the state's ability to obtain confessions. And although confessions may not be indispensable in all cases, they are nevertheless often of major significance to the success of a prosecution. However, the fact that the power of the state may be brought to bear upon an accused to extract information from him, albeit without the threat of a contempt sanction, makes the confrontation one in which the policies behind the privilege are directly involved. There is a danger that state power may be abused to obtain a suspect's confession. If the state uses coercive interrogation methods, serious questions are raised as to whether an appropriate balance between state and individual rights has been maintained and individual privacy sufficiently protected. Civil libertarians have therefore consistently sought broad constitutional protection for individuals subjected to interrogation.

Acceptance of the need for control of the questioning process, as well as the applicability of the Constitution to the methods used in obtaining confessions, does not necessarily lead to the conclusion that all interrogations are subject to the standards of the Fifth Amendment privilege against self-incrimination. To the contrary, there are strong arguments supporting the inapplicability of the privilege to police and other forms of nonjudicial questioning. Historically, the privilege against self-incrimination arose from a background of opposition to official interrogations and administration of the oath *ex officio*, a context characterized by legal compulsion to respond upon threat of contempt. The establishment of a right to remain silent in such proceedings did not halt the process of preliminary examination before trial in which confessions were often obtained from suspects. Here there was no legal compulsion to respond, but suspects could be pressured into incriminating themselves. The historical sources of the modern privilege, moreover, did not reach this form of questioning. Therefore, if history is to be a guide, the privilege today should be inapplicable to the police interrogation, the modern counterpart of the common law preliminary examination. However, this would not leave the police and others unsupervised in the questioning of suspects. The common law developed a voluntariness standard to govern the admissibility of out-of-court confessions, and it could still serve to control this area if the privilege were deemed inapplicable.

Putting history aside, however, there is seemingly much similarity in the logic behind both the privilege against self-incrimination and the voluntariness rule as they relate to the admissibility of pretrial statements. In particular, the modern confession standard in which even reliable statements may be excluded if deemed involuntary suggests that the statement from the suspect must be the product of his free choice. The Fifth Amendment requirement that self-incriminatory statements not be compelled similarly appears directed toward the admissibility of only freely given statements. It might therefore be argued that nothing of any significance hinges on the source chosen to control the interrogation process other than analytical consistency. In response, however, analytical consistency is not without value; the law is obligated to be doctrinally honest in its resolution of disputes and should not permit separable areas of the law to merge without reason. But, more importantly, it is questionable whether the rules governing involuntary confessions are indeed the same as those applicable to the privilege against self-incrimination despite overlapping policy justifications. The fact that each has a different legal source with its own technical requirements may cause the resulting standards to vary. If so, the issue of whether the privilege is applicable to confessions may well determine whether or not a particular confession will be admitted into evidence by a judge. Not surprisingly, therefore, the evolution of confession law has reflected, to a significant extent, controversies over both the content of admissibility standards and the applicability of the privilege against self-incrimination.

Roots of Confession Law

Although the common law possesses a rich history in the development of the right to be free from inquisitorial court procedures, its concern for criminal justice techniques employed prior to trial was both late in developing and not very deeply felt. Intense activity over several centuries marked the resistance to the oath *ex officio*, succeeding ultimately in eliminating the oath and the courts that heavily depended upon it. During the same period, however, pretrial interrogation proceeded at the hands of justices of the peace with little control. Torture was often utilized to obtain self-incriminatory information. Even interrogations conducted without the use or threatened use of torture hardly lived up to the model of criminal justice pursued by the opponents of the oath procedure. They envisioned a fully respected right to remain silent, but what prevailed was a system of coercive and bullying questioning. Moreover, such tactics persisted despite the gradual decline of torture methods, and the courts willingly accepted the statements they succeeded in extracting. As a result, despite the right to silence at trial, which long years of struggle had sought to secure, the fruits of pretrial interrogation were received in evidence. And if the interrogation was coercive, it meant that the privilege of silence was effectively undercut. All that can be conceded to the pretrial questioning process was that it did not employ legal compulsion and thus directly circumvent the privilege but, in countenancing every other method used to obtain pretrial confessions, it was at odds with the policies behind the right to remain silent.[2]

Torture is an obviously efficient method of securing incriminating admissions, but it is equally clear that it cannot be relied upon to produce truthful statements. Under the threat or application of physical force, the suspect is likely to admit to anything. It thus may have been the recognition of the serious reliability problem generated by torture that gradually led to its abolition. The principle of reliability, however, has far more significance than its narrow role in controlling physical force in the interrogation process. Reliability is brought into question whenever an involuntary confession is obtained. Physical force is only one of a wide variety of tactics that can be employed to make the unwilling talk. And any time a statement is obtained from someone who does not want to make it, whether as a result of physical force or other pressures, its truthfulness may be in doubt. The process was a gradual one, but over time the reliability rationale helped to generate the common law rule that confessions must be voluntary to be admissible in court.[3]

Given the relationship between the voluntariness rule and the reliability requirement, it was necessary for the law to identify techniques that would produce unreliable statements. Obviously torture was one such technique, but beyond that there was less certainty as to the connection between particular methods and the production of false statements. Nevertheless, a common law standard emerged over time. One of its earliest formulations came in a passage from Lord Mansfield in which he stated:

> [T]he instance has frequently happened, of persons having made confessions under threats or promises: the consequence as frequently has been, that such examinations and confessions have not been made use of against them on their trial.[4]

Although Lord Mansfield's dictum that confessions resulting from threats or promises were not admissible was not central to the case before him, a ruling from the King's Bench soon thereafter restated the same principle in support of a lower court decision excluding an involuntary confession. In a frequently cited passage, the court held:

> [A] confession forced from the mind by the flattery of hope, or by the torture of fear, comes in so questionable a shape when it is to be considered as evidence of guilt, that no credit ought to be given to it; and therefore it is rejected.[5]

No particular justification was offered by the common law for this standard other than what appears to be an assumption that threats and promises produced unreliable statements. Yet this hardly explains why a simple admonition to answer truthfully would invalidate a confession, but an exception allowed for *spiritual* admonitions to tell the truth. Moreover, the common law appeared to permit confessions to be used where they were the result of official deception.[6] Reliability was the accepted rationale for the early involuntary confession rule, but it is not at all clear that the prohibited techniques were all equally likely to result in unreliable statements.

The earliest U.S. Supreme Court treatment of the confession issue accepted both the content and source of the principle that voluntariness was a prerequisite to the admissibility of an out-of-court statement by the accused. Justice Harlan, speaking for the Court in *Hopt v. Utah*, an 1884 ruling, quoted from English precedent and maintained that admission standards were met if the confession was "freely and voluntarily made,"[7] meaning with no "inducements of a temporal nature" or "threat or promise."[8] In substance the standard was identical to the common law approach. In addition, Justice Harlan emphasized the connection between the voluntariness rule and the policy goal of assuring reliability much as had the earlier English judges. In his words, the voluntariness requirement met the objective of reliability because "one who is innocent will not imperil his safety or prejudice his interests by an untrue statement."[9] The clear negative implication was that an involuntary statement might result in a false admission, thus justifying its rejection. Exclusion of involuntary confessions on both sides of the Atlantic was thus accomplished as a matter of evidence law governed by the principle of reliability. In its American context, this had the further significance of committing the administration of the involuntary confession standard to the states since they controlled rules of evidence in their own courts.

The next logical step in confession law development would have been to continue the refinement of the voluntariness requirement in federal prosecutions as a matter of federal law. Although the Supreme Court ultimately took that step, the development was temporarily sidetracked by a ruling applying the Fifth Amendment privilege against self-incrimination to federal confessions. The 1897 decision, *Bram v. United States*,[10] was literally without precedent and, as it turned out, without much of a future for nearly seventy years after it was handed down. In one sense it was a prophetic ruling in that it presaged the use of the Fifth Amendment as a tool to control interrogations. On the other hand, it was also a decision of its day in terms of the substantive standard the Court used to control confession admissibility.

The case itself involved a murder on the high seas and the confinement of the first officer, Bram, by the ship's crew on suspicion of being the responsible party. Although initially headed for South America, the ship changed course and landed in Nova Scotia where Bram was questioned by a detective. At trial the detective testified over objection to the absence of threats and inducements and then related the substance of the defendant's statements. Rather than treating the controversy as an evidentiary problem, however, the Court stated:

> In criminal trials, in the courts of the United States, wherever a question arises whether a confession is incompetent because not voluntary, the issue is controlled by that portion of the Fifth Amendment to the Constitution of the United States, commanding that no person "shall be compelled in any criminal case to be a witness against himself."[11]

In the Court's view, "the reasons which gave rise to the adoption of the Fifth Amendment" clearly demonstrated that it was "but a crystallization of the doctrine as to confessions."[12] The common law principle of freedom from compulsory self-incrimination was, simply stated, "in its essence comprehensive enough to exclude all manifestations of compulsion,"[13] and this was what the Fifth Amendment was also intended to encompass. Although later cases rejected the approach, the *Bram* Court had, without dissent, given a new dimension to the privilege against self-incrimination.

The Fifth Amendment standard the Court established in *Bram* was, however, essentially the same as the voluntariness test of *Hopt* and prior English decisions. Reliance was placed on Russell's *Treatise on Crimes and Misdemeanors*, which stated that confessions "must not be extracted by any sort of threats or violence, nor obtained by any direct or implied promises, however slight, nor by the exertion of any improper influence.''[14] The standard was to be assessed on a case-by-case basis, each set of facts to be analyzed to determine the voluntariness of the statement in issue. Having settled this much, the Court proceeded to find the statement involuntary in *Bram* itself due to an impermissible threat and promise. The circumstances of the interrogation, the Court believed, convinced Bram that silence would have constituted an admission of guilt, thus threatening him if he failed to respond. And in seeking to urge Bram to identify his accomplices, the Court found that the detective implicitly promised him a benefit if he did so. Although three justices thought the replies voluntary, it is worth restating that they voiced no objection to the Court's Fifth Amendment theory. Rather, they sought to resist the Court's rather liberal construction of the threats and promises that would render confessions involuntary. Yet the decision was not out of line with other rulings of the era in its effort to define the content of the standard.

Voluntariness and State Confessions

Although the Supreme Court in *Bram* sought to subsume confession law under the protective shield of the Fifth Amendment, it immediately put that theory aside and relegated interrogation issues once again to the realm of federal evidence law. In so doing, however, the Court nevertheless continued to use the voluntariness test as its substantive standard in confronting objections to the admission of confessions at trial. But none of the Court's early decisions gave any clue as to how it might react to challenges to state criminal convictions based upon the use of allegedly involuntary confessions. Neither federal evidence law nor Fifth Amendment principles would control since neither at that time governed state criminal procedure. Indeed, even today federal evidentiary rules are not binding upon the states, and it was not until the Court's 1964 ruling in *Malloy v. Hogan*[15] that the Fifth Amendment privilege against self-incrimination was incorporated and made applicable to state action. Prior to that date, Supreme Court authority to review state confession rules required some basis in a constitutional provision governing state procedure. For all practical purposes, this meant federal supervision pursuant to the due process clause of the Fourteenth Amendment. And although there could be controversy as to what was meant by due process of law, there was no doubt that states were obligated to follow its mandate.

The question of how the Supreme Court would handle state confession rulings was an issue of major importance because of the significant role played by state criminal procedure systems in the late nineteenth and early twentieth centuries. State criminal law enforcement has always constituted the major component of the American criminal justice system, but its role was far more significant then than it is now. The federal criminal law enforcement apparatus has grown mostly in recent years. For confession standards to have had a meaningful impact, therefore, meant that controls had to be exercised over state and local police practices. Without any Supreme Court involvement, as was the case before the 1930s, the states were left to supervise their own systems of justice and, given close to fifty separate sovereignties, inconsistency and at least some laxity was inevitable.

The need for some federal floor on state confession standards was not only the result of the major role the states played in law enforcement. Added impetus came from revelations in the early twentieth century of police abuse of criminal suspects to obtain damaging admissions from them, the most dramatic of which were disclosures of the use of third-degree tactics. Edwin Keedy reported on the problem as early as 1912 in connection with Chicago police practices,[16] but public attention did not significantly focus upon it until the 1930s. In 1930 a New York City police reporter published an account of specific instances of police use of third degree tactics.[17] Works by Ernest Hopkins and Edwin Borchard provided further evidence of the prevalence of the problem,[18] but the major contribution was provided by the National Commission on Law Observance and Enforcement's 1931 *Report on Lawlessness in Law Enforcement*. Based upon extensive surveys of police practices around the country, it concluded:

> The third degree—that is, the use of physical brutality, or other forms of cruelty, to obtain involuntary confessions or admissions—is widespread. Protracted questioning of prisoners is commonly employed. Threats and methods of intimidation, adjusted to the age or mentality of the victim, are frequently used, either by themselves or in combination with some of the other practices mentioned. Physical brutality, illegal detention, and refusal to allow access of counsel to the prisoner in common.[19]

While there were undoubtedly those who either denied the existence of or supported the use of third-degree tactics, the law could not formally sanction the practice without departing from basic American principles. Indeed, even in England the use of torture tended to exist more as a disfavored practice than as official state policy. In terms of legal doctrine, the American states were not out of line with this aspect of the common law voluntariness principle. Both federal standards and parallel state rules required the exclusion of involuntary confessions and thus the problem was theoretically well in hand. Yet the revelations of the 1930s demonstrated that such was not the case. Police abuse was apparently widespread, and state courts were not effectively discouraging the practice, nor were there readily available incentives to spur a change in this situation. Instead, it be-

came increasingly clear that supervision of state confession enforcement
was needed which, in practice, meant Supreme Court review. The difficulty
presented, however, was that existing federal confession decisions provided
no authority for the review of state court convictions. Neither federal
evidence law nor Fifth Amendment decisions were at that time deemed controlling with respect to state criminal procedure. This was the background
facing the Supreme Court in 1936 when it reviewed the admissibility of a
state confession in *Brown v. Mississippi.*[20]

The factual context of the case was as dramatic as could be imagined. A
white farmer had been found murdered in his home in rural Mississippi.
Within a few hours the deputy sheriff and several other white men had
seized a black suspect and brought him to the murder scene where he was
confronted by a group of vigilantes. He protested his innocence in the face
of accusations and then, as described by the Supreme Court, the vigilantes
"hanged him by a rope to the limb of a tree, and having let him down, they
hung him again."[21] The suspect continued to maintain his innocence, as a
result of which he was whipped. Two days later, after another beating, he
confessed. Two other suspects faced similar treatment and also confessed.
In what was unusual for these kinds of cases, there was no dispute as to
whether the suspects had been abused. The deputy freely admitted administering the beatings, adding as to how much they had been whipped:
"Not too much for a negro; not as much as I would have done if it were left
to me."[22] The case presented a picture of police methods that was truly
sobering, and one can only wonder how the suspects managed to hold out as
long as they did before confessing.

Under the circumstances, a decision from the Mississippi Supreme
Court upholding the admissibility of the confessions as voluntary would
have been startling. Rather than taking such an approach, however, it ruled
that the defendants' counsel had failed to move for exclusion of the confessions in a timely and appropriate manner. The Supreme Court, however, rejected the procedural technicalities employed by the Mississippi Supreme
Court and vigorously condemned the deputy's tactics as a violation of the
Fourteenth Amendment's due process of law requirement. The significance
of the Court's reliance upon the due process clause was, of course, that it
provided the constitutional authority for setting a standard against which
state confession rules could be measured. To the Court, moreover, the requirements of due process meant providing criminal defendants with the
essence of a fair trial. Based upon precedent, the concept had come to mean
prohibitions against depriving the accused of the aid of counsel, forcing him
to submit to a mob-dominated trial, and presenting testimony known to be
perjured.[23] *Brown* added to this list convictions "resting solely upon confessions obtained by violence."[24] Finally, given the nature of the due process
violation, "the whole proceeding [was] a mere pretense of a trial and ren-

dered the conviction and sentence wholly void,'' and could be challenged ''in any appropriate manner.''[25]

In *Brown* the Supreme Court did not attempt to further define the concept of a ''fair trial'' as it related to the admissibility of confessions, and as a result a number of questions were left unresolved. For example, the Court carefully noted that the conviction of Brown rested solely upon coerced confessions. What then of convictions based only partly on an inadmissible confession, in which either the confession was necessary to support a guilty verdict or the jury could have convicted the defendant even without it? Both cases involve confessions contributing in varying degrees to a conviction without being its *only* basis. But the most important question left unresolved by the Court was the issue of exactly what confession standards were required by the due process clause. Was a fair trial one with merely a reliable verdict, or did it encompass requirements unrelated to verdict reliability? Resolution of this issue in turn would determine whether confessions extracted only by the third degree were to be excluded or whether techniques that did not necessarily affect the confession's reliability were also to be banned.

Ultimately, the Supreme Court moved to a ''rule of automatic reversal''[26] in coerced confession cases. By its terms, the use of an inadmissible confession at trial necessitated reversal of the conviction without inquiry as to the extent to which the confession contributed to the conviction. Logically, no other alternative was acceptable. While the state might have enough evidence to convict even without the use of a challenged confession, the jury could well disbelieve the other sources of proof. Under such circumstances, the confession could serve to tip the scales in favor of conviction. If the confession were used, one could never assess how the jury would have reacted to the other evidence without it. Thus once the confession was ruled inadmissible on appeal, reversal then became the only appropriate remedy. Given the forceful evidentiary character of a confession, principles of harmless error that permit the affirmance of a conviction despite error below, could have no bearing. But the much more difficult question in the implementation of the fair-trial standard was the evaluation of the confession requirements demanded by due process. The facts of *Brown* presented the Court with no real challenge; if due process-fair trial meant anything, it certainly had to require that confessions concededly extracted by physical force be rejected. Having established that, what should follow? The Court spent the next thirty years confronting this dilemma. Trends emerged during this period, but overall there was a singular lack of internal consistency in the involuntary confession cases. Decisions of the Court could not be predicted nor, as a result, could appellate courts supervise trial court and police confession policies with adequate efficiency.

The early state cases, as well as federal precedent on nonconstitutional grounds, suggest a due process rationale closely tied to the reliability of the evidence contained in the confession. For example, in a case involving a District of Columbia homicide, a suspect was apprehended in New York City, and taken by "consent" back to Washington, D.C. He was held incommunicado for a total of twelve days and subjected to "persistent, lengthy and repeated cross-examination"[27] by the police, including some all-night questioning. Moreover, all during this time he was seriously ill. The Court had little difficulty finding the confession involuntary. To the same effect was a 1940 ruling, *Chambers v. Florida*,[28] in which police had rounded up more than twenty blacks after the murder of an elderly white man. The prisoners were informed of possible mob violence and moved. They were subjected to periodic incommunicado interrogation for nearly a week, including an all-night vigil, and finally gave the police a confession. Putting aside the issue of physical abuse, which was disputed in the case, the Court, speaking through Justice Black, nevertheless found that the circumstances conceded by the state demonstrated unconstitutional coercion. These included:

> the dragnet methods of arrest on suspicion without warrant, and the protracted questioning and cross questioning of these ignorant young colored tenant farmers by state officers and other white citizens, in a fourth floor jail room, where as prisoners they were without friends, advisors or counselors, and under circumstances calculated to break the strongest nerves and the stoutest resistance.[29]

The conclusion that the combination of such tactics would produce an involuntary and unreliable confession was hardly surprising.

Nevertheless, the fundamental character of the Court's analysis left substantial room for the utilization of vigorous, if not brutal, interrogation techniques. At its core, the due process-fair-trial standard called for a case-by-case assessment of all the circumstances surrounding the interrogation process. Similarities among cases were impossible to rely upon since they would always be outweighed by the differences. In *Lisenba v. California*,[30] for example, decided by the Court in 1941, the suspect was held in police custody for eleven days and subjected to periodic interrogation, including an all-night session conducted by relays of police officers. No counsel conferred with the suspect, and his arraignment was illegally delayed. The Court, however, found the confession produced by these circumstances to be voluntary. It made a major concession in that its ruling did not rest on the reliability of the statement, accepting instead the view that the "aim of the requirement of due process is not to exclude presumptively false evidence, but to prevent fundamental unfairness in the use of evidence, whether true or false."[31] At the same time, however, the Court indicated that fairness was to be judged by the totality of the circumstances. The significance of this was apparent in *Lisenba* where despite the delineation of fairness as an objective and the general similarity of the tactics to those used in *Chambers*, the Court held the *Lisenba* confession voluntary. It relied upon what it took to be a different subjective reaction by the suspect to the interrogation process. He was characterized as an intelligent and experienced individual, not young nor uneducated nor unfamiliar with criminal proceedings, nor a member of a minority group being subjected to mob intimidation. Presumably, the Court believed that his decision to confess was not involuntary under the circumstances given his personal characteristics. Implicitly, the Court was thus suggesting that the evaluation of interrogation tactics was to be based upon a sliding-scale analysis, with greater pressures being permissible against more resolute and formidable suspects.

It was apparent to some members of the Court that the due process analysis it had embarked upon was a problematic approach to the resolution of confession admissibility questions. One recurrent difficulty was the fact that sharp disputes often characterized the testimony concerning what went on in the police interrogation room. This was particularly true in relation to testimony on the use of force by the police, the reality for suspects who had been beaten being the likelihood that they would not be believed. Admissions by police that force was used were a rarity, especially after *Brown v. Mississippi*. This meant that the Court had to fall back upon analyzing the surrounding and indisputable conditions such as the length of incommunicado interrogation, access to counsel, use of relays of interrogators, and the like. Lower court rulings on disputed testimony relating to the use of force tended to support the police version and served to keep the real issues away from the Court. Additionally, the case-by-case approach, particularly in light of its emphasis on the reactions of the suspect to police pressure tactics, was an exceedingly subjective principle for the Court to administer. It required an assessment of when the will of the suspect had been overborne, but suggested no guidelines for making this determination.

As an alternative to case-by-case analysis, Justice Black urged the Court to adopt a due process standard under which a more objective assessment would be made of the conditions that produced the confession. He developed the argument in *Ashcraft v. Tennessee*,[32] a 1944 Supreme Court decision. The defendant in the case had been charged with murder for hiring the killer of his wife. Justice Black noted that "the usual pattern"[33] of conflicting testimony on the use of physical force was present and went on to analyze the remaining interrogation conditions. He observed that the interrogation was conducted by relays of police officers "because they became so tired they were compelled to rest."[34] And, most importantly, the questioning continued for a total of thirty-six hours. But, rather than attempt to then evaluate how well the defendant was able to withstand the interrogation, Justice Black concluded that enough information was available to rule the confession inadmissible. In his judgment, the entire context in which the confession was obtained was "inherently coercive" and "irreconcilable with the possession of mental freedom by a lone suspect against whom . . . full coercive force is brought to bear."[35] Justice Jackson, writing in dissent, recognized the dramatic shift reflected in the majority opinion and urged that the standard should be whether the confession "was *in fact* involuntarily made."[36] But even accepting the Court's analysis, there was no indication what kind and degree of conditions would violate its inherent coercion standard. The facts in *Ashcraft* suggested that the Court was particularly concerned about the lengthy interrogation process itself, but this left uncertain the issue of how long a period of questioning the Court would have been willing to tolerate and said nothing about the Court's view of other surrounding conditions such as access to counsel and the duration of the suspect's total period of confinement prior to his confession. Moreover, Justice Black's inherent coercion rationale did not identify what it sought to achieve as a policy objective. One possible goal was that of reliability, with the Court seeking to bar coercive tactics that would generally result in poor evidence regardless of the characteristics of the defendant in any particular case.[37] Alternatively, the inherent coercion standard might have been intended as a technique to control abusive police tactics irrespective of their impact on confession reliability, a view consistent with *Chambers*.

After *Ashcraft*, very little can be said with confidence about confession standards under the due process clause. The inherent coercion analysis appeared to lose its majority, and the Court returned to a case-by-case assessment of the circumstances surrounding each interrogation. Admissibility principles were relatively simple to state. Involuntary confessions were the result of the suspect's will being overborne and the "suction process of interrogation"[38] and thus rejected. The Court did not mean by this, however, a confession standard in which statements would be admitted only if "voluntary in the sense that [the suspect] wanted to make them or that they were completely spontaneous, like a confession to a priest, a lawyer or a psychiatrist" since "in this sense no criminal confession is voluntary."[39] But, as a result of their obvious vagueness, the rules provided no guidance and led to seemingly inconsistent decisions. Thus in *Watts v. Indiana*,[40] the defendant's confession was ruled involuntary, having been obtained after he was held in solitary confinement for a week, without decent sleep or food, and questioned by relays of police officers. Yet in *Gallegos v. Nebraska*,[41] a Mexican farm hand who could neither speak nor write English was subjected to four days of confinement in spartan conditions, confronted with persistent interrogation, and the Court held his confession voluntary. The only consistency in the cases of this period was first, that the Court was willing to authorize at least some degree of custodial interrogation and second, that it measured the voluntariness requirement of the due-process clause from a practical standpoint, far short of the abstract notion of voluntariness a purist might demand.

If the cases are assessed over time, however, it is apparent that the Supreme Court was slowly upgrading its standard of voluntariness in reviewing state confession rulings. The decisions continued to survey the totality of facts in each case, but more readily found coercion to be present. *Rogers v. Richmond*,[42] decided by the Court in 1961, held inadmissible a confession obtained from a suspect after only six hours of interrogation concluding at 8:00 p.m. in the evening. During the questioning the suspect was permitted to eat and smoke, but the police did make a fake call indicating that they were bringing in the defendant's wife for interrogation. Also ruled involuntary was the confession obtained in the 1963 case of *Haynes v. Washington*.[43] There, an older and experienced defendant confessed after a sixteen-hour interrogation during which he was permitted to eat and sleep but denied permission to call his wife. It is possible that earlier Courts would have also ruled these confessions involuntary, but decisions such as *Gallegos v. Nebraska* make it more likely that they would have affirmed the convictions in both instances. By the 1960s, however, such decisions were increasingly predictable as the Court itself became more sensitive to the need to protect civil liberties in the criminal justice process. Moreover, the frequency with which minorities were involved in coerced-confession cases and the level of civil rights activity during that era made it likely that the Court's approach to the voluntariness standard was influenced by these factors as well.

That the Court had difficulty in settling on a rule of law to control state interrogation practices is understandable in light of the boundaries it had set for itself. First of all, the voluntariness standard developed as a feature of the Fourteenth Amendment due process clause. This was a major limiting factor since "due process of law" was taken by the Court to mean no more than fundamental fairness in the conduct of state criminal procedure. And while the notion of what constitutes fundamental fairness has increased over time, the concept has never become a tool for exercising detailed control over state affairs. Second, in adopting the common law concept of voluntariness as the governing standard for confisson admissibility, the Court chose a principle with a wide variety of potential meanings. In a philosophical sense, voluntariness looks toward an exercise of free will, although some might argue that no such state of mind exists. But spontaneous declarations and more generally statements obtained without interrogation are arguably close enough to satisfy the minimum essentials of the doctrine. To view voluntariness in this way, however, would effectively bar police interrogation. This was a step the Court was unwilling to take as evidenced by both Justice Jackson's dissenting observations in the face of rulings holding confessions inadmissible[44] and Justice Frankfurter's extended analysis in *Culombe v. Connecticut*.[45] When Justice Frankfurter observed that "[d]ue process does not demand of the states, in their administration of the criminal law, standards of favor to the accused which our civilization, in its most sensitive expression, has never found it practical to adopt,"[46] he was implicitly recognizing that confession law could not be realistically limited to a pure voluntariness requirement.

If police are then allowed to interrogate, what are the appropriate limits of their power? To say that they may only obtain voluntary statements suggests that the confession must be one the suspect wants to make. This should leave room for the police to try to persuade him to make that decision, but such efforts are improper if the suspect responds when he did not want to. This certainly occurs when the suspect confesses to avoid physical or psychological abuse but not necessarily when other factors are involved. For example, what should be the result where the confession is given simply so that the questioning will cease? Is that an involuntary statement? It should be if the circumstances lead the suspect to reasonably believe that a confession would be the *only* way to end the interrogation, but if such is not the case, the result is less clear. This, however, was the kind of line drawing the Court's voluntariness standard called for. And in interpreting the standard, the Court, although purporting to define the word "voluntary," was in reality setting boundaries governing the exercise of state power and the scope of individual liberty in the interrogation arena.

Federal Confessions and Illegal Detention

Although the Supreme Court had indicated in its 1897 *Bram* decision that federal confession admissibility would be judged by the standards of the Fifth Amendment, subsequent rulings did not follow the same path.[47] But if the Fifth Amendment privilege was not to be the controlling standard, another source of authority would have to be found. One of the choices available to the Court was to rely upon federal principles of evidence as it had done prior to *Bram*. Such an approach, however, would very likely have unduly committed the Court to the objective of evidence reliability in its confession rules since reliability was a central concern of evidence law. Alternatively, as the Court moved to control state confession procedures under the Fourteenth Amendment due process clause, it could have imposed similar requirements on federal authorities pursuant to the due process clause of the Fifth Amendment. Arguably, by the 1920s the Court was moving in just such a direction. But when the Court turned its attention to the supervision of state confession practices, it simultaneously deemphasized federal confession cases. It may be that the Court assumed that its rulings on state confessions would also be taken as the governing federal standard. If so, the assumption was a reasonable one. After all, the legal authority for the Court's state confession rulings was the principle of due process of law, and nothing suggested that confession standards pursuant to due process under the Fifth Amendment were any different from the demands of Fourteenth Amendment due process. But the fact that federal confessions would have to be voluntary in the same sense as state confessions did not necessarily mean that the Court was limited to the voluntariness standard in its efforts to supervise federal interrogation practices. While Supreme Court authority over state criminal procedure might be confined to the boundaries of the Constitution, the same was not true with respect to federal practice. The federal court system in general, and the Supreme Court in particular, have special responsibilities to oversee the federal law-enforcement system pursuant to which they may impose demands not specifically called for in the Constitution. This is the realm of the Court's so-called supervisory power, and while its limitations are not fully defined, it was to this source of authority that the Court turned when it began to once again review federal cases challenging the admission of a defendant's confession.

The utilization of the Supreme Court's supervisory power was not, however, converted into a procedure for open-ended review of federal law-enforcement activities. This is an important caveat to bear in mind. Without self-restraint as a controlling principle, the concept of supervisory power would very likely have led to an unwarranted delegation of almost limitless authority to the Court in contravention of basic democratic principles. Rather, the Court chose to carefully exercise its power, and this meant in the confession field that only one area was subjected to supervisory control, the realm of unnecessary delay.

Under Rule 5(a) of the Federal Rules of Criminal Procedure, as well as comparable provisions in many states, an arrestee must be taken before a judicial officer for his initial appearance without unnecessary delay. Certain obvious considerations lie behind the requirement. The rule seeks to prevent the very fact of secret detention without charge or court appearance. Given the constitutional and statutory right to bail on behalf of an accused, the requirement of appearance without unnecessary delay ensures that the right to release will not be circumvented. In a less direct sense, however, the requirement may also have some bearing on the confession problem. This stems from the fact that one of the major advantages law-enforcement officers may seek to obtain from a delayed appearance is the securing of self-incriminatory statements from an accused. A prompt appearance in court obviously reduces whatever opportunity the police might otherwise have to conduct an interrogation. The appearance itself provides the suspect with an opportunity to secure his release by posting bail. Even if he remains in custody, he will have been warned of his rights by a judicial officer and will often be transferred to the custody of correctional officials and therefore no longer subject to ready access by the police. Whether or not the rule was written with these interrogation implications in mind, it nevertheless provided the Court with a vehicle to further supervise federal law-enforcement questioning.

The factual context in which the delayed presentment issue reached the Court arose out of the murder of an officer of the Alcohol Tax Unit of the Bureau of Internal Revenue. The officer had been part of a team of revenue agents investigating the illegal sale of whiskey on which federal taxes had not been paid. Information had been received that members of the McNabb family, a clan of Tennessee mountaineers living near Chattanooga, were about to engage in such a sale and plans were made to apprehend them in the act. The McNabbs, however, escaped when the officers intervened in the attempted sale, but one of the officers was killed by an unidentified assailant while he was emptying the cans of whiskey that had been abandoned. Several hours after the incident, between one and two o'clock in the morning, federal agents went to the McNabb home and arrested three of the McNabb brothers. They were taken to a federal facility in Chattanooga, but no effort was made to bring them before a judge or commissioner. Instead, they were left in a detention cell for some fourteen hours. The cell was totally barren, and the McNabbs were forced to sit or lie on the floor. They were given some sandwiches during this period but had no visitors. A fourth brother was arrested the morning after the shooting and held in a separate cell, and a fifth brother voluntarily surrendered later. All the brothers shared the common characteristics of lack of prior experience with the law, limited education, and a lifetime spent in the area of their birth. They were subjected to a prolonged process of interrogation during which the brothers were questioned singly and together. They were warned before the interrogation began of their right to remain silent. The interrogation process did not cease, however, until some forty-eight hours after the initial apprehension of the three McNabb brothers; only by then had the necessary confessions been obtained.

In detailing the underlying factual context of the *McNabb* interrogation, the Court presented enough information to enable it to assess the voluntariness of the confession on traditional due process grounds. Age, educational background, prior experience with the law, the fact that a warning was given, and the prolonged detention were all factors relevant to such a decision, although the result could have gone either way. To the Court, however, the fact that the case involved a federal interrogation brought with it an additional obligation to carefully scrutinize the procedures. In the Court's words:

> Judicial supervision of the administration of criminal justice in the federal
> courts implies the duty of establishing and maintaining civilized standards

of procedure and evidence. Such standards are not satisfied merely by observance of those minimal historic safeguards for securing trial by reason which are summarized as due process of law and below which we reach what is really trial by force.[48]

In short, even if voluntary in a due process sense, a federal confession might still be ruled inadmissible for other reasons.

Justice Frankfurter's opinion in *McNabb* found the other reason in congressional enactments, which at the time imposed a duty of prompt presentment of federal arrestees before a judicial officer. His opinion characterized the requirement as an "important safeguard"[49] in the criminal process, necessary not only to protect the innocent but also to ensure that the guilty were convicted only by proper means. Moreover, it was obvious that the McNabbs had not been brought before a judicial officer in a timely fashion; the detention of the three initial arrestees had in fact lasted two days. Nevertheless, the fact that the requirement had been violated did not in and of itself dictate any particular consequence since Congress had failed to specify a remedy. This left the Court with the task of either chastising but not punishing the delayed presentment, or devising its own solution. It was Justice Reed's view in dissent that as long as the prompt presentment violations did not detract from the voluntariness of the confessions, their admission into evidence did not require reversal of the convictions. Justice Frankfurter, writing for the Court, disagreed, maintaining that the violations in issue created a "duty of the trial court to entertain a motion for the exclusion of such evidence."[50] While much was left uncertain by the Court's approach, including the question of how much leeway was left to conduct a federal interrogation consistent with the prompt-presentment requirement, it was clear that a potentially powerful new tool for the control of federal interrogations had been forged. And it was also apparent that since the source of legal authority for the Court's conclusion was its supervisory power over the administration of criminal justice in federal proceedings, Congress had the authority to reverse the decision and state criminal justice officials were not subject to its mandate. Only a constitutional decision would have achieved these results.

The *McNabb* decision generated negative reaction on a number of fronts. Lower federal courts displayed some hostility to the ruling as well as uncertainty as to the scope of the decision. Nevertheless, their obligation was to comply as best they could. Congress, however, began to seriously consider legislatively overturning *McNabb*, and law-enforcement officials were openly critical.[51] They were both held at bay and prevented from succeeding in the legislative arena by the pendency before the Supreme Court of *United States v. Mitchell*,[52] a case presenting the Court with an opportunity to clarify what was intended in *McNabb*. Mitchell, much like the McNabb brothers, had been subjected to a period of illegal detention by federal authorities. In fact, a total of eight days elapsed between his arrest and arraignment. Unlike *McNabb*, however, the confession was obtained from the suspect at the very outset, in the Court's words "[w]ithin a few minutes of his arrival at the police station."[53] Yet the District of Columbia Court of Appeals had held the confession inadmissible on the authority of *McNabb*, viewing the fact of illegal detention itself as sufficient to warrant the exclusion of Mitchell's threshold admission. To Justice Frankfurter, this was a misreading of *McNabb*. Since the *Mitchell* confession was not elicited as a result of the police illegality, its admission would not have amounted to the government's benefiting from the wrongdoing of its officers. Such a reading of *McNabb* served to confine the decision within narrower limits than had been suggested by the District of Columbia Court of Appeals. But some of the language in *Mitchell* suggested more. In particular, listing the "decisive features" of *McNabb* as "inexcusable detention" and "continuous questioning for many hours under psychological pressure"[54] seemed to label the decision more as a traditional involuntary confession than a prompt-presentment ruling. This aspect of *Mitchell* looked like a repudiation of *McNabb*. Thus the Court's effort at clarification of the prompt presentment rule was a failure, although it did successfully prevent undue expansion of the principle.

In the years following *Mitchell*, the lower federal courts struggled to identify the precise scope of the requirement of prompt presentment before a judicial officer. One approach was to view delay as a factor contributing to a finding of involuntariness, but that was fundamentally inconsistent with the *McNabb* decision and the Court's stress on the importance of prompt presentment. The alternative reflected in *Upshaw v. United States*[55] involved the development of a fine distinction arguably suggested by the *Mitchell* opinion. Since the Court in *Mitchell* was willing to accept the admissibility of a threshold confession because the illegal detention did not produce it, should not the same result follow when a confession was obtained *during* the period of illegal detention but could be shown not to have been caused by it? Under this theory only confessions that were a *product* of the delay would have been excluded, a standard not necessarily violated by the fact of delay alone. To the Supreme Court, however, this was an unwarranted narrowing of the obligation to produce an arrestee before a judicial officer. Under Rule 5(a) of the Federal Rules of Criminal Procedure, such production had to occur "without unnecessary delay," and the Court took this to mean that "a confession is inadmissible if made during illegal detention due to failure promptly to carry a prisoner before a committing magistrate."[56] The Court rejected any resort to the voluntariness standard as a way to circumvent the prompt-presentment requirement.

Lest any residual uncertainty remain as to the Court's willingness to enforce the prompt-presentment rule, the principle was reaffirmed in a decision rendered nearly a decade after *Upshaw*. The case was *Mallory v. United States*,[57] and like *Upshaw*, it focused on the unnecessary delay provision of Rule 5(a) of the Federal Rules of Criminal Procedure. The suspect, Mallory, had been arrested in the early afternoon and taken to police headquarters in close proximity to arraignment facilities. Rather than produce the suspect before a judicial officer, the police questioned him and conducted a lie-detector procedure. Only after 10:00 p.m. when a satisfactory confession had been obtained was an effort made to bring the suspect before a judicial officer. The circumstances in the Court's view, however, were inconsistent with the prohibition against unnecessary delay in presentment. But of more significance than the simple reaffirmation of *McNabb* was the fact that the *Mallory* Court made an effort to give the rule some meaningful content. The suspect in *Mallory* had been detained some eight hours during part of which he was in the company of family. At least two hours of the period were taken up with police efforts to locate the operator of the lie-detector equipment. The situation was a far cry from the more than a day-long detention experienced by Mitchell and the McNabb brothers. The more extensive detention in the earlier cases had led to an irrebuttable conclusion that the duration of police custody was impermissibly long and unjustified; without any question the suspects were held in violation of the prompt-presentment requirement for the purpose of securing self-incriminating admissions from them. Perhaps given a less dramatic delay, more leeway would be available for the police to justify their actions. If so, the next issue had to be the identification of the reasons which would excuse delay. *Mallory* was the first occasion in which such an effort was made.

Undoubtedly, the list of potential factors that might delay a suspect's presentment is virtually limitless, and the possible variations in the duration of such delay infinite. At one end of the spectrum are the interruptions caused by routine police administrative procedure in the booking process, which usually amount to no more than a matter of a hour and thus only marginally delay the judicial appearance of the suspect. Yet a rigid interpretation of Rule 5(a) and comparable state provisions might invalidate even the booking delay. Rule 5(a) calls for appearance without unnecessary delay and booking procedures, which can be completed after presentment, are strictly speaking unnecessary and in violation of the rule. If "unnecessary" is taken to mean something akin to "unavoidable," little more than the time needed to conduct a search and transport the suspect to court would be authorized. There is a case that can be made for just such a standard, supported by the notion that any extra time given to police between arrest and presentment is likely to be misused and therefore should be barred. That the Court did not view Rule 5(a) in so demanding a manner,

however, is not surprising. Indeed, it is doubtful that the courts would want
to administer a system in which arrestees were taken immediately from the
street to court without an opportunity for completion of necessary paper-
work. Accepting the "necessity" of such delays, however, need not be
turned into an open-ended exemption for longer delays caused by other factors. In fact, tolerance of booking delays could well constitute the limit of
the scope of necessity under Rule 5(a), barring even delays caused by the
unavailability of a committing official during evening or weekend periods.
Here too, however, no apparent effort to strictly apply the necessity standard has been made even though unwillingness to commit the resources required to provide available personnel is the only justifying factor.

To the Court, the provisions of Rule 5(a) "contemplate[d] a procedure
that allow[ed] arresting officers little more leeway than the interval between
arrest and the ordinary administrative steps required to bring a suspect
before the nearest available magistrate."[58] Delays occasioned by booking
and locating a magistrate apparently did not offend the rule. The real problem behind such delays, however, was not the delay itself so much as the
fact that the time would be used to continue the police investigation by in-
terrogating the suspect. If this is permitted, it must be because questioning
that occurs during legitimate delay is not offensive to the rule as long as it
is not the *reason* for the delay. Or, should the rule go further and allow
delay for the explicit purpose of permitting some questioning by police? To
this question the Court responded in the negative, although perhaps not as
forcefully as it might have. The relevant language in *Mallory* provided:

> Circumstances may justify a brief delay between arrest and arraignment, as
> for instance, where the story volunteered by the accused is susceptible of
> quick verification through third parties. But the delay must not be of a
> nature to give opportunity for the extraction of a confession.[59]

The thrust of the language clearly discouraged delay for purposes of interrogation but did not necessarily bar it. In particular, if the interrogation was
not such as would "extract" a confession, as is the case when police employ
high-pressure questioning tactics by teams of officers utilizing
psychologically coercive techniques, but rather amounted to a noncoercive
inquiry, it might be deemed consistent with Rule 5(a). Even conceding that
the police should not "arrest, as it were, at large and . . . use an inter-
rogating process at police headquarters in order to determine whom they
should charge,"[60] not every interrogation necessarily would run afoul of
such a policy objective. The Court was unwilling to say clearly and unequivocally that presentment may never be delayed to permit any type of questioning of the suspect, nor would it bar police from conducting an interrogation
during a period of delay occasioned by some other reason. What was accomplished instead under the guise of the prompt-presentment requirement

was the fashioning of a tool to control relatively serious interrogation abuses that did not necessarily affect the due process voluntariness of the confessions they produced.

Confessions and the Right to Counsel

The fact that the Supreme Court chose to supervise federal interrogation practices pursuant to its supervisory authority over the administration of criminal justice in the federal courts meant that the same strategy could not be employed in reviewing state confession cases. The voluntariness standard under the due process clause of the Fourteenth Amendment of necessity had to carry the load in controlling state interrogations since it alone possessed the necessary constitutional foundation for such a task. Unlike the prompt-presentment standard that was directly and unambiguously aimed at the control of undesirable police tactics, however, the voluntariness standard simply sought to assess whether the decision to confess was the suspect's free choice. The two standards overlapped insofar as at least some improper police tactics normally would result in involuntary confessions, but there remained an area of discord for those police interrogation techniques that, although in violation of prompt-presentment standards, might not lead to involuntary confessions.

A variety of responses can be made to the fact of differing federal and state interrogation standards. One is simply to accept the result that some confessions might be deemed admissible in state prosecutions despite the fact that they would be excluded in federal trials. Indeed, our federal system arguably seeks to encourage state experimentation with its likely consequence of variance between state and federal solutions. If divergence was deemed a serious problem, however, federal confession law could have returned to a Fifth Amendment due process foundation. But since the Court was clearly not inclined to lower the federal standard, a movement toward uniformity had to mean raising the voluntariness standard so that it would meet the essential demands of the federal prompt-presentment rule. In fact, the voluntariness standard did indeed grow more demanding over time, but its character was such that equivalence to the federal standard was unlikely. Simply put, given the direction of the voluntariness standard as a tool protecting free choice, it could not accomplish adequate control of the interrogation process in a manner similar to that of a rule fashioned specifically to supervise police tactics. This left the Court with the task of finding an alternative technique to bring the two standards closer together, and its solution, developed in a series of cases spanning the six years between 1958 and 1964, was to utilize the right to counsel to achieve further control over police interrogations.

Crooker v. California[61] and *Cicenia v. La Gay*[62] were both decided by the Supreme Court in 1958. Each involved an assessment of the voluntariness of a suspect's confession under traditional due process standards. In *Crooker* the suspect had been convicted of the murder of his paramour and sentenced to death. He was 31 years of age and a college graduate who had attended law school for one year. Crooker was arrested the day after the murder victim was discovered, questioned sporadically at the time, and subjected to custodial interrogation from 8:30 p.m. to 2:00 a.m. after he arrived at police headquarters. Moreover, during that period he had made a formal request to consult with his attorney which the police denied. However, the Court noted that he was warned of his right to remain silent and did indeed exercise it at various points during the interrogation. In contrast, the circumstances of the *Cicenia* confession involved a 20-year-old suspect lacking any legal education. He voluntarily surrendered to the police after consulting with counsel, but subsequent requests by counsel to consult with his client and the client to see his attorney were denied. The interrogation lasted from 9:00 a.m. to about 9:00 p.m. Both cases were found to involve confessions meeting the due process standard of voluntariness.

The novelty of *Crooker* and *Cicenia* lay not in the holdings on the voluntariness issue per se but rather in a common feature shared by both cases. The suspects in each instance sought, but were denied, the opportunity to consult with their attorneys. The Court recognized that it had not previously considered the admissibility of confessions based solely upon such a denial and indicated awareness of the possibility of coercion in each case but found the denial "not decisive."[63] Its view was that on a case-by-case basis, and particularly in *Crooker* and *Cicenia*, the denial of a request for counsel need not always undercut the voluntariness of the resulting confession. Also involved, however, was the possibility of a due process violation in the fact of the denial of the right to consult with counsel, regardless of the voluntariness of the subsequent confession. Prior right-to-counsel cases had indeed established such protection for criminal defendants under the due process clause.[64] To the Court, however, the heart of the due process right to counsel focused upon the need for fundamental fairness at trial. While this might be infringed as a result of the denial of an opportunity to consult with counsel during the pretrial stage of the criminal process, such would not always be the case. The circumstances surrounding each confession and denial of counsel were to be individually assessed, the Court thereby rejecting the call for an automatic exclusionary rule in all such cases. Given the fact that the defendant in *Crooker* had some legal background and was aware of his right to remain silent and that the defendant in *Cicenia* had conferred with counsel prior to his voluntary surrender, no constitutional violations were found.

Despite the majority rulings in *Crooker* and *Cicenia*, four members of the Court would have reversed the convictions in both cases solely because of the denial of the right to consult with counsel. Justice Douglas, writing for the dissenters, observed that the suspect who "feels the need of a lawyer and asks for one is asking for some protection which the law can give him against a coerced confession."[65] At a minimum, the right to consult with one's attorney would undercut the secrecy of police interrogation through which coercion flourished. To the dissenters, the "right to have the assistance of counsel [was] too fundamental and absolute to allow courts to indulge in nice calculations as to the amount of prejudice arising from its denial,"[66] whether that denial took place during or prior to trial.

With the addition of Justice Stewart to the Supreme Court, it began to appear that the denial of counsel to a suspect during a police interrogation might become a more significant factor in judging confession admissibility. In *Spano v. New York*,[67] decided by the Supreme Court in 1959, the claim was made that the refusal of the suspect's postindictment request to consult with his attorney was in itself enough to warrant exclusion of the resulting confession. The four members of the Court who had taken this position in *Crooker* were still on the bench. And although the Court ruled in *Spano* that the confession was involuntary as a result of the totality of circumstances surrounding the interrogation, Justice Stewart wrote that "the absence of counsel when this confession was elicited was alone enough to render it inadmissible under the Fourteenth Amendment."[68] Thus it appeared that a total of five members of the Court viewed the single fact of the denial of counsel in a police interrogation as a controlling event in determining confession admissibility, seemingly without regard to whether the voluntariness standard had been met.

It was not until 1964, five years after *Spano*, that the Supreme Court returned to the problem of attempting to define the circumstances that would bar admissions made by a suspect who had been denied counsel. *Massiah v. United States*[69] confronted the Court with the question of the admissibility of incriminating statements secured from an already indicted suspect. Rather than being the product of a police custodial interrogation, however, the admissions were obtained by an undercover informant who engaged the suspect in a lengthy conversation that was simultaneously transmitted. Given the fact that this was a federal prosecution, the Court felt that admissibility had to be judged by the standards of the Sixth Amendment right to counsel and found that right to have been violated "when there was used against [the defendant] at his trial evidence of his own incriminating words, which federal agents had deliberately elicited from him after he had been indicted and in the absence of his counsel."[70]

Although the Court's language may have suggested that the decision might be limited to federal prosecutions, the fact that the Sixth Amendment right to counsel had been incorporated and held applicable to the states in

Gideon v. Wainwright[71] made the *Massiah* principle equally relevant to the states. But *Massiah* was not entirely clear in delimiting the scope of its holding. One reading of the decision would have made critical the fact that the admissions were obtained after the suspect had been indicted. Pursuant to this analysis, since the Sixth Amendment provided for a right to the assistance of counsel in "all criminal prosecutions," the Court needed to merely define the circumstances that constituted a criminal prosecution and then determine whether right-to-counsel standards had been met. The postindictment period clearly fell within the scope of Sixth Amendment protection since at this point the state had sufficiently committed itself to prosecution so as to make right to counsel protections necessary. One could dispute whether surreptitious interrogations, as in *Massiah*, violated the right to counsel, but it was difficult to question the conclusion that the Sixth Amendment applied to the postindictment period. Despite the ease with which this definitional approach to the Sixth Amendment could be stated, however, it was not the only available theory. A criminal prosecution can be viewed not only as an arbitrary line drawn somewhere within the numerous stages of the criminal process from investigation to final disposition but also as a functional standard. Under this theory the protections of the right to counsel would be applied any time a critical event occurred in the criminal process at which the guiding hand of counsel was required. Justice White, writing in dissent, feared that the *Massiah* ruling combined with a functional approach to the Sixth Amendment right to counsel would lead to vastly increased controls on the preindictment police interrogation process, far in excess of the restrictions imposed by the voluntariness and prompt-presentment requirements. And in a matter of just two months, the Court's decision in *Escobedo v. Illinois*[72] demonstrated the accuracy of his prediction.

Danny Escobedo had been arrested by Chicago police for the murder of his brother-in-law. He was held over fifteen hours before his attorney was able to secure his release pursuant to a state habeas corpus writ. Some eleven days later, and as a result of more information that had been acquired during that period, Escobedo was rearrested. From the very outset, as early as the car ride to police headquarters after arrest, Escobedo indicated in response to questions that he wished to consult with his attorney. He repeated the request during the entire course of his interrogation and his attorney, who had arrived at the police station during the questioning, sought to see him. The police, however, denied both requests and continued the interrogation until they had obtained the confession they sought. Escobedo's motions to suppress the confession were denied and he was convicted of murder.

There are obvious differences between the tactics used by the police in *Escobedo* and *Massiah*, but perhaps the most significant is the fact that the *Escobedo* interrogation occurred prior to the institution of formal charges against the suspect. Arguably, therefore, the questioning did not take place during a "criminal prosecution" stage and no Sixth Amendment right to counsel was applicable. If so, the Court's analysis should have proceeded to a determination of the voluntariness of the confession in line with due process of law standards. And given the fact that specific requests to consult with counsel were denied, a significant issue in light of the Court's 1959 ruling in *Spano*, a finding of involuntariness would have been possible. *Escobedo* and *Massiah* also differed in that Danny Escobedo knew he was being questioned by police, unlike Massiah whose conversations with a police informant were surreptitiously monitored. Using the functional analysis, Escobedo had a greater need for legal advice so that he could have intelligently decided whether to answer police questions. Confronted with these alternatives, the Court, in a five-four decision written by the recently appointed Justice Arthur Goldberg, ignored the voluntariness question and held the Sixth Amendment to apply to the circumstances of Escobedo's interrogation and to have been violated.

The Court's earlier decision in *Massiah* applying the Sixth Amendment to postindictment proceedings did not, in the Court's view, imply a limitation of the right to counsel. The *Escobedo* homicide was not a general investigation into an unsolved crime, and Danny Escobedo was the accused even though not yet indicted. Moreover, he was never informed of his absolute right to remain silent, nor was he, as a layman, aware that admission of mere complicity in the murder plot could be as damaging as a confession to having been the principal. The totality of these considerations presented the picture of a suspect desperately in need of legal advice. It was clear to the majority that Escobedo's preindictment interrogation was a critical event in which important rights could be lost if not asserted. In the Court's view, only the exaltation of "form over substance"[73] could justify making the right to counsel depend upon whether an indictment had been secured. Nevertheless, Justice Goldberg was careful to limit his opinion to the facts presented, specifying both the circumstances under which the Sixth Amendment applied and the conditions that would constitute a violation, in ruling:

> [W]here, as here, the investigation is no longer a general inquiry into an unsolved crime but has begun to focus on a particular suspect, the suspect has been taken into police custody, the police carry out a process of interrogations that lends itself to eliciting incriminating statements, the suspect has requested and been denied an opportunity to consult with his lawyer, and the police have not effectively warned him of his absolute constitutional right to remain silent, the accused has been denied "the Assistance of Counsel" in violation of the Sixth Amendment . . . and . . . no statement elicited by the police during the interrogation may be used against him at a criminal trial.[74]

If the Court truly meant to confine its ruling to the listed conditions, it was adhering to its tradition of considering the admissibility of state confessions on a case-by-case basis, albeit from a Sixth Amendment rather than a due process perspective. Presumably, prefocus questioning could generate a different result, although the need for counsel would still be great. The result might also differ if the suspect had not retained his own attorney or failed to request an opportunity to consult with him. But, again, it is not clear why these factors would make a difference despite the fact that they were part of the totality of the conditions actually present in *Escobedo*. However, Justice White in dissent recognized that the implications of the *Escobedo* ruling extended beyond the specific factors that the majority had taken such pains to list. In particular, recent precedent had made especially questionable any reliance upon a suspect's financial inability to hire an attorney or his failure to request one in determining Sixth Amendment rights.[75] If so, the trend represented by the decision suggested vastly increased controls over the police interrogation process and a reduction in the ability of police to secure confessions. Nor was Justice White particularly happy with the use of the Sixth Amendment right to counsel to supervise the interrogation process, which seemed more suitable to regulation by other means. Although his views did not prevail, as long as the *Escobedo* ruling applied only when all the conditions listed by the Court were present, its impact might well have remained limited.

6 Confessions: *Miranda* and Beyond

The development of confession law by the U.S. Supreme Court, at least until its 1966 decision in *Miranda v. Arizona*,[1] was a strange blend of theories. The earliest rulings suggested that traditional principles of evidence law required the exclusion of involuntary confessions. This stemmed from the view that statements obtained as a result of coercion were generally unreliable. In *Bram v. United States*,[2] however, decided by the Court in 1897, the Fifth Amendment self-incrimination clause was held to be the controlling standard for federal confessions. But, later cases ignored the decision, and by 1953 the Court referred to it as "not a rock upon which to build constitutional doctrine."[3] Instead, federal confession law turned to legislation imposing a prompt-presentment requirement in the federal system. Although the obligation, both in statutory form and as incorporated in Rule 5(a) of the Federal Rules of Criminal Procedure, did not encompass a requirement that evidence obtained in violation of the rule be suppressed, the Supreme Court exercised its supervisory authority to achieve that result. The *McNabb-Mallory*[4] line of cases called for the exclusion of statements obtained after unnecessary delay in the production of the suspect before a judicial officer. Since neither the Fifth Amendment nor the prompt-presentment requirement were deemed applicable to the states, the Supreme Court relied upon the Fourteenth Amendment due process clause to supervise state interrogation procedures. Initially, as reflected in the Court's decision in *Brown v. Mississippi*,[5] the Fourteenth Amendment appeared to impose a voluntariness standard akin to the early federal confession decisions in that the focus was upon the trustworthiness of the challenged statements. Over time the content of the due process voluntariness requirement appeared to become more substantial, but the development was not a smooth one, and many inconsistencies were apparent in the decisions. Finally, the Court utilized the Sixth Amendment right to counsel as an interrogation control technique holding, ultimately, that a suspect who is the focus of a criminal investigation must be permitted to consult with his attorney upon request. Any confession obtained in violation of this right, even if voluntary under Fourteenth Amendment standards, would be suppressed.

In bringing together so many alternative rationales to govern the single issue of confession admissibility, the Court was reflecting its basic uncertainty as to what the controlling standards for confessions should be. There was a consensus at the extreme in barring the use of untrustworthy confessions involuntarily secured from a suspect. This progressed to a standard prohibiting the admission of involuntary confessions regardless of their trustworthiness. Nevertheless, the Court was not able to clearly articulate what its voluntariness standard meant nor the objectives it was designed to achieve. Some decisions talked in terms of a goal of protecting the suspect's free choice in deciding whether to make a confession, while others appeared directed more toward achieving control over abusive police interrogation tactics. The cases did suggest a general trend in the Supreme Court's approach to police interrogations reflected in a gradual upgrading of the voluntariness standard. However, the rationale and legal foundation of the Court's confession rules were in continual flux.

Although there were important guideposts in the total array of Supreme Court confession decisions, no single case provided a fully satisfactory explanation of the Court's actions. In part this was due to the Court's unwillingness to utilize the most textually logical legal authority to control police questioning. With the exception of the 1897 ruling in *Bram v. United States*, the Fifth Amendment's self-incrimination clause played no part in Supreme Court confession rulings. Had it been relied upon, there would have been a body of law supervising federal interrogations to apply to the states once the Fifth Amendment was incorporated. But the privilege was not utilized, and as a result ill-suited constitutional and statutory provisions were pressed into service. After incorporation of the Fifth Amendment, however, the Court had the opportunity to achieve uniformity in confession law by applying the privilege to state and federal interrogations with a virtually clean slate to write on at the same time. The case law, particularly by the 1960s, seemed headed in that direction and, with its 1966 decision in *Miranda v. Arizona*, the Court finally took the last necessary step.

The *Miranda* Decision

Miranda v. Arizona presented the Supreme Court with four companion cases all raising interrogation issues. Ernesto Miranda was arrested in connection with a kidnapping and rape investigation. He was identified by the complaining witness and then taken to an interrogation room where two hours of questioning by two officers produced a signed confession. Michael Vignera was subjected to custodial interrogation on a robbery charge that lasted through the afternoon and evening of his arrest. An oral admission and the transcript of his responses to police questions were used against him at trial. Carl Westover's initial detention arose as a result of his arrest by Kansas City, Missouri, police officers. After interrogation on the night of the arrest as well as the next morning, he was turned over to agents of the

FBI. They continued the interrogation at the Kansas City police facility and, within two and one-half hours secured two signed confessions relating to out-of-town robberies that were not the subject of local police interest. Finally, the Court reviewed the conviction of Roy Stewart for robbery and murder. After his arrest by Los Angeles police, he was held in police custody and subjected to interrogation on nine occasions during a five-day period. The final questioning session produced a confession. Although the details of the four cases were varied, several critical features were present in each. All four involved custodial police interrogation; in each case the suspect was under arrest and not free to leave. Moreover, the questioning took place in the privacy of a police station rather than in an area of general access to the public, with typically only the suspect and his interrogators present. Neither neutral observers nor friends of the accused were permitted to watch or participate. Similarly, no visual nor audio record of the entire procedure was made, although some record of the final confession was secured. And finally, in no case did the record demonstrate that the suspect received a warning of the scope of his constitutional rights prior to the start of his interrogation.

Without much ado, and with only a modest attempt at justification, the Court returned to the premise of its decision in *Bram v. United States* that police interrogations are governed by the Fifth Amendment's self-incrimination clause. In part this was achieved by asserting that the decision was "not an innovation in our jurisprudence, but . . . an application of principles long recognized."[6] Thus simply a citation to *Bram* was sufficient. Nevertheless, the Court added that the historical evolution of the privilege against self-incrimination led inexorably to its application to custodial police interrogations. Although the historical context of the privilege focused upon settings in which the state possessed legal authority to compel self-incriminatory admissions, the Court felt there was a larger sense in which the evolutionary process was one that "groped for the proper scope of governmental power over the citizen."[7] Since the process of police interrogation entails the same general policy considerations as those reflected in other Fifth Amendment issues, it therefore was appropriate to use the balance established by the privilege against self-incrimination to regulate such questioning. The fact that the "privilege has consistently been accorded a liberal construction"[8] made the conclusion easier to reach. Moreover, even though Justices Harlan and White, writing in dissent, questioned the Court's extension of the Fifth Amendment to cover police interrogations, their resistance was relatively restrained, Justice Harlan going so far as to call it "perhaps not an impermissible extension of the law."[9] Rather, the dissenters saved the major thrust of their objections for other aspects of the decision.

The application of the Fifth Amendment privilege to police interrogations need not have entailed any dramatic shift in the standards governing the admissibility of the resulting confessions. The privilege bars compulsory self-incrimination, but the language could easily be read as simply requiring that confession admissiblity be judged on the same voluntariness standard developed pursuant to the Fourteenth Amendment. Indeed, voluntary statements are arguably no more than those secured in the absence of compulsion. Such an approach would have meant, furthermore, continuation of the case-by-case style of adjudication the Court had developed over the years with its attendant emphasis on the unique facts of each situation and resulting flexibility of decision making. This, however, is what the Court chose not to do in favor of embarking on a new and in its judgment potentially more effective set of principles to regulate police interrogations.

The essence of the *Miranda* decision was set out in the early pages of the ruling and elaborated upon as it progressed. At its core it provided for a set of warnings to be administered before the police would be permitted to conduct a custodial interrogation and use the fruits thereof at trial. In Chief Justice Warren's words:

> Prior to any questioning, the person must be warned that he has a right to remain silent, that any statement he does make may be used as evidence against him and that he has the right to the presence of an attorney, either retained or appointed. The defendant may waive effectuation of these rights, provided the waiver is made voluntarily, knowingly and intelligently.[10]

The Court explained that the warning of the right to remain silent was necesssary both to alert those who were unaware of the privilege and to demonstrate police willingness to respect its assertion. Explanation of the consequences of forgoing the privilege was deemed essential to ensuring an intelligent decision by the defendant. Finally, the Court saw the right to the presence of counsel as a means of protecting the defendant's will from being overborne. His right of choice must remain "unfettered throughout the interrogation process,"[11] and access to his attorney would aid in achieving that objective.

The *Miranda* decision was not written as a total ban on police questioning. Rather, it contained two features establishing the basis upon which the police interrogation process would have to rely. The first of these was the waiver authority built into the *Miranda* warnings which authorized interrogation after an affirmative waiver of the rights the warning provided. The state, however, was given a "heavy burden"[12] to establish a valid waiver, and that burden could not be met by simply demonstrating that the warning preceded the confession. Second, the terms of the decision were directed only to the process of custodial interrogation defined as questioning of the suspect "while in custody at the station or otherwise deprived of his freedom of action in any significant way."[13] Excluded were "general on-the-scene questioning as to the facts surrounding a crime" and "other general questioning of citizens in the fact-finding process."[14] Finally, the entire decision was qualified by the observation that the warnings were designed to protect the defendant's Fifth Amendment rights, and that other equally protective alternatives might warrant dispensing with the *Miranda* procedure. The Court did not specify what would be an adequate alternative nor have any been developed by other sources.

Of course, there is nothing explicitly stated in the Fifth Amendment that suggests the need for warnings prior to custodial police interrogation, nor is there language calling for police to meet a heavy burden to demonstrate a valid waiver of the privilege. The Fifth Amendment simply provides for a ban against compulsory self-incrimination. Thus if compulsion were exerted in the police questioning process, assuming the applicability of the Fifth Amendment, the resulting statements would be involuntary and inadmissible. Traditional doctrine, however, had allowed the state to introduce a voluntary confession even if no warnings were given. Here is where *Miranda* parted company with the old voluntariness test, for the decision banned the admission of any statement obtained from an unwarned defendant as a result of custodial interrogation regardless of its voluntariness. The challenge the Court had to meet, therefore, was to find a source of compulsion in the custodial interrogation process warranting the interposition of a warning requirement.

The Court undertook an analysis of interrogation tactics to bridge the gap between the traditional application of the Fifth Amendment to settings involving legal compulsion to respond, the historical source of the privilege, and the police interrogation room where no legal compulsion existed and where other forms of compulsion were not always present. The opinion approached this task by analyzing police interrogation manuals, particuarly Inbau and Reid's *Criminal Interrogation and Confessions*. Even though no showing was made that the techniques described were in fact in use, the Court nevertheless found them instructive. Among the strategems the manuals advised were to interrogate in private and show confidence during the questioning. Additionally, the suspect's guilt was to be assumed by the questioner and his blame minimized to induce a confession. The so-called Mutt and Jeff tactics were described, involving a team of harsh and gentle interrogators to play on the defendant's insecurity and fear. The police were also advised to use deception. In assessing the overall process, the Court felt it "obvious that such an interrogation environment is created for no purpose other than to subjugate the individual to the will of his examiner."[15] In turn, this led to the conclusion that compulsion was "inherent in custodial surroundings"[16] during such an interrogation and that "protective devices"[17] were necessary to dispel it. Without the warnings, therefore, no statement could "truly be the product of . . . free choice."[18]

Although phrased as a set of prophylactic procedures to dispel the inherent compulsion of custodial police interrogation, the thrust of the decision can also be viewed as an effort to substantially upgrade the level of voluntariness required as a precondition to the admission of a confession. Prior to *Miranda*, voluntariness was assessed from the totality of the circumstances. The suspect might be unaware of the scope of his right to remain silent or the consequences of waiving it or simply be worn down by the interrogation, but his confession could still be held voluntary. Such a result, in contrast, was at least theoretically barred by virtue of the *Miranda* warning since only statements obtained after the warning and a valid waiver could meet the *Miranda* voluntariness test. Even slight coercion to obtain a waiver was seemingly prohibited despite the fact that the Court traditionally tolerated some pressures on the individual's decision to confess under the old voluntariness test. To Justice Harlan, the end product of the decision was "voluntariness with a vengeance"[19] and ultimately the discouraging of any confessions. Whether or not that was an accurate reading of the decision, there could be little doubt that the majority was indeed establishing a far more demanding standard by which the defendant's decision to answer police questions would henceforth be measured.

The Aftermath of *Miranda*

Despite the fact that the Supreme Court's interrogation rulings were heading toward the *Miranda* decision, reaction did not appear to build in a slow and methodical fashion. Rather, the criticism burst forth after the *Miranda* ruling was handed down.[20] The focus was not unexpectedly the likely impact of Fifth Amendment warnings on the administration of the police interrogation system. Indeed, the *Miranda* decision itself was attentive to the possible impact it might have, both in the majority and dissenting opinions. Justice White, for example, felt that the decision would have a "corrosive effect on the criminal law as an effective device to prevent crime."[21] It was his view that administration of the warnings would decrease the number of confessions secured by the police and thereby lead to a decrease in the conviction rate. Justice Harlan's dissent was more restrained, calling the decision a "real risk" and "hazardous experimentation."[22] But the majority saw the interrogation process as a far more abusive system than the dissent, and deemed the warnings essential to retaining a fair balance between the state and the accused. Its view was that the decision was not an "undue interference with a proper system of law enforcement."[23] The basis of this conclusion appeared to be a judgment that law enforcement had overstated the true need for confessions. And each of the companion cases did indeed involve substantial evidence of guilt aside from the confessions, although how important the confessions were to each conviction was largely unmeasurable. The majority was not conceding that its ruling would deprive the police of a significant number of confessions, but rather felt that the real solution lay in the intensive pursuit of other investigative techniques. The experience of the FBI and Commonwealth countries was, to the Court, persuasive proof that interrogation protections would not have disastrous consequences.

The majority and dissenting views of the likely impact of *Miranda* were, of course, only educated guesses. They could not foresee what would actually occur in the police interrogation room with warnings being regularly administered, nor could one even predict that warnings would indeed be regularly given. Only painstaking research would answer the *Miranda* impact question. New Haven, Pittsburgh, and Washington, D.C., became the sites for the most ambitious of the efforts to assess what *Miranda* really meant to the criminal justice system.

The New Haven study included extensive observations of police interrogation sessions. While revealing no evidence of physical coercion, the study pointed to frequent failures to give full *Miranda* warnings, although performance improved as police became more experienced with the procedures. But even compliance with the letter of the law did not necessarily mean compliance with its spirit. A very formal delivery or hedging in the listing of rights were among the techniques employed. The study noted that "[n]o support was found for the claim that warnings reduce the amount of 'talking,' "[24] but also found some statistical evidence that interrogations were important in only a small percentage of cases. All in all, the study concluded that "[n]ot much . . . changed after *Miranda*."[25] No significant differences were detected in the Washington, D.C., and Pittsburgh studies.[26] The pattern was consistently that of a more limited need for confessions to secure convictions than had been anticipated, and no discernible effect on conviction rates. But the sum total of even these efforts fails to conclusively tell us what *Miranda* would mean if followed in letter *and* spirit, and no comparable research has been undertaken since. Rather, what implementation there has been of the *Miranda* rule suggests less than full compliance and continuing police success in securing confessions.

Neither the fact that the decision was new, nor the serious uncertainties as to its true meaning, were sufficient to stem the tide of criticism of the *Miranda* ruling. American society was very much concerned with the dilemma of crime in the mid 1960s, due partly to its apparent steady rise, but also to its dramatic manifestation in the urban riots of that period. Just the bare possibility that the decision might have impeded law enforcement would have been enough to generate a reaction, but the breadth of *Miranda* suggested the likelihood of a substantial curtailing of police interrogation practices. The response, therefore, was predictably more intense, including calls for a constitutional amendment to overturn *Miranda*. Ultimately, however, the critics coalesced behind a legislative reversal. And the very fact that a legislative route was chosen was indicative of the intensity of the feelings against *Miranda* since the constitutional basis of the decision meant limited legislative power to affect it. Nevertheless, Congress proceeded to enact and the president to sign Title II of the 1968 Omnibus Crime Control and Safe Streets Act.[27] Part of a larger anticrime program, including the provision of financial assistance to state and local law enforcement and federal wire-tapping authority, Title II called for the admission of confessions in federal trials if "voluntarily given." Voluntariness was to be judged by the totality of the circumstances and the statute suggested several factors to be considered including whether or not warnings were administered and whether or not the defendant had the assistance of counsel during his interrogation. But the statute concluded by providing that the presence or absence of any of the enumerated criteria "need not be conclusive on the issue of voluntariness of the confession." *Miranda*, in contrast, sought to abandon the traditional voluntariness test in favor of a fixed requirement that warnings be administered prior to any custodial interrogation. The conflict between the statute and the decision was clear and direct.

Congress, however, was not seeking in Title II to reverse a constitutional decision of the U.S. Supreme Court; that would have been a fruitless gesture since Congress could not enact an unconstitutional piece of legislation and force the Court to accept it. But Supreme Court precedent did suggest some limited role for Congress in defining the contours of constitutional rights. Under one theory, Congress could assess the factual premises underlying the Supreme Court's decision in *Miranda*, and, if it found that custodial interrogations were not inherently compulsive, it would then have removed the foundation of the decision thereby justifying the reinstitution of the voluntariness standard. Alternatively, the legislation could be supported on the theory that Congress has some measure of authority to define the substantive content of the self-incrimination clause. This approach relied on the Supreme Court's ruling in *Katzenbach v. Morgan*[28] in which federal legislation that invalidated New York State's voter literacy test was upheld. The test disenfranchised many New Yorkers of Puerto Rican ancestry and, even though the Court made no independent judgment as to whether it was a violation of the Fourteenth Amendment equal protection clause, it permitted Congress to reach that conclusion. In the same sense, Congress was arguably establishing the elements of a violation of the Fifth Amendment in Title II. Finally, the *Miranda* decision itself left room for Congress and the state legislatures to devise their own measures to protect Fifth Amendement rights, and Title II, especially its delineation of criteria relevant to the voluntariness standard, could be said to be Congress's formulation of an alternative to the administration of warnings.[29]

The legal arguments in support of Title II, however, were subject to serious dispute. It was not at all clear that Congress either meant to or could dispute the factual foundation of *Miranda*. The Court's conclusion that custodial interrogations were inherently coercive was not in fact investigated by Congress. The *Katzenbach v. Morgan* analogy suffered from a different defect. There the Court had permitted Congress to expand the scope and principle of equal-protection when it upheld the Voting Rights Act. Title II, in contrast, was a legislative effort to constrict the reach of the privilege against self-incrimination, and Congress's interpretive power need not necessarily have encompassed such a role. Finally, the argument that the Title II scheme of voluntariness was sufficiently protective of the Fifth Amendment right to warrant dispensing with the *Miranda* warnings was subject to challenge on the merits. Insofar as the statute reflected a return to the voluntariness standard that the Court explicitly abandoned in *Miranda*, it was in reality the substitution of a far less protective shield for the right to remain silent.

In the years since 1968, however, the Supreme Court has not had to confront the issue of the constitutionality of Title II. This stems partly from the fact that the Justice Department has not chosen to abandon the use of warnings in reliance upon the statute and also because of the fact that appellate courts have not had to rely exclusively upon Title II in upholding federal confessions.[30] Beyond that lies the additional consideration that *Miranda* has turned out to be less of an impediment to police questioning than might have been initially anticipated. Through a process of interpreting the substantive limits of the decision, the Court itself has entered into a process of slowly dismantling it, thereby making a confrontation with Title II unnecessary.

The provisions of Title II dealing with the *McNabb-Mallory* rule, unlike those directed toward *Miranda*, have been successfully applied in the federal courts. Pursuant to *McNabb-Mallory*, any statement obtained from a suspect during a period of unnecessary delay in presentment was excluded, but the basis of the principle was the Court's supervisory authority over the administration of justice in the federal courts, not the U.S. Constitution. As a result, Congress presumably had the power to reverse the decision. Title II utilized this power in provisions that required federal courts to consider unnecessary delay as only one factor in the total assessment of the voluntariness of the confession.[31] The Supreme Court has not ruled on the validity of the statute, but lower federal courts have enforced it by admitting statements held to be voluntary despite substantial delays for which there was no apparent justification.[32] As a result, the Court has not had to manipulate the definition of the term "reasonable delay" in order to undercut *McNabb-Mallory* since that has been successfully achieved by legislation. The evolutionary development of the *Miranda* doctrine, particularly the way the Court has defined the critical elements of the decision, thus stands in sharp contrast to the judicial treatment of unnecessary delay. The challenge to *Miranda* has turned into a process of judicially whittling away at the decision, thereby eliminating the need for outright reversal, while *McNabb-Mallory* has been successfully restricted by statute.

Warnings and Custody

The totality of Supreme Court decisions regulating the use of confessions by state and federal courts has been closely tied to the process of police custodial interrogation. Such questioning by law-enforcement authorities has repeatedly created both conceptual and practical difficulties with the Court straining to devise workable controls. The Court's twentieth-century confession decisions, in particular, have repeatedly confronted challenges to custodial interrogations encompassing a wide variety of alleged abuses. The *Miranda* decision itself was simply an outgrowth of an evolutionary process in which the Court, in a sense, experimented with alternative strategies to control custodial questioning, including use of the Sixth Amendment right to counsel, Fourteenth Amendment due process clause, supervisory authority over the administration of justice in the federal courts, and finally the Fifth Amendment privilege against self-incrimination. But there was no question that the Court was intent on achieving some degree of regulatory supervision. Rather, the disputes within the Court, reflected in *Miranda*, focused upon the question of whether the Court's traditionally limited supervision of the interrogation process was adequate.

The wisdom of *Miranda* in terms of its constitutional foundations and practical impact has been a matter of much controversy. The Court could not have been unaware of this likelihood but nevertheless chose to embark upon its experiment with interrogation warnings anyway. But why did it conclude that Fifth Amendment warnings must be administered before the resulting custodial confessions would be received in evidence? What was wrong with the voluntariness test as it had evolved in a long line of Court opinions? The characteristics of the custodial interrogation process and the methodology of Supreme Court review of the results suggest some answers. One overriding characteristic of police stationhouse questioning was the veil of secrecy that surrounded it. Interrogation sessions were conducted in private quarters with access limited to authorized police personnel. The defendant was alone and requests for consultation with friends, relatives and legal counsel were typically denied. The proceedings were not recorded nor filmed in their entirety, although a final confession was often taped. As a consequence of these incidents of the interrogation process, it was possible for the police to abuse their authority without the defendant's being adequately able to reconstruct and prove what actually transpired. Similarly, false claims of abuse could not be conclusively rebutted. In court, the dispute turned into a swearing contest between the defendant and the police, and the decision maker was left with little in the way of hard evidence upon which to assess voluntariness. Moreover, the case-by-case process of reviewing the admissibility of confessions was an exceedingly ineffectual way to supervise interrogation techniques given the Court's inability to hear more than a few of the vast number of confession cases. Finally, police interrogation in the surroundings of the police stationhouse constituted a high-pressure atmosphere within which the questioning process was conducted. The voluntariness standard was thus inadequate to cope with the reality the suspect had to face. The change reflected in *Miranda* responded to each of these concerns by providing for the opportunity to have counsel present during the questioning and imposing a heavy burden on the state to establish a waiver.

There is no doubt that *Miranda* itself involved a custodial interrogation fact situation, as did the companion cases in *Miranda*, and as did many of the numerous pre-*Miranda* confession cases that formed the background for the decision. The Court's holding in *Miranda*, moreover, was keyed to "custodial interrogation," which was defined as "questioning initiated by law enforcement officers after a person has been taken into custody or otherwise deprived of his freedom of action in any significant way."[33] The warnings were seen as "protective devices . . . employed to dispel the compulsion inherent in custodial surroundings."[34] To the Court, "all the principles embodied in the privilege apply to informal compulsion exerted by law enforcement officers during in-custody questioning."[35] These conditions, however, did not necessarily express the limits of *Miranda*. To the contrary, it could be argued that the custodial interrogation process was merely illustrative of one arena in which the suspect "cannot be otherwise than under compulsion to speak,"[36] and the Court intended its warning requirement to apply to all similar inherently coercive environments. If so, *Miranda* was not confined within set boundaries. On the other hand, the decision could be limited by its language exclusively to the context of custodial interrogations. Clearly, this would far more effectively confine the scope of *Miranda* to a narrower range. In the years following *Miranda* the Court was confronted with the problem of resolving this uncertainty.

In *Mathis v. United States*[37] the defendant had been convicted of knowingly filing false claims against the government for income tax refunds. Part of the evidence used to convict him was obtained by a government agent who questioned the defendant while he was incarcerated in a state prison on an unrelated charge. No *Miranda* warnings were given before the questioning, but despite that fact the defendant's efforts to have his answers suppressed were rejected by the lower courts. In support of the lower court rulings, the government argued that the questions were asked as part of a routine tax investigation in which there was no certainty of a criminal prosecution ensuing. Additionally, it was argued that the incarceration was the result of an entirely separate state offense. The Supreme Court, however, characterized the government distinctions as "too minor and shadowy"[38] to warrant a departure from *Miranda* requirements. It noted that tax investigations frequently do lead to criminal prosecution and therefore no exemption was warranted. And, it found no merit in the view that the custody the suspect was under must relate to the subject of the questioning. To the Court, such a position would have gone "against the whole purpose of the *Miranda* decision which was designed to give meaningful protection to Fifth Amendment rights."[39]

The *Mathis* decision appears to be only a modest amplification of the *Miranda* rule and as a result has received scant attention from commentators and lower courts. Yet it does provide a signal as to the *Miranda* majority's view of the scope of the warning requirement in questioning sessions. *Miranda*, as well as its precedents, dealt with the environment of police custodial interrogation and its inherently coercive character. This was the context in which the Court felt that warnings were necessary to protect the right to remain silent. It is true, of course, that incarceration stemming from a conviction on an unrelated criminal charge by another jurisdiction technically fits the *Miranda* language calling for custody or a significant deprivation of freedom, but it is not necessarily the case that such custody entails the same inherently coercive aspects. To the contrary, it may be that the pressures of interrogation in a police station by officers who have arrested a suspect and are questioning him about an offense which is the reason behind the custody *and* the interrogation are greater than those encountered in *Mathis*. That *Mathis* did not undertake an extensive analysis of the characteristics of the suspect's state prison questioning session, however, may have reflected a broader view of the Fifth Amendment and its role in regulating interrogations conducted in situations varying from the precise facts of *Miranda*. At the very least, the *Mathis* opinion clearly demonstrated an unwillingness to bind the *Miranda* rule to the exclusive confines of the police stationhouse interrogation room.

Further demonstration of *Mathis'* view of the circumstances requiring Fifth Amendment warnings was subsequently provided in the Court's 1969 *Orozco v. Texas*[40] decision. Orozco had been convicted of murder by a Texas court and sentenced to a term of from two to ten years. The facts indicated that he had been involved in an argument outside a Dallas, Texas, bar around midnight. A fight ensued, and the other participant was killed. Orozco left the scene and returned to his boardinghouse room where he went to sleep. At 4 a.m. four police officers arrived at the boardinghouse looking for the defendant. They were admitted by an unnamed woman and, upon being informed that Orozco was asleep, entered his bedroom and began to question him. The officers themselves testified that Orozco was under arrest and not free to leave from the moment he identified himself. The questioning, however, proceeded without *Miranda* warnings and produced incriminating admissions that were used at trial. Since the incident preceded the *Miranda* decision but the trial followed it, the admissions could be used as evidence only if *Miranda* was followed or did not apply. The Court, however, ruled that *Miranda* was controlling and that the warning requirement had been violated. Although the defendant was in custody, he was not questioned in a police station, but the Court did not find this factor critical. Moreover, the setting in *Orozco* was the defendant's own room, but this too did not matter. Seemingly, the fact of arrest alone was in and of itself sufficient to generate a need for warnings, a conclusion not necessarily compelled by *Miranda*, which could have been read as limited to the stationhouse environment. But, an expansive view of the opinion of the *Miranda* majority would not warrant confining warnings to police station interrogations. Simply stated, Fifth Amendment warnings were called for wherever needed to protect the right to remain silent from surroundings containing substantial inherent pressures that compelled the accused to talk.

The effort to expand *Miranda* beyond the police station interrogation room had to take into account the fact that the Fifth Amendment nowhere provides for warnings. *Miranda* responded to this by viewing the privilege as requiring the protection of warnings in all coercive environments. By 1969 this appeared to encompass all forms of incarceration as well as all postarrest questioning. *Miranda* had prepared the way for this by establishing custody as a precondition to the application of the ruling. Thus the gap between the custodial coercion of *Miranda* and that of *Mathis* and *Orozco* was minor. There was enough coercion common to all three forms of custody to warrant a similar warning requirement in each. Where no custody existed, however, either in the sense of incarceration or arrest, the same argument would be more difficult to make. The *Miranda* opinion did leave room for its application to situations involving significant deprivations of freedom short of custody, but without an indication of what was intended by that phrase. If, however, *Miranda* was viewed as a set of principles to be applied in all circumstances in which pressure could undermine a suspect's ability to assert his right to silence, that failure was not significant. Each context would simply have to be assessed for its coercive characteristics with *Miranda*, *Mathis*, and *Orozco* available as guideposts. The analysis would not be easy, but on the other hand, by looking at the substance of each questioning environment, it would avoid arbitrary limitations not relevant to the policy considerations underlying the decisions. *Mathis* and *Orozco* seemed headed in that direction by taking a broad view of the custodial features warranting Fifth Amendment warnings. But by the time the Court began to consider what kinds of significant liberty deprivations would, by analogy, require the administration of warnings, its composition and inclination to expansively interpret *Miranda* had changed.

In 1976 the Court returned to the subject of tax investigations in *Beckwith v. United States*[41] to consider the application of *Miranda* in a truly noncustodial context. The taxpayer, Beckwith, was under investigation by the Intelligence Division of the Internal Revenue Service for possible criminal tax fraud. Two agents went to interview Beckwith at a private residence where he occasionally stayed. It was early morning, and the agents were seeking to avoid embarrassing the suspect by interviewing him at his place of work. The Court's description of the circumstances suggested a relaxed atmosphere, reflected in the fact that after the agents were invited in and Beckwith entered the room, they introduced themselves and Beckwith then left to finish dressing. Moreover, the suspect was informed of the character of the investigation and given a standard IRS notification of rights advising him of his right to remain silent and that information obtained could be used against him. Finally, the notification included a provision that alerted Beckwith to his right to seek the assistance of counsel. The actual conduct of the interview that followed was described by the agents as "friendly" and "relaxed," and Beckwith stated that the agents did not "press" him.[42] Beckwith, however, sought to have the fruits of the interview suppressed for failure to comply with *Miranda*. With only Justice Brennan dissenting, the Court rejected his claim.

The argument in favor of requiring warnings in the kind of tax interview at issue in *Beckwith* involves a broad reading of the "custody" and "significant deprivation of freedom" criteria of the *Miranda* ruling. Although these phrases do indeed appear in the decision, they can be seen as only illustrative of those circumstances whose compelling surroundings require warnings to guard the exercise of Fifth Amendment rights. While not strictly custodial, the tax interview, particularly when conducted by representatives of the IRS Intelligence Division whose function is to investigate potential criminal tax violations, entails a significant psychological deprivation of freedom. The atmosphere thus becomes a coercive one in which the suspect's freedom to exercise his Fifth Amendment rights is undermined to an extent requiring the interposition of full *Miranda* warnings. To reach this conclusion, one must focus on the policy considerations of *Miranda* in providing Fifth Amendment protections in order to ensure an unimpeded free choice by the suspect in his decision to speak.

Anyone who has gone through a tax audit or been stopped for a traffic violation or been the subject of questioning by any government authority has no doubt felt pressure to respond. Can it really be said that the pressure is substantially less than traditional police questioning? Rather than assess the question on a case-by-case basis, there is merit to the view that a broad warning should be given in all such confrontations in the manner *Miranda* has clearly chosen for police station questioning. At the very least, if the conclusion is drawn that such environments are less inherently coercive than the *Miranda* context, a view not empirically supported, perhaps scaled down warnings would be appropriate. But whether *Miranda* is viewed as an all or nothing requirement or whether its warnings may be tailored to the degree of compulsion present, some effort to protect the right to remain silent should be undertaken. In contrast, the Court's analysis in *Beckwith* signaled a far more literal reading of *Miranda*. It refused to accept the fact that noncustodial settings might entail sufficiently coercive aspects to warrant applying a requirement of full *Miranda* warnings. In the Court's view, such cases should instead be analyzed solely to determine the voluntariness of the suspect's statement, *Miranda* warnings being merely a factor in that assessment rather than a prerequisite. Voluntariness therefore could be found in the absence of any warning whatsoever, and only custodial settings would then trigger *Miranda*. It is certainly true that custody appears as a criterion in *Miranda*. Whether it was intended to set the outer limit for Fifth Amendment *Miranda* warnings, despite the fact that other questioning situations may have a coercive atmosphere, is not so clear. However, that is the direction *Beckwith* unmistakably took.

The implications of this approach are more dramatically evidenced in the 1977 *Oregon v. Mathiason*[43] ruling. There police were investigating a residential burglary, and the owner of the home, when asked if she suspected anyone, mentioned Mathiason, a parolee and friend of her son. Nearly a month after the burglary, a police officer left a message at the suspect's home asking him to call. Mathiason did so, and the officer asked to meet with him. Since Mathiason expressed no preference as to location, they agreed to meet at the state patrol office, which was housed in a building with several other state agency offices and located close to Mathiason's apartment. When Mathiason arrived, he was met by the investigating officer and taken to an office. The two sat across a desk with the door closed. Mathiason was notified he was not under arrest, informed that the investigation concerned a burlary that the officer thought he was guilty of, and falsely told that his fingerprints were found at the scene. No *Miranda* warnings were administered and, indeed, the suspect was urged to speak by the officer, who indicated that truthfulness might help him with the district attorney or judge. Within five minutes Mathiason admitted having committed the burglary. *Miranda* warnings were then given and a taped confession obtained. Afterward, Mathiason was permitted to leave without being placed under arrest, the officer informing him that the case would be referred to the district attorney for possible prosecution. To the Supreme Court of Oregon, the totality of the circumstances presented a coercive environment in which *Miranda* warnings were essential to protect Fifth Amendment rights. But, to the U.S. Supreme Court, "[s]uch a non-custodial situation is not converted into one in which *Miranda* applies simply because a reviewing court concludes that, even in the absence of any formal arrest or restraint on freedom of movement, the questioning took place in a 'coercive enviroinment.'"[44] The Court added that "*Miranda* warnings are required only where there has been such a restriction on a person's freedom as to render him 'in custody.'"[45]

If the *Beckwith* opinion left any doubt that *Miranda* warnings were to be limited to custodial interrogations, *Mathiason* resolved it. Despite what must have been a highly coercive environment, including a private questioning session in a police facility, the *Mathiason* Court held the *Miranda* requirements inapplicable. *Beckwith* was hardly support for such a result, however, since it had involved low-pressure questioning of a suspect in familiar surroundings. The only coerciveness present was that inherent in the very fact of official questioning. The Court's refusal to demand protective warnings to dispel such coerciveness was far different from its view in *Mathiason* that precustody, police station questioning requires no protective warning. In reality, the coerciveness of the interrogation environment in a police facility does not vary depending on whether or not formal custody has been asserted over the suspect, and therefore protective warnings are equally necessary for all such questioning. Mathiason might well have viewed his situation as effectively an arrest or likely to lead to one, in which case the argument for applying *Miranda* is even stronger. But if the Court's formal custody rule is controlling there is even room for holding *Miranda* inapplicable when a suspect in a "voluntary" interview at a police station is told she should not leave, as one appellate court has held.[46] A dissenting judge in another appellate decision would have held that a Customs interview of a suspect following her subjection to a complete strip search was not custodial for purposes of *Miranda*.[47] That a questioning session reasonably looks like an actual or imminent arrest or is generally a coercive environment has become irrelevant as long as the setting is not technically custodial, and this despite the indistinguishable need for protective warnings.

Of further concern is the Court's apparent willingness to allow police to proceed with noncustodial questioning in the absence of any warnings. If it viewed *Mathiason* as a less coercive environment than custodial interrogation and therefore not in need of full *Miranda* warnings, scaled-down warnings could have been required tied to the level of compulsion deemed present in the particular setting. To the Court, however, any interrogation short of custodial questioning does not require a protective warning. Rather, whether or not a warning has been given, as well as the scope of the warning, are relegated to the status of factors to be assessed in determining the overall voluntariness of the statement. Moreover, the likelihood is that in the final analysis they will be treated as rather insubstantial factors. Given the fact, moreover, that the voluntariness test has traditionally been less demanding than the heavy burden of proving waiver under *Miranda*, the only conclusion that can be reached is that the decision to talk in a coercive but noncustodial setting can be less of a free choice than is required for a custodial statement, even if the pressures upon the suspect are similar. It is questionable whether *Miranda* truly contemplated such a result.

Miranda and the Grand Jury

The applicability of *Miranda* warnings, or some other variety of notification of Fifth Amendment rights, to grand jury proceedings presents issues akin to those encountered in the previous analysis of *Miranda* and custody. Concededly, the *Miranda* Court framed its warning requirement in the language of custody and significant deprivation of liberty. Moreover, the precedents as well as the cases reviewed in *Miranda* itself were instances of custodial interrogation in a private police facility with the suspect isolated from associates and familiar surroundings. Again, however, the rationale behind the decision may not have meant these criteria as arbitrary limits but rather as reflective of an inherently coercive environment in which protective devices to guard Fifth Amendment rights were essential. From this viewpoint, other situations with similar coercive characteristics would require similar protections or, if somewhat less coercive, scaled-down protective devices might be sufficient. This analysis raises the question of whether testimony before a grand jury creates an atmosphere in which the individual's ability to assert his right to remain silent is so undermined that a warning preceding the questioning is required, and if so, what kind of warning is necessary.

United States v. Mandujano[48] presented the Court with the opportunity to consider how best to guard the privilege against self-incrimination in the grand jury room. The case arose out of a grand jury investigation into narcotics traffic in San Antonio, Texas. Mandujano had been approached by an undercover agent who sought to purchase heroin. According to the agent, Mandujano agreed to obtain drugs for the agent and received $650 to make the purchase from his source. The transaction was never completed, but when called to testify before the grand jury, Mandujano denied ever discussing the sale of heroin. Prior to his testimony before the grand jury the prosecutor had informed Mandujano:

> [Y]ou are required to answer all the questions that I ask you except for the ones that you feel would tend to incriminate you . . . . You don't have to

answer questions which would incriminate you. All other questions you
have to answer openly and truthfully. And, of course if you do not answer
those [questions] truthfully, in other words if you lie about certain questions, you could possibly be charged with perjury . . . . [I]f you would like
to have a lawyer, he cannot be inside this room.[49]

Mandujano was indicted for perjury based on his testimony and ultimately
convicted.

The Supreme Court unanimously affirmed Mandujano's perjury conviction but split on fundamental aspects of the Fifth Amendment issue. Accepted without dissent was the notion that even if the defendant has the
right to refuse to answer questions entirely, he may not answer them falsely.
A series of precedents were cited in support of the principle[50] and, given the
defendant's option to refuse to answer self-incriminatory questions, no
compelling policy reasons in support of a perjury option exist. Four
members of the Court, however, went beyond the perjury issue to consider
the potential applicability of *Miranda* warnings to grand jury questioning.
Their approach was parallel to the opinions in *Beckwith* and *Mathiason*
holding *Miranda* inapplicable to noncustodial questioning by law enforcement agents. The plurality in *Mandujano* characterized the *Miranda* warnings as "aimed at the evils seen by the Court as endemic to police interrogation of a person in custody. *Miranda* addressed extrajudicial confessions or
admissions procured in a hostile, unfamiliar environment which lacked procedural safeguards."[51] Extending the warnings designed for the stationhouse interrogation to a grand jury investigation would have been, to
the plurality, an "extravagant expansion"[52] of the *Miranda* decision.

A realistic assessment of the operation of a grand jury and the pressures
its procedures create makes the conclusion that warnings are unnecessary
difficult to support. It is true that the *Miranda* opinion had observed that
"the compulsion to speak in the isolated setting of the police station may
well be greater than in courts or other official investigations, where there
are often impartial observers to guard against intimidation or trickery."[53]
However, these comments were not necessary to the decision and did not
reflect substantive analysis. Grand jury proceedings in fact do have substantially compelling aspects to them. Unlike individuals not in custody who are
free to avoid police interrogations entirely by refusing to participate,
witnesses before a grand jury are under legal compulsion to be present and
must respond to all questions that do not seek privileged matter. Moreover,
they are isolated in an unfamiliar environment and barred from having
anyone with them during the questioning. Although the grand jurors are
present, the witness will not necessarily view them as disinterested
observers. Finally, the questioning may well be intense to the point of being
overbearing, and the witness, even though possessed of the right to refuse to
answer self-incriminatory inquiries, is likely to be unaware of the

incriminatory potential of all the questions. Despite these considerations, however, the plurality concluded that *Miranda* warnings were not required and, without deciding whether any warnings need be given, nevertheless believed the warnings that were in fact related to Mandujano were more than adequate.

Even without following a *Miranda* analysis, it is possible to argue that Fifth Amendment warnings are necessary in *Mandujano*-like circumstances. This view, reflected in Justice Brennan's *Mandujano* concurrence, relies upon the fact that grand jury questioning of a putative or *de facto* defendant is not truly an interrogation of an uninvolved witness. Suspicion already exists as to the criminal involvement of such an individual; indeed, the prosecution may already have sufficient evidence to secure a conviction. The context thus is one in which the government is "acutely aware of the potentially incriminatory nature of the disclosures sought."[54] And it is arguably an undermining of the fundamental character of the adversary system to permit a putative or *de facto* defendant to be called before a grand jury and questioned about the events for which he may be indicted because this entails reliance upon the accused to provide evidence against himself rather than on independent police investigation. Since this touches upon basic interests the Fifth Amendment is designed to safeguard, a knowing and intelligent waiver, preceded by adequate warnings, should be a prerequisite. This non-*Miranda* analysis, however, was equally unpersuasive to the plurality.

Although the Fifth Amendment analysis of *Mandujano* could be set aside as dictum, the same is not true of the Court's 1977 rulings in *United States v. Washington*[55] and *United States v. Wong*.[56] The suspect in *Washington* had been called to appear before a grand jury investigating a motorcycle theft, after previously giving police a highly dubious story of how he had come to possess a stolen motorcycle. The U.S. attorney in charge had not reached a final decision as to whether to seek an indictment of Washington, although he was aware that an indictment could result if the grand jury disbelieved Washington's story. Nevertheless, Washington was not informed of this possibility. Instead he was warned:

> You have a right to remain silent. You are not required to say anything to us in this Grand Jury at any time or to answer any question. Anything you say can be used against you in Court. You have the right to talk to a lawyer for advice before we question you and have him outside the Grand Jury during any questioning. If you cannot afford a lawyer and want one a lawyer will be provided for you. If you want to answer questions now without a lawyer present you will still have the right to stop answering at any time.[57]

Washington proceeded to testify in response to the grand jury's questioning and repeated his earlier explanation of how he came to possess the stolen motorcycle. The grand jury, however, indicted him for grand larceny and receiving stolen property, and his grand jury testimony was admitted at trial over his objection.

The *Washington* fact situation presented issues apparently similar to those confronted in *Mandujano*. In the latter case, after an arguably inadequate warning, the grand jury witness perjured himself, and his grand jury testimony served as the basis of the perjury prosecution. In *Washington* the witness's testimony was used as evidence to prove the charges the grand jury was investigating when it called him as a witness. The difference, however, was of major significance since the fact that the testimony was used at the theft trial in *Washington* precluded utilization of the perjury exception. It was not enough therefore to simply conclude, as in *Mandujano*, that the witness had chosen a course of conduct that was not sanctioned, and thus his lies could be used to convict him of perjury. To establish admissibility in *Washington*, it had to be demonstrated that the testimony was not compelled in violation of the Fifth Amendment. One way to demonstrate this was by looking to the warnings that preceded the questioning, and it was clear that Washington was accorded far more notification than Mandujano received. Moreover, the tenor of the prosecutor's statement in *Washington* placed far more stress on the right to remain silent than the words used by the *Mandujano* prosecutor. The latter emphasized the obligation to answer and downplayed the right to counsel, thus providing more discouragement than support for a suspect seeking to exercise his right to remain silent. In short, even without the *Mandujano* decision, it would have been possible to conclude that Washington testified before the grand jury without compulsion and thus his statements could be used against him.

Both the district court and court of appeals, however, had suppressed Washington's testimony. The district court found that the witness had not made a knowing and intelligent waiver of his Fifth Amendment rights. In particular, it noted the lack of an inquiry into the suspect's educational background and his awareness of the consequences of waiver. The court of appeals expressed concern that Washington was not informed that he was a potential defendant and did not receive his warnings until immediately before the questioning began. Neither of these arguments proved convincing to the seven-member *Washington* majority. Instead, the Court returned to the idea that the grand jury room is not a coercive setting such as that upon which *Miranda* was based. It might constitute an "atmosphere conducive to truthtelling,"[58] but in the Court's view that did not run afoul of the Fifth Amendment. But in so ruling, the Court ignored the existence of grand jury pressure to talk in the first instance which constitutes the core of the Fifth Amendment problem, as opposed to pressure to tell the truth *after* the decision to talk has been made. Again, however, the Court did not rule that warnings could be dispensed with entirely since substantial warnings were given. Rather, its conclusion was that there was no constitutional violation in using testimony obtained by a grand jury after the witness had received the warnings Washington was given. But, by referring to the pre-*Miranda* voluntariness test as the controlling standard, and given the fact that warnings had never been mandated under that approach, the Court may have been hinting that no preconditions to grand jury testimony were necesssary.

United States v. Wong, decided along with *Washington*, was treated by the Court as if the warnings had been misunderstood by the witness before testifying. In fact, Rose Wong, the witness, had come to the United States from China and, though receiving some education in San Francisco, nevertheless understood English poorly. The prosecutor informed her of her Fifth Amendment rights, but she did not understand the warning and believed, to the contrary, that she was obligated to answer every question, even those that were self-incriminatory. From her perspective the choice she faced was the classic cruel trilemma of self-accusation, perjury, or contempt; and Wong chose perjury, for which she was indicted. A unanimous Court, relying upon *United States v. Mandujano*, invoked the perjury exception and ruled that her grand jury testimony was admissible in the subsequent perjury trial. The fact that the witness did not believe she had the right to remain silent, unlike Mandujano, was found not controlling; the Fifth Amendment bars perjury even if the option of silence is thought by the individual to be unavailable.

The only question left to resolve after the Supreme Court's three recent decisions on the necessity of warning grand jury witnesses is whether in the absence of any warning whatsoever the witness's testimony may be used against him in a trial on the charges that were the subject of the grand jury investigation. Here *Washington* would not be controlling since the prosecutor did indeed give Washington substantial warnings. Similarly, the perjury exception would not apply since, unlike *Mandujano* and *Wong*, the state is not prosecuting the perjury charge.[59] Nevertheless, it seems unlikely that the Supreme Court would mandate Fifth Amendment warnings in the grand jury setting. Rather, as one lower court has already ruled,[60] the Supreme Court appears headed toward a return to the voluntariness test in which warnings are but one among a number of factors. This would merely be a continuation of the process of confining the *Miranda* rationale to police stationhouse interrogations and further rejection of the argument that the type of warning should be geared to the particular setting of the questioning. The latter view would permit scaled-down warnings to grand jury witnesses, but the Court seems to be writing off the compulsion of the grand jury room as a sufficient source of coercion to warrant any protective devices to guard the grand jury witness's privilege against self-incrimination.

It is worth noting before leaving this subject that there have been substantial efforts to counteract the Supreme Court's restrictive view of the need for grand jury witness warnings. Among other things, the American Bar Association has adopted recommended standards calling for warnings to be administered prior to a witness testifying.[61] Congress, moreover, has been considering a variety of legislative proposals to deal with this and other alleged grand jury abuses.[62] It is also interesting to note that prevailing practice, at least in the federal system, has been to notify a witness of both his Fifth Amendment rights and his status as a target of the grand jury investigation. This was revealed in litigation in the Second Circuit Court of Appeals in which a perjury indictment secured by a Justice Department strike force attorney was dismissed for failure to adequately warn a target witness, a practice that U.S. attorneys regularly engage in. The district court judge relied on his supervisory power in dismissing the charges rather than on specific constitutional authority. The Supreme Court agreed to review the decision but subsequently dismissed its writ of certiorari as improvidently granted.[63] Thus it is not at all certain that the Supreme Court would permit lower federal courts to impose Fifth Amendment warning obligations upon the grand jury system on nonconstitutional grounds. If the current approach is to change in the near future, reform is more likely to have to come from the executive and legislative branches.

Warnings: Doing It Wrong and Doing It Again

Once a confession or incriminating statement has been made, it may serve a variety of criminal law purposes, including most directly a role as substantive evidence tending to prove the guilt of the accused. Beyond that, however, such statements may also be used to impeach the credibility of a witness whose trial testimony varies from his prior declarations. The holding in *Miranda* clearly established that statements obtained in violation of its dictates would be excluded as substantive evidence of guilt. Whatever implications the decision and language might have had for the impeachment use of pretrial statements was strictly speaking only dicta. Moreover, precedent in Fourth Amendment decisions of the Supreme Court seemingly suggested some room for a distinction between direct and impeachment use of illegally obtained evidence. In *Walder v. United States*,[64] decided by the Supreme Court in 1954, the defendant had been charged with illegal narcotics transactions and took the witness stand in his own defense. He not only denied the charges against him but also, on direct examination by his own attorney, volunteered the further claim that he had never possessed narcotics. In fact, two years earlier he had been charged with the illegal possession of heroin, but the case had been dismissed because the search and seizure through which the heroin was obtained was unconstitutional, thus mandating its exclusion. The judge at Walder's trial, however, allowed the government to establish prior illegal drug possession, even though this meant the use of illegally obtained evidence, but instructed the jury that it could be used only for the limited purpose of impeaching the defendant's credibility. The Supreme Court approved the trial judge's action, observing that while "the Government cannot make an affirmative use of evidence unlawfully obtained," that does not mean that "the defendant can turn the illegal method by which evidence in the Government's possession was obtained to his own advantage, and provide himself with a shield against contradiction of his untruths."[65]

The post-*Miranda* Fifth Amendment situation comparable to *Walder* would involve an unwarned defendant who has made incriminating statements not directly bearing on the immediate charges facing him and who at trial volunteers testimony on direct examination contrary to that contained in his pretrial declaration. The policy of allowing the impeachment use of such a statement in order to prevent the defendant from taking advantage of the government's illegality to hide his perjury would apply. In *Harris v. New York*,[66] however, critical differences were present. In particular, the defendant did not volunteer any "sweeping claim"[67] denying prior criminal activity, and thus there was no collateral matter introduced by the defendant for the state to impeach. Rather, the government used a statement obtained from the defendant without a complete warning to impeach his denial of guilt on the charges for which he was being tried. The situation was not identical to *Walder*, but that did not prevent the Court from reaching the same result.

The justification for the Court's *Harris* decision rested upon its view of the exclusionary rule as a deterrent device; the reason why unconstitutionally obtained evidence is suppressed is to discourage police illegality. The Court maintained that this goal was accomplished by the suppression of the statement as direct evidence of guilt. An officer would not violate *Miranda* to obtain an impeachment statement because what he really wants is an admission that will contribute to the defendant's conviction. Thus since exclusion of the statement for impeachment purposes would not further deter *Miranda* violations, there was no need to invoke the exclusionary rule when the statement was offered as impeachment evidence. But, the Court's deterrence theory was not entirely convincing. Police might very well conclude that holding impeachment evidence would deter the defendant from testifying in his own defense. And if a statement could not be obtained in conformance with *Miranda* and thus available to prove guilt, keeping the defendant off the witness stand or being able to impeach him might be seen as sufficient to warrant the violation. Since the police would have the benefit of the possible impeachment use of an illegally obtained statement, it is more than merely conceivable that they would in fact not be deterred from violating *Miranda*. The *Harris* majority, however, refused to accept this analysis. Moreover, it gave no consideration whatsoever to the view that judicial integrity might be adversely affected if use was made of unconstitutionally acquired evidence, except in the narrow circumstance of a *Walder*-type context, and this despite the fact that Supreme Court precedent had suggested judicial integrity as one of the factors behind the exclusionary rule.[68]

A close look at the *Miranda* error committed by the police in *Harris* reveals a failure to inform the suspect of his right to appointed counsel. The logic of the Court's deterrence theory was that police would not be significantly induced to dispense with this warning in order to secure impeachment evidence when the possibility also existed that if they gave the required warning they might wind up with evidence that could also be used to prove the state's case in chief. But, if the police do give the proper warnings, the suspect in response may either assert or waive his rights. *Miranda* tells us that a complete warning followed by a valid waiver authorizes the prosecutor to use any resulting statements. But if the suspect asserts his *Miranda* rights, the appropriate police response is to cease questioning. Certainly, if the law provides for a potential benefit when the assertion of *Miranda* rights is not respected, deterrence of such violations is undercut. Yet the Court followed its ruling in *Harris* with a 1975 decision, *Oregon v. Hass*,[69] in which the state was permitted to make impeachment use of a statement secured from a fully warned suspect whose demand for counsel was not complied with. As a result of the decision, a police officer confronted with a suspect who invokes his *Miranda* rights will obtain no evidence if he respects the assertion. If he does not, however, he may be able to secure impeachment evidence. With nothing to lose and something to gain from ignoring *Miranda*, such violations are encouraged, a result far more serious than merely lessening the deterrent effect of the exclusionary rule that was the arguable limit of *Harris*.

Harris and *Hass* taken together constitute a virtually total impeachment exception to *Miranda*. Both assume that *Miranda* is a procedural requirement designed to protect Fifth Amendment rights but accept that a statement secured in violation of *Miranda* may nevertheless still be voluntary. And as long as the voluntariness standard is satisfied, a conclusion reached in both *Harris* and *Hass*, the use of a statement obtained in violation of *Miranda* for impeachment purposes is proper. Only if the statement is involuntary is its impeachment use barred.[70] The notion that *Miranda* was meant to upgrade the level of voluntariness required for the admission of confessions has thus been rejected. More specific support for this conclusion arises from *Michigan v. Tucker*[71] in which a state witness was identified as a result of a pretrial interrogation of the defendant following inadequate warnings. The Court noted in upholding the admissibility of the witness's testimony that the violation did not infringe on the defendant's "constitutional privilege against compulsory self-incrimination, but departed only from the prophylactic standards laid down by this Court in *Miranda* to safeguard that privilege."[72] And as further testament to the lowered status of *Miranda* warnings, the Court prohibited the use of postwarning silence to impeach a defendant's trial testimony. But rather than rule that the Fifth Amendment privilege against self-incrimination barred the adverse use of such silence, the Court held that this followed instead from the due process clause.[73] The privilege against self-incrimination as reflected in *Miranda* was not forceful enough by itself to lead to this result given the merely procedural character of the warning obligation.

Police, however, may find it difficult to violate *Miranda* and produce only impeachment evidence as a result of the Court's willingness to tolerate renewed questioning after *Miranda* rights have been asserted. *Miranda* itself did not conclusively resolve the question of how police should respond when, after being warned, a suspect indicates either that he wishes to consult with an attorney or refuses to answer police questions. Several options are concededly present including at the extremes the choices of either barring further interrogation once *Miranda* rights are asserted or merely requiring an instantaneous cessation of the interrogation before questioning could be renewed. The latter choice, of course, would make a total mockery of *Miranda* and would be tantamount to its overruling. But, there is much to support the alternative view that a refusal to waive *Miranda* rights should bar resumption of the questioning. Initially, there is language in the *Miranda* opinion itself strongly suggesting that renewed questioning is prohibited. To the *Miranda* Court it was clear that if "the individual indicates in any manner, at any time prior to or during questioning, that he wishes to remain silent, the interrogation must cease."[74] Logically, an assertion of the right to counsel should also lead to the cessation of questioning, at least until an attorney has consulted with the suspect. Moreover, as a matter of policy the logic of the *Miranda* decision, particularly its concern for the effect of the coercive police custodial environment on a suspect's Fifth Amendment rights, is strongly supportive of a ban against renewed questioning once the individual has refused to waive his privilege against self-incrimination. In such circumstances, it is just as likely that the *Miranda* waiver would be the product of the coercive environment rather than the individual's free choice. To the Court, however, the appropriate solution was to permit the police to seek a *Miranda* waiver after a prior rejection subject to some rather vague limiting conditions.

The setting for this ruling was the Court's 1975 decision in *Michigan v. Mosley.*[75] As a result of an anonymous tip, the suspect, Richard Mosley, had been arrested by Detroit police in connection with two robberies. After being warned, he refused to answer questions about the robberies but did not request a lawyer. The questioning ceased and Mosley was placed in a cell. Some time later he was moved to a different floor of the police building and, after receiving another *Miranda* warning, he was questioned about an unrelated homicide. This interrogation produced incriminating admissions that were used at trial over the defendant's objection. In upholding the admission of the statements, the Court set as the governing standard for renewed questioning after a suspect had indicated his desire to remain silent the test of whether the defendant's "right to cut off questioning" had been "scrupulously honored."[76] In its view, conduct meeting that standard was a sufficient check against the effects of the inherent compulsion of police custodial interrogation. Critical events in *Mosley* satisfying the test were, for the Court, the elapse of over two hours before questioning was renewed, repeat of the *Miranda* warnings, and the fact that the questioning was resumed in a different location and on an unrelated offense. The decision, however, left enough room for other courts to permit renewed questioning in the absence of any one of the enumerated factors.[77] It was a totality of the circumstances test of the kind that had formerly governed the entire question of confession admissibility and which *Miranda* sought to replace with a uniform standard.

Voluntariness and Waiver: The Remaining Criteria

One cannot predict with certainty what the future holds for confession law. *Miranda* warnings, or procedural devices akin to them, may be expanded to cover more interrogation situations or they may be eliminated entirely. We may find ourselves reverting to traditional standards in the assessment of confession admissibility or the courts may break new ground in supervising pretrial interrogations. For the time being, however, the law appears to have evolved into a bifurcated system for reviewing the evidentiary products of pretrial questioning. Those statements secured under circumstances covered by *Miranda* are apparently still governed by the obligation to administer a Fifth Amendment warning, and require a valid waiver of the rights encompassed in the warning as a precondition to the statement's admissibility. After a valid waiver has been obtained, it is still necessary for the statement to be voluntary, but normally a valid waiver of *Miranda* rights will be sufficient to establish the voluntariness of subsequent statements. In contrast, circumstances not controlled by *Miranda*, such as noncustodial questioning and the impeachment use of statements obtained in a custodial interrogation, need only satisfy the voluntariness standard. The twin concepts of waiver and voluntariness have thus become the governing standards of contemporary confession law.

To the extent that the contours of the voluntariness standard must be established, it is of course possible to refer to pre-*Miranda-Escobedo* case law. Indeed, nearly one hunded years of Supreme Court decisions are available for this purpose. These older cases, however, provide only the most general guidelines. They reflect a totality of the circumstances test, which, although highlighting relevant criteria, nevertheless fails to provide the guidance necessary to ensure consistent decisions. Moreover, the early voluntariness cases were predominantly Fourteenth Amendment due process decisions and, while voluntariness may be the standard for Fifth Amendment rulings as well, perhaps application of the privilege should make the standard more demanding. In fact, the mere passage of time could lead to this result.

In the years since *Miranda*, however, the Supreme Court has taken advantage of a number of opportunities to elaborate on the voluntariness standard. This effort has not entirely resolved the question of whether the Fifth or Fourteenth Amendment is controlling, nor has it added much to already existing law. Nevertheless, a few signals are contained in the Court's opinions. Most directly addressed by the Court has been the voluntariness of statements obtained after sustained periods of detention and incommunicado interrogation. In *Davis v. North Carolina*,[78] decided one week after *Miranda* but not governed by it since the trial at issue occurred before the *Miranda* ruling was handed down, the Court confronted a confession obtained after sixteen days of intermittent interrogation. The case also revealed the lack of an adequate warning of rights and a somewhat limited diet for the defendant during his confinement, but the major factor underlying the Court's ruling that the statement was involuntary seemed to be the prolonged detention. Even without intensive grilling, the situation suggested an overbearing of the suspect's will rather than a voluntary decision to confess. Similarly, in *Brooks v. Florida*[79] the defendant confessed to involvement in a prison riot after fifteen days of confinement in a punishment cell on a reduced diet. Again, although other factors were present, the substantial period of punitive separation from the general prison population loomed as the primary consideration leading the Court to conclude that the confession was involuntary. Sustained questioning of over a day's duration also contributed to findings of involuntariness in *Clewis v. Texas*[80] and *Darwin v. Connecticut*.[81] The cases reflected no effort to set time limits, but when matched against *Boulden v. Holman*[82] in which the Court upheld the voluntariness of a confession secured after three hours of questioning, it seemed clear that the tradition of holding suspects beyond a fairly restricted period of time to secure statements was unlikely to be tolerated in the future.

Prolonged detention had, of course, always been a major concern under the pre-*Miranda-Escobedo* voluntariness standard. Nevertheless, confessions obtained after substantial periods of confinement were readily admitted. The Court's involuntariness rulings, instead, tended to rely heavily upon the character of the interrogation process and, in later years, the denial of counsel. Given the *Miranda* decision, however, it is understandable that detention took on increased significance in assessing voluntariness. The assumption of *Miranda* was, after all, that custodial interrogation was an inherently coercive process sufficient to warrant special protective warnings. The inherent coerciveness, however, also applied to the voluntariness of the responses police were able to elicit in the absence of warnings. And, the longer the detention lasted without the dissipating effect of *Miranda* warnings, the more likely it was that the statement was the result of the coerciveness and thus involuntary. *Miranda's* attention to the effects of custodial interrogation, therefore, not only resulted in the imposition of a warning requirement but also increased the significance of detention for purposes of determining a statement's voluntariness. But note must also be taken of the rather limited implications of the new concern for confessions produced after substantial confinement. Even though post-*Miranda* opinions suggested a more rigorous review under the voluntariness standard, the fact of the matter was that post-*Miranda* questioning of individuals who had been detained also had to meet the *Miranda* warning requirement. Questions about the admissibility of such statements were far more likely to revolve around the adequacy of the *Miranda* waiver rather than the voluntariness of the statement.

In a 1978 opinion, *Mincey v. Arizona*,[83] the Court had an opportunity to consider the voluntariness of a confession based on more than just the detention issue. Mincey, a suspect in a drug investigation, was involved in a shoot-out in which he was injured and a police officer was killed. He was immediately taken to the hospital where examination revealed a hip wound which had damaged his sciatic nerve and caused partial paralysis. He was placed in intensive care with tubes inserted into his nose, throat, and bladder, and given various drugs. While in this condition he was visited by a police officer for questioning. He was unable to talk and had to write down his answers, but he was notified that he was under arrest and given *Miranda* warnings before the questioning began. The officer did not stop the interrogation when Mincey repeatedly asked for an attorney, thus violating *Miranda*, but the state sought to use his answers for impeachment purposes. The Supreme Court, however, held the statements involuntary and inadmissible for any purpose, relying on Mincey's repeated requests for counsel and his "debilitated and helpless condition."[84] Significantly, the decision was based upon the due process clause, not the privilege against self-incrimination. However, the opinion was not all that instructive in isolating the basis of the decision. Refusal to provide counsel and the rather extreme infirmity were certainly relevant factors, but it is impossible to tell whether either one was sufficient in and of itself to support the decision. The ruling was well in line with the Court's tradition of assessing voluntariness on the basis of the "characteristics of the accused and the details of the interrogation" including "the youth of the suspect, . . . his lack of education, . . . low intelligence, . . . lack of any advice to the accused of his constitutional rights, . . . the length of detention, . . . the repeated and prolonged nature of the questioning, . . . and the use of physical punishment such as the deprivation of food or sleep."[85] The extreme facts of *Mincey* make it hard to tell whether the old voluntariness standard had changed.

Since voluntariness is determined by the totality of the circumstances, the characteristics of both the individual questioned and the interrogation process must be evaluated. But, exactly what is the assessment looking for? To say that the statement must have been voluntarily made in actuality confronts the legal system with a basic philosophical problem, the need to establish the relationship of the authority of the state to the rights of the individual. For example, if one took the concept of voluntariness in its purest form, only statements that were entirely the product of the individual's free will would be admitted. Police interrogation might have to be prohibited since it could arguably undercut the individual's ability to reach a decision free from external pressure. Similarly, attention would have to be given to nonpolice influences that might undercut the individual's free will such as family pressure and legal advice from an attorney. Ultimately, the standard would raise questions as to whether any statement was truly voluntary as long as the accumulated influences of an individual's life contributed to his decision to confess.

Although the American legal system has traditionally been careful about its reliance upon confessions, it has never suggested that only statements that are voluntary in the purest sense of the word meet legal standards. To do so would place greater emphasis upon the acquisition of evidence by other means and establish the primacy of the individual's right not to assist the state in securing his own conviction. Although these are rational objectives to pursue, their attainment would come at a significant cost to society. First, an extreme view of voluntariness would deprive the courts of a source of evidence that would probably be reliable and might often be critical in determining guilt. There is of course a legitimate state interest in convicting the guilty, and the value of doctrines that undercut that goal should be substantial before convictions are made more difficult. Second, any rule that allegedly reaffirms the sovereignty of the individual by barring the use of all but a small number of confessions may well force the state to utilize other techniques of investigation that are even more distasteful. It is true that searches and seizures, electronic surveillance, and use of undercover agents do not involve state authority exerted on the accused to acquire incriminating evidence from him in the same sense as is entailed in the process of securing an incriminating admission by interrogation. But the extent to which there are subtle differences between the techniques does not necessarily reflect meaningful distinctions. All such techniques may equally or more severely undermine individual freedom, and as a result the goal of placing greater reliance upon them should be cautiously pursued.

Aside from the policy considerations that suggest that voluntariness in its purest form may not be an appropriate standard for confessions, the applicable legal background leads to the same conclusion. If voluntariness is judged under Fourteenth Amendment due process principles, it need merely meet criteria of fundamental fairness, a not particularly demanding standard that would readily accept confessions that are less than exclusively the product of the individual's free will. The privilege against self-incrimination of the Fifth Amendment does not necessarily call for a different result. The language of the Fifth Amendment speaks in terms of a prohibition against being "compelled" to incriminate oneself and undoubtedly bars physical as well as coercive psychological pressures in the interrogation process. The essence of the concept of compulsion suggests that the privilege against self-incrimination is a protection against being forced to assist the state in securing one's own conviction. But a prohibition against the use of any form of force in questioning a suspect does not by itself require the establishment of a pure free-will standard to govern confessions. Certainly, confessions that are the product of an individual's free will are sufficient, but there is a range between the extremes of prohibited compulsion and free will that is not readily classifiable. If compulsion is taken to mean force, lesser pressures might then be permissible. On the other hand, reliance upon a free-will standard would presumably preclude any pressure, however slight.

The use of deception in the interrogation process highlights the philosophical problems inherent in choosing the standard of voluntariness confessions must meet. When police mislead a suspect and thus place him in a situation where he must decide whether to answer questions with only a false picture of the surrounding circumstances to guide him, the exercise of his individual free will has been substantially interfered with. To allow deception to be practiced in such a manner would make a mockery of the free-will standard; indeed, it would prevent individual decision making from being furthered by virtue of the external influences deception brings to bear upon the suspect. Yet such techniques are arguably outside the range of the force barred by the compulsion language of the Fifth Amendment. They may alter the reality within which the suspect must reach his decision of whether or not to talk and may even convey to him a picture of surrounding circumstances that incorrectly influences his judgment, but the pressure is internal to him. The interrogators merely create the environment in which the suspect compels himself to confess and do not thereby forcibly remove the option of remaining silent. In *Frazier v. Cupp*,[86] a post-*Miranda* decision, the Supreme Court implicitly adopted this line of reasoning. There, during the interrogation of the suspect, police falsely told him that the alibi witness he named had in fact confessed to participation in the homicide then under police investigation. To the Court the misrepresentations were, "while relevant, insufficient . . . to make this otherwise voluntary confession inadmissible."[87]

If voluntariness supports the admissibility of a confession obtained after an outright lie, undoubtedly other police interrogation techniques would be deemed constitutionally permissible. Failure to correct a suspect's misunderstanding, for example, should not undercut the voluntariness of a confession if the police are permitted to affirmatively create a misunderstanding.[88] Traditionally, promises of benefit have been held in violation of the voluntariness standard, but *Frazier* may indicate a new tolerance in this area.[89] The decision also implicitly supports at least some persuasion to secure a confession since the police feigned sympathy with the suspect in *Frazier* as part of their interrogation procedure without Court disapproval.[90] Presumably, voluntariness still requires that the suspect have sufficient competence to intelligently decide whether or not to respond to police questions.[91] Although the Supreme Court has not ruled on this issue, lower-court decisions have frequently upheld confessions despite significant competence questions raised by defendants who were allegedly intoxicated or under the influence of drugs during their interrogations.[92] Overall, the voluntariness standard in the post-*Miranda* period does not appear to be a barrier to the police interrogation process except with respect to the issue of prolonged detention. That, however, is the area where the *Miranda* warnings are themselves applicable. If they are administered and properly waived, police may resort to strategems to secure incriminating admissions with the waiver ensuring that the decision to respond is in fact the defendant's own choice. The persuasion and trickery that follow merely ensure that what the defendant relates is the truth. Therefore, to assess the effectiveness of contemporary confession standards, we must look at *Miranda* warnings in the situations in which they are required. If police conduct a custodial interrogation, a difficult question in itself given recent views as to what constitutes an interrogation,[93] the waiver doctrine and its administration in turn determine how protective a principle *Miranda* truly is.

Given the critical significance of waiver principles to the goals of *Miranda*, it is surprising that the Supreme Court has not delineated much of the content of the doctrine. In *Miranda* itself the Court did note that the state has a heavy burden to establish waiver and that the mere fact that an individual confesses after being given a warning is insufficient to meet the standard. Beyond that, little is clear. What constitutes a knowing and intelligent waiver of *Miranda*? If the standard is the same as that underlying the voluntariness doctrine, police have room to employ a variety of their special techniques to secure a waiver. This, however, is unlikely since the *Miranda* Court specifically observed that "any evidence that the accused was threatened, tricked or cajoled into a waiver will, of course, show that the defendant did not voluntarily waive his privilege."[94] Voluntariness of a waiver is thus a different and more demanding standard than the requirement that confessions be voluntary.

Presumably, the kind of trickery that the Court tolerated in *Frazier v. Cupp* would invalidate a *Miranda* waiver. The waiver issue is not whether prohibited force has been employed but rather a search for a knowing and intelligent decision to give up the right to remain silent and the right to the presence of counsel. Painting a false picture of the surrounding circumstances is totally inconsistent with the premises underlying the concept of waiver, even though it may not be a prohibited tactic once a valid waiver has been secured. Threats, of course, are barred under the voluntariness standard as well as in waiver law. And the same is true for cajolery if that means intense and relentless pressure. Having established these limited contours for a valid *Miranda* waiver, everything else is up in the air, and we are left with substantial uncertainties in a number of areas. In particular, what kind of assessment must be made of the competence of an individual to execute a *Miranda* waiver and what procedures must police employ in the process?[95] These are not rigorously reviewed in weighing voluntariness, but that need not be binding in ruling on the validity of a waiver. And of equal concern is the question of whether persuasion short of cajolery may be used to obtain a waiver.[96] Voluntariness cases have traditionally tolerated substantial encouragement in the interrogation process, but it is clear that they were not pursuing a free-will standard. This issue also has not been finally resolved under *Miranda*.

Until 1979 the closest *Miranda* waiver decision from the Supreme Court was its 1977 ruling in *Brewer v. Williams*.[97] Williams had been charged with murder and arraigned, but it was necessary for him to be transported to the city in which the crime had occurred. He was advised by his attorney not to answer police questions, and police were instructed not to conduct an interrogation. Nevertheless, during the drive an officer who knew of Williams's deep religious convictions and prior status as a mental patient stressed to him the need for a decent Christian burial for the as yet undiscovered remains of the victim, observing that if the body was exposed, it would be covered by the snow, and urging that he "think about it."[98] To the Court this was a violation of the Sixth Amendment right to counsel. Building upon *Massiah v. United States*[99] in which the Sixth Amendment was held to have been violated by an informant's surreptitious monitoring of his conversation with an already indicted defendant, the Court ruled that the same restrictions apply to the direct interrogation of a suspect after arraignment. The state courts, however, had ruled that the totality of the circumstances surrounding the confession constituted a valid Sixth Amendment waiver. But, the Supreme Court rejected this test in favor of the view that the state must show "an intentional relinquishment or abandonment of a known right or privilege,"[100] with the "courts indulg[ing] in every reasonable presumption against waiver."[101] The standard was not met because despite evidence of the defendant's awareness of his rights, particularly the fact that he had received several *Miranda* warnings, there was no proof of relinquishment other than his confession.

Since prearraignment interrogations are governed by the Fifth rather than the Sixth Amendment, *Brewer* left room for less demanding *Miranda* waiver standards to be framed. Such a result, however, seems questionable. *Miranda's* delineation of a heavy waiver burden and its citation of the same precedents as *Brewer*, along with the equally important stature of both rights, strongly supports the view that the waiver standard is equivalent in both instances.[102] That, however, does not tell us what the exact flaw in *Brewer* was. If the problem was the lack of a specific waiver prior to the confession, the difficulty could be easily remedied in most cases. Similarly, if the defect was the police failure to observe the attorney's instructions not to question his client, which they themselves had agreed to follow, they needed merely to decline such an agreement. These are minor points compared to the heart of the problem, the question of whether a suspect may be persuaded to waive his rights. In *Brewer* the defendant had indicated his desire to remain silent until he reached the destination and could consult with his attorney, but police played on his sympathies to secure a confession. Conceivably, the Court might have approved of the tactics had an explicit waiver been secured. Such an approach would then have required that a line of permissible persuasion be established. Or the Court might have mandated that any persuasion beyond a simple inquiry as to the suspect's willingness to waive be prohibited.

The effort to accommodate waiver and persuasion is an exceedingly difficult undertaking, one that brings us back to the conflict between interrogation protections as a means of ensuring individual free will versus the view that the applicable doctrines need merely preclude undue pressures. While the free-will standard may have lost out in the assessment of the voluntariness of a confession, it is the more rational theory upon which to judge waiver. The doctrine of waiver seeks to determine if an individual is willing to forgo a right or privilege, an orientation far different from an evaluation of whether there has been impermissible compulsion in the obtaining of a confession. The waiver focus is on the rights being given up, and the Court has traditionally been very cautious when rights are abandoned. Still, however, the fact that waiver does look to the individual's freedom in reaching his decision does not warrant concluding that no external factor may impinge on his choice. Surely, there is enough room to ask a suspect if he is willing to waive. But is there room for more? Since each additional step may substantially influence the individual's decision, great care must be exercised. As a result, if the Court does go beyond permitting the simple request for a waiver, against which a strong case can be made, the limit should be the relaying of objective facts that constitute admissible evidence against the defendant.[103] Arguably, this merely ensures a more informed judgment; the tactics in *Brewer* should not be tolerated.

Although the Fifth Amendment waiver lessons of *Brewer v. Williams* are uncertain, the Supreme Court did clearly resolve at least one *Miranda* waiver issue in its 1979 *North Carolina v. Butler* decision.[104] The North Carolina Supreme Court had held that a suspect's purported waiver of his *Miranda* rights was invalid where he had refused to execute a written waiver and had not specifically waived his rights orally. Instead, the North Carolina Supreme Court imposed a requirement that the *Miranda* waiver be explicit, not one derived from the totality of the circumstances. This was a result perhaps hinted at in *Brewer*, as well as an approach sensitive to the *Miranda* Court's concern for the inherently coercive pressures of custody. Nevertheless, the *Butler* majority was content with permitting lower courts to find a valid waiver in the conduct of the suspect, his words, and inferences from both. Even though it would be a relatively simple matter for the police to secure an explicit answer to a waiver request and despite the fact that allowing courts to rely upon implicit waivers will undoubtedly lead to confusing and unpredictable decisions, the Court did not feel that a per se rule mandating explicit waivers was necessary. Consequently, it will take years of case law development to establish what circumstances will justify a waiver finding, although the lines can never be precise, and in the process substantially more leeway has been given to police to conduct interrogations as a result of being free from the restraint of having to secure an explicit waiver of *Miranda*.

The Supreme Court has also recently upheld the validity of a waiver secured from a juvenile under rather unusual circumstances. In *Fare v. Michael C.*[105] a youth had been apprehended in connection with a homicide and brought to the police station for questioning. After receiving a *Miranda* warning, he asked if he could have his probation officer present. He declined the offer of an attorney, fearing that the police might trick him by sending in a policeman but falsely identifying him as a lawyer. The Court recognized that *Miranda* called for police questioning to cease after a suspect indicated either that he wished to exercise his right to remain silent or have an attorney present. It refused, however, to treat a juvenile's request for the presence of his probation officer as a per se invocation of either of those rights. In the Court's view, the probation officer's role was not sufficiently akin to the protective duties of a lawyer to warrant a pro-phylactic rule that would interfere with otherwise legitimate police question-ing. That the suspect was a juvenile and therefore in need of special protec-tion and the fact that he requested the presence of perhaps the only individual he trusted, criteria of significance to the four dissenters, were not adequate to persuade the majority of the need for any variation from the traditional totality of the circumstances test for assessing the validity of the waiver. Since Michael C.'s waiver was explicit and since he was sixteen years of age and had prior experience with the juvenile court, was of adequate in-telligence to understand what he was doing and was not subjected to coer-cive interrogation techniques, the Court concluded that the state's heavy burden of proving a voluntary and knowing waiver had been met.

Even under a totality of the circumstances test, which permits implicit waivers, the law must still account for the state of mind of the accused at the time he chooses to forgo his *Miranda* rights. Lower-court case law has not been particularly concerned with the intellectual, psychological, and physical characteristics of the accused in reviewing *Miranda* waivers.[106] Yet if the accused's personal situation undercuts his capacity to make a choice, it is difficult to see how the waiver decision can be intelligent and knowing. If a suspect does not realize the implications of his waiver and the source is an infirmity affecting his capacity, accepting a waiver from him amounts to authorizing police to take advantage of the weakest individuals they ap-prehend. This does not mean that waivers can never be secured in such cases but rather suggests a more demanding standard of proof for the state to meet whenever a capacity question arises. The *Miranda* warning and waiver, which may normally be adequate, cannot, in the context of the in-terrogation of an individual whose capacities are impaired, satisfy the knowing and intelligent standard. This may mean, for example, a more detailed explanation of *Miranda* rights in appropriate cases in lieu of the rather sterile warning prescribed by the Court. Or it may mean waiting until a temporary physical condition has been alleviated before an effort to secure a waiver is made. If no special care is taken, the waiver doctrine may find itself not much more effective than the voluntariness standard.

It is critical that the issue of waiver be sensitively evaluated. *Miranda*, after all, has been narrowly circumscribed by the Supreme Court. In its rather restricted domain of custodial interrogation, the arena the Court has judged to be in need of special protection, waiver stands as the only mean-ingful shield available to the suspect. There is a real risk that the inherent coercion of custody, which in pre-*Miranda* days led to involuntary confes-sions, will now lead to involuntary waivers. Moreover, if judicial analysis is not sufficiently precise, courts may well judge the validity of *Miranda* waivers on the basis of standards applicable to the issue of confession voluntariness. If the courts emasculate the heavy burden requirement of proving waiver dictated by *Miranda*, they will have in the process emasculated *Miranda* as well. Guarding against this requires vigilance in the assessment of police requests for a waiver and in the evaluation of the intelligent and knowing quality of the suspect's decision. Unlike the confession voluntariness standard, a *Miranda* waiver should reflect the individual's free choice unaffected by police pressure or signficiant infirmities of the accused.

7

Self-Incrimination Without Interrogation

The heart of the privilege against self-incrimination is surely the right to remain silent in the face of official questioning. The earliest assertions of the principle were made by the victims of inquisitorial proceedings. Most often they were representatives of political or religious minorities who were viewed as threats to the British Crown. By engaging in a process of wide-ranging interrogation, government officials sought to ensure that the dissidents would incriminate themselves, thus justifying their detention. A privilege of silence in response to this process, particularly where the inquisitorial questioning occurred prior to the victim being charged with an offense, was a highly pragmatic goal at that time for it meant significant protection against abuse and harassment by the state. Here history is very much in accord with the contemporary role of the privilege against self-incrimination. The most important aspect of the right to silence even today is its ability to control state-sponsored interrogations. Without the individual's right to refuse to answer self-incriminatory questions generally, and more particularly the right to refuse to answer any police-initiated inquiries, and to decline to take the witness stand at his own criminal trial, the state would be effectively in control of enormous power in the enforcement of the criminal law. The risks of abuse would be great, and the potential cost to individual privacy interests high. The Fifth Amendment's self-incrimination clause is the principle barrier against the inquisitorial mode of criminal procedure and the risks entailed by it. If it were necessary to establish a priority in the application of the privilege, it would certainly be appropriate to make its primary mission the restraint of official interrogation since that would provide the most substantial protective impact.

The fact that the privilege against self-incrimination is an important and effective shield against state interrogation practices—indeed that its most important contribution to civil liberties lies in this area—should not lead to the conclusion that the questioning process constitutes the limits of its applicability. To so restrict the privilege would be a disservice to the principles it represents. The historical background of the privilege may well extend no further than official interrogations and efforts to resist their abusive characteristics, but this need not forever define the boundaries of the right to remain silent. To the contrary, it should not because of two factors. First, the characteristics of modern society are dramatically different from what they were in 1637 when John Lilburne was suspected of bringing seditious tracts into England. Commercial and interpersonal transactions are far more complex today with the result that they often must be set down in documentary form; indeed, the government frequently compels the submission of written regulatory reports. Almost every American has felt the impact of this as a result of the mandatory reporting features of the federal income-tax system, but for many, particularly those engaged in business, the need to document one's activities is a pervasive fact of life. Oral communications are no longer sufficient in our complex world, and as we switch to documentation, we concurrently build up a file of evidence for the state. This presents the government with the opportunity of acquiring highly incriminating information through compulsory reporting, searches, and subpoenas. If the interests reflected in such writings are akin to those the privilege has sought to safeguard from abusive questioning, the fact that the information is in written form should not preclude the applicability of the self-incrimination clause.

Second, there can be little doubt that contemporary America is a far more crowded and intrusive environment than that from which the privilege grew. As a result, privacy is in need of greater protection to ensure some measure of human dignity and value. While it is true that the role of the privilege protects privacy within the boundaries of compulsory self-incrimination, it is important that the privacy protection it offers not be undercut by a narrow and historically controlled interpretation. To do so would deprive contemporary society of an important shield when it is most needed.

The restrictions of history and the countervailing pressures of a complex modern society have generated much debate over the proper scope of the privilege against self-incrimination outside the official questioning arena. Concern focuses primarily upon government efforts to obtain documentary evidence, although similar problems can arise in the quest for nondocumentary property. When such evidence is sought, there may be no need to obtain any oral testimony from the individual providing it, assuming authentication can be secured from another source. Yet such writings may be highly incriminating, and if state compulsion is applied to secure them from the individual who will be incriminated by their contents, it is certainly possible to conclude that the circumstances constitute compulsory self-incrimination. This occurs most directly when the state either compels the submission of a regulatory report that would incriminate the individual submitting it or issues a subpoena for documentary evidence from a suspect who would be incriminated by the writings sought. There are, however, aspects to a search and seizure that arguably constitute sufficient compulsion to also bring it within the domain of the self-incrimination clause. A broad reading of the privilege therefore would not only bar compelled oral self-incrimination but also would prohibit the state from obtaining testimonial evidence in written form by techniques of compulsory self-incrimination.

The Fifth Amendment's self-incrimination clause can be either narrowly or broadly construed. At the very extreme, the privilege might be read as totally inapplicable unless oral testimony is sought. But far too many opportunities for abuse are presented by so rigid an interpretation, and the position has not been seriously urged. In contrast, substantial support does exist for a reading of the Fifth Amendment which, although conceding its applicability beyond oral questioning, nevertheless imposes strict historically based limits on the role it can play in noninterrogation contexts. The choice between a strict reading of the language of the self-incrimination clause and a broad construction of its policy foundations is, however, ultimately a problem of philosophy as much as it is a question of law. Not surprisingly, judicial decisions over the years have reflected no single position on this problem. Instead, there are illustrations of almost every theory in the myriad opinions. The most recent cases, however, have opted for a narrowed scope for the right to remain silent, rejecting older precedent and substantially curtailing individual liberties in the process.

The Era of *Boyd v. United States*

Justice Louis Brandeis called *Boyd v. United States*[1] "a case that will be remembered as long as civil liberty lives in the United States,"[2] while Justice Hugo Black viewed it as "among the greatest constitutional decisions of this Court."[3] For those who view the modern era, particularly the decade of the 1960s, as the period in which individual rights have grown most dramatically, such words of praise for a case decided in the 1880s may appear puzzling. But when the praise comes from such ardent champions of civil liberties as Justices Brandeis and Black, it has to be taken seriously. Upon close analysis, however, it is clear that *Boyd* is indeed a far-reaching decision in its interpretation of the constitutional limitations on criminal investigation techniques. It was for a long time the cornerstone of both Fourth and Fifth Amendment jurisprudence and is the necessary starting point in assessing the role of the privilege against self-incrimination in controlling government acquision of incriminating evidence.

The factual context of *Boyd* was simple enough. The United States brought an action for the forfeiture of thirty-five cases of plate glass that had allegedly been imported in violation of federal customs regulations. Illegal importation of the plate glass was denied, and an effort was made to secure the return of the cases that the government had seized pending forfeiture proceedings. The claim of Boyd and Sons was that it had contracted to furnish a specified foreign glass for the construction of a government building with the understanding that if it had to utilize some of its duty-paid inventory to meet the contract, it could import an equivalent quantity of the foreign glass without payment of duty. Twenty-nine cases of glass were imported on this basis before the concern sought to bring in the additional thirty-five cases duty free. The government maintained that Boyd and Sons fully replaced the foreign glass used to fulfill the government construction contract with the importation of the first twenty-nine cases and that the attempt to avoid duty on the subsequent thirty-five cases was a fraud on the customs laws. To establish its position, the government sought and obtained a court order requiring production of the shipper's invoice covering the twenty-nine-case shipment. The statute pursuant to which the order was issued provided that if a document subpoenaed in connection with a customs proceeding was not turned over without good excuse, the allegations that the document would tend to prove "shall be taken as confessed."[4] Rather than risk this result, the invoice was produced over objection based on the Fourth and Fifth Amendments. It was this objection that the Supreme Court confronted in its review of the ruling forfeiting the thirty-five cases of glass.

Justice Bradley's opinion for the Court in *Boyd* was a majestic philosophical statement about both self-incrimination and the power to search and seize. It had been argued that the limitations of Fourth Amendment Authority had not been exceeded since no search and seizure was undertaken. Rather, the invoice was produced in response to a subpoena. But to the Court the "compulsory production of a man's private papers to establish a criminal charge against him, or to forfeit his property, is within the scope of the Fourth Amendment to the Constitution."[5] Once controlled by Fourth Amendment principles, the order to produce the invoice could not be justified by the long-standing tradition allowing for seizure of stolen or forfeited goods. Seizure of private papers was "totally different" since "[i]n the one case, the government is entitled to the possession of the property; in the other it is not."[6] As proof that private papers were immune from search and seizure, the Court pointed to the 1765 decision by Lord Camden in *Entick v. Carrington*.[7] There a search for private papers under a technically valid warrant had been held illegal and no defense to an action for trespass. Justice Bradley noted that *Entick* was familiar to American statesmen and undoubtedly in the minds of those who drafted the Fourth Amendment. As a result, its reasoning was a persuasive guide to the construction of search and seizure restrictions. Quoting at length from *Entick*, Justice Bradley demonstrated that Lord Camden also believed that the state's authority to search and seize was limited by rights of possession. Indeed, Lord Camden had expressed the view that "[p]apers are the owner's goods and chattels; they are his dearest property; and are so far from enduring a seizure, that they will hardly bear an inspection."[8] Even the argument of utility did not persuade Lord Camden. He observed:

[T]here are some crimes, such for instance, as murder, rape, robbery, and house-breaking, to say nothing of forgery and perjury, that are more atrocious than libelling. But our law has provided no paper-search in these cases to help forward the conviction. Whether this proceedth from the gentleness of the law towards criminals, or from a consideration that such a power would be more pernicious to the innocent than useful to the public, I will not say.[9]

The essence of the *Entick* philosophy, supported by the opinion in *Boyd*, was that restrictions upon the power to search and seize created a sphere of privacy into which the government could not intrude. As long as the individual from whom the private papers were sought had a possessory interest in them superior to the government, the Fourth Amendment barred their seizure. In Justice Bradley's words:

It is not the breaking of his doors, and the rummaging of his drawers, that constitutes the essence of the offence; but it is the invasion of his indefeasible right of his personal security, personal liberty and private property, where that right has never been forfeited by his conviction of some public offence,—it is the invasion of this sacred right which underlies and constitutes the essence of Lord Camden's judgment.[10]

Moreover, by equating an order to produce documents with the search for and seizure of them, the Court's protective shield was made virtually impenetrable; the state could not take the documents nor could it demand that they be turned over. Although it may be argued that the ruling rested on property concepts that are no longer controlling, the Court also used unmistakable language referring to individual liberty and the tradition of resisting unchecked state power in support of its decision. "Privacy interests" were protected regardless of whether the Court used that term in so many words. Papers and documents, even more in need of safeguarding from government intrusion today, appeared immune from state efforts to obtain them at the beginning of the twentieth century as a result of the *Boyd* ruling.

Justice Bradley, however, did not end his analysis with the delineation of Fourth Amendment barriers to the production order in *Boyd*. His opinion also found room to treat the applicability of the privilege against self-incrimination, but two possible approaches were available. First, there was the view that by compelling the production of documents, the individual producing them provided implicit authentication that they were the items sought, and that as such he was compelled to be a witness against himself.[11] Second, it was possible to in a sense view the individual as being embodied in his private papers. Compelling their production even absent the implicit authentication would thus violate the privilege.[12] This latter view would have reflected a broad interpretation of the Fifth Amendment similar in scope to the expansive reading *Boyd* gave to the Fourth Amendment. The

privilege against self-incrimination would have barred the seizure or production of private papers in much the same manner as Fourth Amendment
principles, the only difference being that the Fifth Amendment produced
this result because of the self-incriminatory character of the material while
the Fourth Amendment limitations stemmed from the individual's superior
property interests in the items sought.

Despite the opportunity, Justice Bradley's opinion did not clearly articulate his Fifth Amendment philosophy. He observed:

> [W]e are further of opinion that a compulsory production of the private
> books and papers of the owner of the goods sought to be forfeited in such a
> suit is compelling him to be a witness against himself, within the meaning
> of the Fifth Amendment to the Constitution.[13]

Yet the proposition was stated more as an assertion than a reasoned argument. Elsewhere, the opinion maintained, in referring to *Entick*, that the

> principles laid down . . . affect the very essence of constitutional liberty
> and security. They reach farther than the concrete form of the case then
> before the court, with its adventitious circumstances; they apply to all inva-
> sions on the part of the government and its employees of the sanctity of a
> man's home and the privacies of life.[14]

These fundamental principles prevented the "forcible and compulsory ex-
tortion of a man's testimony or of his private papers to be used as evidence
to convict him of a crime."[15] Again, however, no clear self-incrimination
rationale emerged. To the contrary, the logic read so much like the underlying Fourth Amendment argument that it was hard to distinguish the two.
The opinion itself concluded, not surprisingly, that as to private papers,
"the Fourth and Fifth Amendments run almost into each other."[16]

After *Boyd* it seemed that both the Fourth and Fifth Amendments
barred the government from obtaining private papers from a suspect and
using them to secure his conviction of a crime. The absolute character of the
Boyd principle, however, did not last long. A variety of Fifth Amendment
decisions served to narrow its scope. Corporations were denied the protection of the self-incrimination clause[17] as were custodians of corporate
documents.[18] Similarly, the Court ruled that items transferred to a trustee in
a bankruptcy proceeding[19] and papers introduced in a civil proceeding[20] lost
the protection of the Fifth Amendment. Within the remaining boundaries,
however, *Boyd* remained controlling, and its specific holding was reaffirmed by the Court in *Gouled v. United States*,[21] decided in 1921. Private
papers could not be seized from or used against an individual in a criminal
proceeding even pursuant to a warrant. As in *Boyd*, the *Gouled* search
resulted in the obtaining of documents to which the defendant had a

superior right. Rather than seeking to obtain fruits or instrumentalities of a crime or contraband, the government in both cases was after items of "evidential value only."[22] *Boyd*, followed by *Gouled*, prohibited such a seizure under the Fourth Amendment because of the defendant's superior interest in the papers, as well as pursuant to the Fifth Amendment because the defendant was the "unwilling source of the evidence."[23]

Although the years following *Boyd* had narrowed the range of situations it covered, *Gouled* demonstrated that within its scope the *Boyd* doctrine provided complete protection against government process, be it in the form of a warrant or subpoena. Papers over which the suspect had an ownership interest could not be obtained both because of his superior property rights under the Fourth Amendment and, assuming them to be self-incriminatory, because their use as evidence would compel the owner to be a witness against himself in violation of the Fifth Amendment. The Fourth and Fifth Amendments overlapped therefore with respect to those papers that would be self-incriminatory and as to which the government could not claim a superior right. Such documents were mere evidence and the beneficiaries of constitutional protection under two amendments. In effect, the Court had created a special class of items totally beyond government reach.

The course of the Court's decisions over the next several decades began to cut into the full scope of the *Boyd* principle, even beyond the narrowing achieved as a result of excluding corporations and their officers from its protective umbrella. One illustration was provided by the *Gouled* opinion itself which, although reaffirming *Boyd*, nevertheless observed that there was "no special sanctity in papers"[24] rendering them immune from seizure if they constituted an "agency or instrumentality"[25] of a crime. The import of this qualification was to suggest that private papers were not to be deemed absolutely protected from disclosure after all. Rather, the shield surrounding them existed only so long as they could not be classified as one of the traditional objects of a legitimate search and seizure—the fruits or instrumentalities of crime or contraband. The protection afforded by this standard was obviously less extensive than that of a rule that would have prevented the state from obtaining and using *any* private document. As a result of *Gouled*, some documents could be now denied coverage due to their status as an agency or instrumentality of a crime despite their private and incriminatory character. The decision adopted the position that documents should be treated like other forms of property in that they would be immune from seizure only when they constituted mere evidence.[26] Shifting to this position, with its reliance upon common law property concepts to distinguish items subject to government seizure from those with immunity because of the owner's superior interest, undercut but did not end the special protection afforded private papers. The Supreme Court allowed the category of documents subject to classification as agencies and instrumentalities of crime to grow, but nevertheless did not totally reject *Boyd*. This in turn meant that many documents could still be assumed protected by the Fourth and Fifth Amendment theories of Justice Bradley.

While a traditional property focus may have been a satisfactory basis for interpreting the Fourth and Fifth Amendments in nineteenth-century America, it was less in keeping with the needs of an evolving twentieth-century nation. A 1928 decision of the Supreme Court that permitted the use of the fruits of warrantless wiretapping as evidence in a criminal trial exemplified the problem. To the majority, the lack of a physical trespass in conducting the wiretap precluded the finding of any violation of the Fourth and Fifth Amendments. Its opinion perpetuated the Court's reliance upon property principles in interpreting the protections created by both provisions of the Bill of Rights. Constitutional restraints were effectively tied to what were believed to be the concepts that motivated the framers, thereby leaving the government free to circumvent the restrictions through modern technological developments. The doctrinal weakness of the decision and the need for an alternative rationale were forcefully argued by Justice Brandeis. He stated in his dissent in *Olmstead v. United States* that the amendments reflected the value of personal privacy—the "right to be left alone."[27] He observed:

> Every unjustifiable intrusion by the Government upon the private life of the individual, whatever the means employed, must be deemed a violation of the Fourth Amendment. And the use, as evidence in a criminal proceeding, of facts ascertained by such intrusion must be deemed a violation of the Fifth.[28]

Justice Brandeis did not fully elaborate on the significance and implications of a shift from a property to a privacy rationale in the interpretation of the Fourth and Fifth Amendments. Obviously, the change would mean constitutional regulation of wiretapping, but the larger impact on *Boyd* was left unclear. On the one hand, it is possible to argue that the special characteristics of private papers, be they either mere evidence, or agencies or instrumentalities of a crime, are such that any government effort to obtain them would be an unjustifiable intrusion. This position views private papers as so reflecting our individual personality that they must be immunized from unconsented use against us. Unlike the property focus that rested upon rights of possession to protect documents, the privacy rationale would achieve this result based upon the need to protect the *contents* of the writings from involuntary disclosure. Alternatively, privacy could be taken to mean a concern for the justification behind and manner of the government's intrusion in the securing of private papers. This would not immunize such documents, but would rather ensure that there were grounds to believe they were of evidentiary value before a seizure was authorized, as well as protect against general rummaging through an individual's personal property to obtain them.

The question of the status of private papers under the Fourth and Fifth Amendments grew in importance when the Court finally discarded its property theory in favor of Justice Brandeis' privacy philosophy. The change came in two 1967 decisions of the Supreme Court. The first was *Warden v. Hayden*[29] in which the Court rejected the mere-evidence rule. Noting that the rule had been severely criticized by courts and commentators, Justice Brennan observed that the Fourth Amendment was "a reaction to the evils of the use of the general warrant in England and the writs of assistance in the Colonies, and was intended to protect against invasions of 'the sanctity of a man's home and the privacies of life,' . . . from searches under indiscriminate, general authority."[30] Given a privacy focus, it was clear that the interests protected by the Fourth Amendment were infringed just as much by a search for mere evidence as by an intrusion to secure fruits and instrumentalities of crime, and contraband. The property focus that had governed searches and seizures reflected Lord Camden's view in *Entick v. Carrington* that the "great end, for which men entered into society, was to secure their property,"[31] but over time that position had come to be "discredited."[32] All that could be said in favor of the mere-evidence rule was that "limitations upon the fruit to be gathered tend to limit the quest itself,"[33] but the Court found that rationale too arbitrary to justify maintaining the distinction. Later that same year the Court completed its conversion to a privacy rationale in *Katz v. United States.*[34] The Court reversed the *Olmstead* holding that the Fourth Amendment did not cover wiretapping and formalized a new standard that has come to be known as the reasonable expectation of privacy test.

Both *Hayden* and *Katz* were treated by the Court as Fourth Amendment decisions. *Hayden* involved the seizure of items of clothing which, under what was then the recently adopted view that the Fifth Amendment was limited to testimonial or communicative evidence, placed it outside of the scope of self-incrimination protection. *Katz*, however, involved the seizure of a communicative telephone conversation. As a result, it could have been treated in Fifth Amendment terms since under the traditional view of the "intimate relation"[35] between the Fourth and Fifth Amendments, the violation of one would prevent satisfaction of the other. The finding of a Fourth Amendment violation should thus have been only half of the decision, the remainder of which should have held that Katz had been compelled to incriminate himself. By not assessing the role of the privilege against self-incrimination, the Court might have been suggesting that the Fourth and Fifth Amendments were not in fact related. Combined with the new privacy focus underlying the Fourth Amendment, the implication that the two amendments would henceforth operate independently was a major development. It raised the possibility that the core of items that had previously been immune from seizure by any method might now be obtainable consistent with the Fourth Amendment and without violating the Fifth. Moreover, the Court's revision of this aspect of Fourth Amendment jurisprudence raised the possibility that a similar effort would be undertaken with respect to the privilege against self-incrimination. Both steps clearly challenged the immunity from unconsented transfer that private papers had been accorded. It was now at least conceivable that such documents might be obtained by both search and seizure as well as subpoena. The Supreme Court let the issue rest for a while, but returned to it in the early 1970s to resolve the questions that its opinions had raised.

Papers and Self-Incrimination:
The Current Standards

Determining the extent of the state's authority to acquire private papers consistent with the Fifth Amendment depends upon the identification of the values the privilege is designed to protect. With *Warden v. Hayden* and *Katz v. United States*, the Court had chosen privacy over property as the underlying concern of the Fourth Amendment, qualified by the observation that the scope of privacy protection provided by the Fourth Amendment was from arbitrary government intrusion and that more general privacy protection was a matter of state law. If the Fourth and Fifth Amendments were to continue to be linked, presumably privacy would have become the guiding principle in the interpretation of the privilege against self-incrimination as well, subject to similar qualifications. In support of this position, Justice Douglas had observed that "[t]he Fifth Amendment in its self-incrimination clause enables the citizen to create a zone of privacy which government may not force him to surrender to his detriment,"[36] and the Court in *Murphy v. Waterfront Commission* had included in its list of policy justifications for the right to remain silent the view that it allows each individual "a private enclave where he may lead a private life."[37] On the other hand, there were hints in *Hayden* and *Katz* that the Fourth and Fifth Amendment function independently. Moreover, the prior statements of the Court linking the privilege to the goal of protecting privacy were only dicta in totally unrelated areas, and with different language as well as a separate historical background, the privilege against self-incrimination could easily be disassociated from the privacy interests deemed central to the Fourth Amendment.

These issues confronted the Supreme Court in the 1973 case of *Couch v. United States*.[38] The factual context involved a Fourth and Fifth Amendment challenge to an Internal Revenue Service summons. Couch was the sole proprietress of a restaurant and had for fifteen years used an accountant to prepare her income tax returns. Payroll, sales, and expenditure records were regularly turned over by her to the accountant for this purpose, and the accountant, an independent contractor with numerous other clients, kept possession of the documents. Couch came under suspicion for failure to report her income accurately, and the IRS was considering, among other things, recommending criminal prosecution. A summons was issued to the accountant in connection with the *Couch* investigation for "[a]ll books, records, bank statements, cancelled checks, deposit ticket copies, workpapers and all other pertinent documents pertaining to the tax liability"[39] of the suspect. Although the relevant documents were transferred to the taxpayer's attorney, the objections to producing them were not based upon the interests of either the accountant or attorney. Rather, the taxpayer asserted that her ownership of the records entitled her to object to their compulsory production. The IRS, as a result, sought enforcement of the summons.

How would *Couch* have been handled under *Boyd*? The answer isn't entirely clear since the documents sought in *Boyd* were in the physical possession of their owner while Couch had transferred possession to a third party. Justice Marshall, dissenting in *Couch*, did not, however, believe the distinction to be of constitutional significance. He rejected the view that an owner of documents had an absolute Fifth Amendment right to object to their unconsented use against him. Nor did he accept the alternative position that infringement of the privilege could occur *only* when the owner of the item was also in possession. That theory was based upon the "potential for incrimination inherent in the act of production,"[40] which is a characteristic not present when the owner no longer has the item. Instead, Justice Marshall suggested a policy-oriented analysis in which the Fourth and Fifth Amendments would operate in tandem. He observed that "[b]oth involve aspects of a person's right to develop for himself a sphere of personal privacy. Where the Amendments 'run almost into each other,' I would prohibit the Government from entering."[41] Without delineating its exact contours, Justice Marshall was maintaining in explicit terms the traditional view that the state could not obtain testimonial documents because of the convergence of Fourth and Fifth Amendment privacy interests. In essence, Marshall's opinion sought to reaffirm the *Boyd* principle, merely substituting privacy for property as the motivating rationale.

In terms of its holding, the majority opinion in *Couch* was not all that far removed from Justice Marshall's view. Read narrowly, the Court's opinion merely distinguished *Boyd* on the basis of the fifteen-year divergence of possession and ownership of Couch's financial documents and did not substantively treat her Fourth Amendment challenge, dismissing it in a footnote.[42] *Couch* could still be read as supporting a zone of Fifth Amendment privacy for documents either retained or only temporarily given up by their owner. As such, the zone would be narrower than that called for by Justice Marshall since the majority placed more emphasis on possession, but nevertheless just as impenetrable within its own sphere. Left intact by this reading of the majority's view was the privacy focus for the privilege against self-incrimination and the theory that it worked in conjunction with the Fourth Amendment.

Despite a possible narrow reading of *Couch*, much of its language suggested that the Court had something else in mind. In particular, there were strong hints of a substantial limitation of the privacy rationale. This was indicated first by the Court's ease in concluding that the act of regularly turning over financial records to an accountant for tax purposes meant that the owner no longer had a reasonable expectation of privacy in them even though the complexity of the tax laws frequently makes outside assistance necessary. More significantly, the Court's emphasis on possession as the basis for a claim of privilege suggested that even private documents might lose Fifth Amendment protection if not in the owner's hands. This would make privacy interests subservient to the property concept of posssession and would mean that no document could be absolutely protected from unconsented use by the government. The papers would have to be both private and in the owner's possession to be immune from a summons. Finally, *Couch* hinted that the Court was ready to dispense with the overlap theory of the Fourth and Fifth Amendments. *Boyd* had found Fourth and Fifth Amendment violations in a subpoena to produce private documents. The *Couch* Court, however, noted that the core of the Fifth Amendment's prohibition was directed at "the use of physical or moral compulsion to extort communications"[43] from the accused. Since a search and seizure can be viewed as involving no such compulsion, the Court may have been suggesting that the two amendments function independently in this sphere.

The lower federal courts were unsure of what to make of the "new" Fifth Amendment approach to government efforts to obtain private papers and documents. They could not decide whether the Supreme Court meant to separate the Fourth and Fifth Amendments and thus eliminate the class of papers immune from government seizure, or simply narrow the zone of privilege. *Andresen v. Maryland*,[44] decided by the Court in 1976, settled that question in favor of totally severing the "intimate relation" between the self-incrimination clause and the Fourth Amendment that *Boyd* had established ninety years before. Andresen was a Maryland attorney specializing in real estate transactions who came under suspicion for fraud in some of his dealings. Warrants were obtained to search his law office, as well as the real estate development concern he ran, for documents pertaining to a specific land sale. Less than 3 percent of his office files and less than

5 percent of the development company files were seized on execution of the warrant. Most items were returned to Andresen prior to trial, but several were admitted against him over his Fourth and Fifth Amendment objections. The *Boyd* analysis would have required that the Fifth Amendment characteristics of the items be assessed. If they were found to be testimonially self-incriminating, they would neither be obtainable by a search nor usable as evidence against their owner. Pursuant to *Boyd*, both the Fourth and Fifth Amendments were violated by such procedures. This was the analytical approach *Andresen* rejected.

Justice Blackmun, writing for the Court in *Andresen*, dispensed with *Boyd* and related precedents by classifying them as cases involving violations of the Fourth Amendment that provided the compulsion required for an infringement of the self-incrimination clause. But as a result of the mere evidence rule, which prevailed until *Warden v. Hayden*, most seizures and subpoenas for documents were Fourth Amendment violations and hence also Fifth Amendment violations. The discarding of the mere-evidence rule left the Fourth Amendment with only a limited role in regulating government seizures of documents. No longer was a class of items totally excluded from Fourth Amendment restrictions. Instead, traditional Fourth Amendment protections—prior judicial review, probable cause and particularity—were to govern documentary searches, and these were all satisfied in *Andresen*. Furthermore, the Court viewed the Fifth Amendment as premised on a finding of compulsion that was lacking in *Andresen* since the

> petitioner was not asked to say or do anything. The records seized contained statements that petitioner had voluntarily committed to writing. The search for and seizure of these records were conducted by law enforcement personnel. Finally, when these records were introduced at trial, they were authenticated by a handwriting expert, not by petitioner. Any compulsion of petitioner to speak, other than the inherent psychological pressure to respond at trial to unfavorable evidence, was not present.[45]

The Fifth Amendment protected privacy only "to some extent"[46] and had no bearing when the state did not exert compulsion.

Arguments can certainly be mounted against the ruling in *Andresen*. There are, for example, aspects of a search and seizure that can be said to amount to compulsion, including the force of law behind the issuance of the warrant as well as the prohibition against interference with its execution. Moreover, the majority's characterization of *Boyd* and its progeny as hinging the finding of a Fifth Amendment violation upon an identifiable Fourth Amendment violation is open to challenge. To the contrary, the language of the opinion in *Boyd* seems quite clear in concluding that the effort to obtain private documents was an *independent* Fourth and Fifth Amendment violation. Thus pursuant to the *Boyd* analysis, failure to violate Fourth Amendment principles, a situation more likely to arise since the abandonment of the mere-evidence rule, would not preclude finding a violation of the privilege against self-incrimination. However, the heart of the objection to *Andresen* lies in its partly explicit and partly implicit narrowing of the philosophical objectives of the right to remain silent. The decision makes sense only if there is to be a very limited role for the Fifth Amendment, one that has little to do with protecting privacy and guards against only a particular form of state coercion.

The fundamental point separating Justice Brennan from the *Andresen* majority was his view that the privilege against self-incrimination should be concerned with the content of what the government sought to obtain, not just the manner (compulsion) by which it went about obtaining it. In the same way the mere-evidence rule and the theory of an overlap between the Fourth and Fifth Amendments had been clearly content-oriented approaches that placed particular items beyond the government's reach. Under both theories, the documentation of transactions or thoughts did not bring with it the risk that the act of writing them down would be tantamount to revealing them to others, including the government. Concepts of property may well have been the motivating force behind the *Boyd* approach to documentary protection, but property was in a sense the nineteenth-century equivalent to the contemporary notion of privacy. For all practical purposes, property at that time meant privacy—the right to exercise exclusive dominion over possessions both real and personal. Modern society may not be able to afford the luxury of protecting property rights from any and all intrusions, but in now permitting the state to acquire virtually all private papers, it may be sacrificing far more privacy than circumstances actually warrant. Moreover, the fact that the increasing complexity of society forces far more documentation than was previously necessary should lead to even greater sensitivity to the implications of easy access to private papers by way of search and seizure. Yet the law clearly provided far more protection for documents and the privacy interests they reflect during a bygone era in which documentation was less of a practical necessity. Only in recent years has the law begun to "confine the dominion of privacy to the mind."[47]

Terminating the Fifth Amendment's role in controlling government searches for documents does not, of course, leave the area devoid of constitutional protection. The Fourth Amendment prohibition against unreasonable searches and seizures remains available for this purpose. Yet the protection it affords is only conditional. With the demise of the mere-evidence rule, it appears that every writing is subject to search and seizure if the prerequisites are met, perhaps even including personal diaries, although the issue has been left open by a Supreme Court footnote.[48] Since the *Katz* decision, the Fourth Amendment has become a device to ensure that the manner of search and seizure is reasonable without creating an impenetrable zone of privacy for particular items. The Fifth Amendment, meanwhile, has been left to guard against compulsory testimonial communications, with an emphasis on the oral aspects of communication. These cannot be obtained consistent with the privilege while writings, even if more private in character, are seizable. Thus the privilege against self-incrimination has also become a protection focusing upon the means used to obtain information (compulsion to testimonially communicate), not the content of the item sought. Earlier Courts had found a need to use the privilege along with the Fourth Amendment to prevent unconsented intrusions to obtain testimonial communications in written form. The current Court no longer sees this as necessary, finding sufficient protection in the narrowed Fourth Amendment. This restricts the class subject to documentary seizures to those against whom the state has probable cause to believe are in possession of writings of evidentiary value. Conditional privacy of this sort is better than no privacy at all, but its adequacy in a complex and privacyless society is open to question.

When the police lack probable cause or cannot identify the item they seek with sufficient particularity, the opportunity for seizure provided by *Andresen* is not available. And if consent to its transfer to police custody cannot be obtained, the only available strategy to secure the item is the summons or subpoena demanding its production. Here compulsion of the individual facing possible self-incrimination, in the form of the demand that he turn over the document, is clear. Presumably therefore the Fifth Amendment should bar such a summons or subpoena due to the fact that both constitute compulsion to provide the state with testimonially self-incriminating information. *Fisher v. United States*,[49] however, decided by the Supreme Court in 1976, gave another twist to the interpretation of the self-incrimination clause and opened up the possibility that the state could indeed compel production of self-incriminatory documents.

If the state searched for private papers as allowed by *Andresen*, the Fourth Amendment, and its demand that probable cause be present would control. The result would be a narrowing of the class of individuals subject to such a procedure to those likely to possess the sought-after items. But the Fifth Amendment is free of such limitations. Anyone can be called upon to produce documents even if there is only the faintest suspicion that they have the desired items and despite the fact that the documents cannot be described with particularity sufficient to satisfy the Fourth Amendment. Because police will not be rummaging through private possessions to locate the papers, the law permits the state to use the subpoena and summons with fewer restrictions. If the privilege does not absolutely prohibit the compulsory production of private papers, there may be no restraints left at all.

In *Fisher* there were two separate fact patterns involving IRS summonses

for the production of tax records. In each instance, however, the taxpayers
under investigation were visited by IRS agents, after which they retrieved
tax documents from their accountants for transfer to their attorneys. The
IRS then issued summonses to the attorneys demanding that certain
documents relating to the tax liability of their clients be produced. Enforcement of the summonses was ordered in both instances at the federal district
court level. On appeal, however, the Court of Appeals for the Third Circuit
affirmed one enforcement order,[50] but the Court of Appeals for the Fifth
Circuit reversed the other,[51] creating a conflict the Supreme Court sought to
resolve. And consistent with the Court's general disfavor toward all but the
narrowest view of the privilege against self-incrimination, it held the IRS
summonses valid in both instances.

One aspect of the decision was a refinement of the *Couch* rule denying
Fifth Amendment protection to documents where their owner had surrendered possession to a third party. In *Couch* the papers sought from the
taxpayer's accountant had been held by her as a matter of practice for
nearly fifteen years. The lack of a "reasonable expectation of privacy with
respect to the evidence"[52] was seemingly critical to the conclusion that the
Fifth Amendment offered Couch no protection for the particular items she
had regularly given to him. Although the *Fisher* conclusion was the same,
the reasoning differed markedly from *Couch*. Justice White, writing for the
Fisher majority, found that the privilege was not violated because of the
absence of compulsion on the accused where the summons was directed to a
third party. The opinion thus rejected the notion that the Fifth Amendment
could provide protection for reasonable expectations of privacy with respect
to documents turned over to a third party except in the most restricted of
circumstances where "constructive possession is so clear or relinquishment
of possession so temporary and insignificant as to leave the personal compulsion upon the taxpayer substantially intact."[53] In third-party summons
cases, therefore, compulsion upon the owner of the documents is the controlling standard, not the legitimacy of privacy expectations in the contents
of the documents and the circumstances of their transfer. In the Court's
view, ruling otherwise would have "cut the Fifth Amendment completely
loose from the moorings of its language, and ma[d]e it serve as a general
protector of privacy"[54] when, according to Justice White, the framers intended the privilege to relate solely to the issue of compelled self-
incrimination. As a result, the Court's message was to warn of the risks of
disclosure attendant to the transfer of documents and therefore encourage
their retention.

Justice White's opinion, however, did not end there. Although the taxpayers could not claim the privilege against self-incrimination once they had
transferred the tax documents to their attorneys, there still remained the
matter of the relationship of the attorney-client privilege to the govern-

ment's right to obtain the items. The law recognizes the confidentiality of the attorney-client relationship in order to encourage clients to reveal private information to obtain legal advice free from the risk of divulgence to third parties. Yet, as the Court recognized, the attorney-client privilege does not protect against the disclosure of information that could be compelled from the client. The government's ability to obtain such information, particularly if in written form, would not affect the client's willingness to disclose it to his lawyer. Thus if the client has a Fifth Amendment right to resist a summons for documents, the attorney need not produce them if they were transferred to him in order to obtain legal advice. On the other hand, documents obtainable from the client should also be obtainable from the attorney. Enforcing the summonses therefore necessitated a finding that the clients could not have resisted them on self-incrimination grounds.

In the *Couch* and *Andresen* cases, as well as in that portion of *Fisher* relating to the ability of the taxpayer to assert the privilege to resist production of documents held by his attorney, the Court could dispose of the challenges by focusing upon the absence of compulsion on the accused. With that as the controlling standard, the Fifth Amendment claims were clearly invalid since the summonses were issued to third parties and the search and seizure did not constitute compulsion. Summonses to a third party do not compel the accused to do anything, and a narrow reading of the term also bars its applicability to a search and seizure where no affirmative act by the suspect is required, only the absence of resistance. A summons requiring the production of testimonially self-incriminating papers from the individual who owns, possesses, and will be incriminated by them cannot be analyzed in the same manner. Rather, another framework is necessary to assess whether the privilege is a shield against compulsory production in such cases, and again fundamental questions about the scope and function of the self-incrimination clause must be confronted.

The *Boyd* decision had suggested that one way to deal with subpoenas for the compulsory production of private documents was to bar their enforcement entirely. The rationale for this conclusion rested both upon the mere-evidence rule that excluded most documents from government subpoena or search because of the individual's superior property interest in them, as well as on the view that the Fourth and Fifth Amendments provided interrelated protection against government efforts to obtain private papers. The erosion of both theories, in the words of the Court, left "the prohibition against forcing the production of private papers . . . a rule searching for a rationale."[55] But viewing *Boyd* that way required that one totally ignore frequent Court observations that the privilege against self-incrimination was not *just* a device to protect property interests, including the statement in *Boyd* itself that "it is the invasion of [an individual's] indefeasible right of personal security, personal liberty and private property" that is "the essence"[56] of a Fifth Amendment violation. The *Boyd* approach, therefore, could have been applied to the facts in *Fisher*. In light of the demise of the mere-evidence rule, it would have been necessary to define the category of "private" papers subject to the Fifth Amendment's zone of privacy, but that task, though difficult, would not have been impossible. Justice Brennan, in fact, outlined some guideposts for the classification process, suggesting that personal letters and diaries be accorded maximum Fifth Amendment protection while economic records, although generally covered, should lose their protected status if not handled in a way consistent with a desire to retain their private character.[57]

Not surprisingly, the privacy argument has not fared well in this Fifth Amendment arena, just as it has been rejected in other privilege contexts. The Court has read the history of the privilege as predominantly a battle against compelled oral testimony. As long as the compulsory production of documents does not require oral testimony, the values of the privilege are not infringed. By this reading of the self-incrimination clause, the Court has continued the process of turning the Fifth Amendment into a protection against particular methods of acquiring information instead of a shield surrounding the privacy of the information itself. Both the historical and policy foundations of this approach, however, are open to debate. The framers may well have intended their property-oriented thinking to reflect a barrier to intrusions upon what we today think of as a privacy interest. Moreover, in dispensing with the privacy rationale, the Court may be sanctioning intrusions the framers would have prohibited. Finally, this change has evolved during an era in which the growing complexities of society have left privacy less protected in all spheres of life. To the Court, privacy is now only an incidental value underlying the privilege, and it is outweighed by the state interest in ease of access to evidence to assist in enforcing the law.

The oral testimony rationale, however, creates some difficulty in the enforcement of documentary subpoenas. As Justice White observed, "[c]ompliance with the subpoena tacitly concedes the existence of the papers demanded and their possession or control by the taxpayer. It also would indicate the taxpayer's belief that the papers are those described in the subpoena."[58] Moreover, production of the documents amounts to their implicit authentication. The combination of the implicit admissions of the existence, possession, and authenticity of the sought-after documents would appear to be sufficiently equivalent to oral testimony so that the privilege could be invoked. This view is consistent with Wigmore's position that an individual may resist an order to produce documentary items if the procedure is one *"relying on his moral responsibility for truthtelling."*[59] And it follows McCormick's observation that the role of the privilege in barring documentary subpoenas is premised on the theory that "one who produces documents (or other matter) described in a subpoena *duces tecum* represents, by his production, that the documents produced are in fact the documents described in the subpoena. This representation is a testimonial activity and within the protection of the privilege."[60] Using this analysis, it is possible to conclude, along with Justice Brennan, that the compelled production of private documents should therefore be barred under the Fifth Amendment. Again, however, a strict reading of the exact character of the implicit admissions reflected in the response to such a subpoena convinced the Court that the privilege did not prevent its enforcement.

The precise nature of the papers sought by the government summonses was critical to the conclusion that their production could be compelled. The documents were the accountants' workpapers prepared as a basis for computing their clients' tax liability. In the Court's view they did not belong to the taxpayers, were not prepared by them, and did not contain any of their testimonial declarations. Moreover, their preparation was "wholly voluntary."[61] On the basis of these facts, the Court was "confident that however incriminating the contents of the accountant[s'] workpapers might be, the act of producing them—the only thing which the taxpayer[s were] compelled to do—would not itself involve testimonial self-incrimination."[62] First, the summonses reflected no reliance on the taxpayers' truth-telling since the documents were of a customary sort, and their existence and location were a "foregone conclusion."[63] And although questioning whether there was any incrimination risk as a result of the implicit admissions compulsory production in *Fisher* created, the Court added that even if some testimonial significance was present in the communication, it did not represent "any realistic threat of incrimination to the taxpayers."[64] This conclusion was based upon the view that although the contents of the documents might be incriminating, the compelled act of producing them admitted only that the taxpayers sought accounting help in preparing their tax returns, and the accountants prepared workpapers that they ultimately turned over to their clients. Finally, there was no danger of implicit authentication in *Fisher*; producing the documents could reflect only the taxpayers' belief that the documents were those sought by the government and the taxpayers were not in fact competent to authenticate them.

After *Fisher* it appears fairly clear that documents voluntarily prepared by a third party can be subpoenaed from a suspect even though he may be incriminated by their contents. This stems from the fact that the act of production—the only thing compelled—is either not at all or not sufficiently incriminating. Even ownership of such documents, a factor not clearly present in *Fisher*, would be unlikely to change this result.[65] But the *Fisher* opinion left open the question of whether there are other papers such as those prepared by the individual from whom they are sought, which the Fifth Amendment would continue to protect. Lower courts are proceeding to confront this question, and inconsistency is likely to occur until further direction is given by the Supreme Court. Indeed, a disagreement has already arisen between some of the federal appellate courts over whether an individual's personal tax records are protected by the Fifth Amendment. The Fifth Circuit Court of Appeals expressed "doubt" that the privilege would be violated by a government search for or subpoena of private tax records unless "the actual preparation of the documents or the making of the written declarations which they contain, has been compelled,"[66] while the Ninth Circuit found that the privilege does shield such documents.[67] Going one step further, the Second Circuit Court of Appeals held that the protection of the Fifth Amendment extends to copies of the taxpayer's letters to his accountant that had been retrieved by him prior to the issuance of the summons.[68] Additionally, the Eighth Circuit Court of Appeals found that a doctor's patient files were protected by the privilege[69] and the District Court for the Southern District of Florida held that tape recordings of telephone conversations were covered as well.[70] These decisions reflect the fact that several alternative approaches remain possible even after *Fisher*.

It would be possible, for example, to read *Fisher* as simply narrowing the zone of protected privacy to documents prepared by the individual from whom they are sought. These would be outside the range of a government subpoena while all other documents would be judged by the implicit incrimination reflected in the compelled act of production. But although *Fisher* reserved judgment on the applicability of the Fifth Amendment to "private papers,"[71] it did not suggest that its analysis of the privilege would necessarily depend upon who prepared the documents. At the other extreme lies the Fifth Circuit's suggestion that only documents an individual is compelled to prepare may be shielded from compulsory production; yet this view appears too narrow. The detailed analysis present in the *Fisher* opinion demonstrates enough of an awareness of the potential for self-incrimination in the compulsory production of voluntarily prepared documents to refute this position.

It seems more likely that the *Fisher* problem will have to be analyzed on a case-by-case basis with a focus upon the question of whether admitting the existence, possession, and authenticity of particular papers entails a sufficient risk of self-incrimination to justify withholding them. And a strict assessment of this question might mean that very little can be withheld. Admitting the existence and possession of documents, even one so private as a diary, is rarely incriminatory. This would not be true if the government sought something suspicious such as the note used in a bank robbery, but there is nothing inherently incriminatory about possessing most other papers. That the contents are self-incriminatory is not controlling; only the incrimination encompassed in the act of production is relevant. The implicit authentication reflected in compulsory production, however, is more of an issue when the individual's own papers are sought. But this problem can be circumvented by not revealing the source of the document and authenticating it through the testimony of a handwriting expert. If this is the way the *Fisher* Court intended the privilege to be read, it has eliminated the role of the Fifth Amendment in preventing the compulsory production of *all* documents except those whose very existence and possession are inherently self-incriminatory. Only such writings could generate implicit self-incriminatory admissions in the compelled act of production. For all others no incrimination would arise from the act of production as long as the state secured independent authentication. Coupled with the absence of substantial safeguards in the subpoena process, the government would end up with the power to engage in wide-ranging fishing expeditions for evidence from the accused to secure his conviction, a process that begins to look very much like the kind of open-ended questioning to which John Lilburne so vigorously objected. Only a content-oriented approach to the privilege, a philosophy the current Court views with disfavor, would serve to safely protect against such an outcome.

The Privilege and Government Regulatory Programs

The character of the modern industrial state, particularly the urban environment generated by it, has obvious implications for the scope of personal privacy. The fact of large numbers of people in crowded cities in and of itself is likely to decrease opportunities for people to escape from the intrusions of others. To this is added the loss of privacy resulting from the large amount of information about individuals that is both maintained and readily accessible in the public and private sectors. The government's ability to secure documents from an individual free of Fifth Amendment restrictions only adds to the total of intrusions to which we are all subject. However, to the extent that individuals do not create or retain documents and private papers they can at least avoid this inroad into their privacy. But there is a further aspect of contemporary life that makes even this tactic impossible. Where applicable, the result is not only the normal set of intrusions upon individual privacy but also the additional interference reflected in the compelled creation of papers and information and their submission to governmental authorities.

The obligation to provide information to the government is by now commonplace. It is encountered in myriad situations from filing for government licenses to submitting income tax forms. And the need for information that lies behind filing requirements is concededly an important governmental interest. Information is critical to decision making, and it is appropriate for the state to demand the data it requires from those who possess it. The process of government regulation would be seriously impeded if the power to acquire information were taken away. Such a change would dramatically alter the relationship between the government and the institutions and individuals it regulates. Whether or not this should occur, the fact that our national government continues to rely upon administrative and regulatory agencies to supervise major segments of American society indicates that the current political judgment is not in favor of any significant change. But once the importance of information to the regulatory process and the fundamental role of that process has been established, it is still not necessarily true that the power to acquire such information must be without limit. To the contrary, no justification suggests itself as to why this area of government activity should be immune from limitations on the authority of the state that exist elsewhere. The question, instead, is more appropriately how such restrictions should apply.

When the government seeks to obtain private papers through subpoena or search, recent case law holds that the Fifth Amendment privilege against self-incrimination may not be offended. In the context of a search, there is no compulsion exerted on the individual whose papers are taken and therefore no infringement of the privilege. Subpoenas do compel the production of documents, but at least where the preparation of the documents was voluntary and the accused is not required to authenticate them, there is similarly no Fifth Amendment violation. Protection against abuse instead rests with the Fourth Amendment's guarantee against unreasonable searches and seizures. Where government requires the submission of informational reports, however, it is not so easy to avoid a Fifth Amendment problem. The essence of such requirements is that information be provided to the government with sanctions available for noncompliance. This is unmistakably governmental compulsion focusing not merely on the act of producing the document but also the prior act of preparing it. Where the information is not self-incriminatory, obviously the privilege is not offended. But where the individual obligated to submit the report would be incriminated by its contents, it would appear that the Fifth Amendment has been violated. Literally, the circumstances suggest compulsion to be a witness against oneself and bring into play the values the Fifth Amendment was designed to protect. Over the years, in a variety of contexts, the courts have sought to define how the privilege should apply where the government-reporting requirement would entail such self-incriminatory consequences. In the process, some fundamental issues about the scope of the privilege have been raised.

Appropriately enough, the Supreme Court first addressed the role of the Fifth Amendment as a bar to regulatory reporting requirements in the context of federal income tax submissions. The opportunity was presented in the Court's 1927 *United States v. Sullivan*[72] decision. There the taxpayer had failed to file any income tax return and argued that the privilege against self-incrimination excused his omission since his income had been derived in violation of the National Prohibition Act and disclosure of that fact would have been self-incriminatory. While the argument was successful before the Fourth Circuit Court of Appeals, the Supreme Court, in an opinion by Justice Holmes, disagreed. The Fourth Circuit's view of the application of the privilege to this problem was seen as too extreme, Justice Holmes observing that "[i]f the form of the return provided called for answers that the defendant was privileged from making he could have raised the objection in the return, but could not on that account refuse to make any return at all."[73] No attempt was made to define with precision the specific disclosures the privilege would bar, but Justice Holmes did express skepticism that the revelation of the amount of an individual's income would be protected. Overall, the *Sullivan* opinion focused upon the risk of incrimination to the individual filing the return and suggested that the privilege could be invoked only where such risk was present. The notion of a general exemption from the filing requirement because of the incrimination risk to a particular taxpayer was clearly rejected.

The years following 1932, as the United States sought to pull itself out of the Depression, and later as it entered World War II, witnessed rapid growth in federal regulatory activity. Reporting requirements well beyond those encountered in the tax system grew, and these were given legal sanction under the *Sullivan* principle. But *Sullivan* had retained a role for the Fifth Amendment where an individual risk of self-incrimination existed. Obviously, this presented the regulators with some measure of interference with their information collection responsibilities. Required reports would have to be filed, but specific self-incriminatory information could be withheld. Yet although that was the resolution *Sullivan* pointed to, a 1948 opinion, *Shapiro v. United States*,[74] offered a new doctrine that seemed to read the Fifth Amendment out of the entire arena of reporting requirements.

The factual context of *Shapiro* involved a fruit and produce wholesaler suspected of illegal tie-in sales in violation of the Emergency Price Control Act. He was served with a subpoena issued by the price administrator that, among other things, demanded the production of records that regulations required him to keep. Upon production of the documents, inquiry was made as to whether immunity was being granted to Shapiro, but the presiding official responded that he would receive only the immunity that flowed by law from the compulsory production of the required records. To the Court this meant that immunity was not to be given to the "custodians of non-privileged records"[75] or else the result would have been "a bonus for the production of information otherwise obtainable."[76] The question therefore was whether or not the required records sought by the price administrator were covered by the Fifth Amendment privilege.

The answer provided by the Supreme Court in an opinion by Chief Justice Vinson was that the records sought in *Shapiro* were not protected by the Fifth Amendment despite the fact that they were required to be kept by government regulation. They exemplified the "non-privileged status of records validly required by law to be kept."[77] The premise of this conclusion was the Court's previous holding in *Wilson v. United States*[78] that the president of a corporation could not invoke the privilege for corporate documents that would have served to incriminate him. The Court read *Wilson* as barring an assertion of privilege with respect to public documents and concluded that government record-keeping regulations result in the creation of public rather than private records. Thus required records maintained as a result of government regulation are public records, public records are not protected by the privilege, and therefore required records are not protected by the privilege. The implications of the syllogism so stated, however, were enormous. All Congress apparently had to do to nullify the Fifth Amendment was to create a reporting obligation since the product of such a requirement would be a nonprivileged public document. The *Shapiro* opinion, however, did not wish to state the required-records doctrine so broadly and thus "assumed at the outset that there [were] limits which the Government [could not] constitutionally exceed in requiring the keeping of records which [could] be inspected by an administrative agency and . . . used in prosecuting statutory violations committed by the record-keeper himself."[79]

Nevertheless, the Court's purported qualification of the required-records doctrine was not a fully satisfactory limitation of state authority. The opinion indicated that the test was whether

> there is a sufficient relation between the activity sought to be regulated and the public concern so that the Government can constitutionally regulate or forbid the basic activity concerned, and can constitutionally require the keeping of particular records, subject to inspection by the Administrator.[80]

So stated, the standard invited only minimal control by the courts. It did nothing to prevent normally private records from being converted into public and disclosable records by the simple expedient of a reporting or record-keeping obligation. Indeed, such was the context of *Shapiro* where the records involved were "duplicate sales invoices, sales books, ledgers, inventory records, contracts and records relating to the sale of all commodities,"[81] in short, customarily kept records which, absent the state-imposed obligation, might have been privileged. And it invited the government to demand the creation of new records simply for the state's convenience, perhaps even to the point of dissenting Justice Jackson's concern that expediency might lead to the tactic of requiring citizens to keep account of their whereabouts for government review.[82] Indeed, some courts in fact took an overly broad view of *Shapiro*, including one that read the decision as holding that "all records which Congress in the exercise of its constitutional powers may require individuals to keep in the conduct of their affairs relating to the public interest become public records in the sense that they fall outside the constitutional protection of the Fifth Amendment."[83] Other courts were more restrictive,[84] but even with limitations, Justice Frankfurter aptly characterized as "startling" the position that "whenever Congress requires an individual to keep in particular form his own books dealing with his own affairs his records cease to be his when he is accused of crime."[85] Qualifications on its scope did not alter the fact that the doctrine was simply a means of bootstrapping an argument for nullification of the privilege against self-incrimination.

Put side by side, *Sullivan* and *Shapiro* represented contradictory approaches to the regulatory information problem. *Sullivan* permitted invocation of the privilege in lieu of self-incriminatory disclosures, while *Shapiro* dispensed with the privilege for required records. It was doubtful that the contrasts between the taxing authority at issue in *Sullivan* and the price-administration system involved in *Shapiro* could explain the radical difference in the role played by the Fifth Amendment. More likely, the *Shapiro* required-records doctrine was a reflection of an effort to develop a theory to permit the state to acquire information desperately needed to perform complex regulatory tasks and to do so without conferring unwarranted immunity the effect of which would have been to undercut the enforcement side of the regulatory process. But the accommodation reached in *Shapiro* may well have been an extreme one, unwarranted in its scope and virtually limitless in its applicability. Retrenchment, and the development of an alternative approach, were clearly called for in the face of a doctrine conferring upon the legislature authority to virtually write the Fifth Amendment out of the Constitution.

That Congress was willing to fully utilize its required-record authority and thereby preclude invocation of the privilege against self-incrimination, was well illustrated by the anticommunist legislation enacted during the McCarthy era. In particular, under the Subversive Activities Control Act of 1950,[86] members of the Communist party could be ordered by the Subversive Activities Control Board to register with the Attorney General and admit membership in the Communist party. Such an admission in and of itself might have created a risk of incrimination under other internal security legislation then in force. Indeed, the Supreme Court had held that a claim of privilege could be raised by a witness questioned as to his association with the Communist party,[87] and compulsion to make the same admission in writing would have been in substance no different. Analyzed in terms of *Shapiro*, however, the registration statement might have been viewed as a required record as to which a claim of privilege could not be raised. In support of such a result, it was arguable that the registration form in the internal security context was as much of a public document as the records sought by the price administrator in *Shapiro*. Similarly, the need for the sought-after information was equally great in both cases, and the importance of both regulatory systems equivalent. This analysis would lead directly to the conclusion that the Fifth Amendment had no bearing on requirements that communists register with the Attorney General despite the self-incriminatory character of the information the registrant had to provide.

Instead of pursuing the *Shapiro* reasoning, however, the Supreme Court in a 1965 decision that did not even cite *Shapiro*, held the registration requirements of the Subversive Activities Control Act to be in violation of the Fifth Amendment. In *Albertson v. Subversive Activities Control Board*[88] the Court returned to the *Sullivan* line of analysis, which had authorized a claim of privilege if a required report would be self-incriminatory, but only as to the specific items of information that generated that risk. *Sullivan*, as previously noted, did not create an exemption from the entire reporting obligation. In the context of filing an income tax return, the Court felt it appropriate to require the filing, subject to specific claims of privilege, because it viewed as "frivolous"[89] the notion that a valid self-incrimination claim could be made to every question on the return and to the simple act of filing it. In contrast, subversive activities legislation covered a narrower class of subjects in what had become a highly regulated area, thereby making the assumptions of *Sullivan* inapplicable. The Court concluded:

> In *Sullivan* the questions in the income tax return were neutral on their face and directed at the public at large, but here they are directed at a highly selective group inherently suspect of criminal activities. Petitioners' claims are not asserted in an essentially noncriminal and regulatory area of inquiry, but against an inquiry in an area permeated with criminal statutes, where response to any of the form's questions in context might involve the petitioners in the admission of a crucial element of a crime.[90]

As a result, the Fifth Amendment justified not merely specific claims of privilege but rather a total failure to file.

Albertson, in its holding and rationale, raised more questions than it answered. The focus of the decision was the group subject to the registration requirement rather than the individual faced with the self-incrimination risk. Because of this change in the method of analysis, the Court could excuse a complete failure to file and did not feel bound by the *Sullivan* approach in which the filing itself would have been required but specific questions could have remained unanswered if self-incriminatory. Yet the Court failed to articulate why it felt that an individualized focus was not appropriate in analyzing the Fifth Amendment implications of the Subversive

Activities Control Act. More significantly, the absence of any reference to *Shapiro* could have been taken as an implicit rejection of the required-records doctrine. Alternatively, if meant simply as a narrowing of the required-records sphere, *Albertson* gave no hint as to the factors that separated it from *Shapiro*. And finally, *Albertson* raised questions as to how far its analysis would be applied beyond the narrow confines of internal security legislation. Given the whole range of required reports and records imposed on society at large, and the government's legitimate interest in maintaining the steady flow of information, extensive application of *Albertson* could have led to major problems in the regulatory process. Nevertheless, the logical implications of the group-focus test could not be limited to the Subversive Activities Control Act.

A trio of decisions in 1968 demonstrated the manner in which the group-focus orientation developed in *Albertson* would be applied. In *Marchetti v. United States*[91] the Supreme Court held the Fifth Amendment to be a valid defense in a prosecution for failure to register and pay the occupational tax under the federal wagering tax statutes. *Grosso v. United States*[92] reached the same result with respect to the federal wagering excise tax. And finally, the Court ruled in *Haynes v. United States*[93] that an individual charged with possession of and failure to register one of the defined firearms under the National Firearms Act could raise the privilege against self-incrimination as a defense. Both the fields of wagering and possession of the kind of firearms regulated by the Firearms Act were found to involve individuals "inherently suspect of criminal activities." *Albertson* was thus controlling and justified the failures to register and make required tax payments. Unlike *Albertson*, however, the *Marchetti, Grosso*, and *Haynes* opinions confronted the analytical problems raised by the application of the privilege to regulatory systems having reporting obligations. First, the Court rejected the view that the Fifth Amendment was not affected where the admission called for related only to future criminal conduct. It had previously been held, on the authority of Dean Wigmore, that when an individual is faced with the choice of self-incrimination or forgoing future criminal activity, the choice could not be said to violate the Fifth Amendment.[94] The Court labeled this logic as "twice deficient: first, it overlooks the hazards here of incrimination as to past or present acts; and second, it is hinged upon an excessively narrow view of the scope of the constitutional privilege."[95] Similarly, the Court disapproved of a theory of waiver as applied to *prior* criminal acts. An individual cannot be said to have relinquished his Fifth Amendment rights when he commits a crime; if so, "ingeniously drawn legislation" could lead to "widespread erosion"[96] of self-incrimination protection. The Court was on firm ground in concluding that the commission of a crime, either in the past or the future, was no basis for removing the privilege since its very function was to provide for a right to remain silent that even criminals could invoke.

The *Shapiro* required-records theory, however, did not operate on a waiver or choice rationale to justify compelling the production of self-incriminatory information. Instead, its premise was that certain records that would otherwise be private took on a public character when regulations required that they be kept or submitted. This could have been applied to the Communist party registration requirement of the Subversive Activities Control Act in *Albertson*, but it was not nor was any mention even made of the issue. However, the Court sought to distinguish the price-administration data involved in *Shapiro* and the wagering and firearms information sought in *Marchetti, Grosso,* and *Haynes.* It judged the important differences to be that the wagering and firearms regulatory systems did not call for records that were customarily kept, nor were they public in the sense of the records involved in *Shapiro*, nor were the reporting requirements imposed in a non-criminal and regulatory sphere of activity but rather existed in an area permeated with criminal statutes. Yet despite the fact that the opinions suggested how the *Shapiro* rationale was to be distinguished, they were unclear as to why the controlling criteria should have led to a different result. It is obvious that if the distinctions were of no substance or were irrelevant to the underlying standard, the consequences ought not to have varied. What the Court was subtly attempting to do, however, without so stating, was to begin the effort to delineate what kinds of record-keeping and reporting systems might survive a Fifth Amendment challenge. Obviously, the Court was not willing to let *Shapiro* operate without limits since to do so would cause the protections of the privilege to evaporate. At the same time, however, the Court was not willing to dispense entirely with the required-records doctrine since that would seriously frustrate legitimate government regulatory efforts. The group-focus test may not have been the perfect solution, but it was an appropriate first step in reintroducing Fifth Amendment protections that the required-records doctrine had seemingly dispensed with. It remained for a subsequent decision to develop a more reasoned rationale for reconciling the privilege with the government's need to regulate.

That opportunity arose out of a California decision holding that state's hit-and-run statute in violation of the Fifth Amendment privilege against self-incrimination.[97] The statute required a driver involved in a California automobile accident causing property damage to give his name and address to the car owner or leave a note with that information as well as a statement of the circumstances of the accident in a conspicuous place on the vehicle. In *California v. Byers*,[98] the Supreme Court in a five-four decision reversed the California ruling and held there to be no violation of the privilege. The factual context involved a driver charged with both a violation of the hit-and-run statute and with illegal passing. The hit-and-run charge exposed Byers to a possible fine of up to $500 and/or imprisonment for up to six months, while the maximum punishment that could have been imposed on the illegal passing charge was substantially less. The circumstances raised the classic issues inherent in the relationship between the privilege and reporting statutes and moreover did so in the context of a type of regulatory system in widespread use throughout the United States.

The three-way split in the Court's opinion in *Byers* may well be even more significant than the Court's validation of hit-and-run laws. To the plurality, the hit-and-run statute could not be subsumed under the *Albertson* line of reasoning since the objects of the California statute, namely, all licensed drivers in California, were not at all comparable to such highly suspect groups as Communist party members, bookmakers, and those who possess short-barrel shotguns. As a result, Byers could not defend against the total failure to report by relying on the characteristic of those regulatory systems that narrowed their focus to inherently suspect groups. Moreover, unlike the wagering tax, communist-reporting, and firearms-registration statutes, all of which appeared to be regulatory systems designed to assist criminal law enforcement, the hit-and-run statute had the clearly civil orientation of ensuring that civil liability arising out of automobile accidents would be satisfied. The Court pointed out that most accidents do not in fact lead to criminal liability as an indication that the hit-and-run legislation was not primarily supportive of criminal enforcement efforts. Dispensing with the *Albertson* rationale, however, still left the *Sullivan* principle as a basis for asserting the Fifth Amendment. *Albertson* justified failure to report if the reporting obligation was aimed at a highly suspect group, but *Sullivan* permitted individuals in other regulatory contexts to raise a claim of privilege if they faced specific self-incriminatory risks. The plurality opinion of Chief Justice Burger did not reject this approach but instead found that no such risks of incrimination were present. And, even if a self-incriminatory risk did exist in the disclosures required by the statute, the plurality felt that it would not be sufficiently testimonial to be protected by the Fifth Amendment.

Five members of the Court, however, rejected the plurality's rationale for the disposition in *Byers*. Justice Black observed that the plurality's view that there was no substantial risk of incrimination requiring Fifth Amendment protection could "hardly be taken seriously."[99] He raised the question, "What evidence can possible be more 'testimonial' than a man's own statement that he is the person who has just been involved in an automobile accident inflicting property damage?"[100] Justice Brennan highlighted the fact that the reporting obligation was triggered by an automobile accident, thus supporting Justice Black's position that the relevant class for purposes of analyzing the California statute was really composed of the much more suspect group of drivers involved in accidents, not the larger category of all drivers. And still, even if the class was not sufficiently suspect, there remained the fact that Byers, as an individual, faced a personal risk of self-incrimination. Acceptance of all these points, however, was not enough to invalidate the statute. Justice Harlan, although rejecting the plurality's argument, nevertheless joined in upholding the legislation by assessing it against a balancing test. The determinative issue in *Byers*, therefore, was really the question of whether application of the privilege against self-incrimination to required reports and records, be they written or oral, was to be judged on the basis of a weighing of interests or invoked as an absolute prohibition.

The four dissenters supported an absolutist view of the privilege that would bar compelled self-incrimination, as in *Byers*, regardless of the context and the underlying state interests involved. Yet although nothing in the language of the Fifth Amendment suggested anything but an absolute standard to determine the applicability of the self-incrimination clause, it was nevertheless true that the historical context out of which the privilege grew was many shades removed from the modern regulatory sphere represented in *Byers*. Justice Harlan was thus correct in calling the Fifth Amendment an "uncertain mandate."[101] But, was not the risk of the alternative, as Justice Black noted, "inevitably . . . the dilution of constitutional guarantees?"[102] And did not Justice Brennan accurately observe: "The dangers of which we must really beware are . . . that we shall fall prey to the idea that in order to preserve our free society some of the liberties of the individual must be curtailed, at least temporarily. How wrong that kind of a program would be is surely evident from the mere statement of the proposition."[103] If consistently followed, the Brennan and Black position would have forced the state to choose between its regulatory system being disrupted by claims of privilege and the maintenance of the system through grants of immunity. Application of the Fifth Amendment presented a problem only if the state was committed to maximum efficiency in both areas.

Justice Harlan's balancing theory to determine the applicability of the privilege against self-incrimination to reporting and record-keeping requirements took a different view of the meaning of the Fifth Amendment. It rejected the notion that the self-incrimination clause was an impenetrable barrier whenever a real and appreciable danger of self-incrimination existed and instead required a broad inquiry into the character of the regulatory system at issue to assess whether the privilege would have impeded its enforcement. Such an analysis would not be permissible in a strictly criminal context because the very function of the privilege in such circumstances was to bar compelled self-incrimination. Those were the surroundings out of which the privilege grew and allowing it to be circumvented where its central role was in question would have far too seriously interfered with the Fifth Amendment's core values. However, outside of the criminal sphere, the individual from whom compelled self-incriminatory information was sought retained the same interest in resisting disclosure, but the state would have more than the simple goal of criminal law enforcement supporting its position. And if the state interests were strong enough, the balancing theory would permit compelled reporting despite its self-incriminatory character.

In the specific context of the California hit-and-run statute, Justice Harlan concluded that the state interests were sufficient to justify denying applicability of the privilege. First, if the privilege were applied, the result would be that those who did not report either could not be punished, or immunity against use of the compelled report would have to be granted. But even use immunity would very likely make it impossible in practice to prosecute anyone who committed a driving infraction that led to an accident and the reporting obligation. Therefore, both alternatives, allowing a Fifth Amendment defense or providing immunity, would hamper the enforcement of the reporting obligation and thereby result in the frustration of the state's legitimate noncriminal purpose. On the other hand, in Justice Harlan's view, permitting both the reporting requirement and the criminal sanction to function unimpeded by Fifth Amendment considerations would not have seriously invaded the core values the privilege was designed to further. Unlike *Albertson*, the hit-and-run statute did not involve an inherently suspect activity, and the disclosures demanded were minimal. If the privilege were to be extended to this sphere, one might fear for the continued viability of other reporting statutes. In Justice Harlan's words:

> Technological progress creates an ever-expanding need for governmental information about individuals. If the individual's ability in any particular case to perceive a genuine risk of self-incrimination is to be a sufficient condition for imposition of use restrictions on the government in all self-reporting contexts, then the privilege threatens the capacity of the government to respond to societal needs with a realistic mixture of criminal sanctions and other regulatory devices.[104]

In light of these broad implications as well as the specific characteristics of the hit-and-run statute, including its noncriminal purpose, its necessity as a means of securing the information sought, and the minimal disclosures required, Justice Harlan concluded that the balance was weighted in favor of the state.

After *Byers*, required record-keeping and reporting systems are subject to several possible analyses. At one extreme are regulatory obligations imposed on inherently suspect groups. Here the regulatory structure lies too close to strictly criminal law enforcement goals and an individual who would be incriminated by a required report is free not to file. The identification of sufficiently suspect groups has not been clarified, but it at least includes Communist party members, gamblers, and those who possess specified firearms such as short-barrelled shotguns. If the regulatory system does not have the proscribed group focus, it must then be analyzed in terms of Justice Harlan's criteria: How important is it to retain civil and criminal controls in the regulatory sphere in question; how necessary is the self-reporting system to the acquisition of the sought-after information; what kind of disclosures are required; and how are Fifth Amendment values implicated? If the balance weighs in favor of the state, the individual must comply with the regulatory obligation; if not, his privilege against self-incrimination applies but only as to specific incriminatory disclosures. *Albertson, Marchetti, Grosso,* and *Haynes* provide guidance in applying the group-focus test, while Justice Harlan's concurring opinion in *Byers* illustrates the analysis of a successful state regulatory system under the balancing test.

To complete the picture, the Court's 1976 decision in *Garner v. United States,*[105] demonstrated how the Fifth Amendment functions where only individualized assertions of privilege are permitted. The taxpayer in *Garner* had listed his occupation as a "professional gambler"[106] on his tax return. This information was used as evidence against him in a gambling conspiracy prosecution over his Fifth Amendment objection. The Court ruled that he should have asserted his privilege in response to the incriminatory question and that his disclosure of the information could not be labeled *compelled* self-incrimination. The fact that the privilege would constitute a defense to failing to answer the specific incriminatory question satisfied the Fifth Amendment and allowed the state to use the information submitted on the form against the taxpayer.

Existing doctrine relating to the role of the privilege with respect to required record-keeping and reporting procedures is open to a variety of criticisms. The rules are vague in that they fail to give guidance in determining how a particular system will be categorized. The lines between the categories are extremely difficult to discern. Moreover, the Supreme Court has failed to delineate all the factors relevant to analyzing regulatory obligations that are self-incriminatory, thereby presenting the risk that "the scope of the Fifth Amendment's protection will now depend on what value a majority of nine Justices chooses to place on this explicit constitutional guarantee as opposed to the government's interest in convicting a man by compelling self-incriminatory testimony."[107] Most importantly, however, there is little explanation from the opinions as to why the Court has chosen particular approaches. Neither the absolutist position nor the balancing theory is adequately justified. Why should the privilege be given full sway in a realm of governmental activity far different from the strictly criminal confines out of which the privilege grew? Alternatively why should any inroads be allowed upon the right to be free of compulsory self-incrimination, no matter what the context in which the risk arises? Only the fullest development of the policy foundations of the Fifth Amendment can give us a satisfactory solution that respects the core values encompassed in the privilege, while an abbreviated analysis such as the Court has undertaken is likely to lead to far too much deference to the state's purported regulatory interest.

8   Burdening the Fifth Amendment

The privilege against self-incrimination has received inconsistent treatment from the Supreme Court over the last several decades. During the 1950s and 1960s, for example, Court decisions generally expanded the reach of the Fifth Amendment, while more recent rulings have sought to narrow its scope. Moreover, even during the expansionist era, some limiting principles were established, and selected growth has continued to occur in recent years despite an overall trend toward restricting the privilege. There is an accordion-like quality to the Fifth Amendment's evolutionary development as a result of which its precise sphere of application is difficult to delineate. But even with its ups and downs and despite the vagueness of its role in some situations, there are a number of contexts in which the right to raise the privilege in lieu of providing self-incriminatory information is not in doubt. Thus a suspect has a Fifth Amendment right to remain silent in a police interrogation; a witness may invoke the privilege when asked a self-incriminatory question; a criminal defendant need not take the stand at his trial. In contrast, there is no right to assert the privilege in response to a search for documents, and at best only a limited privilege when documents are sought by subpoena and when the state seeks pretrial notice of an alibi defense.

The Court's recently imposed restrictions on the scope of the Fifth Amendment, even conceding some rulings to the contrary, are not the only manifestation of its effort to narrowly interpret the self-incrimination clause. Even within those spheres concededly covered by the privilege, it is not entirely clear what invocation of the Fifth Amendment means. To be sure, an assertion of privilege authorizes a refusal to answer self-incriminatory questions, but that is a far too narrow perpsective from which to analyze the problem. To say that an individual may refuse to answer self-incriminatory inquiries means that the state is deprived of the information it seeks, but left unresolved are the questions of what the state may do to encourage an individual to choose not to assert the privilege and what powers it has to deal with those who invoke the Fifth Amendment despite state encouragement to the contrary. If the Fifth Amendment were read to legitimize a refusal to answer a self-incriminatory question but to have no role in controlling state inducements against its invocation and the severity of penalities imposed for its assertion, the privilege would be little more than an empty formality. Few would feel able to invoke the Fifth Amendment, and the consequences they would face for doing so might be worse than the results of incriminating themselves.

The words used by the framers in drafting the Fifth Amendment clearly demonstrate an intent to focus upon the circumstances surrounding an individual's decision whether or not to invoke the privilege. The language of the Fifth Amendment provides that no person shall be "compelled to be a witness against himself." Obviously, if information is voluntarily provided, it cannot at the same time be compelled. The task inherent in the self-incrimination clause, however, is to separate voluntary from compelled self-incrimination. To the extent that the state seeks to induce waivers of the privilege or penalizes its exercise but does so in a manner short of compulsion, its actions will not run afoul of the Fifth Amendment. As a result, the interpretation given to the compulsion standard is of major significance in determining the true effectiveness of the privilege. If the Court allows significant state pressures to be brought to bear upon the decision to exercise the privilege, as it arguably has done, the role of the Fifth Amendment, even in areas where it concededly applies, will have been substantially diminished.

The Burden of Silence as Evidence of Guilt

The Fifth Amendment doctrines that control what trial uses can be made of a defendant's exercise of the privilege against self-incrimination have been previously touched upon. More detailed treatment is appropriate at this point, however, because these principles can also be meaningfully assessed from the perspective of the pressures they bring to bear upon the defendant's decision to exercise or forgo the right to remain silent. This is not meant to concede that the Fifth Amendment should tolerate such infringement and, indeed, it can be argued that the language the framers used demonstrates a clear intent not to permit the state to so interfere with the invocation of the privilege. Rather, the problem is illustrative of the fact that every aspect of the substantive doctrine of the privilege against self-incrimination is also in part a potential Fifth Amendment burden issue.

If it were deemed critically important to ensure that the decision to invoke the privilege at trial remained totally unfettered by state-imposed pressures, adverse trial use by the state of the defendant's exercise of the privilege would be barred. Since the criminal trial context is the procedural focus of the evolution of the privilege, there is certainly a historical rationale for prohibiting any negative consequence at the defendant's criminal trial emanating from a decision to invoke the Fifth Amendment. Policy reasons constitute an even stronger argument for this position. The consequence of undue pressure on the defendant's Fifth Amendment decisions at trial may be the near immediate imposition of criminal sanctions. The Fifth Amendment is at the very least aimed at preventing the individual from being forced to convict himself and therefore should have its greatest impact in the forum in which criminal responsibility is to be decided. For the most part, the law has been responsive to the need to protect the criminal defendant's Fifth Amendment interests at trial but not without some important qualifications.

Commenting upon the defendant's failure to testify would constitute the most direct burden upon the exercise at trial of the Fifth Amendment privilege. But, as we have already seen, the Supreme Court held in *Griffin v. California*[1] that such comment is unconstitutional. The Court, in an opinion by Justice Douglas, called it an impermissible "penalty imposed by courts for exercising a constitutional privilege" and a "remnant of the 'inquisitorial system of justice,' . . . which the Fifth Amendment outlaws."[2] The Fifth Amendment, however, bars only compulsion to be a witness against oneself, not all adverse consequences if they are less than compelling pressures. But rather than seeking to determine whether the adverse comment was in fact a compelling form of pressure on the defendant, the Court utilized the penalty rationale. Seemingly, because the setting was the trial itself, the fact that the adverse comment made the assertion of the privilege a "costly"[3] decision was enough to warrant prohibiting it under the Fifth Amendment. Whether or not the adverse inference itself may have been warranted as a matter of logic and despite the fact that the jury might draw it anyway, the exercise of the privilege at trial by the defendant could not be affirmatively singled out to the jury with a direction that it be assessed against him. This resulted not from the fact that adverse comment generated compelling pressures on defendants to waive the privilege, but rather because it was purely and simply unfair.

If the Supreme Court was seriously intending to embark upon a fairness rationale in assessing burdens imposed upon the defendant's exercise of the Fifth Amendment at trial, it did so without any hint as to its conception of fairness in such a context. To call the adverse-comment rule an excessively costly penalty provides no standards for evaluating other consequences. Yet the theory, if sensitively administered, could have supervised state-imposed consequences following invocation of the privilege fairly, particularly those consequences arising at the defendant's trial. Nevertheless, the Court has since chosen to return to a compulsion analysis. This was the result of *Lakeside v. Oregon*[4] in which the Court rejected a defendant's challenge to a jury instruction directing that there be no adverse inference as a result of the defendant's failure to take the stand.

Under the *Griffin* analysis, any direction to the jury that focused attention on the accused's silence would arguably be unfair. Yet the Court correctly observed in *Lakeside* that it was unlikely that a no-adverse-inference instruction would compel an individual to incriminate himself. As a result the Court demonstrated that the compulsion analysis would permit more prosecutorial advantage to be taken of the defendant's decision not to testify, at least up to the point at which it would compel self-incrimination. In line with this the Court recently held that a prosecutor may call the state's case "unrefuted" after the defendant's attorney had indicated in his opening statement that the defendant would testify but then did not.[5] Moreover, at the lower-court level the compulsion theory has tolerated even more explicit highlighting of the accused's silence. As long as the prosecution's references do not run afoul of the compulsion standard, they are generally held to be harmless error.[6]

The Supreme Court's treatment of the doctrine permitting the prosecutor to impeach the credibility of the defendant by referring to his prior invocation of the privilege is also indicative of a narrow view of the Fifth Amendment's role in controlling the adverse consequences that may flow from the defendant's silence. At first glance, one might wonder what relevance a prior decision by the defendant not to testify would have on the establishment of his guilt at trial. The law has, however, traditionally accepted the propriety of utilizing for impeachment purposes the fact that an individual remained silent in the face of assertions he would naturally be expected to deny. Among other things, the defendant's probable belief in the truth of the statement or his desire to adopt it as his own might justify that result. To apply the doctrine fully would mean that the defendant's prior silence under appropriate circumstances could be used by the state as affirmative proof of guilt. But as we have already seen, *Griffin v. California* suggests that this would be a violation of the Fifth Amendment. To use such evidence to impeach the defendant's credibility, however, could be said to be sufficiently different to warrant a contrary result. It might cause the jury to give less weight to the defendant's story but would not necessarily add to the weight given to the state's case.

The Court had in fact upheld the constitutionality of using the defendant's prior silence for impeachment purposes in a 1926 decision, *Raffel v. United States*.[7] There, the state's cross-examination of the defendant brought out his failure to testify at a prior trial. But despite Supreme Court approval of this approach, it raises substantial problems. First, whatever the merits of the evidentiary rule allowing for the substantive or impeachment use of pretrial silence, the application of the doctrine to a criminal defendant at trial touches the very core values the Fifth Amendment is designed to protect. This in itself warrants caution in the application of the rule. Second, it is questionable whether there is an inconsistency between the decision to remain silent and a subsequent change of mind. A variety of factors other than guilt or a lack of credibility might be the explanation. Finally, although the jury might be directed to consider the evidence only for impeachment purposes, there is always the risk that it will view the defendant's prior silence as substantive evidence of guilt, a result seemingly inconsistent with *Griffin*. In recognition of these factors, the Supreme Court, in the exercise of its supervisory authority over the federal courts, barred the impeachment use of evidence of the defendant's previous failure to take the stand.[8] But the ruling was not binding on the states and, given the Court's decision in *Harris v. New York*[9] that statements obtained in violation of *Miranda* could be used for impeachment purposes despite their exclusion as substantive proof of guilt, it appeared possible that a state decision along the lines of *Raffel* would survive constitutional attack.

Perhaps the most dramatic context in which the impeachment use of silence problem could arise would be the case where a suspect is arrested, given an appropriate *Miranda* warning, and then remains silent. While "the *Miranda* warnings contain no express assurance that silence will carry no penalty, such assurance is implicit to any person who receives the warnings."[10] For this reason, the Supreme Court in *Doyle v. Ohio*[11] found it fundamentally unfair and a violation of due process to use a defendant's post-*Miranda* warning silence for impeachment purposes. By interpreting the *Miranda* warning as a guarantee of both the right to remain silent and of the fact that exercise of the right would not come out at trial, the Court could not avoid the conclusion that use of silence for impeachment of the defendant was unconstitutional. A suspect could not, consistent with due process, be given such a promise by the state only to have it broken at trial. But by treating the issue as a due process question, the Court sidestepped the need to apply the Fifth Amendment, and it is not at all clear how the problem would have been resolved had the self-incrimination clause been deemed controlling.

The application of the *Griffin* analysis would probably have led the Court to reject the impeachment use of postwarning silence. Much like comment upon trial silence outlawed in *Griffin*, the impeachment rule could be viewed as a Fifth Amendment penalty that makes assertion of the privilege costly. Indeed, some lower courts had held the impeachment rule unconstitutional on just such grounds.[12] But the result is not crystal clear since the impeachment penalty may not be as severe as the *Griffin* comment upon trial silence, and the Court could have developed penalty standards under the Fifth Amendment that the impeachment rule would not have violated. However, even though it could be argued that the Fifth Amendment is burdened to a greater extent by the knowledge that failure to take the stand would be stressed to the jury as proof of guilt than it would by an awareness that trial testimony could be impeached by prior silence, the difference does not seem to be significant enough to justify contrary rules. Both appear to make the invocation of the privilege sufficiently costly to warrant application of the *Griffin* penalty theory.

The compulsion analysis more recently employed by the Court, as in *Lakeside v. Oregon*, would be far more likely to have tolerated the impeachment use of pretrial silence, even after a *Miranda* warning. Simply stated, the fact that invocation of the privilege might be used to impeach the defendant's trial testimony would not compel him to incriminate himself. The pressures the rule generates are first that the defendant will be burdened in his decision to invoke the privilege by the knowledge that this may later be used to impeach his credibility if he testifies at trial and second that his decision to take the stand will be affected by his prior silence. The risk of impeachment, however, would not compel the defendant to forgo his right not to take the stand since impeachment could only occur if the defendant chose to testify. Furthermore, even though theoretically the defendant might be pressured into waiving his privilege at the time of arrest in order to prevent the risk of impeachment at trial should he later choose to take the stand, a defendant has no right to be free of the "traditional truth-testing devices of the adversary process."[13] On this basis, and in line with the Court's 1926 decision in *Raffel v. United States*, the dissenters in *Doyle* found the impeachment rule constitutional.

Although the relevance of the Fifth Amendment to the impeachment rule might appear to be an academic discussion because of its invalidation under the due process clause, the issue is an important one in light of a number of unresolved questions. The first of these is the issue of whether prior silence may be used for impeachment purposes in circumstances varying from *Doyle*. For example, what if the defendant fails to exculpate himself in a situation where an innocent person would have done so *prior* to the point at which *Miranda* warnings would be necessary. In a noncustodial setting, the police may question a suspect without informing him of his rights and thus there would be no unfairness, as was the case in *Doyle*, in using the silence for impeachment purposes. Absent a warning, there is no implicit assurance against state-imposed adverse consequences if the suspect remains silent. With the due process issue of fairness removed, the resolution of the problem would have to depend upon the Fifth Amendment. And if the Fifth Amendment would permit the impeachment use of silence in the precustody stage, would it allow for the same result in a postcustody setting where the police neglected to give a warning? In *Harris*, the Court allowed confessions obtained in violation of *Miranda* to be used for impeachment purposes even though they could not be used to prove guilt. Why not allow silence obtained in violation of *Miranda* to similarly be used for impeachment purposes? Having decided *Doyle* on Fourteenth Amendment grounds and given the impeachment exception to the use of statements obtained in violation of *Miranda*, the Court left this as an open possibility. And if the Fifth Amendment would tolerate the impeachment use of silence obtained in violation of *Miranda*, the police would wind up with added incentive to dispense with the warning where the signs were that the suspect was prepared to exercise his right to remain silent.

Aside from the use of silence for impeachment purposes, there is still a question whether a suspect's silence may ever be used as substantive evidence of guilt. If so, the state would be helped in cases where the defendant did not testify. We know that comment upon the defendant's silence at trial is barred as a result of *Griffin*. But even though the jury cannot be told to consider the defendant's silence, it is certainly aware of the fact that he has refused to take the stand and may draw an adverse inference on its own. In jurisdictions where the law authorizes a no-adverse-inference instruction under such circumstances, there is at least an effort to avoid this result. But there is no constitutional rule mandating the giving of a no-adverse-inference instruction, and it could be argued that making no reference whatsoever to the defendant's failure to take the stand is not equivalent to the comment upon silence that the *Griffin* case invalidated. *Lakeside v. Oregon*, which approved a no-adverse-inference instruction given over the defendant's objection, interpreted *Griffin* narrowly enough to permit this result.

There is an even stronger argument that evidence of *pretrial* silence might be usable not merely to impeach the credibility of the defendant but also as substantive evidence of guilt. Its basis lies in tacit-admission rule, which provides that silence in the face of an accusatory statement, under circumstances where an innocent individual would be expected to make a denial, is probative of the defendant's guilt.[14] In a criminal context, however, the rule runs into competing policies. In particular, *Miranda* tells us that the environment of police custody is sufficiently threatening to the voluntariness requirement that preinterrogation warnings must be given. The values reflected in this obligation would be too easily circumvented if silence could be used as evidence of guilt. Police could literally manufacture evidence by making accusatory statements to the suspect without giving him a warning. Their hope would be either to use silence as evidence of guilt or to draw out a self-incriminatory response to be available as impeachment evidence should the defendant take the stand. And the custodial environment would assist them in achieving their purpose. The most sensible solution therefore would be to bar the use of postcustody silence for both substantive evidence *and* impeachment purposes whether or not warnings have been given.

The Supreme Court's view of the precustody environment, however, has denied the existence of the inherently compelling atmosphere present in a postarrest police-citizen encounter. Hence no warnings are necessary prior to the suspect being questioned. Therefore if evidence of silence is held admissible, it cannot provide an inducement to dispense with the administration of a warning that would not be given in any event. Based upon this logic, the tacit-admission rule has been accepted in circumstances where warnings of the right to silence were not required.[15] The cases hold that as a matter of evidence policy, the failure to deny is deemed probative of the defendant's guilt, and there need be no fear that the rule would encourage violations of the *Miranda* requirement. Yet there is a risk that the doctrine may be misused as appears to have been the case in a Missouri decision, *State v. Peebles*.[16] The defendant, Peebles, was an inmate in the St. Louis County jail. After he had an altercation with another inmate during the night, guards rushed in and found the defendant with a razor blade in his hand. His failure to make an exculpatory statement at that time was held admissible to prove guilt under the tacit-admission rule. The circumstances, however, were too close to Fifth Amendment-related concerns to justify such a result. The defendant was in custody even though on a charge unrelated to his assault on another inmate, and thus custodial pressures similar to those of *Miranda* were present. More significantly, however, the connection between silence and proof of guilt since *Miranda* has become too tenuous to support its evidentiary use. Knowledge of the right to remain silent is sufficiently widespread to justify concern that the silence was meant as a decision to exercise a constitutional right and if so, it has no evidentiary value.

The Supreme Court has already upheld the validity of an adverse inference based upon an individual's exercise of the privilege against self-incrimination, albeit in a civil context.[17] It might well conclude that an adverse inference based upon precustody silence in a criminal proceeding is also permissible. The inference itself is a purely evidentiary question as to whether the probative value of the evidence outweighs its prejudicial effect. The law, however, appears to have accepted the evidentiary utility of silence, leaving only the privilege against self-incrimination as a potential basis upon which to justify exclusion. Yet the interference with Fifth Amendment values resulting from an adverse inference in a civil proceeding upon invocation of the privilege is less severe than that which would follow an adverse inference at a criminal trial. The historical focus upon the criminal trial in the privilege's evolutionary development amply supports such a position. Consequently, the adverse use of silence, while possibly tolerated in other contexts, should not be allowed to enter the arena in which guilt is to be determined. To ensure that Fifth Amendment interests are not infringed upon at their most central point, the privilege must be taken to mean that where there was any possibility that silence was meant as an invocation of the Fifth Amendment, no adverse use of that silence may be permitted in any criminal proceeding. Whether the Supreme Court will follow this analysis, however, is tied to the determination of how much an individual's decision to invoke the privilege may be burdened.

Nontrial Burdens and the Penalty Theory

We have already seen that the Supreme Court in *Griffin v. California* utilized what appeared to be very open-ended language to bar comment upon the defendant's failure to take the witness stand. The Court labeled such comment a penalty that impermissibly made assertion of the privilege costly. But *Griffin* wasn't the only penalty case of that period. To the contrary, a series of penalty decisions from the Court during the 1960s was seemingly creating a wide protective shield around the defendant's right to silence at trial. The decision whether to exercise that right was not to be burdened by the imposition of penalties against anyone who invoked it. It must be stressed, however, that the penalty theory in its early manifestation was tied closely to the criminal trial context, and the penalties themselves were directly related to the accused's ability to defend himself. They included evidentiary use of the defendant's failure to take the stand but did not end there.

Thus, for example, the Supreme Court in *Brooks v. Tennessee* invalidated a Tennessee requirement that the defendant testify before his other witnesses, calling it an "impermissible restriction on the defendant's right against self-incrimination."[18] *Griffin's* command that the assertion of the privilege not be made costly was quoted with approval. And, in *United States v. Jackson*[19] the Court invalidated the death-penalty provision of the Federal Kidnapping Statute pursuant to which a defendant could be sentenced to death if convicted by a jury, but faced a maximum of life imprisonment if he plead guilty and was sentenced by a judge. The penalty was the risk of death for exercising the constitutional right of pleading not guilty and being tried by a jury. Again citing *Griffin*, the Court ruled the sentencing structure an "impermissible burden upon the assertion of a constitutional right" because it "needlessly encourage[d]"[20] guilty pleas and jury waivers. Finally, in another self-incrimination setting, the Court ruled that testimony a defendant must give in a suppression hearing to establish his standing to challenge a search and seizure could not be used against him at trial. By asserting his privilege against self-incrimination, the defendant suffered the penalty of being unable to vindicate his Fourth Amendment rights. Similarly, assertion of his Fourth Amendment rights would require him to give up the benefits of the privilege. The situation actually presented reciprocal penalties, a "tension" between constitutional rights that the Court in *Simmons v. United States* found "intolerable."[21]

The fact that the penalty cases served to shield important trial rights should not obsure the Court's failure to define the content of the penalty standard it was using. The *Griffin* ruling was the worst offender, lacking any guidance for judging Fifth Amendment penalties. *Brooks, Jackson,* and *Simmons* were only slightly better. Some effort was made in each of them to describe how an individual might be affected by the relevant penalites, but precisely why those consequences were forbidden remained unclear. Yet the issue was of major significance in defining the scope of the privilege against self-incrimination. The controlling language of the Fifth Amendment bars compelling an individual to incriminate himself. Clearly, therefore, any penalty that would compel self-incrimination could not be permitted. But further refinement was necessary as to whether an individual or group focus was to be taken. If an individual focus was controlling, the relevant inquiry was whether the object of the penalty had been compelled to incriminate himself by it; if so, the privilege would have been violated, and the evidence could not be used. By hypothesis, however, anyone who asserted the privilege despite the penalty had not been compelled to incriminate himself, and thus there would have been no Fifth Amendment violation. But even if self-incriminatory information were provided, it would still be possible to use the evidence if it could be established that the penalty did not *compel* the self-incriminatory revelations. The individual focus standard, therefore, was very much a case-by-case determination in which all the facts would have to be weighed to determine whether a specific person was compelled to incriminate himself by the penalty. The fact that none of the penalty cases undertook a detailed assessment of the effect of the penalty on the defendant suggests that the individual focus was not employed. Only those tactics that *always* produce compelled self-incrimination could be allowed to escape such an analysis, but even assuming there exists a totally effective penalty, those that were involved in the Court's decisions could hardly be so classified.

A group focus test bases its assessment of Fifth Amendment penalties upon the general tendencies they produce. If a particular consequence results in compelled self-incrimination with sufficient frequency, it could be labeled an unconstitutional penalty despite the fact some individuals would be able to withstand its pressure. Presumably, the judgment would be based upon a weighing of the penalty's likely impact upon an average individual, since a penalty standard based upon what heroes and martyrs would do might well write the privilege out of the Constitution. The absence of a case-by-case factual inquiry in the Court's penalty decisions is a hint that it may have been employing a group-focus standard. At the same time, however, there was no sign in the opinions that the penalties were thought to ordinarily compel self-incrimination. Certainly, there was no empirical evaluation of how the penalties functioned, but beyond that the Court did not appear to suggest that the penalties had generally compelling characteristics even in its narrative. Rather, the language of the opinions talked in terms of the harshness of the choices confronting the defendants. If so, they were barred on a theory not directly tied to the Fifth Amendment ban against compelled self-incrimination. The Court was not changing its standard of compulsion; instead, it was decreeing that certain consequences could not follow invocation of the privilege because they were unfair, irrespective of whether they were also compelling.

The development of extra protective devices to shield Fifth Amendment rights at trial does not necessarily lead to the conclusion that similar protections are required for out-of-court contexts in which privilege issues may arise. Arguably, the fairness rationale should be limited to Fifth Amendment problems at trial, and the more traditional compulsion analysis would supervise other burdens on the exercise of the right to remain silent. Accepting a hierarchy of values underlying the privilege, and assuming the primacy of the interests of the criminal defendant in the trial setting, it then is possible to justify more than one theory to regulate the advantages the state may take of an individual's decision to invoke the privilege. Yet it can also be argued that when the state applies compulsion to obtain self-incriminatory information outside of the trial courtroom, the effects may well be comparable to the results of efforts made inside. Granting that the immediacy of the risk of a criminal conviction is of course greater at trial than elsewhere, there would nevertheless be an equal intrusion on privacy values regardless of the setting in which an individual was "compelled to be a witness against himself." Moreover, if compelled self-incrimination is viewed as an abuse of power by the state, the particular forum at issue hardly detracts from the abusive characteristics of the state's actions. The policies lying behind the privilege against self-incrimination would appear to call for the same regulatory principles in all applicable situations. Although the Court appeared to accept this line of reasoning for a time, more recent decisions suggest some uncertainty on this issue with the applicability of the privilege now seemingly once again determined by the setting in which the problem arises.

Two cases decided by the Supreme Court in 1967 marked the beginning of an apparent commitment to the application of rigorous standards in controlling all instances of state-imposed burdens on the Fifth Amendment. The first of the decisions was *Garrity v. New Jersey*.[22] The case evolved out of an investigation by the New Jersey Attorney General into the alleged fixing of traffic tickets by local police officers. Individual officers were called in for questioning and informed that they had the right to refuse to answer incriminatory questions but that exercise of that right, under state law, would lead to removal from office, while their answers could be used against them in a criminal proceeding. Later, they were prosecuted for conspiracy to obstruct the administration of the traffic laws, and statements they made in the attorney general's investigation were admitted over their objections. The options available to the officers were either to incriminate themselves or forfeit their jobs, and the Court concluded that the situation was "the antithesis of free choice to speak out or remain silent."[23] Lacking a free choice of whether or not to exercise the Fifth Amendment, the Court reasoned that the statements must have been coerced and were therefore inadmissible. No waiver could be found since the inquiries were answered under the duress of the threat of job forfeiture. The fact that there was a theoretical option of remaining silent was not sufficient for a valid waiver given that the choice was "between the rock and the whirlpool."[24]

As noted by Justice Harlan in dissent, however, the Court's conclusion was ambiguous in delineating its rationale. On the one hand, it hinted that as a factual matter, the statements were coerced, but it did so without even bothering to consider the circumstances under which the statements were made other than the existence of the job-forfeiture penalty. The analysis was far from the sort normally associated with findings of involuntariness. But the majority's approach was also suggestive of the *Griffin* type of penalty analysis in concluding that a statement resulting from the threat of an impermissible penalty is inadmissible at trial. Granting that the penalty made the choice difficult, the Court was either satisfied with that alone as a basis for excluding the resulting statement or felt that something about the penalty in question exceeded acceptable bounds. Exactly what that might have been was not clarified.

In *Spevack v. Klein*[25] the Court reviewed the disbarment of an attorney by the state of New York. Solomon Klein had been one of the objects of a Brooklyn, New York, ambulance-chasing inquiry. He refused to honor a subpoena *duces tecum* to produce various financial records on grounds of privilege and was for that reason disbarred. The entire context was somewhat analogous to *Garrity* in that a penalty was threatened by the state for invocation of the privilege against self-incrimination. Unlike *Garrity*, however, the penalty was the loss of a state license rather than a government job per se, and Klein was able to resist it. Thus while *Garrity* weighed the admissibility of a statement obtained as a result of threatening a penalty, *Spevack v. Klein* focused upon whether the penalty could be invoked if it failed to produce the sought-after information. A 1961 Supreme Court decision, *Cohen v. Hurley*,[26] authorized disbarment in circumstances "on all fours"[27] with *Spevack*, but that ruling had occurred prior to the incorporation of the Fifth Amendment in *Malloy v. Hogan*. Viewing the case from the perspective of the self-incrimination clause, however, the Court reasoned that *Cohen* was no longer good law and that the penalty of disbarment could not be invoked against Klein.

The penalty rationale was the unmistakable source of the Court's ruling in *Spevack*. The majority opinion quoted from *Malloy v. Hogan* to the effect that the Fifth Amendment means the "right of a person to remain silent unless he chooses to speak in the unfettered exercise of his own will, and to suffer no penalty . . . for such silence."[28] And penalty was taken to mean the *Griffin* concept of a sanction that makes exercise of the privilege costly. The Court then concluded without any real analysis that the threat of disbarment was simply too powerful a penalty to withstand a Fifth Amendment challenge. The majority was unwilling to create any special rule for attorneys that would authorize penalties that could not be applied against others.

Despite many similarities, it is apparent that the *Spevack* ruling presented issues not addressed in *Garrity*. It is one thing to conclude that the Fifth Amendment is violated by the use of a statement obtained by threatening a penalty. In *Spevack*, however, no self-incriminatory information was obtained. Thus barring imposition of the penalty could not be based upon the involuntariness of any statement secured from Klein. The decision could be said to represent a finding that the disbarment threat, where successful, would produce only coerced statements, but the Court gave no sign that it viewed the penalty in such a light. Short of that the Court might have considered disbarment as coercive enough to produce an unacceptable number of involuntary statements and thus invalidated the penalty as a prophylactic measure. Again no clear indication of a prophylactic theory was offered, and precedent suggested its limitation to far more coercive surroundings or to sanctions more clearly directed at interfering with Fifth Amendment rights. The custodial interrogation process[29] and adverse comment upon the defendant's failure to take the stand[30] come to mind as appropriate examples. The disbarment process is a much different environment, and its labeling as a prohibited sanction was surely a sign of the Court's concern with the fairness of the Fifth Amendment choice Klein was faced with. The fact that disbarment was the penalty the state would impose upon assertion of the privilege undercut the degree of freedom the Court was indirectly insisting upon in the choice of self-incrimination or silence.

The majority opinion in *Spevack* did not address the relevance of the *Garrity* ruling to the validity of imposing the disbarment penalty. As a result of *Garrity* anything that attorney Klein might have said under threat of disbarment could not have been used against him. In short, he had immunity by operation of law and thus could legitimately have been compelled to respond. Nevertheless, it would have been terribly unfair to hold him accountable for refusing to provide immunized testimony. First, Klein was not told that he had immunity, nor could he have known it since the law at the time did not provide for immunity under such circumstances. Given any possibility that he would have answered the inquiries had he been made aware that immunity was available, imposition of the sanction would have been unjust. More importantly, however, the principle of immunity by operation of law does not encompass the protections present in statutory immunity procedures, including supervision of decisions to grant immunity and the offering of it in open court. The immunity route chosen by the legislature is to be preferred. The exclusion of statements obtained as a result of prohibited penalties is a remedial device to correct for an impermissible Fifth Amendment burden, not an alternative to the formal route available for conferring immunity. In a 1973 decision, *Lefkowitz v. Turley*, the Court seemed to accept this position in stating that "if answers are to be required in such circumstances States must offer to the witness whatever immunity is required to supplant the privilege."[31] In using the word "offer," the Court may have meant that the fact that whatever information was obtained would be ruled inadmissible would not in itself validate the penalty unless there was a "grant of immunity"[32] such as is provided for by statute.

The *Garrity* and *Spevack* decisions not only were ambiguous in explaining these rationales but also used very broad language in ruling the penalties illegal. As a result, the dissenting opinions in both cases expressed concern that the Court was making it impossible for the state to call its servants to account for their conduct in office. In two 1968 decisions, however, the imbalance was rectified. The cases, *Uniformed Sanitation Men Association v. Commissioner of Sanitation of New York*[33] and *Gardner v. Broderick*,[34] both involved Section 1123 of the New York City Charter, which provided for the dismissal of city employees who refused to waive their privilege against self-incrimination in an official inquiry related to their conduct in office. In each instance waiver of the privilege was refused, but the Court ruled that the penalty of dismissal could not be invoked. By merging the *Garrity* and *Spevack* decisions, the Court appeared to suggest that not only would the fruits of an unconstitutional penalty be inadmissible but also that the imposition of the penalty itself was barred. This had been the result for the attorney in *Spevack* and would be no different for public employees even if they were police officers. Despite the special loyalty a police officer owes to the state, the Court still forbade the imposition of unconstitutional burdens on his Fifth Amendment rights.

Up to this point the decisions appear to be no more than reaffirmations of the Court's 1967 *Garrity* and *Spevack* rulings with the added feature that impermissible penalties were held unenforceable against public employees. The Court, however, in opinions written by Justice Fortas, took pains to point out that the state was not barred by the penalty theory from effectively investigating the conduct of public business by questioning public officials. Thus in *Gardner* the Court noted:

> If appellant, a policeman, had refused to answer questions specifically, directly, and narrowly relating to the performance of his official duties, without being required to waive his immunity with respect to the use of his answers or the fruits thereof in a criminal prosecution of himself . . . the privilege against self-incrimination would not have been a bar to his dismissal.[35]

And in *Sanitation Men Association*, the Court stated that the case would have been "entirely different"[36] had not a waiver of the privilege been demanded. In not offering immunity in return for the compelled testimony and requiring the dismissal of those who asserted the Fifth Amendment, New York City was seeking to have its cake and eat it by securing self-incriminatory information that would be available in both a criminal proceeding based upon the official's misconduct and a civil proceeding to remove him from office. If the individual refused to answer, the state could nevertheless have automatically dismissed him for invoking the Fifth Amendment. This was a Hobson's choice the Court refused to tolerate.

Further developments in the *Garrity* penalty theory are reflected in two more recent decisions of the Supreme Court, *Lefkowitz v. Turley*[37] decided in 1973 and *Lefkowitz v. Cunningham*[38] decided in 1977. In *Turley* the penalty for failure to waive the privilege against self-incrimination was the imposition on a contractor of a five-year disqualification from doing business with the state, while *Cunningham* involved a penalty of forfeiture of a nonpaying political party position. Both penalties appear to be of a lesser order of magnitude than the firing of a government employee whose job is his means of support. To the Court, however, the five-year contract disqualification was a "substantial economic sanction"[39] and therefore barred, and the loss of unpaid political party positions was prohibited because it was a "potent"[40] penalty. In each instance the opinions stressed that the sanctions were penalties for refusing to waive the privilege. Left undecided was whether a dismissal and contract disqualification aimed at ensuring fitness to hold a public trust might be acceptable. The McCarthy era cases accepted the legality of this technique[41] subject to the qualification that no "sinister meaning"[42] could be imputed to the assertion of the privilege. In order to survive challenge today, however, given the *Garrity* line of cases, some change in procedure may be necessary. Another decision, *Baxter v. Palmigiano*,[43] hints at what this might have to entail.

Palmigiano was an inmate in the Rhode Island Adult Correctional Institution charged before a prison disciplinary board with inciting a disturbance. After being informed that he could be additionally charged with a criminal violation, he was advised to consult with his attorney, but the attorney could not be present during the disciplinary hearing. Palmigiano was informed of his right to remain silent but also told that his silence could be held against him. The hearing was conducted without the inmate's testifying, and he was found guilty and sentenced to a period of solitary confinement as well as the downgrading of his classification status. The overall procedure appeared analogous to those cases in which the Court invalidated penalties for assertion of the privilege, particularly *Griffin v. California* in which the Court barred adverse comment upon the defendant's failure to take the stand. The *Baxter* opinion, however, adopted the distinction between trial and nontrial burdens and limited *Griffin* to adverse comment in the criminal proceeding itself. Since a prison disciplinary hearing is not a criminal trial, *Griffin* did not bar the use of an adverse inference from silence in such a situation.

Nevertheless, *Garrity* and related decisions barring the imposition of nontrial Fifth Amendment penalties had demonstrated that sanctions imposed outside of the criminal courtroom could violate the Constitution if sufficiently potent. However, these cases were distinguished by the *Baxter* Court on two grounds. First, the opinion observed that Rhode Island had not "insisted or asked that Palmigiano waive his Fifth Amendment privilege,"[44] a factor present in the *Garrity* line of cases. Additionally, a prison inmate "electing to remain silent during his disciplinary hearing . . . [was] not in consequence of his silence automatically found guilty of the infraction."[45] Thus the Court characterized the *Garrity* cases as situations involving the automatic imposition of a penalty upon refusal to waive the Fifth Amendment, a problem not present in the context of *Baxter* since the state of Rhode Island did not directly employ its sanction to obtain a waiver of the privilege. Its use of silence as the basis of an adverse inference occurred in a noncriminal proceeding and was not an automatic triggering device for imposition of the penalty. Most directly, the decision affirmed the validity of drawing adverse inferences for assertion of the Fifth Amendment. But when applied to the *Garrity* type problem, it raised the possibility that invocation of the privilege could lead to job dismissal. However, it would be necessary for the state's goal to be that of assuring the individual's competency to hold office or an official trust, not punishment for a refusal to waive the privilege. Moreover, the silence could be given no more evidentiary value than it deserved and could not be used to automatically trigger a potent sanction.

Dissecting the intricacies of the Court's penalty theory for assessing Fifth Amendment burdens is an obviously complicated undertaking. But the theory's major problem is not so much its complexity as its absolute character. During the developmental phase of the penalty theory, it appeared to be a label that could be conveniently applied to prohibited consequences for assertion of the privilege. As such, it was more of a substitute for detailed analysis than a logically supported principle. It gave the appearance of being an effective shield against improper Fifth Amendment burdens, but with major flaws. Primary among these was the absence of a standard by which Fifth Amendment penalties could be evaluated. To the contrary, the language used by the Court made it appear that nearly every negative consequence might be labeled a prohibited penalty. The fact that all penalties so labeled, whatever the standard, were barred was another drawback. So unyielding a theory can create pressure to evaluate Fifth

Amendment burdens in a way that does not appropriately classify them. Moreover, its absolute character virtually invited the Court to develop a formalistic distinction such as that reflected in *Baxter*.

Balancing Fifth Amendment Interests

As an alternative to the penalty analysis, Justice Harlan pressed for the adoption of a balancing theory to assess the validity of Fifth Amendment burdens. In lieu of the arbitrariness of the rule totally barring the imposition of penalties for assertion of the privilege and excluding all statements obtained on threat of invoking the sanction, he argued that a weighing process should be employed to determine the constitutionality of the penalty. At its core, however, his theory was more of a due process analysis than an offshoot of the self-incrimination clause. But it implicitly constituted a strict reading of the Fifth Amendment as prohibiting the use of only those penalties that would produce *compelled* self-incrimination. Moreover, the admissibility of statements obtained by threat of invoking the penalty was to be handled on a case-by-case basis. The compulsion requirement of the Fifth Amendment was thus taken as representing substantial force, perhaps on the order of the threats of physical abuse and imprisonment for contempt. By relying on due process to protect against lesser penalties, and given the rather tolerant due process standard of fundamental fairness, the balancing analysis was obviously meant as a far more permissive control mechanism. In contrast, the penalty theory of the self-incrimination clause prohibited all adverse consequences by merely labeling them penalties.

As far back as *Garrity v. New Jersey* and *Spevack v. Klein*, Justice Harlan was pressing for the use of the balancing theory. He thought that the absolutism of the penalty analysis was inappropriate, observing that "this broad proposition is entirely without support in the construction hitherto given to the privilege and is directly inconsistent with a series of cases in which the Court has indicated the principles that are properly applicable here."[46] Instead, he proposed a test in which "[t]he validity of a consequence depends both upon the hazards, if any, it presents to the integrity of the privilege and upon the urgency of the public interests it is designed to protect."[47] In the employee termination cases, he saw the relevant state interests as the need to establish reasonable qualifications and standards of conduct for public employees as well as the obligation of the state to require its officers to account for their conduct. And as long as no impermissible inference of guilt was drawn from the exercise of the privilege and the state goal was not to penalize silence, Justice Harlan could find no impairment of Fifth Amendment interests. In his view, the appropriate standard for handling this kind of case had been set by the Supreme Court in *Orloff v. Willoughby*,[48] a 1953 decision in which a physician was denied a commission in the army because he refused on Fifth Amendment grounds to answer questions about his past membership in the Communist party. In upholding the denial of a commission, the Court concluded that the "President of the United States, before certifying his confidence in an officer and appointing him to a commissioned rank, has the right to learn whatever facts the President thinks may affect his fitness."[49] The only limits were those of the *Slochower* case involving prohibitions against imputing a "sinister meaning"[50] to the assertion of the privilege and the requirement that the context be a bona fide inquiry into the officer's fitness as a public employee.

The use of the balancing test as applied to an attorney who refuses to respond in a Bar-related investigation was an even simpler task to resolve. Again, no particular harm to the privilege was entailed other than the general risk that a particular response might be compelled. However, the use of such a statement could be prohibited, and Justice Harlan saw no particular need for a prophylactic rule prohibiting the disbarment sanction. On the other side of the balance lay important state interests in ensuring the professional integrity of attorneys and controlling such evils as ambulance chasing. Moreover, these have been interests historically pursued by the state. Justice Harlan therefore was able to conclude that both the disbarment and dismissal sanctions did not offend constitutional standards. Given the fact that Justice Harlan was writing in dissent, however, his opinion did not have to address the long-range implications of his position, nor was it necessary to consider the wide variety of contexts in which Fifth Amendment sanctions arise. Rather, he was setting forth a methodology of analysis for later cases to elaborate upon. As this occurred, a better sense of the balancing theory would emerge.

Crampton v. Ohio, a companion case to *McGautha v. California*,[51] with Justice Harlan now writing the Court's opinion, provides a substantial elaboration of the balancing theory in a previously unaddressed Fifth Amendment context. Crampton had been convicted of first-degree murder and sentenced to death under Ohio procedure in which both guilt and punishment were determined in a single proceeding by the jury. The essence of his objection was that in order to address the sentencer on the issuer of punishment, he would have had to face the risk of self-incrimination on the issue of guilt. If, for example, he wished to place mitigating considerations before the jury such as prior acts of the victim that might have convinced them not to impose capital punishment, he could have done so only by taking the witness stand and having his testimony be weighed in deciding both whether he was guilty *and* what his punishment should be. He argued that by utilizing the simple expedient of a bifurcated trial in which the jury first determined guilt and then assessed punishment in a separate proceeding, the interference with his constitutional rights would have been avoided. He could then have exercised his privilege against self-incrimination during the guilt phase and later taken the stand solely on the issue of punishment. Some states utilize the bifurcated procedure as a matter of choice; Crampton argued that it was constitutionally required.

One aspect of Crampton's claim was that the Ohio unitary trial procedure violated the constitutional tension theory of *Simmons v. United States*.[52] There it had been held impermissible to require a choice between constitutional rights in the context of a state attempt to use testimony given at a search and seizure suppression hearing against the accused at trial. A recent lower-court ruling has applied the same principle to bar use of an accused's testimony where it was given in support of a claim of double jeopardy.[53] To Justice Harlan, however, the *Simmons* theory was not intended to reflect a general rejection of constitutional tensions but was instead a response to the need to prevent deterring Fourth Amendment claims and thus undermining the efficacy of the exclusionary rule. The Fifth Amendment question in *Simmons* was the validity of the choice between testifying at a suppression hearing and asserting the privilege against self-incrimination, and that was not in itself unconstitutional. The purely Fifth Amendment aspect of *Crampton* and similar cases, after dispensing with *Simmons*, then became the fact that a difficult choice was imposed upon those seeking to assert the privilege against self-incrimination. In the *Garrity* line of cases, the choice was waive the privilege or lose one's job; in *Crampton* the choice was waive the privilege or lose the opportunity to convince the jury not to impose a sentence of death. In one sense the cases were different since the loss of employment was automatic in the *Garrity* situation, but the death sentence was not certain in *Crampton*. But *Crampton* did reflect an automatic penalty of not being able to offer the defendant's own mitigating testimony without loss of the right to remain silent on the issue of guilt. Thus it could well have been analyzed under the penalty theory, and the unitary trial might then have been adjudged a costly burden on the Fifth Amendment and therefore barred. But Justice Harlan had swung a majority of the Court over to his balancing theory, and that was to be the framework for assessing the permissibility of the choice to which Crampton was put.

The first step in the application of the theory was the analysis of the Fifth Amendment interests at stake. In a previous case the Court had held that the mere force of evidence presented by the state that the defendant feels compelled to refute at the cost of his right to remain silent does not constitute a Fifth Amendment violation.[54] Similarly valid is a requirement of pretrial notice of alibi that forces early disclosure of an alibi defense at the risk of its forfeiture as well as the rules that permit wide-ranging cross-examination into otherwise inadmissible evidence when the defendant takes the stand. Given these permissible pressures, Justice Harlan felt that "nothing in the history, policies, or precedents relating to the privilege"[55] warranted a different result for the Ohio unitary trial system. In one paragraph the opinion concluded that the particular problem faced by Crampton had no parallel in the excesses that spawned the privilege. Of the various policies reflected in the Fifth Amendment, Justice Harlan could find only one of possible relevance, the goal of preventing state cruelty to an accused. But since the *Crampton* problem was not akin to the "cruel trilemma of self-accusation, perjury or contempt"[56] which the Fifth Amendment was designed to guard against, Justice Harlan thought it preferable to consider the cruelty argument from the perspective of the "fundamental requirements of fairness and decency embodied in the Due Process Clauses."[57] In light of all the pressures due process tolerates, he could not conclude that yielding to the need to address the sentencer on the issue of punishment and thereby risking self-incrimination on the issue of guilt, even in a capital case, offended fundamental fairness as reflected in the policies underlying the privilege.

The interests reflected in the other aspect of Crampton's dilemma, his desire to plead for leniency in sentencing, were deemed by the Court even less substantial than the self-incrimination considerations. All Crampton was deterred from doing under the Ohio procedure was making the sentencer aware of information "peculiarly within his own knowledge."[58] The Court was skeptical as to the substantiality of the deterrence involved and saw no unfairness in a system that requires "that such evidence be available to the jury on all issues to which it is relevant or not at all."[59] The difficult choice to which Crampton was put therefore did not offend constitutional standards. Even though the burden placed on his Fifth Amendment interests was directly related to the right to silence at trial, he wound up having the privilege balanced away.

Justice Harlan's approach to the balancing theory was also reflected in his concurring opinion in *California v. Byers*,[60] which upheld a statute requiring drivers involved in an automobile accident to stop and identify themselves. The disclosure obligation in his view did have some bearing on the policies underlying the privilege. Specifically, it intruded upon the sphere of privacy protected by the Fifth Amendment and somewhat implicated the privilege's goal of preserving a fundamentally accusatorial system of justice in the face of pressures to introduce inquisitorial tactics. But this was counterbalanced by a strong state interest in ensuring personal financial responsibility for automobile accidents. Moreover, allowing an assertion of privilege in the context of an accident-reporting requirement would have made it virtually a self-executing claim since obviously court review would be nearly impossible. In light of these considerations and the importance of self-reporting systems in contemporary society, Justice Harlan concluded that the Fifth Amendment was no bar to the enforcement of criminal penalties against those who failed to stop and identify themselves after an accident, even if they faced a risk of self-incrimination. Indeed, all such reporting systems were to be judged on the basis of an "evaluation of the assertedly noncriminal governmental purpose in securing the information, the necessity for self-reporting as a means of securing the information, and the nature of the disclosures required."[61] But it was to be a case-by-case assessment that, while balancing in the government's favor in the accident-reporting statute, might authorize nondisclosure elsewhere on the basis of the Fifth Amendment.

Balancing has now become a frequently used legal tool, particularly as in the *Crampton* type of situation where an individual must elect between options that are mutually exclusive. Determining the permissibility of the choice has become a matter of measuring "whether compelling the election impairs to an appreciable extent any of the policies behind the rights involved."[62] Thus *Chaffin v. Stynchcombe*[63] considered whether an individual who succeeded in having his conviction reversed could receive a longer sentence after a retrial. The Court ruled that as long as the jury sentencing the defendant was not informed of the prior sentence and its decision was not shown to have been vindictively imposed, no constitutional violation was present. The risk of a harsher sentence on retrial was only an "incidental consequence"[64] of the jury sentencing system, and the Court denied that it would impermissibly interfere with the decision to appeal the first conviction. An even more dramatic choice confronted the respondent in the Court's 1978 ruling in *Bordenkircher v. Hayes.*[65] The prosecutor had there offered Hayes a plea bargain on a pending forgery charge but threatened to obtain an indictment under the Kentucky Habitual Criminal Act, carrying a mandatory life sentence, if Hayes rejected the bargain. Hayes gambled and lost, winding up with the life sentence he had originally been threatened with. In light of the importance of the plea-bargaining system as well as its special characteristics, the Supreme Court declined to intervene. The burden on the exercise of his right to trial, reflected in the threat of increased punishment, was simply inherent in the plea-bargaining system itself. Similarly, the Court has held that the so-called two-tier trial procedure in which no jury trial right exists at the first proceeding, but the defendant may appeal and secure a trial de novo in which a jury is provided, does not unconstitutionally burden the right to trial by jury.[66] The Court also used the balancing theory to assess the New Jersey homicide statute because of its impact on the right to trial.[67] New Jersey required a mandatory life term for anyone convicted of first degree murder. If a plea of *nolo contendre* or *non vult* was entered to a first degree murder charge, however, the system authorized the judge to impose either a life sentence or the punishment provided for second degree murder. Obviously, the burden of the risk of a higher sentence was placed upon the decision to go to trial, but the Court held that it was not an unconstitutional choice to require a first-degree murder defendant to make.

Clearly, the Fifth Amendment is not the only arena in which the Court has had to confront the problem of reconciling individual constitutional rights with state procedures that burden their exercise. Indeed, the plea-bargaining process has been a particularly fruitful source of doctrine delineating the strategy of the Court in handling such issues. Moreover, it is now apparent that the Court's direction is in favor of a balancing analysis, which it has chosen to uniformly apply to all constitutional burden problems. And as a legal foundation for the balancing test, the Court has chosen to rely upon the due process clause of the Fourteenth Amendment rather than the specific constitutional rights at issue. This means that the fundamental fairness standard must regulate the quality and quantity of pressure the state may exert upon the exercise of constitutional rights. As a result the provisions of the Bill of Rights are left to define the scope of the rights encompassed in the amendments and prevent their denial but do not apply when the state procedures constitute an interference as opposed to an outright rejection. Moreover, the due process approach to balancing is seemingly one in which there are alternative modes of analysis. If the context is one in which an individual is forced to choose between mutually exclusive rights, the degree to which the policies behind those rights are impaired by virtue of the state compelling the choice determines the validity of the burdens that result.[68] The other pattern arises when an individual is forced to run a gauntlet of obstacles before he may exert a particular constitutional right.[69] Here, the weighing process measures the state interest reflected in its mandated procedures against the degree of impairment of the policies underlying the rights that are adversely affected. But whichever pattern the balancing theory is applied to, it must be remembered that in measuring the burden against due process requirements, the governing standard to be met is one of fundamental fairness. The degree to which the state may then burden the exercise of a constitutional right is tied to what the Court views as the baseline of governmental fairness and how willing it is to actively intervene in the supervision of state and federal criminal procedure. These in turn constitute formidable obstacles to strict supervision over Fifth Amendment burdens.

Toward a Presumptive Barrier

The balancing theory has clearly become the primary analytic tool for assessing the validity of Fifth Amendment burdens, and it has been utilized both where exercise of the privilege would result in the loss of other rights and where the privilege has been weighed against state interests. Additionally, however, the balancing theory, based in the doctrine of due process of law, is supplemented by a Fifth Amendment burden theory that bars the automatic imposition of potent sanctions upon assertion of the privilege. The significance of both theories is of course the fact that they stand as the only limitations upon the exercise of state power that penalizes assertion of the Fifth Amendment. The manner in which each doctrine works, however, demonstrates how little value the Court places on the right to remain silent. Neither theory is in practice an effective shield against the misuse of state power.

The cases in which the Court has rejected the automatic imposition of penalties for assertion of the privilege against self-incrimination are deceptive in suggesting the existence of a principle providing meaningful protection against infringements upon the Fifth Amendment. Although the theory initially sought to prevent the use of any sanction that made assertion of the privilege costly and as such would have had the potential to closely supervise state interference with the Fifth Amendment, it could not survive with so broad a framework. First, since just about any consequence could be said to make assertion of the privilege costly, a ban against all costly sanctions might well have swept away too many legitimate state activities. Consequences that would otherwise further important state interests and were rationally related to the invocation of the privilege would have been prohibited. An absolute ban on all costly sanctions might thus itself have been too costly. Second, the fact that the Court's broad prohibition against all costly sanctions encompassed no exception could have led to evasive decisions that would have done even more harm to the privilege. This might have included incorrectly labeling Fifth Amendment sanctions in order to avoid the penalty designation, as well as narrowing other aspects of the privilege such as the definition of the degree of incrimination demanded by it for the like purpose of circumventing the prohibition. It was inevitable that the formalism of the penalty theory would lead to a formalistic narrowing as reflected in the *Baxter v. Palmigiano* decision. But by narrowing the doctrine to bar only those sanctions that were potent and whose application followed automatically, most of the theory's protective potential evaporated. Presumably, sanctions that were not labeled "potent" could be automatically imposed while the more severe penalties could be utilized as long as their invocation was not automatic.

Criticism can also be leveled at the Court's theory of balancing as applied to Fifth Amendment burdens. As it now stands, the prevailing doctrine is set out in *Crampton v. Ohio*:

> The criminal process, like the rest of the legal system, is replete with situations requiring "the making of difficult judgments" as to which course to follow. . . . Although a defendant may have a right, even of constitutional dimensions, to follow whichever course he chooses, the Constitution does not by that token always forbid requiring him to choose. The threshold question is whether compelling the election impairs to an appreciable extent any of the policies behind the rights involved.[70]

Where the pattern is one in which the issue is not a strict choice between rights but rather the imposition of adverse consequences upon invocation of the privilege, the judgment is based on "two factors: the history and purposes of the privilege, and the character and urgency of the other public interests involved."[71] Note, however, that no special significance is given to the fact that balancing is being applied to constitutional rights. The measurement of the impairment to those rights is weighed against countervailing state interests as though apples and oranges were being compared. Existing doctrine does not provide for a preference in favor of the protection of constitutionally guaranteed individual rights. Nor has the actual mechanics of balancing been above reproach. Analysis of Fifth Amendment policy considerations in the context of resolving the legitimacy of state-imposed burdens on the privilege, be they in the form of state sanctions imposed on those who assert the privilege or state-compelled choices between the Fifth Amendment and other rights, has been notable for its superficiality. Fifth Amendment rights have been readily balanced away because the Court has not been inclined to meaningfully consider and evaluate what the privilege means, how various burdens affect the values it represents, and how substantial the state interests underlying the Fifth Amendment burden are.

The character of the privilege against self-incrimination is deserving of far more protection than existing doctrine offers. The Fifth Amendment bars compelling an individual to be a witness against himself. Clearly, the force inherent in the compulsion concept cannot be limited to situations where an individual is deprived of the choice of remaining silent. In the strictest sense there is no such choice deprivation since an individual can always accept the consequences of refusing to give up his self-incrimination protection, even if they reach the severity of torture. This, however, would effectively interpret the compulsion standard of the Fifth Amendment from the perspective of heroes and martyrs and thereby deprive it of any worthwhile content. Instead, the concept of compulsion must be realistically interpreted on the basis of the major interests the privilege guards. And, while its English roots lie in the cruel trilemma of self-accusation, perjury, and contempt, that need not define the Fifth Amendment's contemporary scope. As the Court has already recognized, the privilege both defines a zone of privacy from which the state is excluded and regulates the coercive power of the state in its dealings with individuals. These interests are particularly important in what has become an increasingly intrusive and government-dominated society, and they warrant a more sensitive accommodation to the consequences of burdening the Fifth Amendment than is currently available.

As an alternative, the Fifth Amendment should stand as a presumptive barrier to the imposition of adverse consequences for its exercise. This presumption against burdening the privilege should apply as well to state-compelled choices between the Fifth Amendment and other rights. Reliance upon the due process standard of fundamental fairness represents an unsatisfactory technique for assessing Fifth Amendment burdens. It gives the state vast leeway to circumscribe the right to remain silent because of the fact that due process simply does not provide close supervision over state action. To the contrary, it seeks to bar only those state activities running afoul of principles of fundamental fairness, a criterion intended to permit the state to act on most matters free from judicial control. The Fifth Amendment, however, contains the authority for its own protection. In using the compulsion standard, the Fifth Amendment implicitly authorizes the rejection of whatever would compel self-incrimination. And that should be judged on the basis of what the self-incrimination clause means in contemporary society.

The Fifth Amendment can effectively serve as a presumptive barrier against the imposition of burdens on the right to remain silent. There is sufficient leeway in the language, history, and policy of the self-incrimination clause to regulate interferences with it. The controlling standard therefore must be the compulsion prohibition of the Fifth Amendment itself. But this should not lead to a formalistic theoretical framework in which cases are decided based upon an abstract definition of what constitutes compulsion since no consensus as to the meaning of the word exists. What appears compelling to some is to others acceptable state pressure. Instead, compulsion can be meaningfully interpreted only from the perspective of the policy foundations of the privilege against self-incrimination. These in turn must be scrutinized with care to ensure that they are not unduly infringed as a result of a state-compelled choice between rights or state-imposed sanctions for invoking the privilege. And uncertainties should be resolved in favor of protecting the privilege, it being the state's obligation to justify any infringement. Burdens on the Fifth Amendment therefore should be subjected to a weighing of interests much akin to a balancing process, only with the Fifth Amendment standing as a presumptive barrier to interference with the right to remain silent.

A variety of factors appear to be relevant to the assessment of state burdens on the Fifth Amendment. Consideration should be given to the state purpose underlying its Fifth Amendment sanction, and the privilege should prevail wherever those purposes are directed toward an impermissible object. In *Baxter v. Palmigiano*, for example, the state sought to make use of an adverse inference stemming from a prisoner's invocation of the privilege in a prison disciplinary hearing, despite the fact that he risked self-incrimination with respect to potential criminal charges. Arguably, the purpose of the adverse inference was to assist the state in resolving the question of whether a prison infraction had occurred. But by the Court's own admission, an automatic finding of guilt could not have been based upon the inmate's silence, thus reducing the substantive value of the adverse inference. At the same time, however, the risk of self-incrimination operated as a powerful deterrent against the inmate's defending himself in the prison hearing. The adverse inference thus served as a tool to allow the state to either take advantage of the inmate's silence or coerce him into not exercising his Fifth Amendment rights. A prison disciplinary proceeding, however, will normally incorporate testimony from a guard or a third party that relates facts sufficient to prove a violation. The inmate, moreover, lacks the constitutional right to confront and cross-examine his accusers and has only a qualified right to present witnesses in his own behalf.[72] Under these circumstances, it is difficult to see why the state would even need the adverse inference. If so, and given the presumption against burdening the Fifth Amendment, the adverse inference in a prison hearing could not survive a purpose analysis and should be rejected as an impermissible burden on the Fifth Amendment.

It is also relevant in the weighing of Fifth Amendment burdens to determine whether there are alternative means to achieve the state's goals and how burdensome the alternatives are. The burdens encompassed in a state-compelled election of rights are illustrative since they raise the question of whether the coercion reflected in the compelled choice is truly necessary. If it is not essential, then perhaps the compelled choice should be invalidated. The unitary trial and sentencing procedure used by Ohio in capital cases and approved by the Court in *Crampton v. Ohio* is a suitable example. Under the procedure, the accused could assert his right to address the sentencer on the issue of punishment only by giving up his privilege against self-incrimination on the issue of guilt. This election was compelled despite the simple expedient of a bifurcated trial in which guilt would first be determined and a separate proceeding then used to impose the sentence. Perhaps there is some inconvenience in a mandatory bifurcated trial procedure but surely not enough to justify so heavy a burden on the Fifth Amendment. Nevertheless, the Court did not even bother to consider the availability of alternatives in *Crampton*. Instead, its analysis was limited to a weighing of the impairment of the rights encompassed in the compulsory choice. Yet if there is no good reason to impose a choice, it should not be required. A presumptive barrier theory would demand that reasonable alternatives be pursued before Fifth Amendment rights are infringed.

Additionally relevant in a presumptive barrier analysis is the severity of the sanction to be imposed. In the *Garrity* line of cases, for example, the automatic loss of a civil servant's job was treated as equivalent to Patrick Cunningham's removal as a high New York State Democratic party official. But a sanitation man's loss of his sole means of support is hardly the same as removal from an unpaid position where the individual removed can still continue in his compensated occupation. Similarly, where the circumstances encompass a compelled election between rights, it is necessary to consider the importance of the rights in issue. The *Simmons* constitutional tension theory made an effort in that direction with respect to its invalidation of the requirement that a suspect choose between vindicating Fourth Amendment rights at a cost of sacrificing Fifth Amendment rights. No reason exists for limiting the theory to constitutional rights alone, although they are likely to weigh heaviest on the scale. As a result of *Crampton v. Ohio*, the theory has been virtually buried, but it represents a tool of analysis that warrants resurrection.

Finally, the presumptive barrier theory requires a substantive analysis of the interests affected by the state's Fifth Amendment burden. Pursuant to the Court's current balancing theory, a very narrow approach is taken to Fifth Amendment policy analysis. The interest assessment ends up being superficial despite the fact that it lies at the heart of the Court's judgment. Perhaps a presumptive barrier theory that effectively creates a hurdle the state must surmount will force more depth in the Court's weighing of the competing interests. The state bears the burden of convincing the Court of the overriding significance behind the burden it seeks to impose as compared to the Fifth Amendment interests that are adversely affected. A thumb is on the Fifth Amendment side of the scale, and overcoming its weight will take more than a brief run-through of the countervailing policies. One cannot fully predict what results would follow from a change in the governing principles controlling Fifth Amendment burdens, but a presumptive barrier analysis, including an in-depth policy review, the weighing of the purpose and severity of the state sanction, and the consideration of alternatives, appears to give more appropriate weight to the relevant factors.

9

The Privilege and the Future

Tracing the development of the privilege against self-incrimination from its earliest roots in British common law tradition to its current role in contemporary American law is truly a fascinating undertaking. One cannot help but learn to admire and respect an idea whose historical background is so rich and whose meaning has essentially not lost any of its significance over a substantial period of time. Consistently, through many centuries, the right to remain silent has protected individuals against abuses of state authority and served to establish a sphere of individual personality into which the state could not intrude. It was a right built on the hopes, dreams, and determination of many people of conscience, and their sacrifices have left us with a very special protective shield. But tradition is not the only value the privilege against self-incrimination reflects. As encompassed in the Fifth Amendment, the self-incrimination clause also demonstrates a unique versatility. The character of the protection it affords emerges in a wide variety of contexts, well beyond the rather limited circumstances from which it grew.

It must nevertheless be conceded that the current environment surrounding the privilege is significantly different from that which led to its development. Star Chamber and High Commission proceedings often turned into wide-ranging fishing expeditions against opponents of the British crown and the established orthodoxy. Suspects were questioned without really knowing what they were suspected of and were faced with severe sanctions if they refused to truthfully answer all questions asked of them. Moreover, the questioning often focused upon matters of personal belief and was abusive in character. Official questioning today, however, is dramatically different. The Fifth Amendment stands as a barrier to such activities, but even in its absence, or as has been more seriously urged, its substantial curtailment, it is unlikely that the state would return to full-scale governmental inquisitions of the variety experienced in England during the sixteenth century. Traditions that have evolved pursuant to the First Amendment provide an alternative source of protection for political and religious beliefs, while the due process clause limits other aspects of the interrogation process. Once it is conceded, however, that the surrounding environment has changed, we are left with the problem of what to do with the self-incrimination clause. We can, on the one hand, contract the scope of the right to silence because it is no longer a critical protection. Respected

221

authority suggests that this is the path we should follow.[1] Alternatively, the scope of the privilege might be fixed at some point and held constant; arguably, this is the choice opted for by the current Supreme Court.[2] Finally, if one views contemporary society as one even more in need of the protection of the privilege than previous eras, the Fifth Amendment could be expansively interpreted as dissenting justices in a number of recent cases have urged.[3]

The Foundations of the Contemporary Privilege

If one takes an overview of the Fifth Amendment from the perspective of its status at the beginning of the 1980s, it is apparent that it works well in some respects but is deficient in others. The privilege against self-incrimination has been inconsistently applied and interpreted, at times taking on the character of an impenetrable barrier against state intrusion[4] but on other occasions appearing to be no more than a procedural obstacle to the state's efforts to acquire information.[5] This is particularly apparent when Fifth Amendment decisions are compared over time. The sensitivity of the courts, and the U.S. Supreme Court in particular, to the values reflected in the self-incrimination clause has not been static. To the contrary, each new Court appointment brings with it the potential for a change in judicial philosophy, including attitudes toward the Fifth Amendment. Moreover, to the extent that the judicial appointment process is responsive to the surrounding political environment, and given the shifting patterns of American politics, change is virtually built into the system. Change in perspective over time, however, is not the only reason for the inconsistent quality of Fifth Amendment rulings. The privilege against self-incrimination appears in so many different contexts, not all of which are necessarily deemed to be of equal importance, that courts have refused to provide the same level of self-incrimination protection in every setting. Inconsistency thus emanates from the attempt to apply a single principle in a wide variety of dissimilar situations.

Police interrogations illustrate the evolutionary character of Fifth Amendment doctrine when spread over a sufficiently broad time frame. Initially, the rules barring coerced confessions were a distinct component of the law of evidence, having nothing to do with the privilege against self-incrimination; the latter was deemed to be directed toward the legal compulsion reflected in the contempt sanction. Since police questioning involved no legal requirement to respond, and thus there was in fact a right to remain silent, the privilege against self-incrimination was not relevant. Surprisingly, in *Bram v. United States*,[6] however, the Supreme Court found confession law to be controlled by the self-incrimination clause. In its view, "the reasons which gave rise to the adoption of the Fifth Amendment" represented "but a crystallization of the doctrine as to confessions."[7] Time had certainly changed the scope of the Fifth Amendment's coverage in a substantial way. But in the next nearly seventy years between the Court's 1897 ruling in *Bram* and its 1966 decision in *Miranda v. Arizona*,[8] the Fifth Amendment played no part in confession law. The Court switched back to the view that the privilege against self-incrimination did not encompass any authority over investigatory questioning. *Miranda*, however, returned to the *Bram* philosophy of treating such questioning as governed by the Fifth Amendment.

Having arrived at the conclusion that confessions are covered by the self-incrimination clause, the Court has since had to confront the mechanics of applying the principle to specific interrogation problems. In particular, what constitutes compliance with the Fifth Amendment in the questioning process? Among the problems this question has raised are those of defining the custodial characteristics that generate a warning requirement and setting standards for the assessment of the adequacy of a waiver of the privilege. The Court has also addressed the problem of what remedial action to take in the event of a violation. A statement obtained without complying with the Court's *Miranda* warning requirement must be excluded when the state seeks to use it as substantive evidence of guilt, but the Court has found no constitutional bar in the use of the same statement to impeach the defendant's credibility. This held true when the violation was the failure to give the proper *Miranda* warning[9] as well as when the state failed to comply with the suspect's efforts to assert his *Miranda* rights.[10] The Fifth Amendment thus means different things depending upon the specific confession issue being confronted just as its very applicability to the confession process itself has been inconsistently judged over time.

But what can serve to explain the varying attitudes toward the Fifth Amendment privilege in the realm of confession law as well as the numerous other areas in which there is a right to remain silent? This is indeed one of the most critical issues in Fifth Amendment jurisprudence since the perspective from which the privilege against self-incrimination has been viewed has in turn determined the result in specific Fifth Amendment cases. If the privilege is deemed an important right, one deserving of steadfast protection, it is likely to wind up applicable in a large variety of contexts and consistently enforced in each, with state efforts to circumscribe its effectiveness sharply curtailed. On the other hand, if the right to remain silent is considered more of an obstacle than a valuable personal right, the range of applicability of the privilege is likely to be narrow, and evasions, even within its sphere of influence, readily tolerated.

The task would be much simpler if the words of the Fifth Amendment unequivocally set forth the limits of the privilege against self-incrimination.

It would then only be necessary to apply the literal language of the Amendment to specific fact situations. That, however, is not the character of the problem at hand. First, the language of the Fifth Amendment is far from clear. The Constitution tells us that "[n]o person . . . shall be compelled in any criminal case to be a witness against himself." Is the "no person" language to be taken literally, thereby excluding such entities as corporations and associations? The words themselves do not clearly answer this question. Nor do they specify the degree of incrimination whose compulsory acquisition violates the Fifth Amendment. And perhaps reflecting the greatest ambiguity, the compulsion requirement of the privilege is left undefined. Views as to the point at which pressure becomes compulsion are bound to vary. The framers, however, should not be unduly criticized for their lack of specificity in the Fifth Amendment's self-incrimination clause. The Constitution, and particularly its Bill of Rights, was not meant to fulfill the role of a statute. Legislation is the place for detail while a constitution should be the source of more generalized principles. The process of constitutional interpretation must of course address the problem of applying general principles to specific cases, but one cannot expect constitutional language to solve all uncertainties.

History is another guide often used in the interpretation of constitutional amendments. In the case of the privilege against self-incrimination, however, this means an assessment of nearly eight hundred years of evolutionary development. With so much history to weigh, there is bound to be evidence to support just about any position on the meaning of the privilege. In its fullest sense, the history behind the privilege against self-incrimination is too vast to meaningfully assimilate in the process of interpreting the Fifth Amendment. True, there are key historical events in the development of the privilege, but even these are subject to conflicting interpretations. But even more significant is the question of how controlling history should be in setting the current boundaries of constitutional rights. If history limits constitutional development, the scope of civil liberties protected by the Bill of Rights would remain static. The U.S. Constitution, however, was intended to endure, and this must mean that the framers envisioned some degree of flexibility in the interpretative process, not a rigid document circumscribed by what was known at the time. The absolute necessity of adapting constitutional provisions to new realities has already been recognized by the Supreme Court in decisions interpreting the Fourth Amendment;[11] the same must hold true for the Fifth Amendment's self-incrimination clause. History cannot therefore answer our questions about the appropriate scope of the right to remain silent. That is not to say it is irrelevant just as the words of the Fifth Amendment are not irrelevant in the interpretation of the privilege. Rather, the language and history provide important guideposts, but the more fundamental issue is the relative importance of the objectives the self-incrimination clause achieves as opposed to the costs its entails.

In essence then, the role of the Fifth Amendment must be the product of a balancing process in which state and individual interests are weighed and compared. The Amendment itself, of course, says nothing about balancing. To the contrary, its command is that there be no compulsory self-incrimination. But since we do not know what is encompassed within the prohibition, and history and language are only of limited assistance in resolving the uncertainties, other factors must be considered. Not all Fifth Amendment decisions, however, concede their reliance upon a balancing of competing policies. More often than not, efforts are made to find other bases for important self-incrimination rulings, including the Supreme Court's own precedent and the perceived intent of the framers. Frequently such rationales serve only to obscure the real interests at stake, although they too are not totally irrelevant to the decision-making process.

The primary state interest in opposition to an expansive reading of the privilege against self-incrimination is the objective of crime control. To achieve that goal, the state needs evidence from anyone in possession of relevant information. As a result, the law obliges us to provide whatever the state seeks subject to the limitations set by the Constitution and statutes. The privilege against self-incrimination is one such limitation the effect of which is to deny the state information to which it would otherwise be entitled, even assuming every other requirement has been met. The right to remain silent thus stands in direct opposition to the general principle that we must answer the state's questions if the state has authorized the questioner to compel a response to his inquiries.

It is easy to see the connection between the acquisition of information and the state's efforts to control crime. Our system of justice authorizes a criminal conviction only upon proof of guilt beyond a reasonable doubt, and this imposes an obligation upon the state to acquire sufficient evidence to meet that burden. If it cannot be obtained through voluntary cooperation, which may often be the case, the state must have legal sanctions at its disposal to compel the production of the evidence. In the absence of the power to compel assistance, it will be more difficult to obtain convictions and the security of persons and property will suffer. Since achieving security is an important function of government and securing evidence is tied to the attainment of that goal, the power to acquire the evidence must also be an important state process. Note, however, that carried to its logical extreme, the goal of protecting the security of persons and property would totally undercut the privilege against self-incrimination since the privilege impedes the state's ability to obtain evidence. The fact that the privilege has nevertheless evolved demonstrates that the state's interest has not been deemed so forceful that other considerations could never outweigh it. The adoption of the Fifth Amendment is proof to the contrary. The countervailing interests that lie behind the privilege must therefore be considered in determining what form the right to silence should take.

Primary among the considerations that support the right to remain silent is the fair state-individual balance rationale. Built into our system of government are limitations on the authority of the state that run counter to the larger social interests state action represents. Some kinds of state power are simply too expansive and too corrupting to tolerate. They create their own potential for abuse and may well deny the dignity of human beings when exercised. The framers made the judgment that the power to compel an individual to be a witness against himself fits in that category and should be prohibited. The state would have to shoulder the load of proving guilt without forcing admissions from the defendant; American criminal justice was to be accusatorial, not inquisitorial. Thus the Constitution defined the American sense of the proper allocation of rights between the citizen and state in the specific arena of compelled self-incrimination. But in establishing the basic core of a right to remain silent, presumably focusing upon the criminal trial itself, the Fifth Amendment did not necessarily resolve all questions about the total content of that right. To say that it is unfair to exert compulsion to force an accused to admit guilt at trial does not necessarily lead us to the conclusion that it is equally unfair to subpoena or search for private papers. It may be unfair, but only if we think that the government's need for such evidence is outweighed by the need to prevent it from amassing too much power over the individual. In other words, each Fifth Amendment setting requires its own weighing specifically geared to the kind of authority the state seeks to employ and what it would mean to us if we allowed the authority to be exercised.

The private enclave effect of the privilege adds additional importance to the Fifth Amendment. As a result of the state's inability to compel self-incrimination, certain information in an individual's possession that meets the governing criteria may remain private. To be sure, such privacy is not absolute since immunity will allow the state to compel production and the scope of the privacy protection is limited to that which would be self-incriminatory, despite the fact that some nonincriminatory information may have more of a private character. Nevertheless, given the increasingly crowded and intrusive character of contemporary society, we are best advised to take our privacy where we can get it. Moreover, a state-imposed obligation to admit guilt is a very special kind of state intrusion warranting unique protection. Once again, however, one must be careful not to forget that the values reflected in the protection of a private enclave do not necessarily apply with equal force in every Fifth Amendment setting. They are strongest in guarding the right of an accused not be to forced to testify at his trial; so too they are significant in guarding the privacy of personal papers. Their relevance to the question of whether one may draw an adverse inference from pretrial silence is less apparent.

It is obvious that the delineation of Fifth Amendment principles represents a clash of fundamental values in which neither extreme would provide a satisfactory solution. The elimination of the privilege entirely would leave the state free to engage in the kind of wide-ranging inquisitions that characterized criminal practice in the period prior to the seventeenth century. Such a change would entail a vast increase in state authority over the individual and fundamentally alter the character of our governmental structure. From the perspective of contemporary American standards, the elimination of the privilege against self-incrimination would leave the government much too powerful. Beyond that, the spectacle of compelled admissions of criminal responsibility would violate a very special kind of privacy of conscience the law now protects. On the other hand, if the Fifth Amendment privilege was made an absolute barrier to the acquisition of incriminatory evidence, the state's law enforcement obligation could not be fulfilled. If immunity did not authorize the state to compel testimony, and if a broad notion of privacy became the controlling standard in the interpretation of the privilege, each of us would be left to decide when to cooperate with the government. Both the state's regulatory and law-enforcement roles would be harmed in the process. The state, however, needs more authority than that to meet its responsibilities. With the extremes eliminated, the balancing process leaves us with a right to remain silent whose parameters are difficult to define. In short, the problem is not whether we should keep or dispense with the privilege against self-incrimination, but rather how broad its coverage should be.

The difficulty of making individual decisions setting out the scope of the privilege once its basic core is conceded should not obscure the patterns that have been established by the totality of privilege rulings. No one case in and of itself represents the granting of more authority to the state than is appropriate nor the breakdown of already minimal privacy protection, but the accumulation of a number of privilege rulings may have just that effect. The Supreme Court, however, has avoided considering the impact of individual Fifth Amendment decisions against the background of the scope limits of the privilege previous cases have set. Each case is treated in a relative vacuum. State and individual interests are weighed without any thought being given to the additional dangers to privacy and increases in potentially abusive governmental authority reflected in the gradual erosion of self-incrimination protection. The Court has been able to restrict the Fifth Amendment because no one decision seems that threatening even though the total trend of the rulings may be. The Court's Fifth Amendment decisions also reflect an undue deference to the state's asserted interest in the necessity of securing information by compulsion as well as a lack of sensitivity to the adverse consequences to individuals that may result. The notion that the state may have an interest in promoting individual rights despite some tradeoff in its capacity to control crime has been given no weight. Thus with the balance in each Fifth Amendment case tipped in favor of the state and no effort made to assess the total pattern of decisions, the privilege has ended up sharply curtailed. The core may remain largely intact, and particular features of the privilege may be firmly protected, but the frontiers of the Fifth Amendment have been denied coverage and substantial inroads have been tolerated. It is as though the Supreme Court was not fully convinced of the value of the right to remain silent and thus has only begrudgingly applied and protected it.

A Fifth Amendment Blueprint

The privilege against self-incrimination has been relegated to an unprivileged status in recent years, a conclusion clearly evidenced by the Supreme Court's generally consistent pattern of restrictive Fifth Amendment decisions. In essence, the Court's analysis of the privilege has employed a scale to balance state and individual interests, but with an extra weight on the state's side. Individual claims of privilege have had difficulty overcoming the presumption of validity given to state interpretations of the self-incrimination clause. With the exception of the core Fifth Amendment right of the defendant to refuse to take the witness stand at his own trial, privilege interests are narrowly construed and substantially undercut even where recognized. The result is a pattern consistent with the general obligation individuals have to provide the state with the evidence it seeks, but totally at odds with the equally important principle that state power should not exist without adequate restraints. There are few satisfactory limits left on the state's power to obtain most forms of self-incriminatory evidence. Undoubtedly, increasing use will be made of this newly developed authority to the detriment of the individual's right to be left alone. State pressures will be applied to force the revelation of this very special sphere of privacy of conscience. Since the ultimate government objective is the total well-being of its citizens, it is in the state's interest that the current Fifth Amendment balance be reconsidered. What the current law provides in terms of security of persons and property may well be costing more in the loss of an old and valued civil right.

To reverse the trend toward the constriction of the privilege against self-incrimination, a thorough reevaluation of the entire body of Fifth Amendment doctrine is necessary. The right to remain silent functions in far too may contexts for piecemeal change to make sense. Additionally, such a review requires careful attention to the necessity lying behind the state action under inquiry and the impact it will have upon individual interests. It must also encompass a broad view of the totality of the privilege against self-incrimination, weighing each ruling in light of the results achieved in other Fifth Amendment decisions. Given a sufficiently broad perspective and proper weighing of the underlying interests the privilege serves, major doctrinal change is in order. The following blueprint highlights the fundamental reforms the future should bring to the Fifth Amendment.

Traditionally, a broad view has been taken of the degree of incrimination necessary to justify invocation of the Fifth Amendment. Included, of course, have been complete confessions of guilt and admissions of the essential elements of a crime. Also covered are revelations that would constitute a "link in the chain of testimony"[12] leading toward a conviction. Similarly, testimony that could be used to "search out other testimony to be used in evidence"[13] is covered by the privilege. It is the court's responsibility to judge the validity of the claim of privilege, which should be upheld if there is "reasonable ground to apprehend danger" which must be "real and appreciable."[14] Denial is appropriate only if it is "*perfectly clear*, from a careful consideration of all the circumstances in the case, that the witness is mistaken, and that the answer[s] cannot possibly have such a tendency to incriminate."[15] The practical effect of the incrimination standard is to make rejection of a claim of privilege difficult, thereby frustrating the state's ability to acquire information. But if there is to be a privilege against self-incrimination that cannot be circumvented at the state's whim, such a result is inevitable.

In response, the Court has been hinting that it is ready to develop a number of arbitrary distinctions to permit avoidance of the incrimination doctrine. The first sign was *Schmerber v. California*[16] in which the Court ruled that the Fifth Amendment protects against only testimonial self-incrimination. Nontestimonial evidence can therefore be obtained no matter how incriminatory and regardless of whether the suspect must actually assist the state in order to make it available. *Schmerber*, however, has since been followed by incrimination rulings that are substantial inroads on the supposedly protected sphere of testimonial evidence. *Williams v. Florida*[17] upheld the compulsory pretrial production of the details of an alibi defense, ignoring the risk that such disclosure might constitute a link in the chain leading to self-incrimination. Even more ominously, the plurality in *California v. Byers*[18] found no risk of testimonial incrimination in the requirement that automobile accident participants stop and identify themselves. If this trend continues, the damage to the privilege will be severe. It is already true that the limitation of the Fifth Amendment to the risk of a criminal conviction, excluding substantial noncriminal risks such as parole and probation revocation[19] as well as admissions leading to public disgrace,[20] leaves the privilege with a circumscribed range of operation. Incrimination risks cannot be cavalierly judged without threatening what remains. The testimonial self-incrimination requirement seems firmly entrenched and is unlikely to be discarded. *Williams* and the plurality opinion in *Byers*, however, are little more than evasions of the Fifth Amendment. The links in the chain to compulsory self-incrimination are sufficiently evident to warrant aplication of the privilege to both the alibi notice and accident identification requirements; neither context is one in which it can be said that it is perfectly clear that there is no risk of self-incrimination. That is the standard to which the Court must return if a proper balance is to be retained.

A second major area for reconsideration is the Court's complete about-face in its view of the role of the Fifth Amendment in protecting the sanctity of documents. *Boyd v. United States*[21] had established a sphere of privacy for personal papers stemming from the interrelationship of the Fourth and Fifth Amendments. As a result of *Andresen v. Maryland*,[22] they may now be obtained through a search if the prerequisites of the warrant procedure are satisfied. If they cannot be, the state will have to fall back on the use of a subpoena and, as a result of *Fisher v. United States*,[23] that tactic may be widely employed as long as authentication is secured from someone other than the individual from whom the document has been obtained and its possession is not inherently incriminating. The *Andresen* and *Fisher* rulings, however, suggest the Court's lack of concern for the privacy of conscience the privilege shields. An important priority is for the Court to reevaluate the implications of this orientation. Limiting the privilege to the role of a procedural obstacle to the acquisition of information in a particular manner, thereby denying that it can serve as a barrier to state intrusion into personal privacy, denigrates the value of the individual's right to be left alone. True, the right is not absolute, extending only to compulsory self-incrimination. But the fact that it is limited is all the more reason for ensuring that it is protected within its sphere of influence. It seems strange that during an era in which individual privacy was less intruded upon and less in need of protion, the Fifth Amendment served as an impenetrable shield guarding private documents. Now that our society has become crowded and intrusive, the Fifth Amendment allows personal papers to be obtained by the government despite the need for greater protection of individual privacy. The outcome is a virtual invitation to the government to engage in fishing expeditions for evidence, and the absence of a Fifth Amendment probable-cause requirement means that not even suspicion need be behind the state's efforts. This constitutes too much state authority, subject to high potential for abuse, and far too costly in its impact on individual privacy.

Part of the blueprint for change should include some procedural reform in the administration of the privilege against self-incrimination. The standards for waiver, in particular, are very lax, allowing Fifth Amendment protection to be readily lost. The defendant's decision to testify and a witness's partial testimony may lead to a loss of the right to assert the privilege greater than is necessary to meet legitimate needs. More puzzling still is the fact that the loss can occur apparently without any specific warning having been given. This can affect the defendant if he is called to testify before a grand jury (although he is only a putative defendant at that point), and a witness any time he is required to appear in an official proceeding. In both situations the law imposes an obligation to answer all inquiries except those subject to a valid claim of privilege. As a result, it would be a simple matter for the right to remain silent to be inadvertently lost. Fifth Amendment doctrine, however, should not tolerate accidental waiver under such circumstances. The solution is to require Fifth Amendment warnings in all situations in which the state has the authority to compel responses, including notice of the right to remain silent, the potential for adverse use of all answers, freedom to consult with counsel, and notification of target status in the case of the grand jury's calling of a potential defendant. The provision of less information places the state in the position of potentially taking advantage of an individual's mistake. Current doctrine may have placed too much power in the state's hands, and simultaneously exposed the potential defendant and witness to a risk of unfair treatment. The circumstances are not all that far removed from John Lilburne's concern that his interrogators were trying to "ensnare" him. Warnings are a simple and expedient means of preventing such state overreaching.

The process of preliminary investigation, unlike that of official proceedings, lacks the characteristic of state power to compel responses. Thus when police conduct an interrogation, the suspect being questioned need not answer. The absence of legal compulsion in the questioning process, however, does not necessarily lead to the conclusion that warnings should not be required. The Supreme Court conceded as much in its *Miranda*[24] decision, at least with respect to postarrest police custodial interrogations. If state power must be checked in the interrogation process to prevent its abuse and accord respect to the individual, the Fifth Amendment cannot avoid involvement. The same reasons, however, should make us wary of unduly restricting the privilege's role once its applicability to nonlegal forms of compulsion has been established. Allowing the state to make use of evidence obtained following *Miranda* violations constitutes a step backward from the basic safeguards the decision provides. Warnings serve the same objective in unofficial as well as official proceedings, and only an unduly narrow reading of the compulsion concept can keep them out of the former. If they belong, they should not be undercut by means of winking at police evasions. Moreover, care is needed in the attempt to separate environments subject to the *Miranda* dictates from those in need of no special protection. If the division is to be made by the drawing of arbitrary lines, such as the limitation of *Miranda* to postarrest custodial interrogation, the result will be the triumph of form over substance. Environments in which there is a high risk of state overreaching or individual error leading to loss of Fifth

Amendment protection, regardless of the appropriate formal label for the proceeding, warrant special protection for the right to remain silent.

The personalization of the privilege against self-incrimination represents another facet of Fifth Amendment doctrine in need of review. One reflection of the personalization principle has been the denial of Fifth Amendment protection to organizations. The character of the Supreme Court's opinions on this subject suggest very little likelihood that any group will be able to successfully raise a claim of privilege. An entity as small as a three-man law firm has failed in such an effort before the Supreme Court[25] as has a one-man professional corporation at the lower-court level.[26] Contemporary society, however, is far more group oriented than the environment out of which the privilege grew. To be sensitive to the objectives that lie behind the Fifth Amendment, each set of circumstances should be assessed to determine the degree to which the individual's legitimate interests are adversely affected. The arbitrary exclusion of groups toward which the Court appears headed follows its perception of the privilege's history at the expense of more important interests. The same orientation, moreover, is also reflected in Court decisions denying Fifth Amendment protection to documents that are not at the moment of being subpoenaed in the possession of the owner who would be incriminated by their contents.[27] The problem is not that the Court has barred all claims of privilege whenever there has been relinquishment of the items sought. Similarly, the Court did not rule that associations can never assert the Fifth Amendment. What the Court has done, instead, is to personalize the privilege to a degree that casts doubt on the existence of exceptions to its rulings holding the Fifth Amendment inapplicable in both situations. But what individual interests remain after temporary relinquishment or participation in a group, and under what circumstances should they prevail over the state's efforts to acquire evidence? The Supreme Court has been less interested in answering these questions than in drawing arbitrary lines. Existing decisions need not necessarily have to be reversed, but the method of analysis should be revised to deal with potentially more difficult problems in the future and give needed leeway to lower courts in administering the privilege.

Finally, and most importantly, the Court's approach to balancing Fifth Amendment questions is in need of a total revamping. The weighing of individual and state interests is in reality the heart of the process of interpreting the privilege against self-incrimination. It helps to give content to the language of the Fifth Amendment and determines what consequences may flow from its invocation. Insensitive balancing is a sure sign of indifference to the privilege against self-incrimination, yet that is the most apt characterization of the Court's attitude. High priority has been given to the state's need for information and the individual's obligation to provide it. The fundamental values reflected in the self-incrimination clause, particularly its creation of a private enclave of individual conscience and its role as a check upon unrestricted state authority to force an individual to help secure his own conviction, have not been considered impinged upon in the Supreme Court's recent balancing decisions. Generally speaking, the process of weighing competing interests, which is the essence of balancing, has been rather haphazardly undertaken. Values have been superficially analyzed, and no meaningful effort has been made to accord them any priority status. Since these are constitutional rights that are being balanced, it would be more appropriate for the Court to give them presumptive applicability and delineate the circumstances that would warrant their being overridden.

Although there are innumerable details encompassed within the Fifth Amendment privilege against self-incrimination, it is not necessary to address each and every one of them in making recommendations for revisions in current doctrine. If there is a change in the approach to the core philosophical concerns surrounding the privilege, more particularized problem areas will resolve themselves. An overview of the entire body of Fifth Amendment law, moreover, amply demonstrates that a substantial rethinking of its central features is in order. The Court in recent years has been consistently hostile to the privilege against self-incrimination. Its thinking has been heavily weighted in favor of the state on almost every privilege question, with the result that the Fifth Amendment has taken on the character of an obstacle to information acquisition to be circumvented when at all possible. Lost have been the reasons behind the creation of the obstacle, as well as an appreciation of their importance in contemporary society. To accomplish its goal, the Court has sought to tie current interpretations of the Fifth Amendment to its view of the history behind the development of the privilege. Perhaps the best response to this approach comes from a Fourth Amendment opinion of Chief Justice Burger. Responding to a government argument that history demonstrates that the Fourth Amendment's warrant clause was not directed toward seizures of personal property in public areas, he wrote:

> What we do know is that the Framers were men who focused on the wrongs of that day but who intended the Fourth Amendment to safeguard fundamental values which would far outlast the specific abuses which gave it birth.[28]

Certainly, no less can be said about the Fifth Amendment.

Notes

Chapter 1
The Historical Framework

1. By far the most exhaustive and scholarly treatment of the history of the privilege against self-incrimination is Professor Leonard Levy's Origins of the Fifth Amendment. L. Levy, Origins of the Fifth Amendment (1968). *See generally*: C. McCormick, Handbook of the Law of Evidence (2nd ed. 1972); 8 J. Wigmore, Evidence (McNaughton rev. 1961) [hereinafter cited as 8 J. Wigmore]; Corwin, *The Supreme Court's Construction of the Self-Incrimination Clause* (pts. 1-2), 29 Mich. L. Rev. 1, 191 (1930); Fortas, *The Fifth Amendment: Nemo Tenetur Seipsum Prodere*, 25 Clev. B.A.J. 91 (1954); Kemp, *The Background of the Fifth Amendment in English Law: A Study of Its Historical Implications*, 1 Wm. & Mary L. Rev. 247 (1958); Morgan, *The Privilege Against Self-Incrimination,* 34 Minn. L. Rev. 1 (1949); Pittman, *The Colonial and Constitutional History of the Privilege Against Self-Incrimination in America*, 21 Va. L. Rev. 763 (1935); Silving, *The Oath* (pts. 1-2), 68 Yale L.J. 1329, 1527 (1959); Wigmore, *Nemo Tenetur Seipsum Prodere*, 5 Harv. L. Rev. 71 (1892) [hereinafter cited as Wigmore, *Nemo Tenetur Seipsum Prodere*].

Among traditional biblical references to disfavor with the taking of oaths *see: Matthew* 5:33-37, *Exodus* 20:7, and *Deuteronomy* 5:11. Nevertheless, Christ permitted himself to be sworn. *Matthew* 26:63-64. *See generally*: L. Levy, *supra* at 56; Silving, *supra* at 1333, 1343-44.

2. Cases referring to the history of the privilege against self-incrimination include: Andresen v. Maryland, 427 U.S. 463, 470-71 (1976); Miranda v. Arizona, 384 U.S. 436, 458-60 (1966); Brown v. Walker, 161 U.S. 591, 596-97 (1896). On the role of history and tradition in constitutional adjudication, *see*: P. Brest, Processes of Constitutional Decision-making 102-71 (1975); L. Tribe, American Constitutional Law 572-73 (1978); Ely, *On Discovering Fundamental Values*, 92 Harv. L. Rev. 5 (1978); Kadish, *Methodology and Criteria in Due Process Adjudication—A Survey and Criticism*, 66 Yale L.J. 319, 329-30, 344-45 (1957).

3. Trop v. Dulles, 356 U.S. 86, 101 (1958).

4. United States v. Chadwick, 433 U.S. 1, 9 (1977).

5. United States v. Grunewald, 233 F.2d 566, 581 (2nd Cir. 1956) (Frank, J., dissenting), *rev'd*, 353 U.S. 391 (1957), *quoted in* Miranda v. Arizona, 384 U.S. 436, 460 (1966). Justice Frankfurter observed in Ullmann v. United States that the history of the privilege demonstrates that "it is not to be interpreted literally," 350 U.S. 422, 438 (1956), nor "in a hostile or niggardly spirit," 350 U.S. at 426.

6. 350 U.S. at 438, *quoting* New York Trust Co. v. Eisner, 256 U.S. 345, 349 (1921).

7. Wigmore, *Nemo Tenetur Seipsum Prodere*, *supra* note 1, at 71.

8. 2 W. Holdsworth, A History of English Law 207-16 (7th ed. 1956); L. Levy, *supra* note 1, at 51; 1 F. Pollock & F. Maitland, The History of English Law 171-73 (2nd ed. 1898).

9. L. Levy, *supra* note 1, at 5-7; F. Pollock & F. Maitland, *supra* note 8, at 38-40; Silving, *supra* note 1, at 1361-64.

10. L. Levy, *supra* note 1, at 7-10.

11. L. Levy, *id.*, at 19-23.

12. 9 W. Holdsworth, *supra* note 8, at 199; L. Levy, *supra* note 1, at 23, 28-29; Silving, *supra* note 1, at 1346.

13. The council abolished trial by ordeal at the same time it established the oath. L. Levy, *supra* note 1, at 23-24; Silving, *supra* note 1, at 1345-47. The oath was abolished by the Council of Rome in 1725.

14. L. Levy, *supra* note 1, at 46-47; 8 J. Wigmore, *supra* note 1, §2250, at 270; Wigmore, *Nemo Tenetur Seipsum Prodere*, *supra* note 1, at 72-73.

15. L. Levy, *supra* note 1, at 47-48; 1 F. Pollock & F. Maitland, *supra* note 8, at 152 n. 1; Morgan, *supra* note 1, at 1-3.

16. Dean Wigmore maintained that the crux of the opposition to the oath was the jurisdictional controversy between ecclesiastical and civil courts. Wigmore, *Nemo Tenetur Seipsum Prodere*, *supra* note 1, at 75. Mary Hume Maguire, however, believed that the common law attorneys found the oath repugnant in and of itself. Maguire, *Attack of the Common Lawyers on the Oath Ex Officio as Administered in the Ecclesiastical Courts in England*, in Essays in History and Political Theory in Honor of Charles Howard McIlwain (1936). On the zealous use of the oath by Boniface and the restrictions imposed by the statute "De Articulis Cleri," *see*: 8 J. Wigmore, *supra* note 1, §2250, at 270-71; L. Levy, *supra* note 1, at 48-49.

17. L. Levy, *supra* note 1, at 49-53; 8 J. Wigmore, *supra* note 1, §2250, at 276, 278 n. 43; Kemp, *supra* note 1, at 248-50; Morgan, *supra* note 1, at 4-5.

18. L. Levy, *supra* note 1, at 54-60; 2 F. Pollock & F. Maitland, *supra* note 8, at 544-52; Wigmore, *Nemo Tenetur Seipsum Prodere*, *supra* note 1, at 76. In resisting the oath, Thorpe said: "Sir, if I consented to you thus as yee have herebefore rehearsed to me, I should become an appealer [informer], or everie bishioppe's espie, somoner of all Englande." 1 Howell's State Trials 175, 179 (1407), *quoted in* L. Levy, *supra* note 1, at 59.

19. L. Levy, *supra* note 1, at 60-66.

20. L. Levy, *id.*, at 67-70; 1 W. Holdsworth, *supra* note 8, at 588-92; 2 W. Holdsworth, *id.*, at 444.

21. L. Levy, *supra* note 1, at 73-82; Morgan, *supra* note 1, at 6-7.

22. L. Levy, *supra* note 1, at 98; Kemp, *supra* note 1, at 255-68.

23. Professor Levy specifically disputed Professor Kemp's view that

Catholic resistance to the oath was more substantial. L. Levy, *supra* note 1, at 457 n. 22. *See generally*: L. Levy, *id.*, at 83-106. Some dispute exists as to the exact translation of the entire Latin phrase from which *nemo tenetur seipsum prodere* has been extracted. Dean Wigmore's translation was: "Though no one is bound to become his own accuser, yet when once a man has been accused (pointed at as guilty) by general report, he is bound to show whether he can prove his innocence and to vindicate himself." Wigmore, *Nemo Tenetur Seipsum Prodere*, *supra* note 1, at 83 n.2. This is consistent with the view that there is no absolute right to silence but rather a right to formal accusation before interrogation. The Latin phrase can also be translated as granting an exemption from inquisitorial interrogation. Morgan, *supra* note 1, at 8-9; Silving, *supra* note 1, at 1366-68.

24. 1 W. Holdsworth, *supra* note 8, at 608-10; L. Levy, *supra* note 1, at 109-27; 8 J. Wigmore, *supra* note 1, §2250, at 279; Kemp, *supra* note 1, at 261-63; Morgan, *supra* note 1, at 6-7.

25. L. Levy, *supra* note 1, at 139-50.

26. *Id.*, at 150-51, 164-70. When asked to take the oath, Udall replied, "I will take an oath of allegiance to her majesty, wherein I will acknowledge her supremacy according to statute; but to swear to accuse myself or others, I think you have no law for it." 1 Howell's State Trials 1271, 1275-76 (1407), *quoted in* L. Levy, *supra* note 1, at 164. 8 J. Wigmore, *supra* note 1, §2250, at 286.

27. 8 J. Wigmore, *supra* note 1, §2250, at 277-78, Morgan, *supra* note 1, at 6-9; Pittman, *supra* note 1, at 769-70; Silving, *supra* note 1, at 1366-69; Wigmore, *Nemo Tenetur Seipsum Prodere*, *supra* note 1, at 76-78.

28. The Star Chamber could dispense with normal procedural protections at its own pleasure. L. Levy, *supra* note 1, at 181-84; 8 J. Wigmore, *supra* note 1, §2250, at 281; Kemp, *supra* note 1, at 267-68.

29. L. Levy, *supra* note 1, at 218-21; Corwin, *supra* note 1, at 5-7; Kemp, *supra* note 1, at 270. One such injunction was obtained by Sir Edward Coke in Collier v. Collier, 1 Croke's King's Bench Reports 201, 4 Leonard's King's Bench Reports 194 (1589), although there is some uncertainty as to whether *nemo tenetur seipsum prodere*, the principle that no one is bound to accuse himself, was the basis of the decision. Corwin, *supra* note 1, at 6-7; Morgan, *supra* note 1, at 8; Wigmore, *Nemo Tenetur Seipsum Prodere*, *supra* note 1, at 77.

30. *Of Oaths Before an Ecclesiastical Judge Ex Officio*, 12 Coke's Reports 26, 77 English Reports 1308 (1607), *quoted in* L. Levy, *supra* note 1, at 231. The exceptions were matrimonial and testamentary matters.

31. L. Levy, *supra* note 1, at 241-46, 260; Corwin, *supra* note 1, at 7-8; Kemp, *supra* note 1, at 276-81; Wigmore, *Nemo Tenetur Seipsum Prodere*, *supra* note 1, at 78-82.

32. L. Levy, *supra* note 1, at 266-69.

33. Trial of John Lilburn and John Wharton, for Printing and Publishing Seditious Books. 3 Howell's State Trials 1315, 1318 (1637).

Lilburne's name is spelled both with and without an "e" in the reports of his trials. General accounts of the proceedings are contained in L. Levy, *supra* note 1, at 273-78; 8 J. Wigmore, *supra* note 1, §2250, at 282-83; Kemp, *supra* note 1, at 283-84.

34. 3 Howell's State Trials at 1318 (1637). *See* Corwin, *supra* note 1, at 8-9.

35. 3 Howell's State Trials at 1319-20 (1637).

36. 3 Howell's State Trials at 1320.

37. 3 Howell's State Trials at 1323.

38. 3 Howell's State Trials at 1325.

39. 3 Howell's State Trials at 1341. Lilburne's initial sentence and his tirade against the bishops are described in 3 Howell's State Trials at 1326-40.

40. 3 Howell's State Trials at 1342.

41. L. Levy, *supra* note 1, at 281-83; 8 J. Wigmore, *supra* note 1, §2250, at 283-84.

42. Trial of Lieutenant-Colonel John Lilburne for High Treason, 4 Howell's State Trials 1269, 1270 (1649).

43. 4 Howell's State Trials at 1280.

44. 4 Howell's State Trials at 1285.

45. 4 Howell's State Trials at 1289.

46. 4 Howell's State Trials at 1289.

47. 4 Howell's State Trials at 1292-93.

48. 4 Howell's State Trials at 1294.

49. 4 Howell's State Trials at 1317.

50. 4 Howell's State Trials at 1340-41.

51. 4 Howell's State Trials at 1376.

52. 4 Howell's State Trials at 1393.

53. 4 Howell's State Trials at 1395.

54. 4 Howell's State Trials at 1405. *See generally* L. Levy, *supra* note 1, at 301-09.

55. L. Levy, *supra* note 1, at 309-12.

56. Wigmore, *Nemo Tenetur Seipsum Prodere, supra* note 1, at 82.

57. L. Levy, *supra* note 1, at 324.

58. L. Levy, *supra* note 1, at 332-404.

59. L. Levy, *supra* note 1, at 362, 381, 397-99; Pittman, *supra* note 1, at 782-83.

60. Virginia Declaration of Rights, §8 (1776), in 7 F. Thorpe ed., The Federal and State Constitutions, Colonial Charters, and Other Organic Laws 3813 (1909). *See* L. Levy, *supra* note 1, at 405-08.

61. L. Levy, *supra* note 1, at 409-10; Pittman, *supra* note 1, at 787-88.

62. L. Levy, *supra* note 1, at 410-11; Morgan, *supra* note 1, at 22-23.

63. L. Levy, *supra* note 1, at 414-26.

Chapter 2
The Policy Perspective

1. The major sources on Fifth Amendment policy are: J. Bentham, A Rationale of Judicial Evidence, in 7 The Works of Jeremy Bentham, 445 *et seq.* (Bowring ed. 1843); E. Griswold, The Fifth Amendment Today (1955); L. Mayers, Shall We Amend the Fifth Amendment? (1959); C. McCormick, Handbook of the Law of Evidence, §118, at 251 *et seq.* (2nd ed. 1972); 8 J. Wigmore, Evidence, §2251, at 295 *et seq.* (McNaughton rev. 1961); Friendly, *The Fifth Amendment Tomorrow: The Case for Constitutional Change*, 37 U. Cinn. L. Rev. 671 (1968); McKay, *Self-Incrimination and the New Privacy*, 1967 Sup. Ct. Rev. 193; McNaughton, *The Privilege Against Self-Incrimination: Its Constitutional Affectation, Raison D'Etre and Miscellaneous Implications*, 51 J. Crim. L.C. & P.S. 138 (1960); Nakell, *Criminal Discovery for the Defense and the Prosecution—The Developing Constitutional Considerations*, 50 N.C. L. Rev. 437 (1972); Noonan, *Inferences from the Invocation of the Privilege Against Self-Incrimination*, 41 Va. L. Rev. 311 (1955); O'Brien, *The Fifth Amendment: Fox Hunters, Old Women, Hermits and the Burger Court*, 54 Notre Dame L. Rev. 26 (1978); Orfield, *The Privilege Against Self-Incrimination in Federal Cases*, 25 U. Pitt. L. Rev. 503 (1964); Ratner, *Consequences of Exercising the Privilege Against Self-Incrimintion*, 24 U. Chi. L. Rev. 472 (1957); Williams, *Problems of the Fifth Amendment*, 24 Fordham L. Rev. 19 (1955); Note, *Formalism, Legal Realism and Constitutionally Protected Privacy Under the Fourth and Fifth Amendments*, 90 Harv. L. Rev. 945 (1977).

2. Ullmann v. United States, 350 U.S. 422, 438 (1956).

3. 350 U.S. at 426.

4. Miranda v. Arizona, 384 U.S. 436, 459-60 (1966); Counselman v. Hitchcock, 142 U.S. 547, 562 (1892).

5. Fisher v. United States, 425 U.S. 391, 401 (1976).

6. Murphy v. Waterfront Comm'n, 378 U.S. 52, 55 (1964).

7. McKay, *supra* note 1, at 206-08; McNaughton, *supra* note 1, at 142-43; Meltzer, *Required Records, The McCarran Act, and the Privilege Against Self-Incrimination*, 18 U. Chi. L. Rev. 687, 689-93 (1951); Wigmore, *Nemo Tenetur Seipsum Prodere*, 5 Harv. L. Rev. 71, 86 (1892).

8. Murphy v. Waterfront Comm'n, 378 U.S. 52, 55 (1964), *quoting* Quinn v. United States, 349 U.S. 155, 161-62 (1955). *See also*: Slochower v. Bd. of Higher Educ., 350 U.S. 551, 557-58 (1956); Twining v. New Jersey, 211 U.S. 78, 91 (1908).

9. E. Griswold, The Fifth Amendment Today, *supra* note 1, at 9-10.

10. L. Mayers, *supra* note 1, at 62-63; Friendly, *supra* note 1, at 684 n. 67; Griswold, *The Right To Be Let Alone*, 55 Nw. L. Rev. 216, 223 (1960); Williams, *supra* note 1, at 28-30.

11. J. Bentham, *supra* note 1, at 446.

12. Kastigar v. United States, 406 U.S. 441, 453 (1972); Ullmann v. United States, 350 U.S. 422, 430-31 (1956); Brown v. Walker, 161 U.S. 591, 605-06 (1896).

13. Shelton v. Tucker, 364 U.S. 479 (1960); Sweezy v. New Hampshire, 354 U.S. 234 (1957); Friendly, *supra* note 1, at 697; Griswold, *The Right To Be Let Alone, supra* note 10, at 221; Williams, *supra* note 1, at 34-38. *But cf.*: Uphaus v. Wyman, 360 U.S. 72 (1959); Barenblatt v. United States, 360 U.S. 109 (1959); Fortas, *The Fifth Amendment: Nemo Tenetur Seipsum Prodere*, 25 Clev. B.A.J. 91 (1954).

14. E. Griswold, The Fifth Amendment Today, *supra* note 1, at 9-19; *But see* Williams, *supra* note 1, at 28-30, disputing the validity of Dean Griswold's example.

15. C. McCormick, *supra* note 1, §130, at 272-73; 8 J. Wigmore, *supra* note 1, §2268, at 406-08; Orfield, *supra* note 1, at 526-27.

16. Wilson v. United States, 149 U.S. 60, 66 (1893).

17. United States v. Mandujano, 425 U.S. 564 (1976); C. McCormick, *supra* note 1, §135, at 288-89; 8 J. Wigmore, *supra* note 1, §2268, at 402-06; Orfield, *supra* note 1, at 525-26.

18. L. Mayers, *supra* note 1, at 62-63; Williams, *supra* note 1, at 26-30.

19. Friendly, *supra* note 1, at 686-87; McKay, *supra* note 1, at 206-08; McNaughton, *supra* note 1, at 142-43; Meltzer, *supra* note 7, at 690-91.

20. Griswold, *The Right To Be Let Alone, supra* note 10, at 223.

21. Tehan v. United States *ex rel.* Shott, 382 U.S. 406, 415 (1966).

22. Friendly, *supra* note 1, at 690-91; McKay, *supra* note 1, at 208; McNaughton, *supra* note 1, at 143; Meltzer, *supra* note 7, at 692-93.

23. Cheff v. Schnackenberg, 384 U.S. 373 (1966); Shillitani v. United States, 384 U.S. 364 (1966).

24. United States v. Wong, 431 U.S. 174 (1977).

25. *Id.* at 176.

26. J. Bentham, *supra* note 1, at 446. *See generally* J. Bentham, *supra* note 1, at 445-51.

27. McKay, *supra* note 1, at 208.

28. NcNaughton, *supra* note 1, at 143.

29. Tehan v. United States *ex rel.* Shott, 382 U.S. 406, 416 (1966).

30. *See*: J. Bentham, *supra* note 1, at 452-54; Friendly, *supra* note 1, at 690-91; McKay, *supra* note 1, at 209-10; McNaughton, *supra* note 1, at 147-48; Noonan, *supra* note 1, at 312-13; O'Brien, *supra*, note 1, at 41-45.

31. L. Levy, Origins of the Fifth Amendment 326-27 (1968).

32. 3 Howell's State Trials 1315, 1326-27 (1637).

33. 4 Howell's State Trials 1269, 1317, 1340-41 (1649).

34. 8 J. Wigmore, Evidence, *supra* note 1, §2251, at 296 n. 1.

35. Ullmann v. United States, 350 U.S. 422, 445-46 (1956).

36. United States v. Wade, 388 U.S. 218, 261 (1967). *See also*: Louisell, *Criminal Discovery and Self-Incrimination: Roger Traynor Confronts the Dilemma*, 53 Cal. L. Rev. 89, 95 (1965).

37. Garrity v. New Jersey, 385 U.S. 493, 497 n. 5 (1967).

38. J. Bentham, *supra* note 1, at 452.

39. L. Mayers, *supra* note 1, at 168-69; Friendly, *supra* note 1, at 683, 694-95.

40. NcNaughton, *supra* note 1, at 148.

41. In opposition, *see*: Friendly, *supra* note 1, at 683; O'Brien, *supra* note 1, at 45.

42. Murphy v. Waterfront Comm'n, 378 U.S. 52, 55 (1964).

43. McNaughton, *supra* note 1, at 144 n. 31.

44. McNaughton, *supra* note 1, at 143-44; O'Brien, *supra* note 1, at 37-38.

45. Friendly, *supra* note 1, at 696-97. *See also*: McKay, *supra* note 1, at 212-13; Noonan, *supra* note 1, at 314-15; O'Brien, *supra* note 1, at 38.

46. McNaughton, *supra* note 1, at 151.

47. J. Bentham, *supra* note 1, at 454.

48. Gibson v. Florida Legislative Investigation Comm., 372 U.S. 539, 546 (1963).

49. *E.g.*, Branzburg v. Hayes, 408 U.S. 665 (1972).

50. J. Bentham, *supra* note 1, at 455-58. *See also*: McNaughton, *supra* note 1, at 144 n. 31.

51. *E.g.*, Murphy v. Waterfront Comm'n, 378 U.S. 52, 55 (1964); J. Bentham, *supra* note 1, at 454; Friendly, *supra* note 1, at 691-94; McNaughton, *supra* note 1, at 148-49; O'Brien, *supra* note 1, at 35-41.

52. *See generally* G. Coulton, Inquisition and Liberty (1969).

53. *Id*. at 119-30.

54. Murphy v. Waterfront Comm'n, 378 U.S. 52, 55 (1964).

55. Tehan v. United States *ex rel*. Shott, 382 U.S. 406, 415 (1966).

56. McNaughton, *supra* note 1, at 143, 144 n. 34. This is the essence of what Dean McKay referred to as the "preservation of official morality." McKay, *supra* note 1, at 214.

57. McNaughton, *supra* note 1, at 148.

58. 8 J. Wigmore, *supra* note 1, §2251, at 296 n. 1.

59. J. Bentham, *supra* note 1, at 454.

60. Fortas, *supra* note 13, at 98-99.

61. Friendly, *supra* note 1, at 691-94.

62. 378 U.S. at 55, *quoting* 233 F.2d 556, 581-82 (2nd Cir. 1956), *rev'd*, 353 U.S. 391 (1957).

63. Tehan v. United States *ex rel*. Shott, 382 U.S. 406, 416 (1966).

64. McKay, *supra* note 1, at 210-14.

65. 381 U.S. 479 (1965).

66. *Id*. at 484.

67. *Id*.

68. Roe v. Wade, 410 U.S. 113 (1973). *See also*: Planned Parenthood v. Danforth, 428 U.S. 52 (1976).

69. Stanley v. Georgia, 394 U.S. 557 (1969).

70. Doe v. Commonwealth's Attorney, 403 F. Supp. 1199 (E.D. Va. 1975), *aff'd mem.*, 425 U.S. 901 (1976).

71. Paul v. Davis, 424 U.S. 693 (1976).

72. Fisher v. United States, 425 U.S. 391, 399 (1976).

73. 425 U.S. at 400.

74. Boyd v. United States, 116 U.S. 616, 633 (1886).

75. 116 U.S. at 630.

76. Olmstead v. United States, 277 U.S. 438, 478 (1928) (Brandeis, J., dissenting).

77. Fried, *Privacy*, 77 Yale L.J. 475, 482 (1968). *See generally*: Bloustein, *Privacy as an Aspect of Human Dignity: An Answer to Dean Prosser*, 39 N.Y.U. L. Rev. 962 (1964); Parker, *A Definition of Privacy*, 27 Rut. L. Rev. 275 (1974).

78. Gerstein, *Privacy and Self-Incrimination*, 80 Ethics 87, 91 (1970).

79. Friendly, *supra* note 1, at 687-90. *See also*: L. Mayers, *supra* note 1, at 162-63.

Chapter 3
The Contours of the Privilege

1. *E.g.*, Barron v. Mayor of Baltimore, 10 U.S. 464, 7 Pet. 243 (1833).

2. 8 J. Wigmore, Evidence, §2252, at 318 *et seq*. (McNaughton rev. 1961).

3. *Compare* Malloy v. Hogan, 378 U.S. 1 (1964) (Harlan, J., dissenting) *with* Pointer v. Texas, 380 U.S. 400 (1965) (Goldberg, J., concurring). *See* Brennan, *State Constitutions and the Protection of Individual Rights*, 90 Harv. L. Rev. 489 (1977).

4. 211 U.S. 78 (1908).

5. 83 U.S. (16 Wall.) 36 (1873). *See* L. Tribe, American Constitutional Law 415-26 (1978).

6. 211 U.S. at 97.

7. 211 U.S. at 99.

8. 211 U.S. at 100.

9. 211 U.S. at 113.

10. Adamson v. California, 332 U.S. 46, 74 (1947) (Black, J., dissenting).

11. 332 U.S. at 69.

12. 332 U.S. at 66 (Frankfurter, J., concurring).

13. 332 U.S. 46 (1947).

14. Duncan v. Louisiana, 391 U.S. 145, 149 n. 14 (1968). As Justice Black observed, concurring in *Duncan*, the Court has selectively incorporated specific provisions of the Bill of Rights rather than fully incorporating the entire first eight amendments of the Constitution.

15. This approach combines the Black and Frankfurter theories, thereby using due process both to incorporate the Bill of Rights and as an instrument to independently supervise state criminal procedure. Adamson v. California, 332 U.S. 46 (1947) (Murphy, J., dissenting).

16. Malloy v. Hogan, 378 U.S. 1 (1964).

17. *Id.* at 7.

18. *Id.* at 11.

19. Virginia Declaration of Rights, §8 (1776) in 7 F. Thorpe ed., The Federal and State Constitutions, Colonial Charters, and Other Organic Laws 3813 (1909); L. Levy, Origins of the Fifth Amendment 421-25 (1968); Note, *Applicability of the Privilege Against Self-Incrimination to Legislative Investigations*, 49 Colum. L. Rev. 87, 91-93 (1949).

20. 8 J. Wigmore, *supra* note 2, §2252, at 324-25; Corwin, *The Supreme Court's Construction of the Self-Incrimination Clause* (pts. 1-2), 29 Mich. L. Rev. 1, 3-4; 191, 195-96 (1930).

21. 142 U.S. 547 (1892).

22. People *ex rel.* Hackley v. Kelly, 24 N.Y. 74 (1861).

23. 142 U.S. at 562.

24. McCarthy v. Arndstein, 266 U.S. 34 (1924).

25. *Id.* at 40.

26. Watkins v. United States, 354 U.S. 178, 188 (1957).

27. *In re* Gault, 387 U.S. 1, 49 (1967).

28. *Id.*

29. Boyd v. United States, 116 U.S. 616 (1886).

30. *Id.* at 634.

31. 387 U.S. 1 (1967).

32. 372 U.S. 144 (1963).

33. *Id.* at 168-69.

34. Ullmann v. United States, 350 U.S. 422, 426 (1956).

35. Brown v. Walker, 161 U.S. 591, 631 (1896) (Field, J., dissenting).

36. Ullmann v. United States, 350 U.S. 422 (1956) (Douglas, J., dissenting).

37. *E.g.*, *Ex parte* Lindo, 15 F. Cas. 556 (C.C.D.C. 1807) (No. 8,364). *See* L. Mayers, Shall We Amend the Fifth Amendment? 203-04 (1959).

38. L. Levy, Origins of the Fifth Amendment 313 (1968).

39. 8 J. Wigmore, *supra* note 2, §2260, at 369; §2268, at 406-08. *See also*: United States v. Housing Foundation of America, Inc., 176 F.2d 665

(3rd Cir. 1949); C. McCormick, Handbook of the Law of Evidence §130, at 272-75 (2nd ed. 1972).

40. *E.g.*, Railroad Co. v. Richmond, 96 U.S. 521 (1877). *See also* Hale v. Henkel, 201 U.S. 43, 83-84 (1906) (Brewer, J., dissenting).

41. 201 U.S. 43 (1906).

42. *Id.* at 69-70.

43. *Id.* at 70.

44. *Id.* at 75.

45. Grant v. United States, 227 U.S. 74 (1913); Wheeler v. United States, 226 U.S. 478 (1913).

46. 322 U.S. 694 (1944).

47. *Id.* at 698.

48. *Id.*

49. *Id.* at 701.

50. McPhaul v. United States, 364 U.S. 372 (1960) (Fifth Amendment protection denied to executive secretary of Civil Rights Congress).

51. In addition to the cases cited *supra, see*: United States v. Fleischman, 339 U.S. 349 (1950); Oklahoma Press Publishing Co. v. Walling, 327 U.S. 186 (1946); Essgee Co. v. United States, 262 U.S. 151 (1923).

52. 417 U.S. 85 (1974).

53. *Id.* at 89-90, *quoting* United States v. White, 322 U.S. 694, 701 (1944).

54. 417 U.S. at 92.

55. *Id.*

56. 417 U.S. at 101.

57. 417 U.S. at 100.

58. *See generally* Note, Bellis v. United States: *Denial of Fifth Amendment Protection to Partnerships*, 39 Alb. L. Rev. 545 (1975). Fifth Amendment protection has been denied to a law partnership of four brothers, United States v. Mahady & Mahady, 512 F.2d 521 (3rd Cir. 1975); and a solo practice, United States v. Radetsky, 535 F.2d 556 (10th Cir. 1976).

59. 221 U.S. 361 (1911).

60. *Id.* at 380.

61. *Id.*

62. *Id.*

63. *Id.* at 384-85.

64. *Id.* at 385.

65. 417 U.S. at 97 n. 8.

66. 221 U.S. at 385.

67. 354 U.S. 118 (1957).

68. United States v. Austin-Bagley Corp., 31 F.2d 229 (2nd Cir. 1929). *See also*: Pulford v. United States, 155 F.2d 944 (6th Cir. 1946); Carolene Products Co. v. United States, 140 F.2d 61 (4th Cir. 1944).

69. 354 U.S. at 127.

70. 354 U.S. at 128.

71. *Id.*

72. Brown v. Walker, 161 U.S. 591 (1896). The dissenting opinion of Justice Shiras, joined in by Justices Gray and White, maintained that an act of Congress could not divest an individual of his right to remain silent by granting immunity. The dissenting opinion of Justice Field found a grant of immunity from prosecution for the offense under investigation inadequate but also reacted to the "defamation," "reprobation," and "personal degradation" of being forced to testify with such an immunity grant. 161 U.S. at 636, 637.

73. Ullmann v. United States, 350 U.S. 422 (1956) (Douglas, J., dissenting).

74. *See generally*: 8 J. Wigmore, *supra* note 2, §2281, at 490-508; C. McCormick, *supra* note 39, §143, at 303-08; Strachan, *Self-Incrimination, Immunity, and Watergate*, 56 Tex. L. Rev. 791 (1978).

75. *See* Note, *The Federal Witness Immunity Act in Theory and Practice: Treading the Constitutional Tightrope*, 72 Yale L.J. 1568, 1571-72 (1963).

76. Trial of Lord Chancellor Macclesfield, 16 Howell's State Trials 767, 921, 1147 (1725). *See*: Kastigar v. United States, 406 U.S. 441, 445 n. 13 (1972); National Advisory Commission on Reform of Federal Criminal Laws, Working Papers 1406-11 (1970); 8 J. Wigmore, *supra* note 2 §2281, at 492 n. 2.

77. The context was the investigation of a vote-selling scheme. *See* note 80, *infra*.

78. An executive pardon is deemed to provide sufficient immunity to justify compelling testimony. Regina v. Boyes, 1 Best & Smith 311, 121, Eng. Rep. 730 (Q.B. 1861); 8 J. Wigmore, *supra* note 2, §2280a, at 483-84.

79. 142 U.S. 547 (1892).

80. Act of Jan. 24, 1857, ch. 19, 11 Stat. 155-56. *See* Note, *supra* note 75, at 1571.

81. Act of Jan. 24, 1862, ch. 11, 12 Stat. 333.

82. Act of Feb. 25, 1868, ch. 13, §1, 15 Stat. 37. *See* Note, *supra* note 75, at 1572.

83. *In re* Willie, 25 F. Cas. 38 (C.C. Va. 1807) (No. 14, 692e), at 38.

84. *Id.* at 40.

85. *Id.*

86. 142 U.S. at 584-85.

87. 142 U.S. at 564.

88. 142 U.S. at 585, *quoting* Emery's Case, 107 Mass. 172, 182 (1871).

89. 142 U.S. at 585.

90. Act of Feb. 11, 1893, ch. 83, 27 Stat. 443.

91. 161 U.S. 591 (1896).

92. 201 U.S. 43 (1906).

93. 378 U.S. 52 (1964).

94. *Id*. at 79.

95. *Id*. at 98 (White, J., concurring).

96. 18 U.S.C. §6002 (1970). *See generally* Note, *Federal Witness Immunity Problems and Practices under 18 U.S.C. §§6002-6003,* 14 Am. Crim. L. Rev. 275 (1976).

97. *See*: Piccirillo v. New York, 400 U.S. 548 (1971) (Brennan, J., dissenting from dismissal of writ of certiorari as improvidently granted); C. McCormick, *supra* note 39, §143, at 306.

98. 406 U.S. 441 (1972).

99. 406 U.S. 472 (1972).

100. 406 U.S. at 453.

101. 406 U.S. at 458-59, *quoting* Murphy v. Waterfront Comm'n, 378 U.S. 52, 79 (1964).

102. 406 U.S. at 468 (Marshall, J., dissenting).

103. Note, *Federal Witness Immunity Problems and Practices under 18 U.S.C. §§6002-6003,* 14 Am. Crim. L. Rev. 275, 282 (1976).

104. United States v. Kurzer, 534 F.2d 511 (2nd Cir. 1976). *See also*: United States v. Romano, 583 F.2d 1 (1st Cir. 1978) (Immunity grant does not cover attorney's proffer of evidence to obtain it); United States v. McDonnel, 550 F.2d 1010 (5th Cir. 1977), *cert. denied*, 434 U.S. 835 (1977) (preponderance of the evidence test satisfies independent source burden of proof). The Supreme Court, however, has held that immunized testimony cannot be used to impeach the defendant's testimony at trial. New Jersey v. Portash, 47 U.S.L.W. 4271 (1979).

Chapter 4
Official Proceedings: The Core Concept

1. C. McCormick, Handbook of the Law of Evidence, §130, at 272-75; §135, at 288-89 (2nd ed. 1972); 8 J. Wigmore, Evidence §2268, at 402-10 (McNaughton rev. 1961).

2. 8 J. Wigmore, *supra* note 1, §2260, at 369.

3. United States v. Housing Foundation of America, Inc., 176 F.2d 665 (3rd Cir. 1949); 8 J. Wigmore, *supra* note 1, §2268, at 407; Orfield, *The Privilege Against Self-Incrimination in Federal Cases*, 25 U. Pitt. L. Rev. 503, 526-27 (1964).

4. United States v. Mandujano, 425 U.S. 564, 572 (1976).

5. Wilson v. United States, 149 U.S. 60, 66 (1893).

6. If the defendant chooses to testify at a suppression hearing, the testimony he gives cannot be used against him at trial (at least if the suppression issue is an allegedly illegal search and seizure). Simmons v. United States, 390 U.S. 377 (1968).

7. Brewer v. Williams, 430 U.S. 387 (1977) (issuance of arrest warrant followed by the arrest and arraignment of the suspect constitutes formal accusation for purposes of the Sixth Amendment).

8. Miranda v. Arizona, 384 U.S. 436 (1966).

9. United States v. Washington, 431 U.S. 181 (1977); United States v. Wong, 431 U.S. 174 (1977); United States v. Mandujano, 425 U.S. 564 (1976).

10. 380 U.S. 609 (1965).

11. *Id*. at 610.

12. Adamson v. California, 332 U.S. 46 (1947); Twining v. New Jersey, 211 U.S. 78 (1908).

13. 378 U.S. 1 (1964).

14. 380 U.S. at 620 (Stewart, J., dissenting).

15. 380 U.S. at 614.

16. 435 U.S. 333 (1978).

17. 380 U.S. at 614.

18. 406 U.S. 605 (1972).

19. *Id*. at 610.

20. 402 U.S. 183 (1971). The Fifth Amendment question was addressed in the companion case of *Crampton v. Ohio*, which, along with *McGautha*, also presented the Court with issues related to the death penalty. The official case report, however, is designated under the *McGautha v. California* heading.

21. Malloy v. Hogan, 378 U.S. 1, 8 (1964).

22. Schmerber v. California, 384 U.S. 757, 776 (1966) (Black, J., dissenting); Counselman v. Hitchcock, 142 U.S. 547, 584 (1892).

23. 384 U.S. 757 (1966).

24. *Id*. at 761.

25. Holt v. United States, 218 U.S. 245, 252-53 (1910).

26. 8 J. Wigmore, *supra* note 1, §2263, at 378-79; §2265, at 386-400. *See also*: C. McCormick, *supra* note 1, §124, at 264-66; Dann, *The Fifth Amendment Privilege Against Self-Incrimination: Extorting Physical Evidence from a Suspect*, 43 S. Cal. L. Rev. 597 (1970).

27. 384 U.S. at 764.

28. 402 U.S. 424 (1971).

29. United States v. Wade, 388 U.S. 218, 260 (1967) (Fortas, J., dissenting in part).

30. 388 U.S. at 261.

31. 342 U.S. 165, 172 (1952).

32. Welch v. District Court of Vermont, 461 F. Supp. 592 (D. Vt. 1978) (evidence of refusal to take breath test admissible over Fifth Amendment objection). *See generally*: National Conference of Commissioners on Uniform State Laws, Uniform Rules of Criminal Procedure, Rule 434(d) (1974); Project on Law Enforcement Policy and Rulemaking, Model Rules for Law Enforcement: Eyewitness Identification, Rules 408, 408.1 (1972).

33. *In re* Willie, 25 F. Cas. 38, 40 (C.C. Va. 1807) (No. 14, 692e).

34. *Id.*

35. *Id.*

36. 25 F. Cas. at 39.

37. 8 J. Wigmore, *supra* note 1, §2260, at 376-77.

38. 142 U.S. 547 (1892).

39. *Id.* at 564.

40. United States v. St. Pierre, 132 F.2d 837, 838 (2nd Cir. 1942).

41. Hoffman v. United States, 341 U.S. 479, 486 (1951).

42. Regina v. Boyes, 1 Best & Smith 311, 121 Eng. Rep. 730 (Q.B. 1861).

43. *Id.*

44. *Id.* at 329, 121 Eng. Rep. at 737.

45. *Id.* at 330, 121 Eng. Rep. at 738.

46. 161 U.S. 591, 608 (1896).

47. 8 J. Wigmore, *supra* note 1, §2260, at 376, noting that extension of the privilege to situations in which disclosure would not place the witness in appreciable danger "can only be deplored."

48. 227 U.S. 131 (1913).

49. 244 U.S. 362 (1917).

50. *Id.* at 367.

51. 340 U.S. 159 (1950).

52. 341 U.S. 479 (1951). *See also*: Singleton v. United States, 343 U.S. 944 (1952); Greenberg v. United States, 343 U.S. 918 (1952); Falknor, *Self-Incrimination Privilege: "Links in the Chain,"* 5 Vand. L. Rev. 479 (1952).

53. 378 U.S. 1 (1964).

54. *Id.* at 13.

55. United States v. Coffey, 198 F.2d 438, 441 (3rd Cir. 1952), *referred to in* Emspak v. United States, 349 U.S. 190, 198 n. 18 (1955).

56. 378 U.S. 52 (1964).

57. *See: In re* Grand Jury Proceedings, 532 F.2d 404 (5th Cir. 1976); *In re* Parker, 411 F.2d 1067 (10th Cir. 1969), *vacated as moot*, 397 U.S. 96 (1970).

58. 8 J. Wigmore, *supra* note 1, §2268, at 402.

59. 369 U.S. 599 (1962).

60. 340 U.S. 367 (1951).

61. *Id.* at 369 n. 1.

62. *Id.* at 371. *See also* Brown v. United States, 276 U.S. 134 (1928) (failure to claim Fifth Amendment sufficient as a basis for denying privilege).

63. 349 U.S. 155 (1955).

64. 349 U.S. 190 (1955).

65. 349 U.S. at 157-58.

66. 349 U.S. at 193.

67. 349 U.S. at 163.

68. C. McCormick, *supra* note 1, §137, at 289-91; Orfield, *supra* note 2, at 528-31; 8 J. Wigmore, *supra* note 1, §2269, at 412-13.

69. 352 U.S. 330 (1957).

70. 384 U.S. 436 (1966).

71. *E.g.*, United States v. Wong, 553 F.2d 576 (9th Cir. 1974), *rev'd*, 431 U.S. 174 (1977); United States v. Washington, 328 A.2d 98 (Ct. App. D.C. 1974), *rev'd*, 431 U.S. 181 (1977).

72. 425 U.S. 564 (1976).

73. *Id.* at 582 n. 7; United States v. Wong, 431 U.S. 174 (1977).

74. 425 U.S. at 582.

75. 341 U.S. 479 (1951). The *Hoffman* standard is consistent with Chief Justice Marshall's view that the witness must have primary responsibility in assessing the risk of self-incrimination. *In re* Willie, 25 F. Cas. 38, 40 (C.C. Va. 1807) (No. 14,692e). Elsewhere emphasis has been placed on the witness's obligation to establish the self-incrimination risk presented by the question. Brown v. United States, 276 U.S. 134, 144-45 (1928). *See also*: United States v. Melchor Moreno, 536 F.2d 1042 (5th Cir. 1976) (in camera examination by judge of defense witness after claim of privilege); United States v. Hearst, 563 F.2d 1331 (9th Cir. 1977) (defendant's 41 assertions of privilege on cross-examination invalid).

76. 341 U.S. at 486.

77. 341 U.S. at 486-87.

78. 341 U.S. at 488, *citing* Counselman v. Hitchcock, 142 U.S. 547, 579-80 (1892).

79. 75 Va. 892, 898 (Va. 1881).

80. 340 U.S. 367 (1951).

81. *Id.* at 373.

82. *Id.* at 375, *quoting* Mason v. United States, 244 U.S. 362, 366 (1917).

83. Raffel v. United States, 271 U.S. 494, 497 (1926).

84. Stewart v. United States, 366 U.S. 1 (1961); Grunewald v. United States, 353 U.S. 391 (1957).

85. Stevens v. Marks, 383 U.S. 234 (1966).

86. 8 J. Wigmore, *supra* note 1, §2276, at 459-62.

87. Johnson v. United States, 318 U.S. 189 (1943); 8 J. Wigmore, *supra*

note 1, §2276, at 465-66. A more recent example is provided by United
States v. Beechum, 582 F.2d 898 (5th Cir. 1978).

88. McCarthy v. Arndstein, 262 U.S. 355, 359 (1923) (privilege may be
invoked where previous disclosure was "not an actual admission of guilt or
incriminating facts").

89. 399 U.S. 78 (1970).

90. *Id*. at 111 (Black, J., dissenting).

91. 399 U.S. at 85.

92. 519 P.2d 774 (Alaska 1974).

93. Allen v. Superior Court of Alameda County, 557 P.2d 65, 67 (Cal.
1976).

Chapter 5
Confessions: The Road to *Miranda*

1. Friendly, *The Fifth Amendment Tomorrow: The Case for Con-
stitutional Change*, 37 U. Cinn. L. Rev. 671, 708 (1968). *See also*: 8 J.
Wigmore, Evidence §2266, at 400-02 (McNaughton rev. 1961); Inbau,
Public Safety v. Individual Civil Liberties: The Prosecutor's Stand, 53 J.
Crim. L., C. & P.S. 85 (1962); Kamisar, *A Dissent from the* Miranda
*Dissents: Some Comments on the "New" Fifth Amendment and the "Old"
Voluntariness Test*, 65 Mich. L. Rev. 59 (1966).

2. L. Levy, Origins of the Fifth Amendment 325-26 (1968); O.
Stephens, The Supreme Court and Confessions of Guilt 18-20 (1973), 8 J.
Wigmore, *supra* note 1, §2252, at 327-29.

3. C. McCormick, Handbook of the Law of Evidence §148, at 313
(2nd ed. 1972); 3 J. Wigmore, Evidence §819, at 296-97 (Chadbourn rev.
1970).

4. The King v. Rudd, 1 Leach Cr. C. 115, 118, 168 Eng. Rep. 160, 161
(K.B. 1775).

5. The King v. Warwickshall, 1 Leach Cr. C. 263, 263-64, 168 Eng.
Rep. 234, 235 (K.B. 1783).

6. Dix, *Mistake, Ignorance, Expectation of Benefit, and the Modern
Law of Confessions,* 1975 Wash. U. L. Q. 275, 280-82.

7. 110 U.S. 574, 584 (1884).

8. 110 U.S. at 585.

9. *Id*.

10. 168 U.S. 532 (1897).

11. *Id*. at 542.

12. *Id*. at 543.

13. *Id*. at 548.

14. *Id*. at 542-43.

15. 378 U.S. 1 (1964).

16. Keedy, *The Third Degree and Legal Interrogation of Suspects*, 85 U. Pa. L. Rev. 761 (1937).

17. E. Lavine, The "Third Degree," A Detailed and Appalling Exposé of Police Brutality (1930).

18. E. Hopkins, Our Lawless Police (1931); E. Borchard, Convicting the Innocent (1932).

19. National Commission on Law Observance and Enforcement, Report on Lawlessness in Law Enforcement 4 (1931).

20. 297 U.S. 278 (1936).

21. *Id.* at 281.

22. *Id.* at 284.

23. Powell v. Alabama, 287 U.S. 45 (1932); Moore v. Dempsey, 261 U.S. 86 (1923); Mooney v. Holohan, 294 U.S. 103 (1935).

24. 297 U.S. at 286.

25. 297 U.S. at 287.

26. Kamisar, *What is an "Involuntary" Confession? Some Comments on Inbau and Reid's Criminal Interrogation and Confessions,* 17 Rut. L. Rev. 728, 737 (1963).

27. Ziang Sung Wan v. United States, 266 U.S. 1, 11 (1924).

28. 309 U.S. 227 (1940).

29. *Id.* at 238-39.

30. 314 U.S. 219 (1941).

31. *Id.* at 236.

32. 322 U.S. 143 (1944).

33. *Id.* at 150.

34. *Id.* at 149.

35. *Id.* at 154.

36. *Id.* at 157 (Jackson, J., dissenting).

37. *See* Kamisar, *supra* note 26, at 753-59.

38. Watts v. Indiana, 338 U.S. 49, 53 (1949).

39. Stein v. New York, 346 U.S. 156, 186 (1953).

40. 338 U.S. 49 (1949).

41. 342 U.S. 55 (1951).

42. 365 U.S. 534 (1961).

43. 373 U.S. 503 (1963). *See also*: Blackburn v. Alabama, 361 U.S. 199 (1960); Spano v. New York, 360 U.S. 315 (1959).

44. *E.g.*, Ashcraft v. Tennessee, 322 U.S. 143, 161 (1944) (Jackson, J., dissenting).

45. 367 U.S. 568 (1961).

46. *Id.* at 588.

47. *E.g.*, Ziang Sung Wan v. United States, 266 U.S. 1 (1924); Powers v. United States, 223 U.S. 303 (1912); Perovich v. United States, 205 U.S. 86 (1907).

48. McNabb v. United States, 318 U.S. 332, 340 (1943).

49. 318 U.S. at 344.

50. 318 U.S. at 346.

51. *See generally*: O. Stephens, *supra* note 2, at 63-89; Hogan and Snee, *The* McNabb-Mallory *Rule: Its Rise, Rationale and Rescue*, 47 Geo. L.J. 1 (1958).

52. 322 U.S. 65 (1944).

53. *Id.* at 69.

54. *Id.* at 67.

55. 335 U.S. 410 (1948).

56. *Id.* at 413.

57. 354 U.S. 449 (1957).

58. *Id.* at 453.

59. *Id.* at 455.

60. *Id.* at 456.

61. 357 U.S. 433 (1958).

62. 357 U.S. 504 (1958).

63. 357 U.S. at 438.

64. Powell v. Alabama, 287 U.S 45 (1932).

65. 357 U.S at 443.

66. 357 U.S. at 442, *quoting* Glasser v. United States, 315 U.S. 60, 76 (1942).

67. 360 U.S. 315 (1959).

68. *Id.* at 326 (Stewart, J., concurring).

69. 377 U.S. 201 (1964).

70. *Id.* at 206.

71. 372 U.S. 335 (1963).

72. 378 U.S. 478 (1964).

73. *Id.* at 486.

74. *Id.* at 490-91.

75. Douglas v. California, 372 U.S. 353 (1963); Gideon v. Wainwright, 372 U.S. 335 (1963); Griffin v. Illinois, 351 U.S. 12 (1956).

Chapter 6
Confessions: *Miranda* and Beyond

1. 384 U.S. 436 (1966).

2. 168 U.S. 532 (1897).

3. Stein v. New York, 346 U.S. 156, 191 n. 35 (1953).

4. Mallory v. United States, 354 U.S. 449 (1957); Upshaw v. United States, 335 U.S. 410 (1948); United States v. Mitchell, 322 U.S. 65 (1944); McNabb v. United States, 318 U.S. 332 (1943).

5. 297 U.S. 278 (1936).

6. 384 U.S. 436, 442 (1966).

7. 384 U.S. at 460.

8. 384 U.S. at 461.

9. 384 U.S. at 510 (Harlan, J., dissenting).

10. 384 U.S. at 444.

11. 384 U.S. at 469.

12. 384 U.S. at 475.

13. 384 U.S. at 477.

14. *Id.*

15. 384 U.S. at 457.

16. 384 U.S. at 458.

17. *Id.*

18. *Id.*

19. 384 U.S. at 505 (Harlan, J., dissenting).

20. *E.g.*, Edwards, *The Effects of "Miranda" on the Work of the Federal Bureau of Investigation*, 5 Am. Crim. L.Q. 159 (1966-67); Friendly, *The Fifth Amendment Tomorrow: The Case for Constitutional Change*, 37 U. Cinn. L. Rev. 671 (1968). *See generally Controlling Crime Through More Effective Law Enforcement: Hearings before the Subcomm. on Criminal Laws and Procedures of the Senate Comm. on the Judiciary*, 90th Cong., 1st Sess. (1967).

21. 384 U.S. at 543 (White, J., dissenting).

22. 384 U.S. at 517 (Harlan, J., dissenting).

23. 384 U.S. at 481.

24. Project, *Interrogations in New Haven: The Impact of* Miranda, 76 Yale L.J. 1519, 1563 (1967).

25. Project, *supra* note 24, at 1613.

26. Medalie, Zeitz, and Alexander, *Custodial Police Interrogation in Our Nation's Capital: The Attempt to Implement* Miranda, 66 Mich. L. Rev. 1347 (1968); Seeburger and Wettick, Miranda *in Pittsburgh—A Statistical Study*, 29 U. Pitt. L. Rev. 1 (1967).

27. Omnibus Crime Control and Safe Streets Act of 1968, Title II, Pub. L. No. 90-351, 82 Stat. 210 (codified at 18 U.S.C. §3501) (1969).

28. 384 U.S. 641 (1966).

29. *See generally* Burt, Miranda *and Title II: A Morganatic Marriage*, 1969 Sup. Ct. Rev. 81. *See also*: S. Rep. 1097, 90th Cong., 2nd Sess. (1968); Gandara, *Admissibility of Confessions in Federal Prosecutions: Implementation of Section 3501 by Law Enforcement Officials and the Courts*, 63 Geo. L.J. 305 (1974).

30. Gandara, *supra* note 29, at 311-13; United States v. Crocker, 510 F.2d 1129 (10th Cir. 1975) (dictum upholding constitutionality of Title II in light of finding of no *Miranda* violation).

31. Pursuant to 18 U.S.C. §§ 3501(b)(1) and (c) (1969) a delay of less than six hours cannot lead to a finding of involuntariness if the confession is otherwise found voluntary, while a delay of longer duration may be the sole basis for ruling a confession involuntary. Six hours, therefore, is presumably a reasonable delay.

32. *E.g.*: United States v. Burgos, 579 F.2d 747 (2nd Cir. 1978) (fifteen-hour delay); United States v. Shoemaker, 542 F.2d 561 (10th Cir. 1976) (thirteen-hour delay).

33. 384 U.S. 436, 444 (1966).

34. 384 U.S. at 458.

35. 384 U.S. at 461.

36. *Id.*

37. 391 U.S. 1 (1968).

38. *Id.* at 4.

39. *Id.*

40. 394 U.S. 324 (1969).

41. 425 U.S. 341 (1976).

42. *Id.* at 343.

43. 429 U.S. 492 (1977).

44. *Id.* at 495.

45. *Id.*

46. Barfield v. Alabama, 552 F.2d 1114 (5th Cir. 1977).

47. United States v. McCain, 556 F.2d 253 (5th Cir. 1977) (Gee, J., dissenting).

48. 425 U.S. 564 (1976).

49. *Id.* at 567-68.

50. United States v. Knox, 396 U.S. 77 (1969); Bryson v. United States, 396 U.S. 64 (1969); Dennis v. United States, 384 U.S. 855 (1966); Kay v. United States, 303 U.S. 1 (1938); United States v. Kapp, 302 U.S. 214 (1937).

51. 425 U.S. at 579.

52. 425 U.S. at 580.

53. 384 U.S. at 461.

54. 384 U.S. at 593 (Brennan, J., concurring in the judgment), *citing* Garner v. United States, 424 U.S. 648, 657 (1976).

55. 431 U.S. 181 (1977).

56. 431 U.S. 174 (1977).

57. 431 U.S. at 183-84.

58. 431 U.S. at 187.

59. United States v. Prior, 553 F.2d 381 (5th Cir. 1977), held that statements obtained without any warning having been administered to the grand jury witness may be used in a perjury prosecution.

60. United States v. Plesons, 560 F.2d 890 (8th Cir. 1977).

61. American Bar Association, Policy on the Grand Jury (1977).

62. *See: Hearings on the Grand Jury Reform Act of 1978 Before the Subcomm. on Administrative Practice and Procedure of the Senate Comm. on the Judiciary*, 95th Cong., 2nd Sess. (1978); *Hearings on Grand Jury Reform Before the Subcomm. on Immigration, Citizenship and International Law of the House Comm. on the Judiciary*, 95th Cong., 1st Sess. (1977).

63. United States v. Jacobs, 531 F.2d 87 (2nd Cir. 1976), *cert. dismissed*, 436 U.S. 31 (1978).

64. 347 U.S. 62 (1954).

65. *Id*. at 65.

66. 401 U.S. 222 (1971).

67. 347 U.S. at 65.

68. Mapp v. Ohio, 367 U.S. 643 (1961).

69. 420 U.S. 714 (1975).

70. New Jersey v. Portash, 47 U.S.L.W. 4271 (1979). *See also* Mincey v. Arizona, 437 U.S. 385, 398 (1978).

71. 417 U.S. 433 (1974).

72. *Id*. at 446.

73. Doyle v. Ohio, 426 U.S. 610 (1976).

74. 384 U.S. at 473-74.

75. 423 U.S. 96 (1975).

76. *Id*. at 103, 104, *quoting* Miranda v. Arizona, 384 U.S. 436, 474, 479 (1966).

77. *E.g.*, United States v. Rose, 570 F.2d 1358 (9th Cir. 1978); United States v. Rodriguez-Gastelum, 569 F.2d 482 (9th Cir. 1978) (en banc).

78. 384 U.S. 737 (1966).

79. 389 U.S. 413 (1967).

80. 386 U.S. 707 (1967).

81. 391 U.S. 346 (1968).

82. 394 U.S. 478 (1969).

83. 437 U.S. 385 (1978).

84. *Id*. at 399.

85. Schneckloth v. Bustamonte, 412 U.S. 218, 226 (1973).

86. 394 U.S. 731 (1969).

87. *Id*. at 739. *See also* Oregon v. Mathiason, 429 U.S. 492, 495-96 (1977).

88. Harris v. Riddle, 551 F.2d 936 (4th Cir. 1977).

89. State v. Ferguson, 119 Ariz. 55, 579 P.2d 559 (1978); State v. Martin, 242 S.E.2d 762 (N.C. 1978). *But cf.* United States v. Powe, 591 F.2d 833 (D.C. Cir. 1978).

90. United States v. Charlton, 565 F.2d 86 (6th Cir. 1977).

91. United States v. Frazier, 476 F.2d 891 (D.C. Cir. 1973).

92. United States v. Holleman, 575 F.2d 139 (7th Cir. 1978); State v. Gordon, 387 A.2d 611 (Me. 1978).

93. Brewer v. Williams, 430 U.S. 387 (1977) (Blackmun, J., dissenting); Henry v. United States, 590 F.2d 544 (4th Cir. 1978) (Russell, J., dissenting). *See generally* Kamisar, Brewer v. Williams, Massiah, and Miranda: *What Is Interrogation? When Does It Matter?* 67 Geo. L.J. 1 (1978).

94. 384 U.S. at 476.

95. Pierce v. Cardwell, 572 F.2d 1339 (9th Cir. 1978) (hearing on disputed facts, including intoxication, to determine validity of *Miranda* waiver).

96. The court in Taylor v. Riddle, 409 F. Supp. 631, 636 (W.D. Va. 1976), held that a "gentle probe" to determine whether the suspect wishes to waive his *Miranda* rights is permissible. The court's finding of a voluntary waiver was affirmed on appeal. 563 F.2d 133 (4th Cir. 1977).

97. 430 U.S. 387 (1977).

98. *Id.* at 393.

99. 377 U.S. 201 (1964).

100. 430 U.S. at 404, *citing* Johnson v. Zerbst, 304 U.S. 458, 464 (1938).

101. 430 U.S. at 404.

102. In United States v. Satterfield, 417 F. Supp. 293 (S.D.N.Y. 1976), *aff'd*, 558 F.2d 655 (2nd Cir. 1976), Judge Knapp stated that a more demanding waiver standard is required by *Massiah*. However, the rights encompassed in *Miranda*, including the presence of counsel, are equally critical, and the difficulty of waiver should be the same. United States v. Brown, 569 F.2d 236 (5th Cir. 1978) (en banc) (Simpson, J., dissenting).

103. United States v. Pheaster, 544 F.2d 353 (9th Cir. 1976); United States v. Davis, 527 F.2d 1110 (9th Cir. 1975), *cert. denied*, 425 U.S. 953 (1976).

104. 47 U.S.L.W. 4454 (1979).

105. 47 U.S.L.W. 4771 (1979).

106. *E.g.*, United States *ex rel.* Cooper v. Warden, 566 F.2d 28 (7th Cir. 1977).

Chapter 7
Self-Incrimination without Interrogation

1. 116 U.S. 616 (1886).

2. Olmstead v. United States, 277 U.S. 438, 474 (1928) (Brandeis, J., dissenting).

3. Schmerber v. California, 384 U.S. 757, 776 (1966) (Black, J., dissenting).

4. Act of June 22, 1874, §5, 18 Stat. 186.

5. 116 U.S. at 622.

6. 116 U.S. at 623.

7. 19 Howell's State Trials 1030 (C.P. 1765).

8. 19 Howell's State Trials at 1066, *quoted at* 116 U.S. at 627-28.

9. 19 Howell's State Trials at 1073, *quoted at* 116 U.S. at 629.

10. 116 U.S. at 630.

11. 8 J. Wigmore, Evidence §2264, at 379-80 (McNaughton rev. 1961).

12. Corwin, *The Supreme Court's Construction of the Self-Incrimination Clause*, 29 Mich. L. Rev. 191, 205-06 (pt. 2) (1930).

13. 116 U.S. at 634-35.

14. 116 U.S. at 630.

15. *Id.*

16. *Id.*

17. Hale v. Henkel, 201 U.S. 43 (1906).

18. Wilson v. United States, 221 U.S. 361 (1911).

19. Johnson v. United States, 228 U.S. 257 (1913).

20. Perlman v. United States, 247 U.S. 7 (1918).

21. 255 U.S. 298 (1921).

22. *Id.* at 311.

23. *Id.* at 306.

24. *Id.* at 309.

25. *Id.* at 310.

26. Go-Bart Importing Co. v. United States, 282 U.S. 344 (1931); Marron v. United States, 275 U.S. 192 (1927).

27. 277 U.S. at 478.

28. 277 U.S. at 478-79.

29. 387 U.S. 294 (1967).

30. *Id.* at 301, *quoting* Boyd v. United States, 116 U.S. 616, 630 (1886).

31. 19 Howell's State Trials at 1066.

32. 387 U.S. at 304.

33. 387 U.S. at 309, *quoting* United States v. Poller, 43 F.2d 911, 914 (2nd Cir. 1930).

34. 389 U.S. 347 (1967).

35. Boyd v. United States, 116 U.S. 616, 633 (1886).

36. Griswold v. Connecticut, 381 U.S. 479, 484 (1965).

37. 378 U.S. at 55, *quoting* United States v. Grunewald, 233 F.2d 556, 581-82 (2nd Cir. 1956) (Frank, J., dissenting), *rev'd*, 353 U.S. 391 (1957).

38. 409 U.S. 322 (1973).

39. *Id.* at 323.

40. *Id.* at 347.

41. *Id.* at 349.

42. *Id.* at 325 n. 6.

43. *Id*. at 328, *quoting* Holt v. United States, 218 U.S. 245, 253 (1910).

44. 427 U.S. 463 (1976).

45. *Id*. at 473.

46. *Id*. at 477.

47. *Id*. at 487 (Brennan, J., dissenting).

48. Fisher v. United States, 425 U.S. 391, 401 n. 7 (1976), *citing* United States v. Bennett, 409 F.2d 888 (2nd Cir. 1969).

49. 425 U.S. 391 (1976).

50. United States v. Fisher, 500 F.2d 683 (3rd Cir. 1974).

51. United States v. Kasmir, 499 F.2d 444 (5th Cir. 1974).

52. 425 U.S. at 424 (Brennan, J., dissenting).

53. 425 U.S. at 398.

54. 425 U.S. at 401.

55. 425 U.S. at 409.

56. 116 U.S. at 630.

57. 425 U.S. at 424-27 (Brennan, J., dissenting).

58. 425 U.S. at 410.

59. 8 J. Wigmore, Evidence, *supra* note 11, §2264, at 379 (emphasis in original).

60. C. McCormick, Handbook of the Law of Evidence §126, at 268 (2nd ed. 1972).

61. 425 U.S. at 409.

62. 425 U.S. at 410-11.

63. 425 U.S. at 411.

64. 425 U.S. at 412.

65. *In re* Fred R. Witte Center Glass No. 3, 544 F.2d 1026 (9th Cir. 1976).

66. Fagan v. United States, 545 F.2d 1005, 1007 (5th Cir. 1977).

67. United States v. Helina, 549 F.2d 713 (9th Cir. 1977).

68. United States v. Beattie, 541 F.2d 329 (2nd Cir. 1976).

69. United States v. Plesons, 560 F.2d 890 (8th Cir. 1977).

70. *In re* Bernstein, 425 F. Supp. 37 (S.D. Fla. 1977).

71. 425 U.S. at 414.

72. 274 U.S. 259 (1927).

73. *Id*. at 263.

74. 335 U.S. 1 (1948).

75. *Id*. at 15.

76. *Id*. at 16.

77. *Id*.

78. 232 U.S. 563 (1914).

79. 335 U.S. at 32.

80. *Id*.

81. 335 U.S. at 4. *See also*: *In re* Grand Jury Supoena to Custodian of Records, Mid-City Realty Co., 497 F.2d 218 (6th Cir. 1974) (realty escrow deposit records); United States v. Silverman, 449 F.2d 1341 (2nd Cir. 1971) (attorney closing statements filed with court in contingent fee cases).

82. 335 U.S. at 70-71 (Jackson, J., dissenting).

83. Beard v. United States, 222 F.2d 84, 93 (4th Cir. 1955).

84. *Shapiro* has been held inapplicable in United States v. Blank, 330 F. Supp. 783 (N.D. Ohio 1971) (illegal gambling business records); United States v. Remolif, 227 F. Supp. 420 (D. Nev. 1964) (business records required to be kept by persons subject to federal wagering excise tax); United States v. Ansani, 138 F. Supp. 451 (N.D. Ill. 1955) (records of sales and deliveries of gambling devices).

85. 335 U.S. at 54 (Frankfurter, J., dissenting).

86. 64 Stat. 987 (1950).

87. Irving Blau v. United States, 340 U.S. 332 (1951); Patricia Blau v. United States, 340 U.S. 159 (1950).

88. 382 U.S. 70 (1965).

89. *Id*. at 79.

90. *Id*.

91. 390 U.S. 39 (1968).

92. 390 U.S. 62 (1968).

93. 390 U.S. 85 (1968).

94. Lewis v. United States, 348 U.S. 419 (1955); United States v. Kahriger, 345 U.S. 22 (1953); 8 J. Wigmore, Evidence §2259c, at 349 (3rd ed. 1940).

95. 390 U.S. at 52.

96. 390 U.S. at 52, *citing* Morgan, *The Privilege Against Self-Incrimination*, 34 Minn. L. Rev. 1, 37 (1949).

97. Byers v. Justice Court for Ukiah Judicial District, 80 Cal. Rptr. 553, 458 P.2d 465 (1969), *vacated sub nom*., California v. Byers, 402 U.S. 424 (1971).

98. 402 U.S. 424 (1971).

99. *Id*. at 460 (Black, J., dissenting).

100. *Id*. at 462-63.

101. *Id*. at 450 (Harlan, J., concurring).

102. *Id*. at 463 (Black, J., dissenting).

103. *Id*. at 474 (Brennan, J., dissenting), ,*quoting* J. Harlan, *Live and Let Live*, The Evolution of a Judicial Philosophy 285, 288 (D. Shapiro ed. 1969).

104. 402 U.S. at 452 (Harlan, J., dissenting).

105. 424 U.S. 648 (1976).

106. *Id*. at 649-50.

107. California v. Byers, 402 U.S. at 463 (Black, J., dissenting).

Chapter 8
Burdening the Fifth Amendment

1. 380 U.S. 609 (1965).

2. *Id.* at 614, *quoting* Murphy v. Waterfront Comm'n, 378 U.S. 52, 55 (1964).

3. 380 U.S. at 614.

4. 435 U.S. 333 (1978).

5. Lockett v. Ohio, 438 U.S. 586 (1978).

6. *E.g.*, Lussier v. Gunter, 552 F.2d 385 (1st Cir. 1977); United States v. Bursten, 453 F.2d 605 (5th Cir. 1971).

7. 271 U.S. 494 (1926).

8. Stewart v. United States, 366 U.S. 1 (1961); Grunewald v. United States, 353 U.S. 391 (1957).

9. 401 U.S. 222 (1971).

10. Doyle v. Ohio, 426 U.S. 610, 618 (1976).

11. 426 U.S. 610 (1976). The same result had previously been reached for federal trials on the basis of the Court's supervisory authority. United States v. Hale, 422 U.S. 171 (1975).

12. *E.g.*, Walker v. United States, 404 F.2d 900 (5th Cir. 1968).

13. Harris v. New York, 401 U.S. 222, 225 (1971).

14. C. McCormick, Handbook of the Law of Evidence §270, at 651-55 (2nd ed. 1972).

15. *E.g.*, United States v. Vega, 589 F.2d 1147 (2nd Cir. 1978).

16. 569 S.W.2d 1 (Mo. App. 1978).

17. Baxter v. Palmigiano, 425 U.S. 308 (1976).

18. 406 U.S. 605, 609 (1972).

19. 390 U.S. 570 (1968).

20. *Id.* at 583.

21. 390 U.S. 377, 394 (1968).

22. 385 U.S. 493 (1967).

23. *Id.* at 497.

24. *Id.* at 498.

25. 385 U.S. 511 (1967).

26. 366 U.S. 117 (1961).

27. 385 U.S. at 513.

28. 385 U.S. at 514, *quoting* Malloy v. Hogan, 378 U.S. 1, 8 (1964).

29. Miranda v. Arizona, 384 U.S. 436 (1966).

30. Griffin v. California, 380 U.S. 609 (1965).

31. 414 U.S. 70, 85 (1973).

32. 414 U.S. at 84.

33. 392 U.S. 280 (1968).

34. 392 U.S. 273 (1968).

35. *Id*. at 278.

36. 392 U.S. at 284.

37. 414 U.S. 70 (1973).

38. 431 U.S. 801 (1977).

39. 414 U.S. at 82.

40. 431 U.S. at 805.

41. Invocation of the privilege was held to justify dismissal because it created a variety of doubts about the fitness of the official to hold office, the possible reasons including insubordination, Nelson v. County of Los Angeles, 362 U.S. 1 (1960); reliability, Lerner v. Casey, 357 U.S. 468 (1958); or because the assertion of the privilege obstructed the investigation, *In re* Anastaplo, 366 U.S. 82 (1961); Konigsberg v. State Bar of California, 366 U.S. 36 (1961).

42. Slochower v. Bd. of Higher Educ., 350 U.S. 551, 557 (1956). *Slochower* involved a city employee's dismissal after assertion of the privilege in a federal hearing and was distinguished where a city employee was dismissed for similar reasons following a city hearing. Beilan v. Bd. of Pub. Educ., 357 U.S. 399 (1958).

43. 425 U.S. 308 (1976).

44. *Id*. at 317.

45. *Id*.

46. Spevack v. Klein, 385 U.S. 511, 525 (1967) (Harlan, J., dissenting).

47. Garrity v. New Jersey, 385 U.S. 493, 507 (1967) (Harlan, J., dissenting).

48. 345 U.S. 83 (1953).

49. *Id*. at 91.

50. Slochower v. Bd. of Higher Educ., 350 U.S. 551, 557 (1956).

51. Crampton v. Ohio is reported along with McGautha v. California at 402 U.S. 183 (1971).

52. 390 U.S. 377 (1968).

53. United States v. Stricklin, 591 F.2d 1112 (5th Cir. 1979).

54. Williams v. Florida, 399 U.S. 78 (1970).

55. 402 U.S. at 214.

56. 402 U.S. at 215, *quoting* Murphy v. Waterfront Comm'n, 378 U.S. 52, 55 (1964).

57. 402 U.S. at 215.

58. 402 U.S. at 220.

59. *Id*.

60. 402 U.S. 424 (1971).

61. *Id*. at 454.

62. Crampton v. Ohio, 402 U.S. 183, 213 (1971).

63. 412 U.S. 17 (1973).

64. *Id*. at 32.

65. 434 U.S. 357 (1978).

66. Ludwig v. Massachusetts, 427 U.S. 618 (1976).

67. Corbitt v. New Jersey 47 U.S.L.W. 4055 (1978).

68. *E.g.*, Crampton v. Ohio, 402 U.S. 183 (1971).

69. *E.g.*, Ludwig v. Massachusetts, 427 U.S. 618 (1976).

70. 402 U.S. at 213.

71. California v. Byers, 402 U.S. 424, 449 (1971) (Harlan, J., concurring), *quoting* Spevack v. Klein, 385 U.S. 511, 522-23 (1967) (Harlan, J., dissenting).

72. Wolff v. McDonnell, 418 U.S. 539 (1974).

Chapter 9
The Privilege and the Future

1. *E.g.*, L. Mayers, Shall We Amend the Fifth Amendment? (1959); Friendly, *The Fifth Amendment Tomorrow: The Case for Constitutional Change*, 37 U. Cinn. L. Rev. 671 (1968).

2. *E.g.*, Schmerber v. California, 384 U.S. 757 (1966).

3. *E.g.*, Beckwith v. United States, 425 U.S. 341 (1976) (Brennan, J., dissenting); Couch v. United States, 409 U.S. 322 (1973) (Douglas, J., dissenting).

4. Griffin v. California, 380 U.S. 609 (1965).

5. Andresen v. Maryland, 427 U.S. 463 (1976); Fisher v. United States, 425 U.S. 391 (1976).

6. 168 U.S. 532 (1897).

7. *Id.* at 543.

8. 384 U.S. 436 (1966).

9. Harris v. New York, 401 U.S. 222 (1971).

10. Michigan v. Mosley, 423 U.S. 96 (1975).

11. *See* United States v. Chadwick, 433 U.S. 1, 9 (1977), observing that the "Framers were men who focused on the wrongs of that day but who intended the Fourth Amendment to safeguard fundamental values which would far outlast the specific abuses which gave it birth."

12. *In re* Willie, 25 F. Cas. 38, 40 (C.C. Va. 1807) (No. 14,692e).

13. Counselman v. Hitchcock, 142 U.S. 547, 564 (1892).

14. Brown v. Walker, 161 U.S. 591, 599 (1896), *quoting* Regina v. Boyes, 1 Best & Smith 311, 330, 121 Eng. Rep. 730, 738 (Q.B. 1861).

15. Hoffman v. United States, 341 U.S. 479, 488 (1951), *quoting* Temple v. Commonwealth, 75 Va. 892, 898 (1881).

16. 384 U.S. 757 (1966).

17. 399 U.S. 78 (1970).

18. 402 U.S. 424 (1971).

19. *E.g.*, State v. Mangam, 343 So.2d 599 (Fla. 1977); State *ex rel.* Flowers v. Dept. of Health and Social Services, 81 Wis. 2d 376, 260 N.W.2d 727 (1978).

20. Brown v. Walker, 161 U.S. 591 (1896).

21. 116 U.S. 616 (1886).

22. 427 U.S. 463 (1976).

23. 425 U.S. 391 (1976).

24. 384 U.S. 436 (1966).

25. Bellis v. United States, 417 U.S. 85 (1974).

26. United States v. Radetsky, 535 F.2d 556 (10th Cir. 1976).

27. Fisher v. United States, 425 U.S. 391 (1976); Couch v. United States, 409 U.S. 322 (1973).

28. United States v. Chadwick, 433 U.S. 1, 9 (1977).

Bibliography

There is a vast literature on the Fifth Amendment privilege against self-incrimination, and only an abbreviated bibliography of the relevant materials is possible here. Nevertheless, an effort has been made to include the most important sources for each Fifth Amendment issue.

American Bar Association, Policy on the Grand Jury (1977).

Baker, *Self-Incrimination: Is the Privilege an Anachronism?*, 42 American Bar Association Journal 633 (1956).

Bator and Vorenberg, *Arrest, Detention, Interrogation and the Right to Counsel: Basic Problems and Possible Legislative Solutions*, 66 Columbia Law Review 62 (1966).

J. Bentham, A Rationale of Judicial Evidence, 7 The Works of Jeremy Bentham (Bowring ed. 1843).

Berger, *Burdening The Fifth Amendment: Toward a Persumptive Barrier Theory*, 70 Journal of Criminal Law and Criminology 27 (1979).

Berger, *The Unprivileged Status of the Fifth Amendment Privilege*, 15 American Criminal Law Review 191 (1978).

Bloustein, *Privacy as an Aspect of Human Dignity: An Answer to Dean Prosser*, 39 New York University Law Review 962 (1964).

Boiarsky, *The Right of the Accused in a Criminal Case Not to Be Compelled to Be a Witness against Himself*, 35 West Virginia Law Quarterly 27 (1928).

E. Borchard, Convicting the Innocent (1932).

C. Bowen, The Lion and the Throne: The Life and Times of Sir Edward Coke (1957).

Brennan, *State Constitutions and the Protection of Individual Rights*, 90 Harvard Law Review 489 (1977).

P. Brest, Processes of Constitutional Decisionmaking (1975).

Brodsky, *Self-Incrimination in White-Collar Fraud Investigations: Practical Approach for Lawyers*, 12 Criminal Law Bulletin 125 (1976).

Burt, Miranda *and Title II: A Morganatic Marriage*, 1969 Supreme Court Review 81.

Coke, *Of Oaths before an Ecclesiastical Judge Ex Officio*, 12 Coke's Reports 26, 77 English Reports 1308 (1607).

Comment, *A Paper Chase: The Search and Seizure of Personal Business Records*, 43 Brooklyn Law Review 489 (1977).

Comment, *Compulsory Immunity Legislation: Title II of the Organized Crime Control Act of 1970*, 1971 University of Illinois Law Forum 91.

Comment, *Compulsory Mental Examinations and the Privilege Against Self-Incrimination*, 1964 Wisconsin Law Review 671.

Comment, *Hit-and-Run Statutes, Required Information and the Fifth Amendment*, 1970 Washington University Law Quarterly 79.

Comment, *Impeaching a Defendant's Trial Testimony by Proof of Post-Arrest Silence*, 123 University of Pennsylvania Law Review 940 (1975).

Comment, *Papers, Privacy and the Fourth and Fifth Amendments: A Constitutional Analysis*, 69 Northwestern University Law Review 626 (1974).

Comment, *Privilege Against Self-Incrimination Denied as to Documents Recovered by Taxpayer from His Accountant and Transferred to His Attorney*, 59 Minnesota Law Review 751 (1975).

Comment, *"Refusal to Cooperate" as a Basis for Exclusion from the Bar*, 47 Iowa Law Review 507 (1962).

Comment, *Reporting Illegal Gains as Taxable Income: A Compromise Solution to a Prosecutorial Windfall*, 69 Northwestern Law Review 111 (1974).

Comment, *Required Information and the Privilege Against Self-Incrimination*, 65 Columbia Law Review 681 (1965).

Comment, *Self-Incrimination and the Federal Excise Tax on Wagering*, 76 Yale Law Journal 839 (1967).

Comment, *The Fifth Amendment and Compelled Testimony: Practical Problems in the Wake of* Kastigar, 19 Villanova Law Review 470 (1974).

Comment, *The Fourth and Fifth Amendments—Dimensions of an "Intimate Relationship,"* 13 UCLA Law Review 857 (1966).

Comment, *The Grand Jury Witness' Privilege Against Self-Incrimination*, 62 Northwestern University Law Review 207 (1967).

Comment, *The Marijuana Tax and the Privilege Against Self-Incrimination*, 117 University of Pennsylvania Law Review 432 (1969).

Comment, *The New Definition: A Fifth Amendment Right to Counsel*, 14 UCLA Law Review 604 (1967).

Comment, *The Privilege Against Self-Incrimination in Civil Litigation*, 1968 University of Illinois Law Forum 75.

Comment, *The Protection of Privacy by the Privilege Against Self-Incrimination: A Doctrine Laid to Rest?*, 59 Iowa Law Review 1336 (1974).

Comment, *The Search and Seizure of Private Papers: Fourth and Fifth Amendment Considerations*, 6 Loyola of Los Angeles Law Review 274 (1973).

Comment, *The Self-Incrimination Privilege: Barrier to Criminal Discovery?*, 51 California Law Review 135 (1963).

Comment, *Use of the Privilege Against Self-Incrimination in Civil Litigation*, 52 Virginia Law Review 322 (1966).

Corwin, *The Supreme Court's Construction of the Self-Incrimination Clause*, (pts. 1-2), 29 Michigan Law Review 1, 191 (1930).

G. Coulton, Inquisition and Liberty (1969).

Dann, *The Fifth Amendment Privilege Against Self-Incrimination: Extorting Physical Evidence from a Suspect*, 43 Southern California Law Review 597 (1970).

Dershowitz and Ely, Harris v. New York: *Some Anxious Observations on the Candor and Logic of the Emerging Nixon Majority*, 80 Yale Law Journal 1198 (1971).

Dix, *Mistake, Ignorance, Expectation of Benefit, and the Modern Law of Confessions*, 1975 Washington University Law Quarterly 275.

Dix, *Waiver in Criminal Procedure: A Brief for More Careful Analysis*, 55 Texas Law Review 193 (1977).

Dixon, *Comment on Immunity Provisions*, National Commission on Reform of Federal Criminal Laws, Working Papers, Vol. II. (1970).

Driver, *Confessions and the Social Psychology of Coercion*, 82 Harvard Law Review 42 (1968).

Edwards, *The Effects of* "Miranda" *on the Work of the Federal Bureau of Investigation*, 5 American Criminal Law Quarterly 159 (1966-67).

Ely, *On Discovering Fundamental Values*, 92 Harvard Law Review 5 (1978).

Falknor, *Self-Incrimination Privilege: "Links in the Chain,"* 5 Vanderbilt Law Review 479 (1952).

Fortas, *The Fifth Amendment: Nemo Tenetur Seipsum Prodere*, 25 Cleveland Bar Association Journal 91 (1954).

Fried, *Privacy*, 77 Yale Law Journal 475 (1968).

Friendly, *The Fifth Amendment Tomorrow: The Case for Constitutional Change*, 37 University of Cincinnati Law Review 671 (1968).

Gandara, *Admissibility of Confessions in Federal Prosecutions: Implementation of Section 3501 by Law Enforcement Officials and the Courts*, 63 Georgetown Law Journal 305 (1974).

Gerstein, *Privacy and Self-Incrimination*, 80 Ethics 87 (1970).

Griffiths and Ayres, *A Postscript to the* Miranda *Project: Interrogation of Draft Protesters*, 77 Yale Law Journal 300 (1967).

E. Griswold, The Fifth Amendment Today (1955).

Griswold, *The Right to Be Left Alone*, 55 Northwestern University Law Review 216 (1960).

Gross, *The Concept of Privacy*, 42 New York University Law Review 34 (1967).

Harlan, *Live and Let Live*, The Evolution of a Judicial Philosophy (D. Shapiro ed. 1969).

Hogan and Snee, *The* McNabb-Mallory *Rule: Its Rise, Rationale and Rescue*, 47 Georgetown Law Journal 1 (1958).

W. Holdsworth, A History of English Law (7th ed. 1956).

E. Hopkins, Our Lawless Police (1931).

Inbau, *Public Safety v. Individual Civil Liberties: The Prosecutor's Stand*, 53 Journal of Criminal Law, Criminology and Police Science 85 (1962).

Kadish, *Methodology and Criteria in Due Process Adjudication—A Survey and Criticism*, 66 Yale Law Journal 319 (1957).

Kamisar, *A Dissent From the* Miranda *Dissents: Some Comments on the "New" Fifth Amendment and the Old "Voluntariness" Test*, 65 Michigan Law Review 59 (1966).

Kamisar, Brewer v. Williams, Massiah, *and* Miranda: *What Is "Interrogation"? When Does It Matter?*, 67 Georgetown Law Journal 1 (1978).

Kamisar, *Kauper's "Judicial Examination of the Accused" Forty Years Later-Some Comments on a Remarkable Article*, 73 Michigan Law Review 15 (1974).

Kamisar, *What Is an "Involuntary" Confession? Some Comments on Inbau and Reid's Criminal Interrogation and Confessions*, 17 Rutgers Law Review 728 (1963).

Keedy, *The Third Degree and Legal Interrogation of Suspects*, 85 University of Pennsylvania Law Review 761 (1937).

Kemp, *The Background of the Fifth Amendment in English Law: A Study of its Historical Implications,* 1 William and Mary Law Review 247 (1958).

E. Levine, The "Third Degree," A Detailed and Appalling Exposé of Police Brutality (1930).

L. Levy, Origins of the Fifth Amendment (1968).

Louisell, *Criminal Discovery and Self-Incrimination: Roger Traynor Confronts the Dilemma*, 53 California Law Review 89 (1965).

Maguire, *Attack of the Common Lawyers on the Oath Ex Officio as Administered in the Ecclesiastical Courts in England*, Essays in History and Political Theory in Honor of Charles Howard McIlwain (1936).

Mansfield, *The* Albertson *Case: Conflict Between the Privilege Against Self-Incrimination and the Government's Need for Information*, 1966 Supreme Court Review 103.

L. Mayers, Shall We Amend the Fifth Amendment? (1959).

C. McCormick, Handbook of the Law of Evidence (2nd ed. 1972).

McKay, *Book Review*, 35 New York University Law Review 1097 (1960).

McKay, *Self-Incrimination and the New Privacy*, 1967 Supreme Court Review 193.

McNaughton, *The Privilege Against Self-Incrimination: Its Constitutional Affectation, Raison d'Etre and Miscellaneous Implications*, 51 Journal of Criminal Law, Criminology and Police Science 138 (1960).

Medalie, Zeitz and Alexander, *Custodial Police Interrogation in Our Nation's Capital: The Attempt to Implement* Miranda, 66 Michigan Law Review 1347 (1968).

Meltzer, *Privilege Against Self-Incrimination and the Hit-and-Run Opinions*, 1971 Supreme Court Review 1.

Meltzer, *Required Records, the McCarran Act, and the Privilege Against Self-Incrimination*, 18 University of Chicago Law Review 687 (1951).

Morgan, *The Privilege Against Self-Incrimination*, 34 Minnesota Law Review 1 (1949).

Nakell, *Criminal Discovery for the Defense and the Prosecution—The Developing Constitutional Considerations,* 50 North Carolina Law Review 437 (1972).

National Commission on Law Observance and Enforcement, Report on Lawlessness in Law Enforcement (1931).

National Commission on Reform of Federal Criminal Law, Working Papers (1970).

National Conference of Commissioners on Uniform State Laws, Uniform Rules of Criminal Procedure (1974).

Noonan, *Inferences from the Invocation of the Privilege Against Self-Incrimination*, 41 Virgina Law Review 311 (1955).

Note, *A Reconsideration of the* Katz *Expectation of Privacy Test*, 76 Michigan Law Review 154 (1977).

Note, *Applicability of Privilege Against Self-Incrimination to Legislative Investigations*, 49 Columbia Law Review 87 (1949).

Note, Bellis v. United States: *Denial of Fifth Amendment Protection to Partnerships*, 39 Albany Law Review 545 (1975).

Note, California v. Byers: *Hit-and-Run Statutes and the Privilege Against Self-Incrimination*, 38 Brooklyn Law Review 728 (1972).

Note, *Extending* Miranda *to Administrative Investigations*, 56 Virginia Law Review 690 (1970).

Note, *Failure to Testify—Should the Prosecutor Comment?*, 38 Southern California Law Review 167 (1965).

Note, *Federal Witness Immunity Problems and Practices Under 18 U.S.C. §§6002-6003*, 14 American Criminal Law Review 275 (1976).

Note, *Forcible Administration of Blood Tests*: Schmerber v. California, 14 UCLA Law Review 680 (1967).

Note, *Formalism, Legal Realism, and Constitutionally Protected Privacy Under the Fourth and Fifth Amendments*, 90 Harvard Law Review 945 (1977).

Note, Garner v. United States: *Fifth Amendment Protection for the Taxpayer*, 34 University of Pittsburgh Law Review 510 (1973).

Note, *Immunity from Prosecution and the Fifth Amendment: An Analysis of Constitutional Standards*, 25 Vanderbilt Law Review 1207 (1972).

Note, *Lack of* Miranda *Warnings for Virtual Defendants Results in Suppression of Perjurious Testimony:* United States v. Mandujano, 53 Texas Law Review 156 (1974).

Note, *Mental Examinations of Defendants Who Plead Insanity: Problems of Self-Incrimination*, 40 Temple Law Quarterly 366 (1967).

Note, *Prison Disciplinary Proceedings and the Fifth Amendment Privilege Against Self-Incrimination*, 55 North Carolina Law Review 254 (1977).

Note, *Revocation of Conditional Liberty for the Commission of a Crime: Double Jeopardy and Self-Incrimination Limitations*, 74 Michigan Law Review 525 (1976).

Note, *Right to Counsel in Investigative Grand Jury Proceedings: Washington Criminal Investigatory Act of 1971*, 47 Washington Law Review 511 (1972).

Note, *Supreme Court Delineates the Relationship Between the Fourth and Fifth Amendments*, 1967 Duke Law Journal 366.

Note, *Tacit Criminal Admissions*, 112 University of Pennsylvania Law Review 210 (1963).

Note, *Tacit Criminal Admissions in Light of the Expanding Privilege Against Self-Incrimination*, 52 Cornell Law Quarterly 335 (1967).

Note, *The Federal Witness Immunity Act in Theory and Practice: Treading the Constitutional Tightrope*, 72 Yale Law Journal 1568 (1963).

Note, *The Life and Times of* Boyd v. United States *(1886-1976)*, 76 Michigan Law Review 184 (1977).

Note, *The* Marchetti *Approach to Self-Incrimination in Cases Involving Tax/Registration Statutes*, 56 Minnesota Law Review 229 (1971).

Note, *The Scope of Testimonial Immunity Under the Fifth Amendment*, 67 Northwestern University Law Review 106 (1972).

Note, *Waiver of the Privilege Against Self-Incrimination*, 14 Stanford Law Review 811 (1962).

O'Brien, *The Fifth Amendment: Fox Hunters, Old Women, Hermits, and the Burger Court*, 54 Notre Dame Lawyer 26 (1978).

Orfield, *The Privilege Against Self-Incrimination in Federal Cases*, 25 University of Pittsburgh Law Review 503 (1964).

Parker, *A Definition of Privacy*, 27 Rutgers Law Review 275 (1974).

Pittman, *The Colonial and Constitutional History of the Privilege Against Self-Incrimination in America*, 21 Virginia Law Review 763 (1935).

F. Pollock and F. Maitland, History of English Law, Vol. I, II (2nd ed. 1898).

Project, *Interrogations in New Haven: The Impact of* Miranda, 76 Yale Law Journal 1519 (1967).

Project on Law Enforcement Policy and Rulemaking, Model Rules for Law Enforcement: Eyewitness Identification (1972).

Ratner, *Consequences of Exercising the Privilege Against Self-Incrimination*, 24 University of Chicago Law Review 472 (1957).

Recent Case, *Fifth Amendment Privilege Against Self-Incrimination Applicable to States-Federal Standard Determinative*, 18 Vanderbilt Law Review 744 (1965).

Recent Statute, *Title II of the Omnibus Crime Control and Safe Streets Act of 1968*, 82 Harvard Law Review 1392 (1969).

Ritchie, *Compulsion that Violates the Fifth Amendment: The Burger Court's Definition*, 61 Minnesota Law Review 383 (1977).

W. Schaefer, The Suspect and Society (1967).

Schiller, *On the Jurisprudence of the Fifth Amendment Right to Silence*, 16 American Criminal Law Review 197 (1979).

Schwartz and Bator, *Criminal Justice in the Mid-Sixties:* Escobedo *Revisited*, 42 Federal Rules Decisions 463 (1966).

Seeburger and Wettick, Miranda *in Pittsburgh—A Statistical Study*, 29 University of Pittsburgh Law Review 1 (1967).

Silving, *The Oath (pts. 1-2)*, 68 Yale Law Journal 1329, 1527 (1959).

Sowle, *The Privilege Against Self-Incrimination: Principles and Trends*, 51 Journal of Criminal Law, Criminology and Police Science 131 (1960).

O. Stephens, The Supreme Court and Confessions of Guilt (1973).

Stone, *The* Miranda *Doctrine in the Burger Court*, 1977 Supreme Court Review 99.

Strachan, *Self-Incrimination, Immunity and Watergate*, 56 Texas Law Review 791 (1978).

F. Thorpe, ed., The Federal and State Constitutions, Colonial Charters, and Other Organic Laws (1909).

Tormel and Daniel, Miranda *in Prison: The Dilemma of Prison Discipline and Intramural Crime*, 21 Buffalo Law Review 759 (1972).

L. Tribe, American Constitutional Law (1978).

Westen, *Away from Waiver: A Rationale for the Forfeiture of Constitutional Rights in Criminal Procedure*, 75 Michigan Law Review 1214 (1977).

Westen, *Order of Proof: An Accused's Right to Control the Timing and Sequence of Evidence in His Defense*, 66 California Law Review 935 (1978).

White, *Police Trickery in Inducing Confessions*, 127 University of Pennsylvania Law Review 581 (1979).

3 J. Wigmore, Evidence (Chadbourn rev. 1970).

8 J. Wigmore, Evidence (McNaughton rev. 1961).

Wigmore, *Nemo Tenetur Seipsum Prodere*, 5 Harvard Law Review 71 (1892).

Williams, *Problems of the Fifth Amendment*, 24 Fordham Law Review 19 (1955).

Wyman, *A Common Sense View of the Fifth Amendment*, 51 Journal of Criminal Law, Criminology and Police Science 155 (1960).

Table of Cases

References are to text and notes by chapter.

North Carolina v. Butler, 99 S.Ct. 1755 (1979): ch. 6, 158, and n. 104

Oklahoma Press Publishing Co. v. Walling, 327 U.S. 186 (1946): ch. 3, n. 51
Olmstead v. United States, 277 U.S. 438 (1928): ch. 2, 43, and n. 76; ch. 7, 168, and nn. 2, 27-28
Oregon v. Hass, 420 U.S. 714 (1975): ch. 6, 148, and n. 69
Oregon v. Mathiason, 429 U.S. 492 (1977): ch. 6, 139-142, and nn. 43-45, 87
Orloff v. Willoughby, 345 U.S. 83 (1953): ch. 8, 210, and nn. 48-49
Orozco v. Texas, 394 U.S. 324 (1969): ch. 6, 136-137, and n. 40

In re Parker, 411 F.2d 1067 (10th Cir. 1969), *vacated as moot*, 397 U.S. 96 (1970): ch. 4, n. 57
Paul v. Davis, 424 U.S. 693 (1976): ch. 2, n. 71
People *ex rel.* Hackley v. Kelly, 24 N.Y. 74 (1861): ch. 3, n. 22
Perlman v. United States, 247 U.S. 7 (1918): ch. 7, n. 20
Perovich v. United States, 205 U.S. 86 (1907): ch. 5, n. 47
Piccirillo v. New York, 400 U.S. 548 (1971): ch. 3, n. 97
Pierce v. Cardwell, 572 F.2d 1339 (9th Cir. 1978): ch. 6, n. 95
Planned Parenthood v. Danforth, 428 U.S. 52 (1976): ch. 2, n. 68
Pointer v. Texas, 380 U.S. 400 (1965): ch. 3, n. 3
Powell v. Alabama, 287 U.S. 45 (1932): ch. 5, nn. 23, 64
Powers v. United States, 223 U.S. 303 (1912): ch. 5, n. 47
Pulford v. United States, 155 F.2d 944 (6th Cir. 1946): ch. 3, n. 68

Quinn v. United States, 349 U.S. 155 (1955): ch. 2, 26-27, and nn. 6, 8; ch. 4, 90, and nn. 64, 66-67

Raffel v. United States, 271 U.S. 494 (1926): ch. 4, n. 83; ch. 8, 196-198 and n. 7
Railroad Company v. Richmond, 96 U.S. 521 (1877): ch. 3, n. 40
Regina v. Boyes, 1 Best & Smith 311, 121 Eng. Rep. 730 (Q.B. 1861): ch. 3, n. 78; ch. 4, 86, and nn. 42-45; ch. 9, n. 14
Rochin v. California, 342 U.S. 165 (1952): ch. 4, 83, and n. 31
Roe v. Wade, 410 U.S. 113 (1973): ch. 2, n. 68
Rogers v. Richmond, 365 U.S. 534 (1961): ch. 5, 111, and n. 42
Rogers v. United States, 340 U.S. 367 (1951): ch. 4, 89, 93-94, and nn. 60-62, 80-82

Schmerber v. California, 384 U.S. 757 (1966): ch. 4, 81-82, and nn. 22-24, 27; ch. 7, n. 3; ch. 9, 229, and nn. 2, 16
Schneckloth v. Bustamonte, 412 U.S. 218 (1973): ch. 6, n. 85

Index

About the Author

Mark Berger is currently associate professor of law at the University of Missouri-Kansas City School of Law. He received his undergraduate education at Columbia College and his law degree from Yale Law School. He previously served as legal advisor for the New Haven, Connecticut, Police Department and executive director of the New Haven Pretrial Services Council. He is a frequent participant in Bar Association programs and has published numerous articles in legal periodicals.